From the Virginia Plantation

TO

The National Capitol

OR

The First and Only Negro Representative in
Congress from the Old Dominion

JOHN MERCER LANGSTON

ILLUSTRATED.

Self-reliance the secret of success

HARTFORD, CONN.
AMERICAN PUBLISHING COMPANY
1894

Copyright 1894
By JOHN MERCER LANGSTON
(*All rights reserved*)

This Book Is Respectfully Dedicated

To the young, aspiring American, who, by manly and self-reliant effort, would gain standing and influence, serving his day and generation by such personal accomplishment and useful, heroic achievement, as show him worthy of his citizenship.

God and Destiny shall prove themselves the sure supports of such person, bearing him to victory in every contest. He has only, therefore, to be true, brave and faithful, to win the highest rewards of dignified life, as bestowed in honors and *emoluments by his fellow-citizens.*

ILLUSTRATIONS.

	PAGE.
FROM PLANTATION TO CAPITOL,	*Frontispiece*
PORTRAIT OF JOHN MERCER LANGSTON, 1894,	*Facing Page* 11
LEAVING THE VIRGINIA PLANTATION,	31
THE RETURN OF COLONEL GOOCH AND JOHN,	50
THE ADMISSION TO THE OHIO BAR, 1854,	125
PRESENTATION OF COLORS TO 5TH U. S. COLORED TROOPS, CAMP DELAWARE, OHIO, 1863,	210
ADDRESSING THE COLORED TROOPS AT NASHVILLE, TENN., 1864,	228
AFTER THE SPEECH AT LOUISA COURT HOUSE, VIRGINIA, 1867,	270
VISITING THE GRAVES OF HIS PARENTS,	272
BOARD OF HEALTH, OF THE DISTRICT OF COLUMBIA,	318
PORTRAIT OF SALOMON, PRESIDENT OF HAITI,	393
ADMISSION TO THE HOUSE OF REPRESENTATIVES, WASHINGTON, SEPTEMBER 23RD, 1890,	498
MAKING HIS FIRST SPEECH IN THE HOUSE OF REPRESENTATIVES, JANUARY 16, 1891,	514
HILLSIDE COTTAGE, WASHINGTON, D. C.,	521
PORTRAIT OF MISS. NETTIE D. LANGSTON,	527
PORTRAIT OF MRS. J. M. LANGSTON,	531

CONTENTS.

CHAPTER I.

Parents and Birthplace—Emancipation Deed of his Mother—Will and Testament of his Father—The Four Orphans, . . . 11

CHAPTER II.

Settlement of his Father's Estate—Changes upon the Plantation—Uncle Billy Quarles—The Fugitive Slave—The Preparation and Departure for Ohio—Arrival at Chillicothe, ... 23

CHAPTER III.

Becomes a Member of the Gooch Family—Col. Wm. D. Gooch—The Family—Early Education—" Westward, Ho!" the Popular Sentiment—Starts for Missouri with the Goochs—The Court Interferes and Requires his Return—The Separation from his Friends, ... 37

CHAPTER IV.

The Great Change—Receives needed and valuable Discipline under Mr. Long—Goes to Cincinnati—The Limited Educational Advantages Offered the Colored Youth there—Deep Seated and Growing Sentiment against the Colored People—Cowardly and Deadly Attack upon them in 1840—Dark Days, . . . 54

CHAPTER V.

Colonel Gooch visits him—The Promise which he did not Keep—Returns to Chillicothe—High Record in School—" You Have in you, John, all the Elements of an Orator," 68

CHAPTER VI.

Decides to go to Oberlin College—His Arrival—First Impressions—The First Year—Success as a Country School-teacher—Returns to College—" We do not Entertain Niggers "—Graduates, 1849, ... 77

CONTENTS.

PAGE.

CHAPTER VII.

Oberlin, its Community and its College—The "Oberlin Movement"—The Founders of the College—Oberlin, a Leader and Reformer—The "Liberty School"—Fugitive Slave Population—"What shall I do?" 97

CHAPTER VIII.

Seeks Admission to a Certain Law School, but is Denied—"I am a Colored American"—"I Do not need Sympathy," . . . 104

CHAPTER IX.

Studies Theology—Refuses many Desirable Calls—Studies Law in Judge Bliss' Office—Makes Rapid Advancement—Admitted to the Bar, 1854, ... 111

CHAPTER X.

Purchases a Farm—Rural Life—His Disagreeable Neighbor—A Negro-hater—His First Case—Success and Pocket Full of Retainers—Strong Anti-negro Sentiment in Ohio—"That Darkey is too Smart for You"—His Marriage, . . . 126

CHAPTER XI.

Anniversary Meeting, American Anti-Slavery Society, May, 1855—His Speech, ... 147

CHAPTER XII.

Sells his Farm and Settles in Oberlin—His new Home—"*A Nigger Lawyer*"—Resents an Insult and is a Winner—His Practise and Success as the Colored Lawyer of Ohio—His First Colored Client, ... 156

CHAPTER XIII.

A Rare and Interesting Case which Tested his Powers, . . 171

CHAPTER XIV.

Prophetic Events Preceding the great Struggle and Overthrow of Slavery—Negro-catchers in Oberlin—Kidnapping of John Price—The Rescue—Arrest of Citizens, their Conviction and Release—John Brown, Jr. visits him—Three Oberlin Men Join John Brown's Immortal Spartan Band, ... 181

CHAPTER XV.

Recruits Colored Troops for the National Service—The 54th Massachusetts—The 55th Massachusetts—The 5th United States Colored Troops, ... 198

Contents.

CHAPTER XVI.

First Official Errand to the National Capital—General Lee's Surrender—Assassination of Lincoln—Colored Camp at Nashville—The Fugitive Slave Again, ... 218

CHAPTER XVII.

Early Labors and Observations among the Freed People—First Official Trip through the South—His Faith in his People—The Colored Women, ... 232

CHAPTER XVIII.

First Professional Call to Washington—Appointed General Inspector of the Bureau of Refugees, Freedmen and Abandoned Lands—Mr. Langston and the Republican Party—Visits his old Home—Lousia Court House, ... 249

CHAPTER XIX.

His Labors in the South—Their Influence and Effect—President Johnson opposed to General Howard—Action of General Grant—Prosperity of the Colored People in the Old North State—His Popularity in the Carolinas, ... 275

CHAPTER XX.

Founds and Organizes the Law Department of Howard University—Is made its Vice and Acting President—Ralph Waldo Emerson visits the University—First Lady Law Student, . . 296

CHAPTER XXI.

President Grant Appoints him a Member of the Board of Health of the District of Columbia—*Personnel* of the Board—Resignation—Resolutions and Gifts of his Associates, ... 318

CHAPTER XXII.

Three Great Enterprises—Charlotte Scott—The Lincoln Monument—Freemen's Saving and Trust Company—Minor Normal School, ... 335

CHAPTER XXIII.

Appointed Minister-resident and Consul-general to Haiti—Arrival and Reception—First Impressions—Haiti and the Haytians—Port-au-Prince, ... 350

CONTENTS.

PAGE.

CHAPTER XXIV.

The Legation and Residence of the American Minister—*San Souci*—Diplomatic and Consular Services and Achievements—Our Trade with Haiti greatly Increased—" The Haytians have gone crazy on American Blue Denims," 375

CHAPTER XXV.

Suit against the United States Government for Balance of Unpaid Salary—Judgment Secured—Paid in Full—The Case a Precedent of Importance, ... 401

CHAPTER XXVI.

Accepts the Presidency of the Virginia Normal and Collegiate Institute—His work of Organization—The School Flourishes under his Guidance—Gen. Fitzhugh Lee, ... 409

CHAPTER XXVII.

Resigns the Presidency and Leaves the Institute—Beloved by his Scholars—Their Expressions of Friendship, ... 425

CHAPTER XXVIII.

Nominated to the Fifty-first Congress—Opposed by General Mahone—" *No colored man would be allowed to stand* "—The " *Nigger* " must be Beaten—The Black Belt of Virginia—The Campaign—" Harrison, Morton and Langston's Invincibles," 438

CHAPTER XXIX.

Election Day, November 6, 1888—Represenatives at Every Polling Place—Voting in Petersburg—The Result—Counted Out—Fights for his Seat and Wins—Admission to the House of Representatives, September 23, 1890, ... 474

CHAPTER XXX.

Congressional Experience and Record—Close Observation of House Affairs—The Fifty-first Congress and its Leaders—Its Important Enactments—Mr. Langston Returns to his District at Close of Session—Visiting his Constituents—First Speech—Bills Introduced—Declines Nomination to Fifty-third Congress, . . 504

CHAPTER XXXI.

Description of Hillside Cottage and Surroundings—The Family—Arthur, Ralph, Nettie and Frank ; their Education, Marriage, etc.—The Grandchildren—Mrs. Langston—Mrs. Fidler—Miss Percival—The old Home in Virginia, ... 521

PORTRAIT OF JOHN MERCER LANGSTON, 1894.

CHAPTER I.

PARENTS AND BIRTHPLACE.

JOHN MERCER LANGSTON was born upon a plantation, located three miles from Louisa Court House, in Louisa County, Virginia, on the 14th day of December, 1829.

The plantation was a large one, beautifully located and well appointed in every respect. It was fully furnished with slaves, according to the custom of the times, and being of rich, fertile soil, was made valuable in the cultivation of products peculiar to that section of the State and the country.

Upon this plantation, after the manner and habit of the wealthy slave-holding classes, there were found the Great House, occupied by the owner for his own special accommodation; the smaller, though in this case the equally important one, used as the residence and home of the *favored slave* of the place; with such usual quarters as were necessary to meet the demands of the common slaves, engaged in ordinary field and other services.

The owner of this plantation was Captain Ralph Quarles, a man of large wealth, having in his own right great landed possessions, with many slaves. His social relations were of excellent character, as his name imports, among those acquainted with his family. He was a person of broad and varied education, with a love of learning and culture remarkable for his day; while his habits of leisure, natural inclination and circumstances, offered abundant opportunity, with such influences as contributed to the enlargement and perfection of his general information. His views with regard to slavery and the management of slaves upon a plantation by overseers, were peculiar and unusual. He believed that slavery ought to be abolished. But he maintained that the mode of its abolition should be by the voluntary individual action of the owner. He held that slaves should be dealt with in such manner, as to their superintendence and management, as to prevent cruelty, always, and to inspire in them, so far as practicable, feelings of confidence in their masters. Hence, he would employ no overseer, but, dividing the slaves into groups, convenient for ordinary direction and employment, make one of their own number the chief director of the force. Of course, on this plan, care must be exercised, in his judgment, to prevent any feelings of jealousy, or misunderstanding, among those whose benefit was sought. With such views put in practice upon his plantation, it is not difficult to perceive, that his course would attract attention, with comment not always approving; often, in fact, severe and condemnatory. Besides, such course, finally, as was natural and inevitable, under the circumstances, wrought social ostracism, compelling one holding such views and adopting such practices, to pursue exclusive life among his own slaves, with such limited society otherwise, as might be brought by business interests, or merely personal regard, within his reach. Thus situated, it was not unnatural for such person to find a woman, a companion for life, among his slaves, to whom he gave his affections; and, if forbidden by law to sanctify, in holy wedlock, their relations, to take and make her, Heaven approving their conduct, the mother of his children.

Captain Quarles came of an ancestry distinguished for the vigor of its intellect and the robustness of its manhood. Once fixed in its convictions and determinations, nothing seemed able to hinder or change its course of action. The son of such ancestry was loyal and patriotic, not only as a matter of duty, but by reason of the very elements and instincts of his nature. So that, at the call of his country, in the Revolutionary times, he made quick response and served with such courage and devotion, as to win not only the military title ascribed to him, but distinction among her best and bravest sons.

The woman for whom he discovered special attachment and who, finally, became really the mistress of the Great House of the plantation, reciprocating the affection of her owner, winning his respect and confidence, was the one whom he had taken and held, at first, in pledge for money borrowed of him by her former owner; but whom, at last, he made the mother of his four children, one daughter and three sons. Her name was Lucy Langston. Her surname was of Indian origin, and borne by her mother, as she came out of a tribe of Indians of close relationships in blood to the famous Pocahontas. Of Indian extraction, she was possessed of slight proportion of negro blood; and yet, she and her mother, a full-blooded Indian woman, who was brought upon the plantation and remained there up to her death, were loved and honored by their fellow-slaves of every class. Lucy was a woman of small stature, substantial build, fair looks, easy and natural bearing, even and quiet temper, intelligent and thoughtful, who accepted her lot with becoming resignation, while she always exhibited the deepest affection and earnest solicitude for her children. Indeed, the very last words of this true and loving mother, when she came to die, were uttered in the exclamation, "Oh, that I could see my children once more!"

As early as 1806, as her emancipation papers show, Captain Quarles set Lucy and her daughter Maria, then her only child, at liberty. Subsequently, three other children, sons, were born to them; and, though it may be indirectly, they were certainly and positively recognized by Captain Quarles, as his children, in his last will and testament.

The emancipation deed of Lucy and her daughter Maria reads as follows:

"Be it known to all whom it may concern, that I, Ralph Quarles of Lousia "County, do hereby liberate, manumit, and set free my negro slaves Lucy, a "woman, and Maria a girl, daughter of said Lucy; and I do hereby renounce "forever all right, jurisdiction, authority, and power, which I have, or may "lawfully exercise, over the said slaves. And I do hereby declare the said "slaves to be henceforward free persons, at liberty to go when and where they "please, and to exercise and enjoy all the rights of free persons so far as I can "authorize, or the laws of Virginia will permit; and I hereby bind myself, my "heirs, executors, etc., to warrant and forever defend to the said Lucy and "Maria their right to freedom, clear of the claims of all persons whatsoever. "In testimony whereof, I have hereunto affixed my seal and signed my name, "this first day of April one thousand eight hundred and six.
"(Signed)   RALPH QUARLES."

The three sons born to such parents were Gideon Q., Charles H., and John M. Langston; the children under the circumstances following the condition of their mother and bearing her name.

That portion of the last will and testament of Captain Quarles, which has to do with the three sons here mentioned, is contained in the following words:

"In the name of God, Amen! I, Ralph Quarles, of the County of Louisa, and "State of Virginia, reflecting on the uncertainty of human life, have thought "proper to make and ordain this my last will and testament in manner and "form following, that is to say:

"1st. I desire that out of the money that I may have at my death and the "debts that may be owing to me at that time, all my just debts and necessary "expenses may be paid.

"2d. I give and devise to Gideon Langston, Charles Langston, and John "Langston, the three youngest children of Lucy, a woman whom I have eman- "cipated by a deed of emancipation bearing date the first day of April one thou- "sand eight hundred and six and duly admitted to record in the Clerk's Office of "the County Court of Louisa, to them and their heirs forever all my lands lying "on Hickory Creek and its waters in the County of Louisa together with all my "stock of horses, cattle, sheep, hogs and bees, and household and kitchen fur- "niture, and plantation and all other utensils of every sort whatsoever, including "wagons, carts and still, and all the grain of every kind, and all the hay and "fodder, and dead victuals that I may have on the above-mentioned lands at the 'time of my death, and also all the crops of every kind that may be growing there- "on at that time to be equally divided among them whenever they may think "proper to divide it. But if the said Gideon Langston, Charles Langston, and "John Langston should wish to remove to some other place during the time "between my death and the time of the youngest of them coming of age, then and "in that case it is my will and I do hereby direct that my executors, the survivors "or survivor of them may sell the above-mentioned lands and lay out the

PARENTS AND BIRTHPLACE.

"money arising from the sales thereof in such other lands as they the said
"Gideon Langston, Charles Langston, and John Langston may wish it laid
"out in. And I also give and devise to them the said Gideon Langston.
"Charles Langston, and John Langston and their heirs all the money that I
"may have at the time of my death, and also all the debts of every description
"that may be owing to me at that time except what I have hereinbefore
"particularly disposed of and what I may hereinafter particularly dispose of,
"and I desire that my executors, the survivors or survivor of them may
"either lay out that part of the above-mentioned money and debts which they
"the said Gideon Langston, Charles Langston and John Langston may be
"entitled to in lands or put it out at interest for their benefit until they
"severally attain the age of twenty-one years, and as they attain that age pay
"them their equal parts. And I moreover give to them the said Gideon
"Langston, Charles Langston and John Langston and their heirs all my
"United States Bank Stock, and also all my Virginia Bank Stock, and desire
"that my executors the survivors or survivor of them may receive the dividends
"as they become due on the said Bank Stock and apply the money to the
"support and maintenance of them the said Gideon Langston, Charles
"Langston, and John Langston if necessary, if not put it out at interest till
"they severally attain the age of twenty-one years, and as they attain that age
"pay them their equal parts of the said Bank Stock and interest, if any, that
"may have accrued.

*　　*　　*　　*　　*　　*　　*　　*　　*　　*

"And lastly I do hereby constitute and appoint Mr. Nathaniel Mills and Mr.
"William D. Gooch, and my nephews David Thomson and John Quarles
"executors of this my last will and testament, hereby revoking all other or
"former wills or testaments by me heretofore made. The foregoing will is
"wholly written by myself and will therefore require no subscribing witnesses
"to prove it.

"In witness whereof I have hereunto set my hand and affixed my seal this
"18th day of October in the year of our Lord one thousand eight hundred and
"thirty-three.

"(Signed)　　　　　　　　RALPH QUARLES."

It is apparent from the gifts of landed and personal property made in his will that Captain Quarles regarded the sons of Lucy, described therein, as sustaining peculiar relations to him as well as to her; and, hence, his unusually generous and considerate treatment of them. Could his tender care of them, in their extreme youth, and his careful attention to their education, as discovered by him as soon as they were old enough for study, be made known, one could understand, even more sensibly, how he loved and cherished them; being only prevented from giving them his own name and settling upon them his entire estate, by the circumstances of his position, which would not permit either the one or the other. He did for his sons all he could; exercising paternal wisdom, in the partial distribution of his property in their behalf and the appointment of judicious executors of his will, who understood his purposes and were faithful in efforts necessary to execute them. Thus, he not only provided well for the education of his sons, but, in large measure, made allowance for their settlement in active, profitable business-life.

The Virginia plantation upon which John, like the other sons, was born, and spent the first and tenderest years of his life, was one of the very best and most wisely-ordered of his native State. It was fertile, handsomely located, in the midst of a beautiful section of the country, and surrounded by other extensive, rich and productive farms, distinguished for their improvements of valuable and excellent character. The owners of several of these plantations, the most desirable, were blood connections of Captain Quarles. All of such plantations were cultivated by slave labor. Whatever may have been the rigor of its management upon other plantations of the neighborhood, upon that upon which the sons of Lucy Langston were born and spent their early lives, no one witnessed, in dealings had with the slaves thereupon, any other than mild, well tempered and considerate treatment.

For twenty years before his death, no white man resided upon his plantation other than Captain Quarles himself. No overseer was employed; and none other than a single young colored boy, one of the slaves, was punished in any wise during such period. He had persistently disobeyed the orders of his superintendent after being several times warned and directed by his owner; and, thus, incorrigible, deserved and received merited correction only.

Indeed, Captain Quarles, by reason of his personal convictions and opinions, with respect to the humane and considerate treatment of all slaves, sought to demonstrate, upon his own plantation, the wisdom and advantage of such plans of management, as were calculated to develop the self-respect and self-reliance of every slave. He allowed and tolerated, therefore, no abuses, outrages, or severe and unnatural scourgings upon his place; but cultivated kind, and so far as practicable, indulgent treatment of every one. So he gained the respect and confidence of all, and might very well trust his people, as was his habit, to govern and direct, largely, their own movements. To this end, he divided his slaves, as already stated, and furnishing superintendents and managers of their own number, easily accomplished his purposes.

In the midst of such conditions of slave life and the social environments connected therewith, the boy John began life, influenced by such knowledge of his father, who always treated him tenderly and affectionately, and by such loving care of his mother, as seem natural and inevitable.

In their advanced age, as late as 1834, Captain Quarles and Lucy Langston, after brief illness, on the part of either, died upon the plantation, where they had lived so long together. The former, as he neared his end, requested and ordered, that Lucy, when she died, should be buried by his side, and, accordingly, upon a small reservation in the plantation, they sleep together their long quiet sleep. While the humblest possible surroundings mark the spot of their burial, no one has ever disturbed or desecrated it.

During his last sickness, Captain Quarles was attended only by Lucy, her children, and his slaves. During the two days his body lay upon its bier, in the Great House, it was guarded, specially and tenderly, by the noble negro slave, who, when his master was taken sick suddenly, and felt that he needed medical assistance, without delay, but a few nights before, hurried across the country to the home of the physician, and secured his aid for his stricken owner.

The beautiful day on which he was borne from his house to his last resting-place, by his slaves, and, in the midst of their tears and sobs, committed to the earth till the great Resurrection, was only surpassed in its brightness, its splendor and glory by the other day which quickly followed, when Lucy, who had fallen asleep in her own house, at the other end of the garden, was borne thence to her grave by his side, in the arms of the same true, considerate, Christian people, many of them, then slaves, but on the verge of their emancipation and freedom.

Among those who followed their aged parents to the grave, were their own children, the one daughter and three sons, already named. Of such children, Maria was the only one who, born before her mother was set free, was like her a slave; and, hence, was made the subject of emancipation. Far older than either of the other children, she had not only experienced, in this single way, the deep interest which her father took in her; but in every attention given to her support, education and improvement, she had enjoyed the most abundant evidence of his fatherly disposition toward her, and his constant solicitude for her welfare.

At the time of her emancipation, Maria was esteemed a young girl of fine looks, intelligent and well behaved. Early care was shown for her improvement; and though she was not taught with the same thoroughness as her brothers, who were by many years her junior, her education was not neglected, and her knowledge of books was unusual, certainly for a girl of her class—even for any young girl of her times. She spelled, read and wrote well, being reasonably advanced in all the ordinary elementary English branches. Besides, she was not without that sort of general culture, gained at home, in rather intimate association with her father, who, as already stated, was not only a man of excellent native endowment, but learning and refinement.

Attractive as Maria was, for the reasons indicated, as well as others, it may not be considered surprising that she married early in life, upon the approval of her father, who thereupon located her, in handsome manner, upon a plantation in his own neighborhood, which he bought and gave her. He purchased the person, who was her husband, as he did several other slaves, men and women, and gave them all to his daughter. For many years, this remarkable woman, the only daughter of Ralph Quarles, conducted not only all her household and domestic affairs generally, with wisdom and success; but all her business matters, growing meantime a large number of sons and daughters, maintaining her family, constantly, in respectable and prosperous social condition. Through her influence and her own efforts, every son of hers and every daughter was given a reasonably fair English education, with instruction in every sort of domestic and plantation industry, with sound moral and religious training. Her children numbered in all twenty-one persons. And, it is not known to-day, when or where, any son or daughter of hers, has failed in manly or womanly duty to the community. Besides being persons of fair looks, substantial physical development and sound mental endowment, the children of Maria have not failed to so improve themselves as to be able to exert wholesome educational and moral influence upon their own offspring; and thus perpetuate the character and teachings of parents and grand-parents, who must ever be loved, honored and revered.

Maria lived to be an aged woman; and she and her husband, Joseph Powell, were grateful enough, as they were permitted to see one after another of their family to better their condition, as believed, some married, others still single, leave their old home for a new and improved one, in what was then the western State of Ohio.

Finally, these excellent parents, the wife dying first and the husband following shortly thereafter, were gathered in their long sweet sleep to the father and mother of the wife, who had gone before them.

The other children, the fruits of the union between Captain Quarles and Lucy Langston, were the three boys named, born, respectively, in 1809, 1817, and 1829. The first of these boys was Gideon, born on the 15th day of June in the year indicated. Cared for by his mother and nurse in tender affectionate manner, he soon reached his seventh year in playful, interesting life on the plantation. At this age, he was a bright, intelligent, active, promising young lad, of remarkably good looks and manly bearing. His father manifesting the deepest interest in him, sought by his own efforts and influence to give him such thorough English education, with general information and mental and moral improvement, as to make him a useful man. The boy was in no wise wanting in native aptitude for intellectual accomplishments—even for earnest, persistent and protracted study. Nor was he found averse to any one of the requirements enjoined upon him by his instructor. He was required to appear, for his recitations, in his father's special apartments, the year round, at five o'clock in the morning; and be ready after his duties in such respect had been met, at the usual hour, to go with the slave boys of his age to such service upon the plantation as might be required of them. Thus his father adopted in his case, the rule of intellectual and manual training at one and the same time; so that when he reached his majority, he was well-developed in body, and strong and firm; while in intellect, he was well advanced in English study, with his powers, mental and moral, in good trim for earnest, scholarly labor, within the measure and limits of his opportunities.

So much had Gideon followed in look, in physical conformation, mental endowment, temper, taste and disposition, his father and those of his father's family, that, at his twenty-first birthday, a very significant addition was made to his name. Thereafter, he was called Gideon *Quarles* Langston. He was a young man then of fine appearance, and impressive and agreeable presence; and among his friends, he was always admired as an excellent type of manly character, made even more admirable by his gentle and pleasing manners. His physical peculiarities were all of Anglo-Saxon stamp. He was naturally of religious turn of mind; and discovered under all circumstances becoming interest in those about him, however humble and lowly, seeking where possible to render them some service. These traits of character, especially, were calculated to create and sustain strong attachments for him, not only among those who resided on the plantation with him, but among those, who, residing on neighboring plantations, had made his acquaintance.

Charles was sixteen years of age, only, at the death of his father. In blood, mind and disposition, he partook of the lineage of his mother. He was not large nor apparently firm of body; but well endowed intellectually. His disposition and temper though ordinarily well controlled, were not naturally of the easy and even sort. In his constitution, he was impetuous and aggressive; and under discipline and opposition, he was always restive, yet, he yielded with reasonable docility and obedience to the training to which his father, interested in his education, sought to subject him.

From seven years of age or thereabout, brought under the tuition of his parent, he made, under the circumstances, disturbed as he was often by attacks of ill health, unusual progress in manual and mental improvement. The discipline which was adopted in his case was precisely the same as that followed in dealing with his brother, Gideon ; and was, naturally, adapted to the one and the other, in special sense only, as they differed somewhat in mental make and moral traits and peculiarities. The difference between the two boys, in such respects, was as marked and noteworthy as the diversity in their physical construction. Nevertheless the discipline adopted for their improvement proved to be advantageous, certainly, in large measure to both of them.

Charles was peculiar in this respect, however, as we shall see in the sequel, that his knowledge and power in an emergency never failed him ; and, as a rule, was even then more vigorous and marked. Early this trait of character manifested itself. If he mastered study with less facility and with greater difficulty, by reason of any want of taste in such regard and application, he was never wanting in originality and special individual power.

The start which his father gave him in study was of large service throughout his life ; and although his education as gained by such means was not so thorough and perfect as that of his brother, it made deep impression upon him and did more than anything else connected with his life, to induce him to pursue the after-course of study which made him stronger, more intelligent and useful in his matured manhood. Not possessed of Gideon's personal presence, nor so fortunate as he in favor or manner; in debate, or in urgent trying rhetorical effort, while they were both, finally, men of decided influence in such respects, he far surpassed his brother, and, as between the two, was by far the most successful and masterly disputant and orator. Less religious, naturally, than Gideon; intolerant from his very boyhood of everything like superstition; demanding always of his fellow the reason for his faith; more retiring, more sensitive, and less communicative, while respected and admired by all who knew him, he was, always, less a favorite, generally, than his brother.

John, the child of the advanced years of his parents, was in his fourth year when they died. However affectionately treated by his father, he was too young for any attempt to be made at his education. His mother was so situated as to make it necessary that care and attention be given him constantly by a nurse. From his birth he was committed to the care of a slave woman, Lucky. When his father died and was buried, this woman carried him to the funeral and the grave. When his mother was dying, she bore him to her bedside, that the dying mother might give her child her parting caresses with her lasting benediction. And, when his mother was buried, it was this woman who took him to her funeral and grave, and soothed and solaced his agitated, aching little heart with sweet, gentle, affectionate caresses.

CHAPTER II.

THE SAD SEPARATION AND DEPARTURE FOR OHIO.

How many changes depend on death! The moral and legal changes which it works are often as marvellous and surprising as the physical! Through its agency one goes to his long home, and his endless sleep! Another is called to that condition of active life thereby, in society, sometimes in wealth, often in responsibility, which tests all his powers, and makes, or shipwrecks, his future.

The time had come when, through the death of Captain Ralph Quarles, everybody upon his plantation, his children and all his slaves, had not only to change their situation, but most of them to experience a long and final separation. Property of whatever character, as enjoined by the law, or directed by the provisions of his last will and testament, might be distributed and settled upon those in interest without difficulty, or moral shock. The land even, which composed the plantation, which had been for so many years the home of all now grief-stricken and full of anxiety and solicitude for their future, might pass without legal jar by devise to those who were fortunate enough to have won the consideration of a generous testator. All his property, personal or real, must now pass, in accordance with lawful or testamentary regulation, to those who, in such regard, might be esteemed representatives of the dead.

It is easier much to mark divisions in ownership of property and alien title and possession thereto, than to separate, even in prospect of a more fortunate position in life, those, who have, in constant, intimate, friendly association, spent their days together, giving one another those evidences of sympathy and kindly affection, which win and hold the heart of man to his fellow.

Any slaves disposed of, in this case, must go now to those to whom given. Any of the same class emancipated, must seek by independent individual effort, in freedom, their living and support. At all events, the time had come for each and all upon this plantation to say good-bye and farewell, the one to the other. A separation, under such circumstances, certainly has features that are sad enough to those who had lived so long together and so agreeably, even though most of them had been held as property and inured to daily tasks, often heavy and trying. Even those who had been given their freedom found it hard to leave any of their old comrades, especially as they were to remain in slavery. Certainly, those allotted to such condition, could experience no feelings of satisfaction and pleasure, or resignation of soul, even in a separation which might send any of their former associates into such liberty as they might enjoy in a free State of the North. The scene of grief and sorrow produced by the separation here described, as the same appears now, in memory, to one, then but a child, who witnessed it, was sad and affecting beyond human endurance; and anyone who was witness to it may never lose the effect produced upon his heart.

The last will and testament of Captain Quarles, in accordance with whose provisions, he ordered the distribution of his estate, including all slaves, stocks, and cash, was made by himself, as he declares, upon due reflection and without the least undue influence. It is a remarkable paper, and when understood in the light of the circumstances which surrounded the testator when published, must be regarded as one noted for its wisdom and sagacity. In order to the accomplishment of his purposes with respect to his children, it was necessary for him to exercise here the largest care and caution; and yet his will must be considered as expressive in important senses, beyond doubt, of the peculiar views and maxims which had governed his life.

That which occupied the chief purpose of his mind, filling the largest place in his heart, commanding his attention first of all, in making it, was how he could most effectively and certainly provide for his sons. Though partially colored, and the children of a woman whom he had owned and set free, he made them his principal legatees, giving them in large measure his real and personal property. Distribution of portions of his estate was so made to near kinsmen, and in such character and quantity, as to prevent attempt to set aside his will and nullify his purposes with respect to his children. Could he have done so safely, he would have, doubtless, through bequest and devise, bestowed upon them, large and valuable as it was, his entire estate, except his slaves. So far as the slaves were concerned, could he have followed his desires and convictions, he would have emancipated every one of them. He feared, however, that should he attempt such settlement of his property and the freedom of his slaves, all his purposes, in such regard, would have been defeated. According to his best understanding, he distributed his property, including his children as specially interested, as already shown; and went so far as to emancipate several of the principal and most valuable of the slaves described in his will. The language used by him in that section of the will, which respects the liberation of such slaves, is very remarkable. It reads:

"I do hereby liberate, manumit, and set free my slaves, Billy, Burrel, James, "Jr. and Arthur, and all other slaves that I may have any right or title to, not "hereinbefore particularly disposed of; and I do hereby declare the said "slaves to be henceforward free and at liberty to go when and where they "please, and to exercise and enjoy all the rights of freedom so far as I can "authorize or the laws of Virginia will permit. And I do hereby give to the "said Billy two hundred and twenty dollars; and to the said Burrel, James, "Jr. and Arthur, I give each one hundred and twenty dollars, to be paid out "of the debts that I may have owing to me at the time of my death."

It will not be doubted that Captain Quarles did all in his power, situated as he was, to serve his own sons, and to promote the welfare of his servants. In the appointment of the executors of his estate, it is a fact, that he chose four of the wealthiest and most influential men of his county; all slave-holders to be sure, but persons well known and deservedly esteemed. One of them, Col. William D. Gooch, did not qualify and serve in such capacity, though a special personal friend of the testator, whose advice was often sought in matters of business, and upon general subjects of importance and interest, and whose judgment was wont, always, to be regarded with sincere consideration and confidence. Colonel Gooch did not serve because before Captain Quarles died he had concluded to leave the State of Virginia, and having disposed of his possessions there, settled with his family in Chillicothe, Ross County, Ohio. The other three gentlemen, however, did qualify, and acted accordingly, as an item of the court record of Louisa County will show. They did not proceed, however, without giving their several bonds, which aggregated one hundred and eighty thousand dollars, conditioned that they would honestly and faithfully discharge their duties as defined and prescribed in the last will and testament under which they had been appointed. Perhaps, if Captain Quarles had searched the whole State of Virginia, he could not have found three persons who would have more impartially, and sincerely and efficiently executed the purposes and objects of his will; and, in this connection, it may not be inappropriate to express, even now and here, the deep gratitude which all concerned ever felt toward these men, who failed, in no respect, in the honest and just discharge of their duties. It is true that the men who thus acted have been dead many years; and it is equally true that all those who were most directly interested in their management of the estate upon which they administered, have, also, been buried for many years past, save the one who writes these words; and yet, he, moved as he is by feelings of obligation himself, would record, in earnest phrase, the indebtedness and appreciation of those who are no longer able to speak for themselves.

THE SAD SEPARATION.

But at last the sad separation comes! It is final and decisive in the lives of all those immediately concerned! Jacob and his wife, Winney, with their daughter, Lucy and her children, Lucky, Johnson, Martha, Anthony, Edward, Henry and Ann, are seen busy in preparation for their departure from the plantation. They spend an hour or such matter in gathering together the remnant of their little effects scattered here and there. Abram and Lawrence are employed with looks and manner, significant enough, as they occupy themselves in like manner and to the same purpose. At last, these are all ready to take their leave. Messrs. Ralph and John Quarles, nephews of the testator to whom these slaves had been given, had already come to take them to their own neighboring plantations.

Those who were making preparation to leave soon for Ohio, Gideon, Charles, and John, with Billy, Burrel, James Jr. and Arthur, appear at the door of the great deserted mansion, near which their friends, so long their associates, for whom they bore such cordial attachment, are gathered, to bid them farewell! This meeting and this separation were touching and pathetic enough! And it was not unnatural that the white men present, seeing those dark-hued friends, all in tears, hearing their sighs, and witnessing other manifestations of their deep grief, should turn their faces aside, to hide their own agitated feelings, as they themselves were moved by this heartrending scene of parting.

Abram and Lawrence go off in one direction with their new master to his plantation. Jacob, with his family, not separated as to a single member, thank God! take up their way, under the guidance of Mr. John Quarles, whom they shall thereafter serve, to their home a little more distant.

Those who are to take another journey, so entirely different—one to freedom in a far-off State—at a day so near at hand, watch, in affectionate solicitude, those who leaving are soon lost to sight in the distance. These turn in silence, then, with heavy hearts to thoughts and duties which press upon them, in view of those necessary preparations, incident to the movements which they must undertake and accomplish before their own departure from scenes and surroundings, in the midst of which they were all born, and which becoming familiar and pleasant in the growing days of their lives, have won and held their affections.

Two months elapsed in preparation, with such assistance as the executors, Nathaniel Mills, David Thomson and John Quarles, could give, by those who would soon make their westward trip.

During this period, Uncle Billy Quarles, designated in the will Billy, the most aged, the most largely experienced, and naturally the most intelligent of the company still remaining upon the plantation, became by general consent its guardian and protector. He was withall a very religious man, noted throughout the neighborhood for his deep piety and the unction with which he always expressed himself in favor of pure and undefiled religion. His utterances always discovered his constitutional, positive superstition, which largely influenced and determined his spiritual faith, and explained, generally, his acceptance, or rejection, of any appearance, fact, or unusual movement in nature and conduct. He was a staunch believer, also, in ghosts. And not unfrequently, sounds and movements, which excited his attention and attracted his interest, were ascribed to such agency, at work for man's good, as he would claim, by appointment of divine Providence. Had he not been thus superstitious, afraid of ghosts, and easily disturbed by strange noises and curious sights, so commonly found figuring in the imagination of the too credulous Virginia slave of the olden time, he would have been by reason of his natural endowments and general qualities of character, with his experience and observation, eminently successful in any efforts which he might have been called to make, in such capacity.

For several years anterior to the time here mentioned, the neighborhood in which the plantation spoken of was located, was famous for the presence of several remarkable characters, who had left certain plantations located there, and as fugitive slaves spent their days concealed in the adjoining forests; while, during the night-season, they paid visits to any negro quarters, and sometimes even to other portions of such places as they desired to, for food or other necessary thing. Frequently, by their presence as they first appeared, or were heard, they caused great fear and trepidation even to those of their dusky friends who knew them well, and would do whatever they might to shelter and sustain them.

The most noted among these characters, was a black man of towering build, strong and sinewy, with hair and beard quite abundant for his complexion, unkempt and unshaken, who, with solemn tread and thrilling voice, periodically leaving his hiding-place, came among those who had known him from his very youth. Now, however, they had invested him by reason of his wild, mysterious, weird character, with all those peculiarities of awe and dread calculated to inspire fear and trembling in all those who might witness his ghostly and terror-inspiring approach. It had been a long time since this particular person had made his last visit; and it was generally believed that he had gone to other more safe and agreeable parts. Some felt that he had gone to the North. It might be even to Canada.

The night was a dark one, but not unpleasant by reason of rain, storm, or chill. It was not unpropitious for such visit as this fugitive slave now made to the Great House, where were congregated Uncle Billy and those hoping so soon to quit the plantation. The hour was early; and the promise of a quiet and pleasant night, to all indoors, was apparent. James was the only one who proposed to disturb the pleasure of the company by absenting himself. He decided to visit a neighboring plantation. Against this Uncle Billy offered serious objection, urging among other things that, since he had been set free and was about leaving the country, it became him, as it did all the others, to be exceedingly careful how he undertook such enterprises, under the circumstances. James, however, was persistent, stating in reply that he was well known to all persons upon the plantation which he would visit, and no one there would certainly fail to appreciate, as all would be pleased, with his call. He had not more than passed the garden gate, when a strange unusual rap was heard at the door, which threw Uncle Billy, at once, into great perturbation of mind, as shown in his exclamation: "There! Somebody is after that boy, Jeems, now!" Agitated as he was, he inquired: "Who is there?" A stentorian, oracular voice replied: "Open the door." Uncle Billy was not at all reassured; but whispered to those about him: "That voice is strange, and yet it seems to be one I have heard before." Still the old man was greatly disturbed, and even trembled, as admission was demanded again by the newcomer, at the door. Burrel, however, came to his relief, saying as he threw the door open: "Come in!" A strange towering black figure entering, said: "Boys, I have come for something to eat!"

All present, save John, recognized this wonderful, mysterious person, coming from the wilderness, as one whom they had heretofore seen, and whose presence, and manner, and words, were not wholly unfamiliar to them. They had known him to be one who was always terribly in earnest, never trifling; and while he found his home in the swamps and the desert places of the neighborhood, as a fugitive slave, he would serve no master other than the God who made him. Such a visit, at such a time, from such a person, was to Uncle Billy the augur of a prosperous future to those who would go hence to freedom and the blessings which it might bring. From this time forward, through his influence, moved as he was by the impression just described, the whole company pressed the preparations for their departure with redoubled vigor and enthusiasm.

Gideon, who was a young man of real courage and business ability, understanding well what was to be done and how to do it, led and directed in the arrangement of all those things which must precede their departure for Ohio. First of all, he secured authenticated copies of free papers, not only for himself, Charles and John, but for the other

30a

30b

LEAVING THE VIRGINIA PLANTATION.

THE SAD SEPARATION. 31

four persons, whom he would conduct safely to their prospective homes in another State. He obtained of the executors all the means necessary for the journey for the entire party; and further insisted that Uncle Billy, Burrel, James, Jr. and Arthur, be paid the respective amounts due them under the will.

At this time, no railroads had been built in this section of the country, and no easy, quick, convenient methods of travel had been established between the different States through which they must pass. Special provisions had, therefore, to be made for a trip such as is here contemplated. Conveyances as well as necessary teams must be provided; and to this end Gideon selected and purchased for himself and his brothers a vehicle in those days called a carry-all, with necessary harness and horses; and for Uncle Billy and his companions a light wagon, with harness and horses, suited to their use. So far as personal outfits, clothes, hats, shoes, and other necessary things, were concerned, ample provision was made.

All things had been made ready. The final words of counsel from the executors, especially those of the good and excellent Nathaniel Mills, had been spoken. The last kindly farewells of a host of true friends, white and colored, had been said. And now, early upon a bright and beautiful October morning in 1834, just as the dawn touched the eastern sky, these inexperienced wayfarers, at the time appointed, quitted the old plantation upon a journey which should prove to be to them all a new revelation. No one of them had ever gone beyond the neighborhood, except Uncle Billy, who had gone once or twice to Richmond, with the wagon, to carry tobacco and wheat. The road over which they were to journey was beset with inconveniences and difficulties. Besides being mountainous and rugged, it lay across a country largely without comfortable and accommodating stopping-places for travellers situated as these were. It was distinguished as well for the number of small streams, easily swollen by too frequent rains, which they must ford, however dangerous to strangers; and rivers which could only be crossed by ferries, with appliances of the crudest character.

They contemplated their situation, however, with real courage, and entered upon their journey with true spirit and purpose. Some anxiety was provoked, in view of the tender age and rather feeble constitution of John, then a child in his fourth year only. It was feared, especially by Uncle Billy, that he could not stand such a hard and fatiguing trip. Gideon soon quieted such apprehensions by assuring everyone that he could and would take due care of his young and delicate brother.

They had journeyed on without special noteworthy incident for several days, until they had reached the foot of the Allegheny Mountains, pressing on to the north and westward. They had driven on, gradually, day by day, pitching their tents and camping out by night, feeding and caring for the teams as thoroughly as they might; eating cold food, with warm drinks of tea and coffee, themselves, according to such supply as they had on hand. The sun had just gone down, on the evening of the first week after they had left Louisa Court House. They had just unhitched and unharnessed the teams; some were engaged in pitching the tents, while others went to the limpid mountain stream near at hand, to bring water for men and beasts; when a man on horseback, with saddlebags, attired as a traveller, was seen coming down the highway.

As this man came in sight, Gideon advanced upon him promptly, as if he recognized him, which was in fact the case. He addressed him in tender affectionate words, displaying the most cordial conduct towards him; when all joined in giving the stranger a warm and hearty welcome. This person was one possessing large conversational power, well informed and entertaining. The night was far spent, the moon had reached well-nigh its setting, before he had finished his interesting conversation to the tired travellers —old friends in fact of his, who composed his auditors. He told much of his home in Ohio: how he lived, and what he did there; how he was treated by all classes; when he left

THE SAD SEPARATION.

home, and what his experience had been as he journeyed alone southward to meet those who were now made so happy by his presence and his prospective assistance. He had left the town in Ohio, to which these friends and relatives of his were wending their way, upon the same day, as he supposed, that they had left Louisa Court House; and had expected to meet them sooner; and, if possible, so near their starting-point, as to make it practicable for him to hurry on even so far; spend there at least one day, and pressing his horse and himself in his return, overtake them within fifty miles, certainly, westward of the spot where this agreeable meeting occurred. Now, however, he concluded to go no further; but returning at once, direct and guide those who must travel the road over which he had just passed.

He had known all the persons in this company of travellers well, before he met them here, except the boy John, to whom he seemed drawn at once, and whom he constantly caressed with warm and deep affection. He seemed glad to hold and fondle him. At one time, he would declare that the child was the very picture of his mother; at another, that he was the very image of his father. From day to day, however, his affection as his interest in and for the boy seemed to grow and deepen, being manifested, continually, by loving and tender treatment. Finally, as an expression of his love for him, having arranged the stirrup-leathers of his saddle to fit his little legs and feet, he gave him, as he said, his horse, saddle and bridle. While he directed the horse, with the greatest care, he placed the child in the saddle to ride, and held him there to his great delight and satisfaction. Such treatment he accorded him, daily, to the very end of the journey; and, in a thousand other ways, he manifested his attachment to him, and won thereby his fond confidence.

This man, whose name we have not yet given, was William Langston, the eldest of the three first children—one son and two daughters—born to Lucy Langston, before she was taken from the plantation into the Great House, made housekeeper, and, finally, became the mother of the three sons of Captain Quarles heretofore mentioned and described. He was the half-brother, on the mother's side, to Gideon, Charles and John.

In this solitary place, at the foot of the mountains, for the first time William met his half-brother John, whom he had never seen; for, years before his birth, he, with Mary and Harriett, his sisters, had been emancipated by Captain Quarles and sent to Ohio. The sisters, constitutionally feeble, not standing the severe cold climate of the North, did not live many years after their settlement in that State. The brother, however, found himself very much at home there, and pursuing his trade as a carpenter and joiner, became permanently located at Chillicothe, in Ross County; and, at this time, led a most respected and prosperous life. Having passed over the road which was now being travelled by those whom he sought to aid, he was well prepared to give them valuable assistance. This he did; and by his presence and guidance contributed not a little to relieve them of much of the tediousness and fatigue of their journey.

Pushing on, it was not long before the party reached and crossed by ferry the Kanawa river. Holding steadily on their way, shortly thereafter they came in sight of the great Ohio; and coming upon its banks opposite the town of Gallipolis, they were at once set across in the same manner, creating, as they landed in this first town of Ohio, as they had done in several small ones through which they had passed in the State of Virginia, no little interest and concern among its people.

All seemed anxious at first to know who they were; where they were going; what they were going to do; whether they were really free; or whether Gideon was not a white man and the owner of them all. Any one save the child of the party was able to answer all such questions to the satisfaction of any intelligent person; while William kept all in good courage by his stout assurances, that these were good people—inquisitive to be sure, but that they meant and would do them no harm.

THE SAD SEPARATION.

Tarrying in Gallipolis for a single night only, they pushed on through Gallia and Jackson Counties, reaching a small negro settlement near Berlin Cross-roads, about noon on the third day after leaving that town. Here Uncle Billy, Burrel, James, Jr., and Arthur concluded to end their journey and settle in new homes. So they did. They had been careful in the use of their means and were able to buy small pieces of land, cheap as it was at that time and in that neighborhood, upon which they might respectively locate, and by their industry and accustomed frugality live in reasonable comfort.

Their numbers thus reduced, the other persons composing the party, with William still accompanying them, having in view now only their own destination and settlement, within the next two days found themselves in the battered and worn carry-all, with horses reduced in flesh—all, persons, animals and conveyance bearing a wretched and forlorn appearance—entering the famous, beautiful city of Chillicothe, once the capital of the State of Ohio.

The excitement produced by the arrival of these strangers ran high. The inhabitants of this city as well as those of the neighboring country were, for the most part, Virginians. Many of the families located here were composed of persons who had known these new-comers as they were situated and lived in Louisa County. Their arrival had been expected by many of such persons, who hoped to receive through them direct and reliable news from friends and relatives who still resided in the state of their birth, and in the county from which the Langstons had just come. They were, therefore, quickly surrounded by representatives of such families; and upon the streets, even before they had been able to locate themselves, were plied with questions, which discovered the anxiety and interest of those seeking tidings, in this way, from those whom they loved, and in whose welfare they cultivated constantly the deepest concern. All such inquiries were answered as made; sometimes briefly and in haste, but at all times with becoming respect and consideration. It is true, that such was the behavior of Gideon and Charles, in such respects, that they won at once marked attention and favor from those who questioned them.

Gideon and Charles, by the assistance and guidance of William, soon found comfortable stopping-places for themselves and their team; while John was carried directly to the house of Col. William D. Gooch, who had promised his father before his death, at his own home in Virginia, that when sent to Ohio, he would take, care for, and educate him.

CHAPTER III.

COL. WILLIAM D. GOOCH AND FAMILY.

THE family of Colonel Gooch consisted of himself, his wife and three daughters. Their residence, at the time John was taken into the household, was situated on the outskirts of the city of Chillicothe, to the southeastward, near Paint Creek; and the house which they occupied was peculiar for the place, as it was built of stone. Not long after John's advent, the colonel bought a large and valuable farm, one mile below the town, in the most fertile part of the Scioto Valley, upon the Ohio Canal, then the chief public thoroughfare of the State, running from Cleveland upon Lake Erie to Portsmouth on the Ohio river.

The home of this family was, in all respects, a model one. The parents and children were persons of remarkable qualities of character, possessing and cultivating such amiability of disposition, evenness of temper, and considerate regard for others and their happiness, as to win and hold every one's admiration and esteem.

Colonel Gooch himself, in personal appearance and bearing impressed one directly with the exalted chivalrous manhood which he possessed. In bodily build and development he was a prince, discovering in his fine head, pleasant face, full blue eyes, and well-formed nose, mouth, and chin, as well as the luminous display of conscious rectitude and strength found always in his generous countenance, that he was one who could, indeed, be trusted as husband, father and friend. There was no responsibility and no risk, which he was not ready to meet, to promote, defend, and protect all the interests committed to his care and keeping in such relations. At times, especially under circumstances which required of him earnest and deep reflection, he seemed stern; and yet, he was possessed of a sensibility as tender as possible, responsive, ever, to human necessity and trial.

Mrs. Gooch was a woman, wife and mother of rare elements of disposition and wisdom. Small of stature, but possessing great natural strength and endurance, she was constantly and judiciously engaged in cares and duties connected with her family and household. She neglected no obligation to her husband, or her children; nor did she hesitate, or fail, in respect to any courtesy, or service, however disagreeable, due from her to anyone. Her spirit and temper, in this last particular, were strikingly manifested in her reception and treatment of the new-comer to her home and care. It is not difficult to understand what must have been the condition of John, in person and clothing, neglected as he had been, in fact, for months, before he left the plantation in Virginia, and, then, directly thereafter spending all of three full weeks upon the road, in camp at night, and in carry-all by day. His male relatives and friends, who never so anxious to serve him, neither possessed the knowledge nor the patience necessary to the proper care of one so young. It is true that his brothers and friends did all that they could for him. But, at his age, and in his situation, he needed, daily, if not the attention of an intelligent mother, that of a judicious and painstaking nurse. At a glance, Mrs. Gooch saw his plight; and though the task of renovating his condition was truly a trying and unpleasant one, she displayed, in view of it, no evidences of hesitation or dread. So far from this, in less than two hours after arrival and welcome to the house, he had been thoroughly cleansed in person, changed in clothing, and given his seat by her own side at the table about which all gathered for supper. The various members of the family plied the boy with questions suited to his age, calculated to inspire him with feelings of contentment and satisfaction, manifesting in every word and act of theirs the deepest interest in him.

Mrs. Gooch at once became his mother to all intents and purposes; and during his residence in her family, in health or sickness, treated him in an endearing, affectionate manner. She won completely his confidence and fondness. It is true that John never loved anyone, as mother and parent, as he did, finally, this worthy woman, behind whose apron he felt, as against the whole world beside, that he was in a walled town. Such was the care given him in every way, that he soon became well known among the friends of the family throughout the community. And, by reason of such constant considerate treatment as the whole family accorded him, he lost measurably his own name in another given him, and by which he was usually called—Johnnie Gooch.

The daughters of the family were young ladies of such culture, beauty and influence, so esteemed in the community, as to command the special attention of the highest and best elements of social life. The two elder were so far advanced in age, and were of such attractive and pleasing person and character, that within the first two years after his adoption into the family, John witnessed their marriage to two foremost business gentlemen of Chillicothe, Messrs. Fisher and Eggleston. Immediately, they left their parents, and entered upon earnest substantial life in their own homes.

Virginia, the youngest daughter, born in the State after which she was named, was in personal appearance and behavior the very likeness of her father, modified only by her charming womanhood; while in disposition and temper she reflected the best possible image of her mother. At this time, she was a pupil of the then famous and flourishing Young Ladies' Seminary of the city of Chillicothe. Her conduct and record, as such student, attested the sobriety of her disposition and her exalted mental endowments. While apt and ready, as a scholar, she possessed, naturally, such diligence and application as to master and retain in her vigorous memory, the most difficult and intricate things of learning, with the greatest apparent ease. Her love of books was very great and unusual; and she never seemed to be really so happy as when engaged in their study.

Within a very few days after John became a member of the family, Virginia was directed by her parents to instruct him, according to his tender ability and understanding. Upon this duty she entered with such enthusiasm, diligence and wisdom, as to advance the boy, by means of her oral instructions, rapidly; not only in improved conditions of speech and manners, but so as to impart a reasonable knowledge, under the circumstances, of many of the elementary things of learning. Under her tuition and management, always so patient and tender, John's progress was so commendable that not infrequently Colonel Gooch and his wife applauded him, in view of his success, while they praised and encouraged their daughter for her good work done in his interest.

In such happy circumstances, with a guardian entirely considerate of his welfare in person and property, becoming to him indeed a father, full of solicitude and affection; taking him into his own family, where he found in Mrs. Gooch all that he needed in a kind and gentle mother, and in Virginia all that he might hope to find in a devoted sister and teacher, John spent the early happy days of his life in the charming home of his father's true and faithful friend.

In his last conversation had with Captain Quarles, just before he left Virginia for Ohio, Colonel Gooch had disclosed to him the earnest purpose of his friend to provide more thoroughly for the education of his three sons, by settling upon them a reasonable part of his estate; and by sending them to a free State, where he was assured they could gain public educational advantages, and secure such academic and collegiate opportunities as they might desire. Captain Quarles insisted that it was his desire, as it was his purpose, to have them so advanced and improved by study and learning, as to make them useful, influential members of society. In this conversation, he advised Colonel Gooch, with earnestness and emphasis, of his anxieties and desires with respect to his son John. He had not been able himself to give him a single lesson, nor to make upon his mind a single educational impression. With pressing solicitude, he dwelt to Colonel Gooch upon his wish that he would take John upon his being sent to Ohio, and while acting as the guardian of his person and property, look well and diligently to his education. Upon this last, and seemingly most important matter to Captain Quarles, Colonel Gooch gave his hearty and sincere promise that he would spare no pains, no effort and no reasonable outlay, to accomplish in the case of this boy what his anxious parent requested.

It was in keeping with such engagement, that the boy John was received at the house and home of Colonel Gooch, and was directed and taught in all those elementary branches of study which proved to be so beneficial to him. And opportunities of social advancement and improvement were for like reason accorded him ever, in Colonel Gooch's own family and among his own wealthy and cultured associates and friends. Colonel Gooch meant to keep to the letter, in its broadest sense, the obligation which he had assumed with respect to the care, education and culture of this boy. And the sequel will show even more fully how his purpose, in such behalf, was firm and decided.

John spent during his stay in the Gooch family, the principal part of his time at their beautiful home upon the canal. To this place the family had moved after he joined it; and it was the scene of his chief doings, while a member of the household. After the family had become located there he seemed to settle down to real permanent earnest life and duty. He acted as if he had in prospect a future, apparently as propitious and happy as the son of any home could have sought or desired. Every want and whim of his was noted and answered; and every attention given to his general nurture and admonition. No one tired of effort in his interest; and as he grew in years and knowledge, new plans and endeavors were adopted and made to render him, if possible, more satisfied and contented. His cup of happiness seemed to be ever enlarging itself, and filled to its brim. His recognition and treatment by the colonel and Mrs. Gooch were of the most fatherly and motherly character. In his presence and society, as they seemed to feel, the boy met a want in the household. Among their children, these aged parents had not numbered a son; and now this lad had become a veritable scion of their affection and family.

Located upon a farm of such dimensions and value, with such appointments and service as seemed to be indispensable, the situation of this family became as conspicuous as it was convenient and agreeable. It did not fail to excite comment, in connection with close observation of the acts of its members and inmates, comment which was often of unhandsome and unkind character. One inquired, Where did Gooch get the money to make this purchase and establish such a home? Another ventured the opinion that it came through the Langston boys, whose Virginia father, as he said, had made them wealthy. For two of them, as this person claimed, Colonel Gooch was a retained agent; and for the third and youngest, the duly appointed guardian of person and property. And, hence, allowed a third wiseacre, he treats his ward as a very son. Like a true and brave man, Colonel Gooch paid no attention to such absurd speculations; and the family grew day by day more and more respected, honored, and influential. Not a single change was made in the treatment of John, except as already stated, it became constantly more cordial and pronounced, at home and abroad.

Time had passed so rapidly, in the midst of such congenial, interesting, busy and fortunate circumstances, that John had already reached and entered upon his eighth year. At this juncture, the question of starting him to school regularly was discussed. The distance, quite a mile and a half, which he must walk morning and evening daily, constituted a very serious objection, as urged by Mrs. Gooch, in view of his age, size, and inexperience in self-management. And this objection was urged so stoutly by her, and sustained by Virginia, that he was not put to school for all of three months after the first consideration of the subject. Finally, Colonel Gooch decided to enter him as a pupil of the public school, and took the necessary steps to that end.

His regular training by his first, his best, and truest teacher, was to be interrupted. She had taken him well on in the easy primary lessons of spelling, reading, geography, and arithmetic, with simple instruction in printing and writing the English alphabet; and had taught him how to recite, with comparative childish effect, portions of the Sermon on the Mount, as well as other special selections of the Bible. She would, however, still give him such general, weekly attention, especially as respected his manners and behavior, as might be required.

It was upon a beautiful Monday morning, early in 1837, that Colonel Gooch, with John by his side, left home and other engagements, to put the lad at school. The novelty of the enterprise and the interest which it excited, made it very agreeable to the one to be most deeply affected. With his little new dinner bucket, so clean and bright, full of nice things for his lunch, in one hand, and his books in the other, he moved off, in his neat, trim dress of roundabout and pants of Kentucky blue jeans, with stylish, fashionable cap and shoes, in cheerful spirits, to the experience awaiting him, which might make, or destroy all his hopes. For school experiences often handicap and ruin even promising children, boys and girls.

The distance from home to the schoolhouse seemed short, and Colonel Gooch with his charge soon stood confronting the stern but learned principal, with whom he made quick arrangements for John's entry of the school. This school was composed of two departments; one for the larger and more advanced scholars, and the other for the pupils who were generally small and of the juvenile classes. To one of the more advanced classes of the latter department the boy was assigned and given in charge of a very attentive, kind-hearted, affectionate teacher, Miss Annie Colburn.

Her pupils occupied the gallery of the Methodist Church, in which in the absence of a school building, school was kept. The seats used were made of slabs, supported upon long round shaven legs at either end and in the center, without rest of any sort for the back. Nor were desks of any kind furnished. For six hours daily, however, with a brief intermission at noon, the pupils of this department were supposed to be engaged in school duty. Here was a new and trying experience to John, reared tenderly and in comfortable conditions as he had been.

As he sat upon his seat, his little legs so short that his feet did not touch the floor, with no support for his back or any part of his person, his whole body became so filled with pains, acute and annoying, that no twisting or turning or stretching could or did give relief. In such sad condition, John, young as he was and inexperienced in any ways of deception, occupied his time mainly, at first, in concocting a plan, and made a story accordingly by which he succeeded, for a few days, in getting out of the school at the noon intermission to go home. To accomplish this object, he told his teacher that he was needed at two o'clock every day to aid in getting up the cows. His statement was taken as true, and for a week at least, Johnnie Gooch, as he was then called, might have been seen making his way down the towpath of the canal to his home.

Finally Colonel Gooch inquired of him, how he got home so early. He replied briefly, "The teacher lets me come." He persisted for one or two days more, in coming directly home at the same early hour, when Colonel Gooch said to him on the last day, "To-morrow morning, I will go with you to school to see what this means." Accordingly, the next morning Colonel Gooch for the second time accompanied his ward to the school. Miss Colburn was called, and upon her explanation of the matter, Colonel Gooch without even the least admonition to the boy, stated to the teacher, "that he was not needed at home at all; that his whole business was to attend school; and that he expected him to do so promptly, according to rule." He had hardly quitted the school, when Miss Colburn coming to John and caressing him in her own tender, sweet manner, asked, "if he was not sorry that he had told such stories." Feeling even then, as he sat upon a bench too lofty and unguarded in every way for his size and comfort, the approach of the old pains, which he dreaded, he replied honestly. "No, madam!" However, such was her kind treatment of him thereafter, due pains being taken to improve his condition, that he became earnest in his school work, and although it was environed by every imaginable inconvenience in the old church, it was made pleasant and profitable through the efforts of his patient and faithful teacher.

About this time, people in the State of Ohio, around Chillicothe, began to have their attention called to the importance and advantage of other movements further westward. Hardly a single gathering of any sort—social, political, or business—was had where the saying, "Westward the star of Empire takes its flight," was not reiterated, as the expression of the growing popular sentiment of the neighborhood. Many had their attention turned especially to the then new State of Missouri. Agents handling real estate were not only numerous, but urgent and emphatic, in their descriptions and offers for sale of what they termed the fertile, productive lands of that State; which, purchasable at that time at merely nominal figures, must prove to be at a near future salable at advanced and greatly improved prices. Many farmers of the Scioto Valley sold their great landed possessions, sometimes at even what was deemed low figures, and made haste to invest in lands recommended by such agents.

The Gooch family, beautifully situated as it was, and, apparently, settled without any desire ever to change its excellent and desirable home, even though another investment might greatly increase its wealth, did not escape the feeling here indicated. Debate ran high and became warm between Colonel Gooch and his sons-in-law, Fisher and Eggleston, on the one part, and the ladies of the family on the other, with respect to the sale of their possessions and their removal to and settlement in the State of Missouri. The reasons, pro and con, were presented in many conversations at the table and in the parlors of their home, with warmth, tact, and often eloquence, by both the ladies and gentlemen. At last, however, Colonel Gooch having brought his wife to his own way of thinking, gave his casting vote, as he said, in the interest of his own family, and those of his sons-in-law. He sold without much effort and at great profit, his Ohio lands, including especially the rich and beautiful farm upon which he resided. According to the terms of sale, possession was to be given within a very limited time; and so Colonel Gooch found it necessary to make hurried arrangements for his removal. He determined to leave the State, when he left the farm; and, hence, his duties were, for that reason, various and complex. First of all, he must, according to his desire, arrange for the purchase of such lands in the State of Missouri, as upon his personal inspection, on his arrival there, he should find in situation, quantity and character, suited to his purposes; for now his sons-in-law and their families, going with him, proposed to settle upon portions of the lands which he might buy. Arrangements were very soon made, and to his satisfaction, in such respect, when he gave his attention with energy to the sale of his personal property, and to providing for the conveyance of his own family and those of Messrs. Fisher and Eggleston, with such implements, teams, wagons, and other property as they might find proper to take with them.

At this time there was, in fact, but a single method of public conveyance practicable from Chillicothe to St. Louis, Missouri, the city to which Colonel Gooch would make his way. This was by canal-boat from his farm to Portsmouth, Ohio; and from the latter place by steamboat, on the Ohio and Mississippi rivers, to the chief city of Missouri. He determined, therefore, to charter for his purposes a canal-boat to Portsmouth, and to employ a steamboat from there to St. Louis. Thence, he would use his wagons and teams for conveying the members of the

COLONEL GOOCH AND FAMILY.

different families and their effects to the lands, which, though he had not seen, upon reliable descriptions which he had accepted, he had bought and decided to occupy.

All this was accomplished, and the family was ready to vacate the premises at the appointed time, with full and ample arrangements made for the use of the needed canal and steamboat accommodations for all concerned. In the pressure and hurry incident to the settlement of the affairs described, the boy John seemed to have been forgotten, though never neglected. At last, his case came up for formal and decisive consideration between Colonel and Mrs. Gooch, when they decided to let him say whether he would go with them or remain in Ohio. He was called and, when he had entered and seated himself in the special apartments of these excellent persons, his best friends, as he felt and believed, Colonel Gooch explained carefully to him, as to how he had sold his property, and that he was going to move out of the State; he also told him when and where he would settle, hoping thereby to advance the interests and promote the welfare of his entire household. He then asked the boy the question, "Will you go with us, or do you prefer to remain here?" His answer was promptly given, and affirmatively, he saying, "I will go with you."

John had learned to love these estimable people as his father and mother, and with them, under their care and protection, he felt as if he moved in absolute safety. Indeed, he had come to feel that Mrs. Gooch would not only do everything for him, indulging him as her own child, but that she was able to, and would protect him against all harm. These venerable persons loved him in return, as every act of theirs from the time he came to them, when they received him as described, abundantly showed. The words came, in answer to his statement, without the least hesitation, from the lips of Colonel Gooch, "You shall go." From that time, everything was made ready for his journey, as for that of any other member of the family. His outfit of clothing, his dogs, hunting and fishing tackle, to say nothing of a thousand other things, provided for his comfort and pleasure, were secured against the day of their departure.

That day came quickly! The canal-boat which had been chartered to carry the families and their effects forty-five miles away to Portsmouth, brought immediately in front of the pathway leading, not over twenty-five yards, from the house to the canal, was made fast there, so as to be easily and readily loaded. Within three days the loading was entirely completed; and, at nine o'clock at night, after all the members of the families, including the boy John, had gone aboard, and two teams of valuable horses and three famous dogs of high blood had been carried and secured upon the boat, it was ordered by the captain that everything be made ready without the least delay for departure. Within one hour the boat was moving off. So soon as its motion was felt, the eight persons who composed the Gooch party—four ladies, three gentlemen, and the boy John—took their places upon the deck to get their last look at the beautiful home which they were leaving, with its charming grounds, orchards, garden, and fields, across the full length of whose extended acres the canal ran. At last, within a very short time, the boat passed the southeast limit of the farm; when all, fatigued from late anxieties and labors connected with the necessary preparations for moving, betook themselves, respectively, to their places of retirement.

John had taken leave of his school and teacher only one week before he started upon this journey.

To the surprise of all concerned, on rising the next morning after their departure, it was found that they had only gone fifteen miles, and were still inside of Ross County. They were confronted, also, by the sad intelligence that there was a break in the canal below them, and that in consequence the boat was aground. It was apparent that nothing could be done, in the way of moving on, till repairs were made, and that this might cause a detention of several hours.

COLONEL GOOCH AND FAMILY.

In due season, breakfast was taken, and each one betook himself to such occupation or amusement as seemed to be practicable and agreeable. John was permitted to go upon the shore and amuse himself, as best he might, in finding and throwing pebbles into the river. He had not been engaged in this pastime long, when turning his attention to the distant view, stretching on for miles up the towpath, he discovered certain objects which seemed to be in motion and coming towards him.

It was soon discovered that these objects, now in near approach, were two men on horseback, riding at full speed, as they pressed their animals forward. They commanded the attention of everyone, as stopping, they dismounted and inquired for Colonel Gooch. One of these persons was a white man, the sheriff of the county; the other William Langston, half-brother of John. They had come, as the sequel proved, to serve process upon Colonel Gooch, and to require his return, with his ward John, to the city of Chillicothe, to appear before the court, which would inquire as to whether he could lawfully carry his ward beyond its jurisdiction.

Colonel Gooch made his appearance promptly, and the sheriff served upon him the process which he bore. Going upon the boat, he hurriedly informed his wife that the officer had come after him, and that he would be obliged to take John and return with him. He ordered one of his horses bridled and saddled, while he made his personal preparations to obey the order of the court. In the meantime, Mrs. Gooch, Virginia, and the other members of the family, busied themselves in attentions to the boy, who seemed to be utterly overcome by dread and alarm. All were moved to tears; but none wept and sobbed, as utterly heart-broken, as Mrs. Gooch and John.

Painful as it was, the separation was not delayed; and at once, led by the officer and the man who accompanied him, Colonel Gooch upon his horse, with the boy riding behind him and clinging tightly to him, was on his way back to Chillicothe, to answer the proceeding instituted against him.

It is true, as already stated, that Captain Ralph Quarles had requested Colonel Gooch to act as the guardian of John; but, in order that the authority which he would exercise, as to his person and property, might be in all respects legal and binding, he had been appointed by the Common Pleas Court of Ross County to that position. Such being the case, he was held amenable to the court appointing him, and as claimed by the friends of the boy, he could not take him justly beyond its jurisdiction. Having attempted such thing, he became vulnerable to the action instituted against him; and was, accordingly, served with the process within the limits of Ross County, and compelled to answer upon such charge.

It was past midday when Colonel Gooch reached the court house where the case was to be heard, and it was quite three o'clock before it was called. The excitement caused by Colonel Gooch's conduct was very great, and such was the popular feeling against him on the part of many, that he was charged with attempting to kidnap the boy. The colored people, mistaken as to Colonel Gooch's real feelings and purposes and aroused and exasperated by such a charge as the one just mentioned, gathered in immense numbers in and about the court house and the city, expressing in words and acts the deepest interest in the decision of the court. Colonel Gooch was vulnerable to no charge of wrong to his ward; and this must ever stand as firm and positive assurance in his behalf. Influenced by a fatherly indulgence, to which he was largely moved by the words and actions of his wife, as well as his solemn promises to Captain Quarles, Colonel Gooch attempted to continue his care and protection of John, even carrying him, with all its risks, from a free to a slaveholding State.

The County Court was holding a regular session, at this time, with Judge Keith, a personal friend of Colonel Gooch, and a lawyer of acknowledged ability and name, seated upon the bench. The Chillicothe Bar was the first of the State; and the attorneys in practice before it, were in most cases learned, able, and eloquent. Several of them

THE RETURN OF COLONEL GOOCH AND JOHN.

50b

became subsequently the most accomplished and distinguished members of the American Bar. Thomas Ewing, Henry B. Stansberry and Allen G. Thurman, were then youthful but promising lawyers, who have since by masterly displays of their various sound legal learning and professional skill and integrity, made their names famous and their reputations enduring.

The last named of these three lawyers appeared in this case, as he had been retained and employed by William Langston. Colonel Gooch was represented in the trial by another of the foremost lawyers of that Bar, the Hon. John L. Taylor, who, at that time, was a member of the United States Congress. The action was one founded upon the writ of *habeas corpus*, having for its object inquiry as to the detention of the boy John by Colonel Gooch, in his attempt to carry him beyond the jurisdiction and power of the court by which he had been made his guardian, and to which he was legally held to be amenable. In his attempt to move the boy, and any property, cash or other, which he controlled, without the authority given by the court and sustained by law, he was justly held liable to this action; and the release of the boy from his management and control was manifestly just and proper.

Such was the high esteem in which Colonel Gooch was held, and the desire of all concerned to accommodate him under the circumstances, that the cause which was in hearing when he came into court was by general consent suspended for the time, and the action against him was at once called. The lawyers on both sides appearing promptly, declared themselves ready for the hearing. Statements upon the merits of the case involving the law and the facts were made upon either side; when at last the formal arguments were presented by the attorneys, Mr. Thurman opening and closing while Mr. Taylor offered his full statement in a single address. It is due the former attorney to state that in his comments upon the law as he cited it, and his management of the facts as he adduced them, that he not only discovered remarkable learning and skill but forensic eloquence of a very high order. Immediately upon the close of the arguments the court decided that Colonel Gooch could not carry the boy, his ward, beyond its jurisdiction, outside of the county of Ross and State of Ohio. Besides, it ordered the boy into its own custody, and directed the sheriff to take possession of and care for him until otherwise ordered by it.

While these proceedings were taking place the boy sat in the court room, weeping as if his heart was breaking in the deep bereavement which he experienced. As the judge closed his decision, and the excited assembly expressed its approving relief, not in outburst of applause but changed and pleasing countenances, Colonel Gooch bade John good-bye, tarrying only to leave with him his fatherly caress and benediction.

The Goochs were gone! But the memory of the separation from them has been, all these years, a living thing in the mind and heart of the one who seemed most deeply affected for weal or woe by the proceedings here detailed.

How like a succession of pleasing delightsome dreams the life and experiences of John in the Gooch family, so fortunate and happy, have always appeared to him! His prayer shall ever be in view of them, one of earnest gratitude, with a holy sincere invocation of God's blessing upon any member of that family, who served him in the early day, the one of his greatest need!

Though William Langston manifested special interest and determination in keeping his brother in Ohio, even instituting, as advised by friends and his lawyer, proceedings in the court to accomplish that end, he never lacked confidence in Colonel Gooch and his family, as earnest and honest in their attachments to John, and as honorable and sincere in their purposes to protect and care for him. He did fear, however, that should he be carried to Missouri his education would be neglected; and should Colonel Gooch or Mrs. Gooch die, or serious change be made in the circumstances of the family, his freedom might be endangered in a slave-holding State. Such feelings were natural, and he was wise in acting upon them.

COLONEL GOOCH AND FAMILY.

Thirty years and more had passed! The young lawyer who had managed the case, had won distinction as well in politics as in his profession, and had become a noted and distinguished United States senator. His client himself had become an educated man, passing through the several courses and departments of the schools and the college, and had been numbered among men of prominence in the country. The two met and had their first conversation in regard to the suit and its consequences after such lapse of time, in the city of Washington, and at the senator's own home. This meeting was brought about after the following manner. A person from Ohio, the State represented in part in the senate by Judge Thurman, having in charge a very important school interest located in that State, needing the services of a senator of special fitness and ability to present and advocate such interests in Congress, asked his former client to introduce and commend him and his cause to Senator Thurman. This was done with ease and effect. And after conversation with respect thereto had been finished, allusion was made to the former relations of the lawyer and his boy-client, as they appeared years before in the Chillicothe court. The young client, now hard by forty years of age, told the senator frankly how for a long time he really hated him; because he felt that he had heartlessly taken him from his best and truest friends—from those whom he loved and honored as his father and mother! So soon as the senator recognized in the grown man standing before him, his weeping, heartbroken boy-client, as he saw and plead for him in the court, he advanced, gave him his hand, and in chiding, yet tender manner, asked why he had not long ago called upon him and made himself known. He said with deep feeling and great emphasis, "Langston, I saved, I made you; and so far from hating, you should love me."

But how could a fatherless and motherless boy, without explanation, and the knowledge which it would impart, love one who had seemed to take from him his best friends, when he needed them most?

CHAPTER IV.

THE GREAT CHANGE!

IT was a great change indeed which came to the lad not quite ten years of age, when he passed from the guardianship and home of Colonel Gooch, to the temporary residence and new habits of self-care and labor in the household of Mr. Richard Long. When he was asked whether he would like to continue upon the beautiful farm which Colonel Gooch and his family had just left, it seemed so much like coming near to them again, that he said yes, he would. The present owner and proprietor was the gentleman whose name has just been given, who consented to take John and care reasonably for him.

Mr. Long was originally from New England. He had inherited and gathered from experience all the severer elements of Puritan purpose and life. Quite severe enough in his management of boys, his idea of the highest style of boyhood was realized, when it could be said of one that he was a good worker. Of his own son, who was, like his mother, remarkably talented, kind-hearted, and refined by nature, as well as fair culture for his age, he had a very low opinion, because, as he claimed, he was no worker. He could not milk; he could not manage horses; he knew neither how to drive nor to groom them; he could not chop, saw, nor split wood; he did not know how to do ordinary general farm work; and besides, seemed to have no inclination to do such things, as those which his father deemed to be of the greatest importance ; and, to be able to do which, demonstrated the possession of the best possible youthful character and promise.

The first question Mr. Long put to John was, "What, sir, can you do?" To which the boy made prompt, honest reply, according to his past experience and the truth, in the answer, "I can't do anything." His second question was a terrible one, when, seemingly, astonished at the answer which the young boy had made, he asked with deepest earnestness, "How do you expect to live?" Such questions and the manner of Mr. Long very quickly convinced the young Virginian, who had been living at leisure in the Gooch family, that a change was coming on ; and that life, at last, might prove to be, even in his case, a solemn and earnest thing.

When the matter of John's location was debated among his friends, and it was suggested that it might be well, since he seemed desirous of returning to the old farm, and the owner and proprietor of it, Mr. Long, would take him, it was concluded that such arrangement might prove to be specially favorable, as this gentleman was an Abolitionist. This word was new to the boy, and he ventured to ask its meaning, when some one present replied, saying it means that he loves colored people, and would have them all treated very kindly. John's observation of affairs did not justify the belief that Mr. Long would make any distinctions in his dealings with mankind, favoring anyone in the least on account of his color. He found him severe enough in dealing with any and all classes, always counting the balance in his own favor.

Quite timid, and yet determined to make the most of a bargain, which seemed even in his untutored imagination, by contrast, hard enough, John commenced with Mr. Long, thinking every day of the Goochs, and wondering whether Mrs. Gooch had forgotten him.

The first work given him to do was that of driving the horse and cart, hauling brick from the kiln at a distant part of the farm to the yard, where a new building was to be erected. The lad discovered great love of horses, and considerable skill in the management of the one which he drove. His third day's work with the horse and cart had just been finished, when Mr Long coming up and observing his movements with no little interest, complimented him by saying, "You are doing well, sir, and if you continue, you will make a good driver." What he predicted here was not long thereafter realized; and by the time John had reached his eleventh year, he drove skillfully, and to the satisfaction of even Mr Long, his pair of beautiful sorrel horses, as employed during the week in the wagon, and in the family carriage on Sunday.

After the first six months, John, under the supervision and direction of a nephew of the Long family, a young man of excellent character and kindly disposition, gave attention to general farm work, and according to the measure of his strength, for a boy, became a good and useful worker. The soil in every part of the farm, extremely rich and productive, was easily worked with hoe or plow. So far as the light plow was concerned, he handled that, finally, with skill and ease; and in the use of the hoe and other small implements, he was serviceable. In fact, he made himself useful, generally, and was often complimented by the superintendent for his diligence and efficiency.

Mr. Long was a person of stern and rigid Presbyterian principles. He was a member and deacon of the Presbyterian church of Chillicothe, at that time called "Old School"; and his zeal in behalf of church work was manifest, and apparently sincere. Sustaining such relations to the church, and, of course, obligated to such duty of life and conduct as would naturally tend to advance its general interests and maintain its influence, he daily gathered his family about him to hear the Word, as he himself read and expounded it in family worship. All connected with the family, even the colored cook and hired man, were required to lay aside, for the time being, any duty which might claim attention, and attend upon such religious services. Of course, the members of the family proper—the sons and daughters with others, relatives and friends resident therein—were expected, and did give, special attentive regard to all such matters of spiritual devotion. As the other children were required to have opened before them, on such occasions, the Old or New Testament, according to the morning or evening selection of the reader, John was, from his attendance upon the first of such exercises, given a Bible, and directed to observe the same habit. Not always, but according to the convenience of the family, frequently everyone with the Bible in hand took part by reading a single verse of the lesson in regular course. The exercises consisted of singing and praying as well as reading, and were often really interesting and edifying. Often it was the case, by reason of the relations of the family to the church, that distinguished ministers of the Presbyterian persuasion, spending a little time in visits to the city, made the home of the Longs their place of sojourn; and so their special conduct of the religious exercises lent additional interest and zest to them. It is not difficult to understand what the influence of a Christian family, conducted as indicated, must have exerted upon a young boy like John, of inquisitive, impressible understanding.

Following such family influence, came the attendance upon church, regularly, and the Sabbath-school. For it is due Mr. Long to state that, while he was a man always diligent in business and exacting of those about him and in his service, he would not tolerate the neglect of the moral and religious culture of the humblest of his dependents. It was true that John had his chores, which required his attention on Sunday, as well as upon any ordinary day of the week; and that he was, especially, charged with the care of the family carriage, as he drove the team every Sunday to the Sunday-school and church; and yet he was required to exercise such diligence and promptness, with respect to such duties, as not to lose a single privilege or advantage offered in his Sabbath-school class and the church. He was required to attend, regularly, too, to the study, weekly, of his Sabbath-school lesson, precisely as the other children of the family; and with them, he belonged to the regular Sabbath-school class, and attended church, seated always with the family.

This family consisted of the parents, five children—three boys and two girls, the latter being quite young ladies—and a nephew of Mr. Long, named in his honor, and made by him the special manager of his farm. John found himself quite at home, finally, with them all; for besides receiving from all the younger members of the family kind-hearted and considerate treatment, Mrs. Long proved to be an amiable person, discovering, always, a reasonable amount of interest in him.

The associations of the family were quite extended in the community; and its home was often made the place of social gathering and enjoyment. Those who shared its hospitality, were persons generally of the very first grades of society, representing its highest culture and refinement. Mrs. Long sustained the name and character of one of the very first ladies of the community.

On the whole, by reason of the excellent associations which he enjoyed with the children of the family and their companions; the moral and religious culture which he gained; and the instruction and training given him, in the ways of industry and self-reliance, John lost really nothing by the change which was made in his case from a loving and indulgent family, to one in which the strict and severe discipline of life prevailed. Tender of age as he was, and frail in physical constitution and health, his treatment in the latter family was calculated to improve his condition, while fitting him, mentally and morally, for those trying and taxing duties which must soon come upon him.

How strange the ways of Providence, in its dealings with those who may be called through the hard ways of human existence, to duties for which they can only be prepared through their own experiences! To such, experience is not, in the language of Coleridge, "like the stern lights of a ship." It is rather the full-orbed day, surrounding them with the light, which shall be their wisdom and salvation.

THE GREAT CHANGE!

But philosophize as one may, crediting a kind Providence with the good results which certainly came from the experiences of the boy, of whose condition and advancement record is here made, it is due him, as well as those who had treated him so lovingly and tenderly, to state that the days and weeks multiplied themselves in their grave, solemn tread, till they made months in duration and verged on years, before he could even think of what seemed to be his dire loss, in the great change which had come to him, with the least degree of resignation or satisfaction.

After leaving Mr. Richard Long improved in physical strength, with a better conception of the earnest side of life, John, by arrangement of his friends, and especially through the influence of his brother Gideon, was sent to Cincinnati, where it was supposed he could gain favorable school advantages.

At this time, in the State of Ohio, there were no public school opportunities furnished colored youth. The educational advantages offered them could only be found in private schools, and these were very limited in number, and often difficult to reach and attend.

The best and most accessible school of this character in the State for all such youth as lived in its southern section, was the one located in the city named, kept by Messrs. Goodwin and Denham, two scholarly white men, well-disposed to the colored race, and willing to labor for its education. To this school, occupying the basement story of the Baker Street Baptist Church of Cincinnati, John was sent, his brother who resided at that time in that city, engaging to look after and care for him.

He spent about two years in this city; and both at school and in general association, in the observation and experience and the knowledge which he acquired, he gained an amount and quality of practicable wisdom which proved to be of large profit to him.

His teachers were men of high scholarly attainments, apt at the management and control of their pupils, winning constantly the confidence, as they enjoyed the respect of any scholars attending their school. The attendance was large, being composed of boys and girls more or less advanced and easily classified, so that the discipline of the school was by no means difficult, and its management made conducive with the least trouble to the greatest good of the whole number. It is not saying too much to assert that the morality of this school was of high order, and as thoroughly guarded in all respects as its general standard of scholarship was exalted and maintained. The temper of the teachers, too, was always even and well sustained; while all classes advanced by steady progressive movement, and made reasonable proficiency and accomplishment in study.

Such was the improvement which John had already made in his studies, and such were his application and diligence, that he was not long in this school before he had secured such promotion as to place him in its advanced classes. It is due him to state, that by his good conduct he soon won the respect, confidence and favor of his teachers. And so much did he become a general favorite in the school with his fellow-pupils, that he was never left out when any special play or exercise calculated to increase and sustain the influence of the school was contemplated. And when thus honored and engaged, he acted the part assigned him with enthusiasm and propriety. He very soon discovered special love for, and interest in, any exercise, either confined to ordinary school observances or public exhibitions, which required rhetorical effort or display. He succeeded so well in this school that, during his last year, he was one of two boys who composed its very first, most advanced class. In such studies as ancient history, advanced arithmetic and grammar, with such other subjects of science, in elementary form, as comported with his stage of advancement, he maintained, with his associate and classmate, a record of which he needed not to be ashamed.

His associations while in Cincinnati were had with the best colored families, their children and intimates, located at the time in that city. For the first six months of his sojourn there, he boarded in the family of Mr. John Woodson;

who was a colored man of prominence and influence, occupying with his family high social position with his class. He was a carpenter and joiner by trade, doing considerable business in that line. Fairly educated, he made an efficient superintendent of the Sabbath-school of the colored Methodist church, of which he was a member of acknowledged name and standing. While in his family, John attended the Sunday-school and church with him; and was made welcome to the families which composed, mainly, their membership and congregation.

His boarding-place was subsequently changed, and he was given quarters in the family of Mr. William W. Watson, the leading colored barber, at that time, in Cincinnati. Besides being a man of vigorous mental parts, with limited education, Mr. Watson was a prominent and influential member and trustee of the Baker Street Baptist Church. He was also the superintendent of the Sabbath-school of that church, and taught himself its leading Bible class, of which John became a member on going into his family. If his was not the first family in colored society in Cincinnati at that time, it was certainly equal to any other, and its place in such society and in the Baptist Church was, surely, conspicuous and influential. His house was one to whose well-furnished and pleasant rooms and parlors, the very best and most highly educated and cultured young colored persons were wont to come; and where, by reason of the generous hospitality and kindness of the whole household, they were always at ease. Possessed of considerable means, and conducting a profitable and prosperous business, Mr. Watson did not fail to provide a home for his family which was pleasant and attractive in every way itself, and in its appointments and surroundings wholly agreeable.

If there has ever existed in any colored community of the United States, anything like an aristocratic class of such persons, it was found in Cincinnati at the time to which reference is here made. Besides finding there then a large class of such persons, composed in greater part of good-looking, well-dressed and well-behaved young people of considerable accomplishment, one could count many families possessing a reasonable amount of means, who bore themselves seemingly in consciousness of their personal dignity and social worth.

Perhaps no colored church in any city of the country was more largely composed in its congregation than the old Baker Street Baptist Church of such better class. Its pastor was at first the Rev. Charles Satchell. He was succeeded by the Rev. William P. Newman. Both these gentlemen were possessed of large ability, piety and eloquence. In its efficiency and influence, the Sabbath-school of this church was deservedly noted. Other churches, the Methodist and Presbyterian notably, belonging to the same class, had large and flourishing congregations, with well-attended and ably-conducted Sabbath-schools. In fact the entire negro community of the city gave striking evidences, in every way at this time, of its intelligence, industry, thrift and progress; and in matters of education and moral and religious culture, furnished an example worthy of the imitation of their whole people.

It is not to be denied, nor may it be overlooked here, that at this time in the Cincinnati community, generally, there existed a deep-seated and growing sentiment against the colored people. White persons who were friendly to them, and who dared to avow their sentiments, were in many cases proscribed and made objects of the severest hatred. The influence of slavery, established just across the Ohio river, made itself felt in the then Queen City of the West, in more ways than one, and sometimes to the most terrible effect. Often fugitive slaves crossing the river and coming into the city found succor and refuge; sometimes with white persons, at others with colored ones. When pursued and their hiding-places were discovered it mattered little what the color of the protector was, popular feeling was quickly aroused and in not a few cases manifested itself in violence against those concerned in such transaction. It was not difficult, nor did it require great effort or much time under the circumstances, to generate and sustain such mob-spirit as ultimately showed itself in murderous, destructive methods.

The last outbreak of this character, which John was permitted to witness and which made a lasting impression upon his youthful mind, was that in which the press of Dr. Gamaliel Bailey, the editor and publisher of the "Philanthropist," was seized and by the infuriated rabble thrown into the Ohio river. For several weeks feeling against the Abolitionists, so-called, friends of the colored people, and against the colored people themselves, had been showing itself in high and open threats, conveyed in vulgar, base expressions, which indicated the possibility and probability of an early attack upon both the classes mentioned.

It was early upon a certain Friday evening, in the late fall of 1840, that excited groups of men, some white and others colored, were seen about the streets of the city and showing by their words and gesticulations, that their minds were dwelling upon, and that they were stirred by some deeply serious and fearful matter. By reason of the fact that many found among the white classes were strangers, and evidently persons from the State of Kentucky; and the further fact that the colored people seemed to be specially moved by the apprehensions of assault, which they feared might be coming upon them and their friends, one could very easily understand that the mob, which had been expected, was about to show itself. Such fear proved to be well grounded; for about nine o'clock, a large ruffianly company, coming over from the adjacent towns of Kentucky, called together a large number of the baser sort of the people of Cincinnati, and opened, without the least delay, an outrageous, barbarous and deadly attack upon the entire class of the colored people. They were assaulted wherever found upon the streets, and with such weapons and violence as to cause death in many cases, no respect being had to the character, position, or innocence of those attacked. The only circumstance that seemed necessary to provoke assault, resulting even in death, was the color of the person thus treated.

After the first sudden surprising attack, the colored people, measurably prepared for such occurrence by reason of the condition of public feeling manifested latterly, as already described, certainly in their expectations of it, aroused themselves, seized any means of defence within their reach, and with manliness and courage met their assailants. One of their number, Major Wilkerson, was made their leader; and never did man exhibit on the field of danger greater coolness, skill and bravery, than this champion of his people's cause. A negro himself, he fought in self-defence, and to maintain his own rights as well as those of the people whom he led. They had full confidence in his ability, sincerity, courage and devotion, and were ready to follow him even to death. The record of the number of deaths which occurred during that eventful night, among both the white and the colored people, can never be made. It is well known, however, that the desperate fighting qualities of the latter class were fully demonstrated in the great number of fatal casualties which were noted. All night the fight continued. Many of the white attacking party were carried directly from the fight to the grave; and not a few of the colored men fell in gallant manner, in the struggle which they made in their own defence.

Saturday morning as it dawned upon the stricken city, witnessed a lull in the struggle; and many felt and hoped that the riot with its frightful incidents had ceased. But the day had not grown old before by regulation of the city authorities, swarms of improvised police-officers appeared in every quarter, armed with power and commission to arrest every colored man who could be found. It was claimed that these arrests were made for the purpose of protecting such persons against the further attacks of the mob. Such, however, was by no means the case. The arrests were made, and the colored men were imprisoned, because it had been thoroughly shown by their conduct that they had become so determined to protect themselves against whatever odds, that great and serious damage might be expected were they again assaulted. Hundreds of them concealed themselves at home, and in other hiding-places, and thus escaped arrest.

Early in the day, the family of Mr. John Woodson, living across the canal in Broadway, in that part of the city known as "Germany," and where John boarded at the time, was visited by a colored neighbor, who called to tell Mr. Woodson what was occurring as to the arrest of the colored men, and to advise him both to conceal himself, and to have his foreman, Mr. John Tinsley, do the same thing. The boy waited to see Mr. Woodson hide himself in one chimney of his house, and Mr. Tinsley in another, when he told them both good-bye; and leaving the house through the back yard and garden, jumped over the fence into the alley, and made his way as rapidly as possible, by Main Street, to the canal bridge. He had reached the middle of the bridge crossing the canal, when he heard behind him the voice of officers ordering him to stop. Fleet of foot, with his speed quickened by such orders, he ran with all his might, without the least abatement of his speed, over a mile, to the corner of Main and Fourth Streets, where he entered a drugstore, through which he was compelled to pass to reach his brother Gideon. His brother was concealed at the time, with five other colored men, employed by him in a barber-shop, which he owned and conducted, located near this point. Overcome by excitement and fatigue, no longer in control of his powers, the boy fell to the floor of the drugstore, as if dead, alarming those in charge there, who, seeing his condition, came at once to his relief. He was carried thence into the rooms of his brother, just at hand, where he was cared for, with restoratives promptly administered, and soon recovered himself.

His brother's shop was closed and fortified to the extent of his ability, as to doors and windows, when it ought to have been opened and all the men at work. All found there were agitated, disturbed and anxious about their safety. The arrival of the boy, with such experience as he had to describe after his recovery, did little, indeed, toward reassuring these frightened persons. They feared that the boy would be pursued and they be found and arrested. Subsequent events showed, however, that the good men who kept the drugstore mentioned, were watchful of their interests and ready to protect them against harm. As the night came on, and the darkness rendered it practicable to do so, the owners of the store took John out with them to a confectionery, not far distant, where they purchased a full supply of needed edibles, which, under their care and protection, he carried to his brother and his men, then hungry enough from fasting for more than fifteen hours.

The diabolism of this mob reached its highest pitch, when thousands of infuriated, ungovernable ruffians, made mad by their hatred of the negro and his friends, came down Main Street with howls, and yells, and screams, and oaths, and vulgarities, dragging the press of Dr. Bailey, the great Abolition editor, which they threw, in malignant, Satanic triumph, into the river.

The days and nights made memorable by the deeds here detailed, must ever stand as the blackest and most detestable in the history of the great city of Cincinnati! And how all the black features which distinguish and intensify their horrid character, forever stand impressed upon the memory of the lad who witnessed, as he was terrified by them!

Such cowardly and unjustifiable abuse of their white friends and attack on the colored men, did not tend in the slightest degree to destroy the growing anti-slavery sentiment of Cincinnati and Ohio. Lewis, Chase, Hayes, Smith and other great leaders of the Abolition movement were made thereby the bolder, braver, more outspoken and eloquent in their utterances in such behalf. Nor did such treatment close the lips and hush the voices of the eloquent colored men themselves, who through such experiences, were learning what their rights were, and how to advocate and defend them. It was about this time that the black orator, John I Gaines, made his debut upon the platform, pleading the cause of his people; that Joseph Henry Perkins, another colored speaker of fine talent and great eloquence, appeared in his early efforts of the same character; that Andrew J. Gordon, of the same class, not only discovered signal ability with his pen, but unusual power with his tongue, as the negro's defender; and that Gideon Q. Langston, also manifested large ability and learning with commanding and surprising qualities of oratory, in advocating the cause of his race. Other names of this class might be mentioned here, as fearless and able defenders of the rights of their people, all of whom, it was the privilege and advantage of the boy John to hear and know, their eloquent efforts serving him in large measure as inspiration and purpose.

The Sabbath following these occurrences was one of the greatest beauty and loveliness. The quiet of the city was truly impressive; and but for the hundreds of horsemen, the mounted constabulary forces found necessary to parade the streets and maintain the good order of the city, while protecting the lives of its people, it would have been a day fit for the calm and peaceful worship of our Heavenly Father in a civilized and Christian community. As it was, however, the horrid sight of the vast company of such policemen, the solemn, awful tread and tramp of their march, with the recollection of the sad, dire events of the preceding nights and days, drove every feeling of love and veneration out of the hearts of those who had thus been outraged and terrified.

Those were dark days! And they who still survive them, may never forget the circumstances of their occurrence, and the public sentiment, which, no longer prevalent, made them possible at that time!

CHAPTER V.

THE PROMISE WHICH HE DID NOT KEEP.

JOHN was in attendance upon school, in the city of Cincinnati, where he had been about one year, when to his surprise Colonel Gooch made him a visit, calling at his school rooms. At this time the colonel was on his return from Chillicothe, where he had been to make final settlement of all business connected with the sale and transfer of his farm. He had hoped to meet his former ward at that place. When he failed to find him where he had expected, he inquired after him and his whereabouts;—determined to see him, at all events, and wherever he might be. Whatever might have been his own feelings in the matter, he could not do otherwise and comply with the wishes of his wife and daughter. As he alleged, he acted in obedience to the earnest desire and request of Mrs. Gooch and Virginia, that John should be found and his condition truthfully reported to them. They were still anxious as to his welfare, and desired to learn what he was doing, and with what prospects of advantage.

The boy was not seated far from the door at which Colonel Gooch knocked, and at which he was met by Mr. Goodwin, one of the teachers. The inquiry was at once made of the teacher, "Have you a young boy in your school by the name of John M. Langston?" The boy caught the tones of the voice using such words, and was moved by their seeming familiarity. Indeed, they sent a thrill through his whole being. Why, at the moment, he did not undertake to debate. Addressing him then, Mr. Goodwin said, "John, a gentleman at the door wishes to see you." He stepped forward promptly, when to his surprise and pleasure, he found himself confronted by his old guardian, whose demonstrations of affection and joy were ardent and abundant.

Taking the boy by the hand, while he threw the other arm about his neck and shoulders, they walked together to the steps leading down from the street into the school-yard, where seating themselves, with the boy's head drawn against his friend's person, they remained in close, confidential, loving conversation for quite two hours. First of all, their talk was of Mrs. Gooch and Virginia, the two persons above all others about whom, as was well understood, the boy desired to hear. As Colonel Gooch told of them; how often they called John's name, wondering where he was, how he was, what he was doing, and whether he was happy, the boy's heart was moved with the deepest gratitude, while his love for those thoughtful, kind and affectionate friends, who had not forgotten him, was deepened and intensified. As he described their beautiful home in Missouri, telling how large his farm was, how valuable it must soon become, since the country was being settled rapidly with good people from the South and East, and declaring that the State itself, in the near future, would be one of the first of the Union, he stirred the hopes and expectations, not less than the desires and love of the youthful listener.

He proceeded thereafter to assure the boy that Mrs. Gooch and the daughter lacked only one thing to make them more happy, in their new home, than they had been in Ohio. They loved the country and the people well, and were greatly pleased with their surroundings, generally. However, he continued, "They made me promise them that I would find you, and, in their name, gain from you the earnest and sure promise, that when you reach your majority, you will come to us, and make yourself again at home with your best friends—those who are ready to share all they have, their very best and most valuable things, with you."—" Mrs. Gooch," he urged, "told me not to come back without such promise"; "and," he added, "you know Virginia wants to see you, and we would all make you welcome. Our home you will find a lovely one; and we can furnish you everything needed to make you perfectly happy. You must come!" These last words were used with peculiar tenderness and warmth.

To this urgent, affectionate appeal, the boy, moved by the love he bore for Mrs. Gooch and the family, made prompt, sincere promise, that he would come, on reaching his majority, to the home of those who had been to him in earlier days all that he could desire in loving devoted parents.

Colonel Gooch and John, then, rising, walked leisurely back to the door of the school; and there took affectionate leave of each other. Returning to his studies, pressed with school duties, although deeply affected by the unexpected visit which had been made him, and the promise which he would not forget nor neglect, he could, at most, give to such things, however important and impressive, but a boy's thoughts. He meant, nevertheless, at the time, all he had said and promised as to going to Mrs. Gooch. For he loved her; and hoped to see her again; and, if possible, make her happy in seeing the boy to whom she seemed more his mother than any other woman.

Time moved on apace; changes followed each other in quick succession; and long before his twenty-first year had been reached, the boy had learned things of Missouri which made him feel even satisfied enough that he had not been permitted, at first, to go with his friends to that State. He had learned that slavery existed there! He had come to understand that where that institution was allowed and fostered, he could have, really, no rights; and that his friends might not be able to protect him against approaching danger should it come. He could not consent to live in a State where his personal liberty would be in constant, imminent peril. But more than all this, when he had

THE PROMISE WHICH HE DID NOT KEEP.

reached his majority, so defiant and strong had the Slave Power of the country become in every part of the land, and so audacious in its demands, that he was afraid to go, even for temporary purpose, anywhere within its reach and control.

He did not, because he could not safely, keep his promise as given. And, when much later, slavery had been abolished in the State of Missouri and throughout the whole country, the Gooch family could not be found, not even a single member. The boy, who was then a man, far beyond his majority in age, and still entertaining a deep regard and reverence for his whilom friends, made earnest, special effort to find if not the family in its original entirety, some member of it. For, he would manifest, in suitable form and manner, were it possible, to anyone bearing the blood and lineage of a family so faithful, loyal and true to him, his deep and abiding appreciation of its feelings and conduct.

During his stay of two years and a little more in Cincinnati, John was by no means an idle boy. Faithful and diligent in all school duties for five days in the week, after he had made his home in the family of Mr. William W. Watson, he worked every Saturday about his barber-shop and bathhouse. He was allowed all he could collect, voluntarily given by those whom he served; and he discovered such aptness for the service, with such spirit of accommodation, politeness and industry, that the amount paid him often aggregated, as the results of a single day's labor, quite a considerable sum.

Peter Watson, a brother of the proprietor of the establishment, and Daniel Marshall, his chief assistant, were John's good friends, and did much, in the general management of business, to call attention to him and thus improve his opportunities and advantages. At the close of the week's work on many Saturday nights, these persons would not only discover special interest in him by inquiries as to what his success had been, rejoicing with him when it was considerable, but they encouraged him often to renewed effort, in view of the growing results of his energy and labors. It was frequently the case that they praised him for his thoughtful and intelligent behavior, assuring him that he might expect, should he cultivate properly such elements of business reflection and effort as marked his conduct, to be a successful and thrifty man.

In this shop and bath-house, all business was closed promptly at twelve o'clock Saturday night; and was not resumed, for any reason whatever, or any service however urgent, till Monday morning, at five o'clock. The proprietor and everybody connected with the service therein, were scrupulous in their observance of the Sabbath, and not one of them absented himself, as a rule, from the church on that day. It will not be difficult to comprehend the fact, that the service of which such men had control, was conducted upon the highest moral principles; and, in such way as that while perfect order and decorum were maintained, every customer and visitor was entirely pleased and won. The work, too, was done in the most skillful and satisfactory manner. The influence of all persons employed, and with whom the boy was brought in contact, was of good effect. Naturally penurious rather than extravagant, both in their general liberal outlays and their wise economical habits, they taught him valuable lessons with respect to the expenditure and preservation of any money which he received. He was, therefore, not only possessed of a reasonable amount of funds, the fruit of his own efforts, but he constantly added thereto, and took delight in the labors which brought him such gains. It is easy to perceive that the boy, now fond of the position described, and pleased with all those connected with it, must have given it up finally with no little regret.

It is due John to state, that the record of good behavior and study, which he made under Messrs. Goodwin and Denham, being well known, endeared him to the teachers and the pupils of the school. When he was about to leave them, many attentions were paid to him, and the warmest kindly expressions reached his ears. The families with whom he had lived, had formed for him an affectionate friendly regard; and expressed, as he bade them farewell, respectively, deep feeling and anxiety for his future prosperity and happiness. Both Mr. Woodson and Mr. Watson urged him to feel that their doors were open always to him; and that should he ever visit the city, they would be pleased to have him accept and enjoy their hospitality.

Business matters of importance to him, which could no longer be postponed, connected with the settlement of his father's estate, made it necessary for John to return, without delay, to Chillicothe. This he did. And as soon thereafter as the Court of Common Pleas could convene, he was required to name a guardian for himself and property. He named to such position, and the court confirmed, his half-brother, Mr. William Langston.

From the time he had met this brother, in the mountains of Old Virginia, when on his way to Ohio, John had loved him very greatly. William, since that time, in every practicable way had given special and constant attention to his little half-brother; and upon his visits to him, which were quite frequent, always brought him some beautiful, or interesting, or pleasant thing. Thus endeared to him, it was altogether natural, under the circumstances, for John to choose him for his guardian. His brother Gideon resided, at the time, in Cincinnati; while his brother Charles was away attending school at Oberlin.

His half-brother had not married as yet, and having no family of his own, put his ward in that of a friend for board and care. This family consisted of an aged venerable man, an equally aged kindhearted wife, and a single female domestic. The first two exerted themselves in every way to answer every want and interest of the youth; and the domestic declared that, "she knew nothing but to take care of their little Virginia gentleman." This family was made up of Virginians, and entertained the highest conceivable ideas of Virginia character. They really felt that Virginia alone supplied the best looking, the best behaved, the most excellent men and women, boys and girls. With them Virginia blood was the very best, and to be proud of. Mr. and

Mrs. Harvey Hawes, the persons here spoken of, have fallen asleep long, long, ago. Peace to their ashes! But the domestic of whom mention is made, now quite a hundred years old, still lives, and is never so happy, apparently, as when she is occupied in telling curious anecdotes of the boy whom she was wont to serve years ago. When this aged friend, Aunt Patsy Tucker, shall die, a thousand good people who have known of her virtuous, Christian, useful life, will join with the man of whom she was so fond as a boy, in celebrating her deserved praises.

While thus situated John was once more started to school. He had for his teacher at first Mr. George B. Vashon, who was, at the time, a student of Oberlin College, and a member of its Junior college class. This school was kept for three months only in the winter term. His next teacher, for the following winter, was Mr. William Cuthbert Whitehorn, also a student of Oberlin College, and one year the junior of the former person, in his course of study. Both these young men were colored persons, and were favorably known as scholars, teachers and orators. They were the first colored persons who graduated, regularly, from the Oberlin College; the one taking his first degree, Bachelor-of-Arts, in August, 1844; and the other taking his first degree of the same character in the following August, 1845. The influence exerted by these teachers upon their pupils and the community at large, was widespread and salutary. To the more thoughtful and aspiring scholars of the school and members of the community, their examples of application, diligence, and success in the cultivation of scholarly attainment, and the wise and efficient discharge of the high duties connected therewith, were inspiring and encouraging. They were the first persons of their race, who having engaged thus in exalted, various and profound artistic and scientific study, had so far accomplished their aims and purposes as to reach the high classes in a college course, of which they were members. Forerunners, as they were, for a whole race, in the ways of the highest scholarship, with their peculiarly handsome endowments of manner and address, winning while they attracted popular attention and applause, they were well calculated to exert a large and commanding influence upon such youths as were brought within their reach.

It was under these teachers that John discovered his highest and best elements of scholarly power, making such impression that his friends began to discuss seriously the propriety and wisdom of having him take a regular thorough course of college training. In this discussion large account was made in favor of such a course, of the facts concerning the success attending the efforts of the two colored scholars—the young persons who had made such favorable impression as teachers, scholars and gentlemen upon the community. It may be asserted without much doubt, that had not Messrs. Vashon and Whitehorn appeared in Chillicothe and pursued the course as teachers and scholars indicated, young Langston would not in all probability, have ever left that town to pursue a protracted collegiate and professional course of study elsewhere. His brother Charles, however, who had spent two years in study at Oberlin College, favored this opinion and was outspoken and positive in maintaining it. He had at this time, just returned to his home in Chillicothe, all full of college enthusiasm and hope; and his argument in favor of such course for his young brother was earnest and eloquent. He even went so far in the earnestness of his expression as to declare " that his brother was smart and promising, and should be as thoroughly educated as might be." Besides, Mr. Vashon, who was then his teacher, a member of the senior class of Oberlin College, a person of rare scholarly character, attainment and name, standing at the head of his class in every study, and a teacher of unusual ability, supported Charles in his views. Finally Gideon, hearing of this debate and having himself known of his brother's success and record as a pupil in the school in Cincinnati, wrote favoring also such opinion. He had full knowledge of his father's desires and purpose as to the education of John, and the excellent opportunities which Oberlin College offered to such end, as he himself had spent a year there in taking certain special studies. His second letter came very soon, addressed to John's guardian, advising that he should be sent to the college to take its preparatory and college courses. The guardian at last consented to send him for one year; believing as he claimed, that his education was already sufficient, he having a reasonable knowledge for his age of reading, writing, grammar, arithmetic, geography, history, ancient and modern; and that the best thing to be done for him was to put him to a good trade. Accordingly provisions were made for his going to Oberlin College, and his stay there for one year.

While these matters were commanding the attention of his friends, the boy was advancing in handsome manner under the tuition of his able and skillful teacher, whose second and last winter session of the Chillicothe colored school was rapidly nearing its close. These occurrences took place in the winter of 1843-44, when John had reached his fourteenth year. He was small and light for his age, but nervous and enduring. He had put all his powers to the test in this last session of his school. For his schoolmates, boys and girls, especially those of his own classes, besides being young persons of the finest possible bodily and mental endowment, had taken hold of and pursued their studies with zeal and purpose. To maintain his name and standing it was necessary, therefore, for him to work with his entire devotion and strength.

At the close of the school, the record which he had made was shown to be high; and he was specially honored in the public exercises which were given. In these he appeared to good advantage; and won the public commendation of his teacher and the Board of Managers of the school. More than this, his guardian commended him in unstinted praise; while his brother Charles, after listening to his declamation and witnessing its pleasing effects, said to him, "You have in you, John, all the elements of an orator."

CHAPTER VI.

HE GOES TO OBERLIN COLLEGE.

LEAVING Chillicothe Thursday morning, March 1, 1844, it was not until one o'clock in the morning of the following Sunday, that Mr. George B. Vashon and his former pupil reached the hotel, the only one then in the incorporated village of Oberlin. It was only after considerable knocking and calling that they succeeded in gaining admission and securing entertainment. The last forty-eight miles of their journey, from Mansfield to Oberlin, were difficult and severe, by reason of the depth of mud and the well-nigh impassable condition of the roads. It took them from five o'clock in the morning, the hour at which they left Mansfield, to the hour named, to make the distance indicated. They were compelled to employ a team and wagon, at extravagant cost, to do even this. Railroads were not then known in Ohio, furnishing to the ordinary traveller speed and comfort, at reasonable rates.

The Sabbath morning of their arrival, though the streets and sidewalks of the town were wet and muddy, and to a stranger wholly forbidding, afforded opportunity to see the community in one of its peculiar and most active conditions. By nine o'clock everybody seemed to be upon the streets, pressing on, with earnest purpose depicted in his face, looking neither to the right nor left, in the effort which he was making to get either to the early prayer-meeting or the Sabbath-school. At that time in Oberlin, the whole community was moved by its deep religious sentiment, and spared no effort, as it spared no sacrifice, to maintain every Christian, spiritual instrumentality calculated to impress and save those coming to live in its midst.

Mr. Vashon was familiar, of course, with the sight presented, and made haste to advise his boy friend, that he must soon adjust himself to this new order of things, would he make the most of his Oberlin life, in intellectual, moral and spiritual progress. However, the most remarkable and the most impressive sight had not yet been witnessed. If the whole community seemed to be in motion at the early hour mentioned, it is a fact that it was in actual movement when the time came for going to church.

At half-past ten o'clock, the chapel bell was tolled. The crowd which had hitherto appeared on the streets, and impressed the stranger as being large, seemed small now, as compared with the vast swelling company of students and people pressing to the great church, the only one in the place. Here the greatest pulpit orator at that time was to deliver one of his thrilling, matchless discourses. To this church, Mr. Vashon conducted his protegé, telling him on the way how he would see and hear what it had never been his good fortune to have come within his personal knowledge. What he said in such regard was soon made the inexpressible, pleasing experience of the youth.

How the singing of the great choir of the church, in which more than a hundred voices were blended, sustained by instruments of vast compass and power, and yet with tone sweet and soul-moving, impressed and charmed his youthful mind! How the touching, effective, eloquent rendition of the Scripture lesson made by the faultless, incomparable elocutionist, Prof. John Morgan, led him to see new beauties and gain new ideas from the ever-memorable passage of the Sermon on the Mount, made doubly dear to him, as he recollected how Virginia Gooch had taught him to read and value it! The deepest effect however was produced upon his mind, when the reader had reached and pronounced these matchless words:

GOES TO OBERLIN COLLEGE. 79

"And why take ye thought for raiment? Consider the lilies of the field, how "they grow; they toil not, neither do they spin: And yet I say unto you, that "even Solomon in all his glory was not arrayed like one of these."

The tender sensibility of the reader, expressed in the accents of his voice, moved the souls of his hearers, in such manner and to such effect, as to fill their eyes and moisten their cheeks with tears.

When the orator of the occasion stepped forward, the attention of the audience while every eye was turned towards him, became, as shown in the faces of the people, intensified. The announcement of his text and its rendition, were a sermon. However, in his exposition and illustration of the Truth, as contained in the passage of Scripture which he read, he occupied quite an hour and a half, during which time the vast assembly gave profoundest attention to every word he uttered, hearing him apparently as if for life itself. An intermission of three-quarters of an hour followed his discourse.

Every man, woman and child then came again to the church, to hear the last words of the moving eloquent utterance of the Rev. Charles G. Finney. He continued the discourse commenced by him in the morning, displaying in its further treatment and application, in the afternoon, a power marvelous and indescribable. The wild torrents which sweep the sea; the mighty storms that lay in utter waste mountains and plains, may be as easily described as the fetterless and bounding power which moved this irresistible, vanquishing son of eloquence.

John had never heard such preaching. He had never had his soul moved by such utterance. Like all others who had been listening, at the close of the meeting he left the house so impressed that he moved away in silence, seemingly afraid to speak. Thus he commenced his life in Oberlin; and the impressions made upon his mind by the observations and experiences of his first Sabbath there, were so indelibly written in his thoughts and memory, that no lapse of time, or worldly care, has been able to efface them.

On the following day, as conducted to the office of the secretary and treasurer of Oberlin College, and introduced to Mr. Hamilton Hill, who held that office, by Mr. Vashon, young Langston settled his tuition and incidental expenses, according to rule, and arranged for his studies and classes. When asked what studies he would pursue, whether English branches, or Greek and Latin, as he hesitated a little, his old teacher answered for him, saying, " He will study Greek and Latin, taking up the grammars of those languages at once." Arrangements were made for his location in classes, accordingly, and he did enter upon such studies.

Then followed a visit to the house of Prof. George Whipple. In introducing the new student to this learned professor of mathematics, Mr. Vashon expressed the hope that in taking him into his house and family, consenting to act as his guardian and protector while at school, he would find him obedient, docile and agreeable. The professor received his prospective ward and the future inmate of his family with every manifestation of kindly feeling, assuring him, that so far as his treatment was concerned, while under his watchful care and under his roof, everything should be done to make his sojourn pleasant and advantageous.

At this point, as Mr. Vashon was leaving, Mrs. Whipple, the wife of the professor, came in and was introduced to the student who was to take his place from that day at her table and make his home in her house. A woman of superior appearance and personal attractions, handsomely endowed in every sense by nature, highly educated and cultured, of pleasing manner and address, the near relative of the great Daniel Webster, she made the happiest possible impression at once upon the youth. She had but commenced conversation with him, inquiring as to his studies and classes, when the daughter of the family appeared, and John was introduced to her. It was found to his delight upon explanations which he had made to the mother, that he would be in the same classes with her daughter.

While such occurrences were transpiring in the study of Prof. Whipple, a person, as directed by Mr. Vashon, came to the door bringing the young man's trunk, which was carried directly to the room in the second story of the building, where he was to find his quarters. There was only time given for the most hurried survey of the room, its furniture and conveniences, all of which made pleasant impression upon the prospective occupant, when dinner was announced. Promptly the members of the family, and students, boarders and inmates, gathered in the dining-room, and each took the seat at the table appropriated to him or her. There was a single vacancy, and this was allotted to the new-comer. He took it as directed and found himself near the lady of the house, just to her left, with a noted female teacher and scholar, Miss Mary True, seated immediately beyond him to his left. Seated thus and a stranger in whom no little interest centered, he was so thoroughly questioned, especially by these ladies, that even if he had not been greatly embarrassed, he could not have found time for eating his meal and relieving fully his boyish appetite, for all meals were closed promptly.

However, as the days passed and he made the acquaintance and the friendship of the entire family, he became wholly at home and at ease in his most agreeable surroundings. Besides himself, there was in this family but a single other colored person—a young lady very cordially treated by all, because of her excellent behavior and her natural, appropriate bearing. Situated thus, brought in contact constantly with pleasant persons, associating daily with congenial classmates, with every influence exerted upon him calculated to develop and sustain his scholarly qualities and character, young Langston passed his first year at Oberlin College, pursuing with assiduity and vigor the study of the Greek and Latin languages, advanced arithmetic and algebra, with such lessons in the Bible and instructions in elementary exercises of rhetoric as were given at that time in the preparatory department, to students fitting themselves for examination and entry of the regular college course.

By this time his taste for study, with more matured purpose as to his general and thorough culture, had grown and developed itself, and he had been moved by an earnest desire and serious determination to secure for himself at all hazards a complete academic, collegiate and professional education. At the end of the fall term of the college, he bade his teachers, fellow-students and friends good-bye, in the assurance, in his own mind, that he would meet them again at the opening of the spring term of 1845.

Returning to Chillicothe from Oberlin, in obedience to the orders of his guardian, John spent two weeks with his brother Charles, at his quarters and as his visitor. While there a committee of colored men coming from Hicks' Settlement, eight miles away in the country, called upon Mr. Charles H. Langston to advise with him as to the employment of a school-teacher for the Settlement during the winter. They desired to have the school open on the first Monday of November, and continue through to the first day of the following February, three full months. They were able to pay the teacher for his services ten dollars per month in cash, and furnish him board, as he consented to pass a week in each family patronizing the school, repeating his visits to the various families as necessity might require. Finally they asked their adviser, upon his approval of their plan of opening and conducting their school, to name some suitable person whom they might employ as teacher. He was not able to name for them such person as he believed by reason of his age, experience and attainments was qualified to serve them in such way as might be desirable. One of them finally inquired whether his young brother could not be employed. He replying, told them frankly that he thought whatever might be his brother's accomplishments, he was too young and too small to undertake to teach and manage their school. He was told that the school would be easily managed; that it would be composed chiefly of young men and young girls, who would be diligent in study and well-behaved; and that the work of the teacher would consist, mainly, in hearing recitations and making necessary explanations in the elementary English branches of spelling, reading, arithmetic, geography and writing. To this Mr. Langston replied that his brother was near at hand, and could be seen and consulted.

John was called; and on being introduced to the persons composing the committee, after full explanation by them, with reply by him, with his brother Charles to counsel all concerned, the young man was employed upon the terms already stated, and agreed to open the school promptly on the morning of the first Monday of the following November.

As agreed, young Langston one month before he had reached his sixteenth year, or thereabout, commenced his labors as a country school-teacher. He was the smallest person in the school save a single boy, Samuel Cox. His attention was in no important sense required for matters of discipline, and after the ringing of his bell for opening in the morning, or at noon, not the least possible disorder of any sort could be noted to disturb or annoy the teacher or any pupil. Thus for the full three months of the term, everything in the school moved on to the entire satisfaction of all interested.

Only one week had passed, when a gentleman residing in the Settlement five miles from the schoolhouse, the father of a young son to whom he would have special instruction given because he was too young and small to attend school in the winter season, and who desired also to secure for himself lessons in reading and explanation of the Bible, proposed to the teacher to give him his board in his own family, and keep and care for his horse, provided he would teach as indicated himself and his son. This proposition of Mr. John Jackson, a man of prominence among his class, whose home was in all respects pleasant, and whose influence was worth a great deal to any teacher in the Settlement, was accepted. Thereafter, in addition to his daily duties in the schoolroom, the young teacher gave attention every morning and evening to these scholars at their home. His success in this regard rewarded his labors in manifold, pleasant manner.

Every month as it closed, was marked by a visit from one or the other of the three persons composing the committee, by whose authority in the name of the community the teacher had been employed. The object of such visit was not only to learn the condition of the school, but to bring to the teacher as collected from its patrons the amount due him monthly for his services. The ten dollars paid him consisted in the main of five- and ten-cent pieces, with a few coppers, sometimes a twenty-five cent piece, but at no time a larger one, the money being always the very identical coins collected by voluntary payment of the supporters of the school. It is to be remembered that at this time there were no public-schools provided in Ohio for colored persons, and no public money given for the support of any schools which they might establish among themselves for the education of their children. So far as such education was concerned, it depended wholly upon their own efforts and their own special outlays. It will be understood then, that the organization of the committee named, and the establishment of this school with the employment of the teacher, depended entirely upon the enterprise and purpose of the colored people, composing, mainly, the population of the Settlement.

Having no demands of any kind upon him, whether for board, washing or other necessity, and having in fact no opportunity for spending his money had he been moved by desire to do so, young Langston closed the three months term of his first school with every cent of his thirty dollars kept in the very money which had been paid him.

The closing exercises of the school consisted of examinations upon studies which had been pursued, with simple rhetorical performances such as compositions, declamations and discussion. Such exercises were largely attended, and the scholars and patrons manifested special interest in them. They took place on the afternoon of the last day of the term; and since the school had been kept in a building provided and used for church purposes, the accommodations for a large gathering were very convenient and satisfactory.

The expressions, formal and other, made in brief addresses heard from several leading patrons of the school, with respect to its management by the committee and the conduct of the teacher, were in every way agreeable, especially as they were received by the most cordial endorsement of the great assembly. After taking leave of his scholars and thanking both them and the patrons of the school for their kind, considerate treatment, the teacher closed his services in the midst of great popular applause.

Going directly to Mr. Jackson's house on the way toward town, he tarried there for a short time only. Here he had made his home, and by the family had been treated in the most kindly, hospitable manner. He went at once to his room, where he counted and arranged the money which had been paid him, in the most convenient condition for carrying it with him on horseback to Chillicothe. Carefully wrapping it in a newspaper, he made it even more secure by tying it up tightly in the best white pocket handkerchief which he owned. His horse stood ready for him at the door. As he descended the stairway he met in the hall and sitting-room the good school committee with a few friends, who, on their way home stopped to express their cordial regards for him, and to offer their thanks for the earnestness and diligence with which he had served as their teacher. Having paid his respects to each one, expressing in the warmest terms his feeling of gratitude to the committeemen and Mr. Jackson and his family, he left the house with his package of money in his hand. Inconvenient as he found it in mounting the horse, he handed it to Mr. Jackson who stood near by, with the request that he hold it. As he took it he smiled, seemingly amused at the care with which the owner handled it; expressing his deep regret as he returned it to him, now seated upon his horse, that it was so small in amount though large in bulk. The feeling which moved the teacher himself was his thankfulness that, even if it was large in bulk and small in amount, it was his, and the fruits of his own labors.

He had borrowed for his school service a fine animal of his brother Charles, and as he rode into town on this creature, with his first school-teaching experience impressed favorably upon his mind, his money held tightly in his hand, and his prospect of an early pleasing report to be made to his brother and to his guardian, he did in fact exhibit in word and conduct feelings of pride with a little sense of self-sufficiency. His brother Charles and his guardian gave diligent attention, each, to the account which he gave of his experience and success as a teacher, and rejoiced with him in the good results which had rewarded his first efforts.

Not many days after his return he was visiting his brother Charles at his home in Chillicothe, when the teacher of the city colored school, Mr. Samuel Deveaux, successor in that service to Mr. George B. Vashon, called to see whether he could secure the services of Mr. Langston to take charge of his school for two or three weeks. Important, pressing business required his attention and presence in another part of the State, and to secure release he must supply his substitute in the school. In reply to Mr. Deveaux's request Mr. Langston stated that he could not serve him; but jocosely remarked to him, "John is the teacher of our family; he has just accomplished what he considers a feat in teaching the school in Hicks' Settlement, and his success there has made him quite bold enough and self-reliant to attempt almost anything in the line of school-teaching." The young man was present and heard these comments of his good brother, when he felt not a little rebuked, and would have been glad had he been permitted to make answer and explanation in his own defence. Mr. Deveaux turning to him without the least hesitation, asked him to take his school, promising to pay him for two weeks' work two-thirds of what he had received for three months. At first he refused, as he knew that the school was largely made up of boys and girls who had been his playmates and schoolfellows. He knew, too, that several of the scholars were generally unruly and difficult of management. But Mr. Deveaux pressed him, assuring him that he would leave the

GOES TO OBERLIN COLLEGE. 87

school in such condition that he would have no trouble. He had confidence enough in his ability to do the teaching. He feared only that the boys and girls might form a combination of such strength and purpose as to overcome and set at naught any effort which he might make to maintain good order and discipline.

Finally, as greatly persuaded by Mr. Deveaux and assured by him that he would have no trouble, with an encouraging word from his brother Charles, he consented to take the school for two weeks from the following Monday morning, or until the teacher should return, not exceeding three weeks. As he entered the schoolhouse at the appointed time, the pupils, especially those of the more advanced classes, who had known him, manifested a goodly degree of kind feeling towards him. In fact, all things were commenced smoothly and moved off in excellent order. The two weeks soon passed, and with the exception of a severe punishment administered to one of the smartest and one of the most mischievous small boys of the school, nothing occurred to render his experience in his second attempt at managing a school unpleasant or regretful. On his return, Mr. Deveaux complimented the young teacher, and after thanking, paid him according to promise. The sum which he had thus gained, added to the thirty dollars which he had already earned and collected, aggregated fifty dollars, as his first winter's earnings at schoolteaching. With this amount in his possession, moved by the consciousness of his success, he became greatly inspirited and encouraged, and was more than ever inclined to be proud of his achievement and ambitious to do even greater things.

It was the rule at Oberlin College at this time, to have the long vacation of the school during the winter months, so that any students desiring to engage in teaching for such term, either in public or private schools, could do so. This regulation proved to be of the greatest possible benefit to all interested; for it not only gave opportunity to those teaching to increase their means, but, where success attended their efforts, to promote their desire and determination to make the most of themselves as scholars and useful members of society.

The time had arrived when decision must be made with regard to John's future course of life. According to the law and public sentiment, for the time being at least, under age as he was, this decision must be determined by his guardian, who had control both of his person and his property. The year before that person had consented to his going to Oberlin College for nine months or a single academical year, and had determined then that he must thereafter go to a trade.

William Langston was a thoughtful man. It was a rare thing to find him talkative. He must be deeply interested in any subject, with his feelings greatly moved in view of it, to draw from him many words. When he had reached conclusions upon any matter, he held his judgment with tenacity, and refused to surrender or modify it till he had exhausted every resource in its defence. He was not a man of large logical ability, nor nice and extended sagacity. It was not always the case that he predicated his opinion upon sufficient knowledge, while regardful of the ultimate moral effect which might follow its adoption. Besides, he was not possessed of such fulness of even English education, nor had he such observation of men and things, nor had he gathered such general information from ordinary reading or advantageous association, as to give him liberality and accuracy in regard to any subject of large, special importance, concerning which differences might exist in ingenuous minds. His judgment therefore, even where he might otherwise be generous and just, concerning the life and education of a young man prompted by exalted aspiration in keeping with his natural ambition, must be taken with due vigilance and care. Hence, it was not unnatural for him at the time when it was necessary to make decision with regard to the education of his ward, especially in the light of the influences then operative upon his mind, to be at fault on such subject. And it was very

GOES TO OBERLIN COLLEGE. 89

fortunate for the one who was most concerned in such transaction, to find near him a bold, fearless advocate, who would sustain, in his desires and purposes, the youth who by education and culture would fit himself for exalted place of usefulness and influence.

Two things conspired to save young Langston from a course of life which might have doomed him to such conditions of ordinary mechanical labor as would have thwarted every aim of his ambition and choice of his taste and judgment. In the first place, his brother Charles, a man though comparatively young, of sound English attainment, large reading, and general information gathered from contact as well as study, knew the value of education and how much depended in life upon sustaining and directing rather than opposing and crossing the natural inclination, the moral trend of a young person. Besides, he knew and appreciated the fact that his brother had been sent by direction of his father even in his childhood to Ohio, that he might secure a liberal education—the best furnished at that time by any school to one of his class. Such views as a person of his character and knowledge would entertain on the subject his brother urged in favor of John's return to Oberlin College, emphasizing the fact that he had so far discovered application and diligence as a student, with great docility and obedience, and had made such progress in study generally, as to indicate what he might accomplish even in the higher walks of social and professional life were he given the opportunity to which his talents and circumstances entitled him.

The second circumstance that operated greatly in favor of John's return to Oberlin, was found in the letter which Prof. George Whipple had sent by him to his guardian on his return to Chillicothe. The professor stated in the letter that his conduct and his progress in study while at Oberlin, justified the opinion that he should be sent back and given a full and thorough course of collegiate training. To this letter, and the opinion of a person so well qualified for its expression, his brother finally referred with special and decisive effects, so moving the guardian that he said, with entire earnestness and good feeling, "John shall decide for himself."

Permitted thus to speak for himself, the young man said, "I will return to Oberlin, and fit myself as thoroughly as may be at once to enter college and take the college course." The guardian who had at best small confidence in such education, with larger faith in a trade for a boy, put to his ward the question, "Then, what will you do?" Without waiting for an answer, he spoke of Mr. George B. Vashon, who had graduated the past August from Oberlin College, asking, "What will he do?" Then he mentioned Mr. William Cuthbert Whitehorn, who would graduate from the same college at the next August Commencement, asserting "that the only thing which he would be able to do really, was to return to the West India Islands, from which he had come to the United States, and perhaps he might find something there to do." To all this his brother Charles made quick and earnest reply, saying, "Time will take care of the boy's interests! Let us do our duty!"

This conference and discussion held by the kinsmen of the boy, the guardian who was his half-brother and Charles his whole, resulted at last in the best possible understanding between them and in the greatest good to the young man, who was directed to prepare for his return to Oberlin.

Leaving Chillicothe within the next four or five days, upon a stage-coach running from that city to Columbus and northward, the Neil House, the chief hotel in the capital city, was reached late in the evening of the same day, after a ride of forty-five miles. Here the coach would stop for the night, and every passenger left it to get supper and take lodging accordingly. The coach had been crowded all day, the number of passengers being large and everyone seeming to be going over the entire route. All trunks and baggage were taken from the coach and placed upon the pavement for removal into the hotel. John's trunk was included among the others, to be treated as one would

GOES TO OBERLIN COLLEGE.

naturally suppose under the circumstances, precisely as the other baggage. Following the other passengers who made their way to the office of the hotel, he was just in the act of entering, when a person seemingly in authority stopping him, asked, "Where are you going?" He replied naively, "Into the hotel." This person replied in gruff, coarse, vulgar manner, "No, you are not! We do not entertain *niggers!* You must find some nigger boarding-house." It was a dark, rainy, disagreeable evening on the first day of March, 1845. Every trunk was carried into the hotel except the boy's, and he denied admittance stood by his as an outcast, heartbroken, not knowing what to do nor where to go. A black man in passing seeing his condition, addressed him, asking, "What is the matter?" In the midst of his surprise and sore indignation, he told the stranger of his situation; when in a most kindly manner, taking his small trunk in his hand, he said to the unfortunate lad, "Follow me! I will take you to a stopping-place, where you shall be well cared for." And so in fact it turned out.

Through this experience, which was absolutely more deadly in fact to John's feelings than the quickest poison could have been to his body, he gained the acquaintance of a man and his family, colored persons, whom he learned subsequently to respect and honor. He passed the night with them, and at eight o'clock the next morning the stage-coach in which he had travelled from Chillicothe appeared at their door to take the young man on his journey northward, according to agreement made when he paid his passage to Oberlin. The same person who had met him the night before at the hotel and treated him so illegally and cruelly, appeared with the coach, acting, apparently, as the agent of the company owning it. As the young man came out and advanced to take his seat as a passenger, after his trunk had been put upon the coach, this person ordered him to take his place on the outside and ride with the driver. It was still raining and quite chilly, in the very first days of Spring. Young Langston very properly objected to such an order, asserting that he would do no such thing.

Seated in the coach already, on his way to Cleveland, was a gentleman who had come over the day before from Chillicothe, and who had paid considerable attention to this young man; and when the order of the agent was given, as stated, he objected, saying, "No! He will not take a seat upon the outside of this coach." As he uttered these words, with great earnestness shown in his face and deep agitation discovered in the tones of his voice, he got out of the coach himself, and insisted that every other man do likewise, and that the passengers should take their seats as their names appeared on the way-bill as read by the agent. This was quickly agreed to, and the first name appearing upon the way-bill was that of John M. Langston. He took his seat inside the stage-coach, making such choice of seats, since there was no lady present, as suited him. His friend's name stood next on the way-bill, and when called he entered the coach and took his seat by the one whom he had befriended. Thereafter, on that journey, neither at the hotels nor upon the coach, did John's color figure in the matter of his treatment. The treatment which was accorded him at the Neil House made indelible impression upon his mind, and although he has been a thousand times since entertained, being well and considerately accommodated, he has never forgotten his first experience there.

Otherwise, the trip from Chillicothe to Oberlin was without special incident worthy of note. John reached the college in good season, and arranged his course of study with reference to examination and admission to the college department in the following August. This required on his part vigorous and persistent prosecution of his studies, which necessitated early rising, with late retirement, and devotion of all his powers and time to study and recitations, allowing no time for needed exercise and rest. His record as a student was good, and his examinations for admission to the college were of such character as to give him easy and satisfactory entry thereto.

GOES TO OBERLIN COLLEGE.

His four years in the college course were marked by diligence, good behavior and success. He maintained in every department of study an excellent name, graduating in August, 1849, with high honors. In his college course he manifested, ultimately, in connection with his class, society and public rhetorical exercises, special aptness in debate and address, with large and commendable powers of composition. He sustained an enviable position among the best writers and speakers of the institution.

A single incident of his experience in early college life deserves special mention, for it had much to do with his standing at college and his success in subsequent life. He had but entered college when different persons, members of the two literary societies of the institution—the Young Men's Lyceum and the Union Society—called upon and invited him, as they did other members of his class, then Freshmen, to join the one or the other association. Having several special friends in the Union Society who pressed him to join it, and understanding that this society sustained a very high name, he did join it, and was welcomed as a member by marked and pleasing consideration. He was immediately called to duty by being given position in a debate which was to take place one week from the date of his membership. The question to be discussed, and one which created no small interest at the time in the society and throughout the college, was, "Do the teachings of phrenology interfere with man's free moral agency?" The expectations had in the society and among the students generally with respect to this exercise were high, as at least three of the ablest student-orators of the college were to take part in the debate, and the subject was one which then excited large interest even in the community. The ablest speaker of the students was made the leader of the discussion in the affirmative of the question, and young Langston was made his colleague. Mr. Edmund B. Wood, by far the brightest scholar of the college department, and second to no one of his associates as a debater, had spoken, and a young gentleman of skill and ability as a disputant, had answered him, when the president of the society announced Mr. Langston as the next speaker. He came forward, taking his position upon the platform and addressing the presiding officer as "Mr. President." He was unable to proceed further. Every thought, every feeling, every sentiment, every mental experience and condition, with every word he had ever known, took wings and flew away, leaving his mind a complete blank. How long he occupied his standing position he never knew. When, however, he recovered himself, he was seated in his place, and immediately a flood of strange feeling and saddening experience poured itself through his being, filling his heart and understanding in such manner that he could only find relief in the bitterest and the most copious tears. His condition seemed deplorable, and as the exercises were closed shortly thereafter, every young gentleman proffered his sympathy to the unfortunate member. He could not, then, accept sympathy. Its expression tended to increase and intensify his grief and humiliation. His feelings were too deeply moved; as he thought of his failure, he felt himself wholly unworthy of the slightest attention. With his handkerchief wet with his tears, his cap and his coat sleeves as deeply immersed, in the deepest dejection and mortification he hurried himself away from his kind friends to his own room in Tappan Hall. There all alone he could give himself up to that anguish of soul which he felt, and to its expression in tears, as they came in floods. As he entered his room he locked the door, and throwing himself upon his bed, he continued to give unrestained, though silent vent to his sorrow. His pillow, bed and clothing were saturated with his tears. The morning bell of the institution rang at five o'clock, calling the students to their daily duties, before he seemed able to master and control himself. Then, as if moved by some power above and outside of himself, he arose, and with swollen face and inflamed eyes confronting himself as he stood before the little looking-glass hanging upon the wall of his room, he made the solemn vow of his life. It was that, God helping him, he would never fail

GOES TO OBERLIN COLLEGE.

again in any effort at making a speech ; and that he would never allow, while mental and bodily vigor lasted, any opportunity to make one pass unimproved. Thereupon he made his toilet, and proceeded as usual with the review of his lessons preparatory to his recitations. At the sound of the bell, summoning him and all other students to breakfast, he found himself ready to move. As he descended the stairway of the hall on his way to breakfast, he was overtaken by Mr. Wood, his colleague in the debate, who was still inclined to offer him his sympathy. He was not in tears now, and said to his friend, "I thank you! But, never mind!"

It is true, however, that he was not long at the breakfast table, and did not do much talking that morning. On being excused from the usual family prayers, which the students were required ordinarily to attend, he left his boarding-place, and coming upon the street, met a young man, a member of the same society as himself, who said to him, "Langston, I have just been called home for the week, and I want you to take my place in the society debate next Thursday evening. Do not say no! Do it for me!" The proposition was promptly accepted in the words "I will do so!"—and at the appointed time, when this young man's name was called and the president of the society had explained why he was absent, Mr. Langston was named as his substitute, and introduced accordingly. He came forward without the least delay, and proceeded to the delivery of his speech, occupying the ten minutes allotted to him ; and when it was found that he had not completed his argument, on motion of his colleague in the former discussion, he was given, upon unanimous vote, an extension which exactly doubled the usual time. Upon the completion of his address, which had been delivered with ease and spirit, the applause which he received was reassuring in the largest possible measure. Now his joy and satisfaction were quite equal to the deep mortificacation and dejection that had overtaken him in his failure one week before. Saved thus, he has not failed to redeem in vigorous observance the vow which he made as just recorded.

Young Langston always felt that he and his classmates met a great misfortune, when on Commencement day in August, 1849, the public health in the neighborhood of Oberlin was such, with cholera prevailing at Sandusky City, that no public Commencement exercises could be held. Decision in this matter had not been made before he and his classmates had selected subjects and prepared their Commencement addresses. He had chosen the theme, " The Sacrifices and Recompenses of Literary Life," and very much desired to deliver his address. He felt when denied that privilege, that a special and valuable opportunity had been lost. However, his class, with a reasonable audience in attendance, was addressed by Prof. John Morgan, and the diplomas, as awarded, were conferred by Rev. Asa Mahan, the president of the college.

CHAPTER VII.

OBERLIN, ITS COMMUNITY AND ITS COLLEGE.

THE famous and historical town of Oberlin was founded by two of the most remarkable men ever known in this or any other country. These men were controlled in their purposes by the religious idea. They would build a city, a community and a college, upon their Christian faith, as embodied in the saying, "They knew Christ only and Him crucified."

It has always seemed to be the case, that, in searching for a site on which to build their ideal city, community and college, they sought the most unpropitious and unpromising that could be found. On lands secured of Messrs. Street and Hughs of Connecticut, located in Lorain County, Ohio, ten miles south of Lake Erie, Messrs. Philo P. Stewart and John J. Shipherd, the founders of the town, selected its site. The first house was erected in 1833. Sixty years have wrought such change in the conditions of a situation so inauspicious, that the incorporated village of Oberlin, with its four thousand inhabitants, its well-regulated streets, its public grounds, its college buildings and private residences, designed and erected upon approved models of architecture, constitutes a town of rare New England character and beauty.

These men were no more peculiar in the seeming search they made for a site upon which they must build their enterprise in faith, rather than wisdom, than they were in the great overshadowing purpose which they had in founding it at all. They sought to build in city, community and college, a source whence should issue influences exalted and Christian, which should be elevating as they were missionary, to save the people of the great Mississippi Valley through the teachings and illustrations of Christian maxims and faith. In order to such end, it was necessary to find men and women, whole families, who sympathized heartily with such founders and builders. As they found a site for their city, however forbidding in its natural features and condition, so quickly redeemed and made seemly and pleasant, they found the men and women, in not a few cases whole families, ready to constitute and maintain their community.

In order to the full realization of the Christian, missionary conception of these men, it was understood by them that a school should be established at which men and women might receive, on equal terms, the advantages of thorough liberal instruction, with full accurate knowledge of such spiritual doctrines as might fit them for the earnest labors to which they were called. The school contemplated was established, and its growth and development have been even more marvelous than those of the city and the community.

In 1835, when Lane Theological Seminary, located near Cincinnati, interdicted the discussion of slavery, and thus drove two-thirds of its best students away from it, with several of its ablest instructors, alienating many of its most valuable patrons, the Oberlin school, in numbers and talent, was made gainer thereby in the very best and highest sense. At this time, and because they were earnest in their opposition to slavery, and would speak against it themselves and insist that others should have the right to do likewise, even students, Messrs. Asa Mahan and John Morgan quit their connection, the former as a trustee and the latter as a professor, with Lane Seminary, and both went to Oberlin. Mr. Mahan was made the first president of the Oberlin school, now become a college, and Mr. Morgan one of its leading, most scholarly professors. Thus reinforced as to instructors as well as students, with a president of acknowledged ability and various accomplishments, well adapted to his work, efficient as teacher, and learned, eloquent and effective as a pulpit orator, Oberlin College, starting upon improved conditions of life and power, gave promise of enlarged permanent success.

The "Oberlin Movement," headed by the men already named, and the "Abolition Movement," led by William Lloyd Garrison and his associates, had their origin in the same year. In the former, equality was conceded so far as educational advantages were concerned, without distinction of sex; and through the influence of the latter, whose aim was the unconditional abolition of slavery and the elevation of the negro, the founders and supporters of Oberlin College were forced early in its history, as early as 1835, to consider and determine the question of the coeducation of white and colored students within its halls. Fortunately for the colored race, the Rev. John Keep had been made a trustee of the college, and been elected president of the Board of Trustees. When the question upon this subject came up, the debate was protracted, earnest and exciting. The gravest doubt prevailed as to the final decision to be reached, and when a vote was taken, the board stood equally divided, one half for and the other half against the proposition. It was for the president of the Board of Trustees to give the casting vote, and settle the question in favor of the admission or the rejection of colored students. All honor to his memory and heroic conduct, John Keep gave his casting vote for justice, equality and freedom, when he voted for the admission of the colored student to Oberlin College.

The preamble and resolution submitted to the Board of Trustees on this subject read as follows:

"Whereas, there does exist in our country an excitement in respect to "our colored population; and fears are entertained that on the one hand they "will be left unprovided for as to the means of a proper education, and on the "other that they will in unsuitable numbers be introduced into our schools and "thus in effect forced into the society of the whites; and the state of public "sentiment is such as to require from the board some definite expression on the subject;

"Therefore, resolved, that the education of the people of color is a matter of great interest, and should be encouraged and sustained in this institution."

It was at a meeting of the board of trustees held February 9, 1835, that this action was taken; and ever since that time colored students have enjoyed like opportunities and advantages in the school as white persons.

In such manner the purposes of the founders of the Oberlin community and college have been realized in the wisest and most comprehensive sense, so far as the management of the latter is concerned, as endorsed and sustained by the former. In accepting all persons of every nationality, native and foreign born, white and black, male and female, as students to be fitted in head and heart for the arduous manly and womanly duties of life, the highest ideal of its Christian founders must have been completely, grandly realized. Therefore to Oberlin belongs the honor of being the first institution of learning in the world to give woman equal educational opportunities and advantages with man. To it, too, belongs the honor of being the first college of the United States to accept the negro student and give him equal educational opportunities and advantages with the white. And to the Oberlin community belongs the distinguishing honor of being the first one on the face of the earth to realize in its teachings, its practices and its manners towards every human being, the high central Christian sentiment, " that whatsoever ye would that men should do to you, do ye even so to them." While the town of Oberlin has grown steadily in all the years of its life in every way of improvement and excellence, and the community in every redeeming and desirable quality of popular progress and advancement, the college, multiplying its numbers, improving its methods and appliances for its educational work, has constantly elevated and broadened its standards of scholarship.

From the beginning in Oberlin, extreme radical views were held and maintained on all matters of reform, religion, education and anti-slavery. Correct habits of diet and dress, as approved by the founders of the community, conducive to one's health and in keeping with his circumstances, were advised and urged. The principles of religious faith and life, as inculcated in the severest teachings and philosophy of Jesus Christ and the Apostles, were accepted and pressed as indispensable to individual and popular obligation. Education, which meant the development of the whole human being in intellectual, moral and spiritual powers, with due consecration of all learning, genius, talent and influence to God and humanity, without distinction of sex or color, was recognized as the duty and privilege of every child of man. And upon all subjects of freedom— the unconstitutionality of slavery, its utter violation of the maxims of the Bible, and its outrage of all the fundamental doctrines of genuine democracy—its position was clear, comprehensive and decisive.

To such a community, maintaining such principles and insisting upon their application to and enforcement in favor of all persons, whatever might be the sacrifices or the dangers to be incurred, it was natural to find the fugitive slave, in search of a place of refuge and protection, gathering in large numbers. So it was; and as early as 1844, when young Langston arrived, he found among other remarkable things true of the people, that they had provided a schoolhouse, situated in a conspicuous part of the town, employed solely for the education and improvement of any fugitive slaves who had come to and settled in the place and who were moved by the desire and purpose of elevating themselves educationally and morally. This schoolhouse was known, as it was called, the Liberty School. Here was his Faneuil Hall, in which the negro made his most eloquent and effective speeches against his enslavement. And no fugitive slave resident of Oberlin, attending such school or hearing such utterances, ever feared any successful assault upon his freedom, even though the attacking party came armed with the muniments of the law in such behalf, state or national. The major part of the colored persons residing in Oberlin at this time were fugitive slaves, who remained there in the consciousness that they were safe against the capture of any slave-holder or his agent, any officer of the government or other.

But the real spirit and metal of Oberlin were not tested, so far as its purpose with regard to the fugitive slave and his succor were concerned, till 1858, and in connection with what stands now in history as the "Oberlin Wellington Rescue Case." This was a case in which the whole people, men and women, leaving the town absolutely deserted, went forth under the frenzy of their conviction in favor of freedom, to rescue the black boy, John Price, from a United States deputy marshal who had arrested and attempted to spirit him away to that bondage from which he had by flight emancipated himself.

The treatment accorded colored people in Oberlin socially at this time was most remarkable; in keeping, however, with the professions religiously, politically and educationally made by the founders of the community. Every Sunday colored persons could be seen seated in conspicuous eligible places in the only church in the town, worshipping after the manner of those in whose midst they lived, and no one molested or disturbed them. Such persons were made welcome as equals in the best families, as they were in every part of the institution, and thus were given the best social, as they were the highest educational advantages. Such was the recognition and the consideration accorded the colored American, whether student or resident, in Oberlin, in the earlier days of its history.

Of the leading men of the community and the college, if they may be classified in such way, it would be well-nigh impossible for one duly advised to speak in too high praise. In addition to Messrs. Stewart and Shipherd, already named, Messrs. Asa Mahan, Charles G. Finney, John Morgan and John Keep must be numbered among those who are to be honored as the founders and the promoters of Oberlin, its community and its college, distinguished as it has always been for the high tone of its Christian sentiment, its lofty standard of equal popular education, and its intelligent, sincere devotion to impartial liberty and human rights.

In such a community, at such an institution of learning, under such influences, young Langston was located early in life, and received his education and training.

CHAPTER VIII.

HE SEEKS ADMISSION TO CERTAIN LAW SCHOOLS, BUT IS DENIED.

YOUNG Langston had completed his academic and collegiate studies. He had completed his twentieth year and was nearing his majority. He had taken a course of study calculated to fit him for such further prosecution of some professional course as might properly pursued make him a useful man, and his guardian and friends expected him to go forward in reasonable hope and courage to the end. He had the health—although his natural physical condition had been somewhat disturbed by indiscretion in over-study, want of proper diet and necessary exercise—the means and the ability to justify and determine such course. Here the question came to him, as to all young men similarly situated, "What shall I do?" He would study and practice law. There was not however a negro lawyer in any part of the country, and there never had been one from the foundation of the Government. Besides, there was no public sentiment in any part of the country favoring such course on the part of any young colored man however endowed, educated, qualified and well situated for such profession. The public feeling of the country seemed to be entirely against it, and no promise of success in such behalf could be discovered in any quarter. The colored people themselves were not prepared to sustain a person cultivating the legal profession even where they had business of such character as to require professional attention. For the courts were all composed of white men and so were all the juries, and on the part of the former and the latter alike prejudice, strong and inveterate, existed against the colored litigant. Moreover the very language of the law was so positively against the colored man in many cases, and construed often so as to affect his interests so vitally and seriously, that he very justly felt that he must do his utmost, even in the employment of his lawyer, to gain so far as practicable, favor with the court and jury. He felt that he must not certainly do the least thing tending to engender or arouse any feeling or sentiment against himself as a suitor for justice. Thus the young colored man was invited to this calling by no prospect of success, by no example of a daring and courageous forerunner.

But where could a young colored man find a place to study law? Who would take him, among all the lawyers of the country, into his office as a student, and give him from day to day such attention, with instruction, as he might require? To what law school could he be admitted? Was there one in the whole land which would give him admission and welcome? Our young colored student, well furnished in every way with every natural endowment of mind, education, moral character and fortune, a graduate of Oberlin College, and a citizen of the United States and of the State of Ohio, was confronted by such questions, and stood in doubt and wonder as to whether he could find a place, office or school, where he might pursue professional study. Where could he pursue the study of the law and qualify himself for the duties of an attorney and counsellor?

While in this condition of anxiety and perplexity, an aged colored man who had large observation and experience, with no little thought upon the situation and prospects of his class, and who was esteemed and treated, generally, as a sort of wise man, *par excellence*, advised the young colored graduate not to think of doing such an absurd thing as studying law, declaring in a most oracular manner that the practice of the law was something in which only the very smartest white men could succeed. About the same time the young man received a letter from a lawyer of great prominence in his profession, an anti-slavery man and special friend of the negro race, in answer to one which young Langston had written him asking for a place as a student in his office. After saying in this letter that he could not take him as a student, he kindly advised him to leave the United States and seek a home in the British West India Islands, where, perhaps, as he stated, he could study law, and maybe succeed in its practice. The denial made to the young man, and the counsel vouchsafed to him, were natural enough under the circumstances, and came as prompted by generous consideration in his interest.

Thereupon, the would-be colored law-student manifested greater decision with respect to his desires in such regard than ever; for he at once wrote Mr. J. W. Fowler, who owned and conducted a law school at Ballston Spa, New York, inquiring whether he could be admitted as a student into his school. He wrote frankly and truthfully about himself, telling who he was, all about his race, complexion, qualifications and character, assuring Mr. Fowler that he could not only furnish all needed recommendations and endorsements of standing, but was able to meet every charge for tuition, board, or other demand, in advance. Answer was soon received from this gentleman to the effect that he had submitted his case to his Board of Trustees and Board of Faculty, and that the decision was on the part of both unanimous against his admission, because of his color. Mr. Fowler advised him, however, to come to Ballston Spa and let himself be seen, stating that it might be that he would be received. Anxious as he was to enter this school, feeling and believing that his presence and appearance might be of service to him, and having a young friend attending there who urged him to come on, with the assurance, as he felt, that he would be given admission, he did visit the school. He arrived in time to attend the ordinary Commencement exercises of 1850. He had the pleasure and advantage of seeing and hearing David Paul Brown, the great and famous lawyer and orator, on this occasion, who addressed the graduating class in his usually masterly manner upon "The Aristocracy of Eloquence!" The figure of his address, the striking, marvelous illustration of its truth, was witnessed in his own majestic power, displayed in elocution, manner, gesture, sentiment and effect. And so the picture of the occasion remains in the memory and imagination of the young man, who hearing this orator by the merest chance, had his determination to press on stimulated and confirmed.

Afterward young Langston called upon Mr. Fowler, and renewed verbally, with suitable explanations, his application for admission to the school. The principal promised him that his case should be fairly and impartially considered and decided. He said, however, it would have to be submitted to his Board of Trustees and his Board of Faculty. Accordingly, within the next twenty-four hours, Mr. Fowler called upon Mr. Langston at his hotel, and after paying his respects to him, proceeded to give in full the adverse conclusion, with the reasons therefor, which had been reached in his case.

Among other things he said John C. Calhoun, of South Carolina, had visited the school the year before at Commencement and addressed the graduating class, and upon leaving had promised him that he would see to it that the number of his students should be largely increased by a good and numerous accession of young persons from his State. Continuing he said, "We feel that should we take a colored person into the school as a student, and it should become known, we would offend thereby these friends of ours and the school become loser to that extent, at least, and doubtless to even a greater." Young Langston expressed his deep regret and his profound chagrin in terms and manner which seemed in some sense to move Mr. Fowler's feelings. "You have my sympathy," he said, "and I would be pleased to do something to help you on in your studies. I will tell you what I will do. I will let you edge your way into my school. Or, if you will consent to pass as a Frenchman or a Spaniard hailing from the West India Islands, Central or South America, I will take you into the school." When he had finished his statement, Mr. Langston asked, "What, Mr. Fowler, do you mean by your words 'Edge your way into the school'?" He answered, "Come into the recitation-room: take your seat off and apart from the class; ask no questions; behave yourself quietly; and if after a time no one says anything against, but all seem well inclined toward you, you may move up nearer the class; and so continue to do till you are taken and considered in due time as in full and regular membership."

With the close of these words, Mr. Langston, moved by a deep sense of the humiliation of his manhood under the circumstances, rising from his seat and yet in most respectful but feeling terms, expressed himself after this manner: "I thank you, Mr. Fowler! But, however much I may desire to enter your school, I will do so upon no terms or conditions of humiliation! I will not edge my way into your institution! Nor will I yield my American birthright, as a citizen of the United States, even in the pretense that I am a Frenchman or a Spaniard, to gain that object! I was born in Virginia and upon a plantation. Neither of these facts will I deny. I expect to live as I hope to die, in my own country in the service of my own fellow-citizens! Mr. Fowler, before I would consent to the humiliation and degradation implied in either of your propositions, I would open my veins and die of my own act! I am a colored American; and I shall not prove false to myself, nor neglect the obligation I owe to the negro race! You will pardon the vehemence and positiveness of my utterance."

Mr. Fowler heard Mr. Langston in kind considerate manner. No feeling was exhibited on his part other than that of approbation of his decision and its earnest, manly expression. However, he finally said as he addressed Mr. Langston, "You have my sympathy, but I cannot take you as a student." To this the young man made prompt reply, "I do not need sympathy! I need the privileges and advantages of your law school." Here the interview was ended, Mr. Fowler bidding the would-be colored law-student a cordial and kindly farewell. However, he tarried to say to Mr. Langston, "You lecture sometimes, do you not?" The answer was, "I do." He then asked, "Would you not like to speak to us, and in our great lecture-room?" The answer was, "I would." Then Mr. Fowler inquired, "What shall be your subject?" Quickly Mr. Langston replied, "Your treatment of a young educated colored man, the first of his class to ask admission as a student to any American law school." With the subject announced, Mr. Fowler declined to have the lecture delivered, leaving the young man with his hurried words, "Good-bye! Good-bye!"

Mr. Fowler had learned of Mr. Langston's lecturing sometimes on Anti-Slavery and kindred popular themes from Mr. Thomas Higgins, a young white man, who had formerly attended school at Oberlin, and who was a special friend of the colored student. At this time Mr. Higgins was a member of the Ballston Spa law school, and had taken great interest in Mr. Langston's entering the same institution. Among other high and distinguished evidences of his friendly regard and appreciation of his colored friend worthy of note is the fact that through his influence Dr. St. John, a prominent and active member of the *élite* society of this beautiful little town of New York, invited Mr. Langston to his home, to a very imposing and agreeable dinner party. There were present among others at this dinner, Mr. Fowler, with three or four of the leading professors of his school, and Mr. Higgins and several of the students. The dinner was given the following day after the interview just narrated as occurring between Mr. Fowler and Mr. Langston.

The honor thus conferred upon Mr. Langston was a very signal one, and rendered especially emphatic when, as the company had seated themselves about the table, Dr. St. John, an avowed and positive friend of the colored American, addressing him at his own table in the midst of his very excellent and refined guests, said, "I am glad you have come to live among us, for two or three years at least, and to study in our law school. We shall treat you well. Mr. Higgins has told us all about you." "No," said Mr. Langston, "I shall have to leave you to-morrow morning for Ohio." "Why?" quickly asked Dr. St. John. "Mr. Fowler will answer," replied Mr. Langston.

Mr. Fowler at first was inclined to avoid a frank, truthful answer. But Dr. St. John was earnest and positive in the matter, and would tolerate nothing like indirection or evasion, and pressed his inquiries on the subject in such way that Mr. Fowler was compelled to make proper answer in the case. Dr. St. John thereupon opened his mind freely, offering such utter condemnation of Mr. Fowler's action, in the presence of his friends and to their delight, as really seemed to make the president of the school heartily ashamed of his conduct. That the true sentiment of those who heard Dr. St. John in his criticism of Mr. Fowler's conduct in this case may be fully appreciated, it is proper to present here a circumstance of great interest and satisfaction to Mr. Langston. The next morning after the dinner, one of the gentlemen present, a lawyer of learning and distinction, and a lecturer of the school, residing at Saratoga and doing a flourishing business in that city, called upon Mr. Langston at his hotel, and kindly offered, should he conclude to remain in New York and study law in that State, to take him into his office as his student, and give him a home in his own family. This kind and generous offer, however, was declined; and Mr. Langston returning to Ohio, sought to gain admission to the law school located at Cincinnati, conducted and taught by Judge Timothy Walker. He was denied admission, also, to this school, Judge Walker writing him that he could not receive him, "because his students would not feel at home with him, and he would not feel at home with them."

CHAPTER IX.

HE STUDIES THEOLOGY AND LAW AND IS ADMITTED TO THE BAR.

PROFESSOR JOHN MORGAN was, at once, the friend of the colored student and the negro race. The principles which he accepted as the basis of his character, actuating and guiding his whole life, were those which moved as they stimulated the activities of Daniel O'Connell in behalf of both the British and the American slave. Morgan, an Irishman by birth and lineage, had lost nothing in the inheritance and cultivation of the principles indicated, especially as they had been in his case sanctified through his Christian faith, as discovered always in his noble Christian ardor in behalf of every meritorious and worthy cause. He was, under all circumstances, the valued friend of any student who had been fortunate enough to secure his instruction and his paternal attention and interest; so that any student graduating from Oberlin College, left his Alma Mater assured of his deep abiding interest in his general welfare. It was not, then, unnatural that young Langston, situated as he was, should have appealed to this worthy, kind-hearted scholar, for counsel and direction, so indispensable to wise and proper decision as to the course of study which he should pursue. He well understood that any advice and direction given him by that person, would be offered in the deepest sincerity and in the intelligent hope of the best possible results. Knowing the character of the man whom he addressed, that he was sagacious, earnest and solicitous for his highest good, Mr. Langston did not hesitate to take the judgment of his old teacher as the decision in the most important and solemn matter of his life. As advised, without further debate he determined to return to Oberlin, and to pursue the regular course of theology in that college, as preparatory to his study and practice of the law.

Mr. Langston had studied the Hebrew to some extent and with unusual success, before he left his college course. He had given special attention to the Greek as well as the Latin language, so that so far as the original languages of the Old and New Testaments were concerned he was in good preparation to enter upon theological study. Besides, he had been taken over such branches as mental and moral science in his college course with the greatest care and thoroughness by President Mahan, perhaps one of the most skillful and successful teachers in such studies known in this country. More than this, his student had been unusually fond of such subjects, and under the direction of his teacher had made large proficiency. In the elements of criticism, literature, English and classic, logic and rhetoric, theoretic and practical, he had been instructed with diligence and painstaking by Prof. James A. Thorne, a master indeed in his calling. In addition to such qualifications this student possessed large natural taste and talent for the sacred, divine science whose study he would pursue. He accepted without the least hesitation or question every duty enjoined in the course, and persevered with vigor to the end. Entering with suitable preparation, with proper spirit and purpose, he pursued the new course of study with zeal and enthusiasm, succeeding beyond the expectations of those who felt that he would be industrious and faithful.

The course covered three years, and the studies were most interesting, developing the highest order of scientific, metaphysical, logical, linguistic and literary taste and power. As furnishing a preparatory course for the ultimate study and practice of the law, nothing could be superior to the theological curriculum of studies and lectures pursued under and conducted by the able and distinguished professors, Charles G. Finney, John Morgan, Henry Cowles, Henry E. Peck and their assistants, then in charge of the theological department of Oberlin College. The training secured in the department of sacred rhetoric and sermonizing and the general exercises connected therewith, as the same tended to fit one for ordinary public speaking, whether from manuscript or orally, proved to be of the greatest advantage to one having in view forensic labors, especially arguments to courts and juries. The whole field of didactic theology, embracing in its foundation a system of metaphysics which must attempt the explanation of every phenomenon of the human understanding and every condition of the human heart concerning virtue or vice, contradicting seemingly sometimes, or ever and consistently sustaining the teachings of the Scriptures, New and Old, afforded a subject which commanded the loftiest thought of the most vigorous and accurate intellect. The intricate and profound system of hermeneutics and exegesis as taught and applied to our sacred writings—to the matchless utterances of Isaiah, the master prophet of the Old Dispensation, and the teachings of Paul, the transcendent philosopher of the New—required, while they developed in their utmost strength, all the powers of the stoutest understanding. Such subjects exciting the profoundest interest of the student, educated and sustained his highest conceptions of truth, with his best logical powers, in such manner and to such extent as to prepare him for the hardest and most difficult tasks connected with the exacting and trying intellectual problems of any science, even the law itself. Such was the natural and inevitable effect of this course of study upon Mr. Langston, who though taking the same for mental discipline and culture alone as supposed, could not fail to be reached by its moral and religious results. Herein he was greatly benefited, as he was morally fortified for conscientious service at the Bar.

Mr. Langston was the first colored student who entered a theological school in the United States, and his success in that character was awaited with considerable interest by those who knew of his course in this respect. It was held by many persons then that theological and metaphysical study treated as matter of science was too profound and intricate for the negro brain and intellect, and that therein the untried colored student must prove to be a failure. It was conceded that the colored man had sensibility enough and that religious truth could be taught him to such degree and in such measure as to excite and arouse his feelings, moving him even to eloquent utterance after his own peculiar manner in its advocacy and appeal. To measure its depths intellectually, and to comprehend and master its fundamental principles in thought and in the light of reason as affirmative in its unerring divine approval of its essence and verity, was considered a thing in no sense practicable or possible. Hence, by such persons, those holding this opinion of the inability and incapacity of the colored student, this new experiment of negro education was regarded as little less than a wonder.

Often persons of this character, those without faith or confidence in negro talent or genius, attending the recitations of the classes of which Mr. Langston was a member, when he was called to recite would, especially in look always, and very frequently in words even to him, express their surprise that he handled the subjects under consideration with such ease, facility and skill. Sometimes they would go so far as to inquire of the professors how their colored student was getting on; whether he maintained his standing with his fellow-students; and when answered that he was doing well they would often press their inquiry by asking, "Does he really seem to understand and comprehend the truths, the profound principles of theology?" It is not to be understood that any one of his professors or fellow-students ever entertained any such absurd notions. By them the colored student was simply treated impartially and put upon his own metal, and thus made to make his own way over the course of study in competition and rivalry with his classmates for fair and equal standing as to excellence of achievement and record in general scholarship. How well he did is evidenced in the fact that by reason of his high standing with his instructors and the members of the several classes of the department, he was elected as one of the orators therefrom to appear on its behalf at the Commencement of August, 1852.

His address was received with manifestations of the liveliest interest by the vast audience to which it was made, and its delivery was greeted by demonstrations of the heartiest applause. His professors gave Mr. Langston many words of commendation, while his classmates and fellow-students offered him their cordial praises. He was at once invited to preach specially, at several different important places. Besides, he was offered more than a dozen permanent desirable positions as a settled pastor. To all such propositions however he promptly replied that he was only fitting himself for the Bar, and was taking this course of study because he had not been able to gain admission to a law school.

Many seemed surprised at such a decision and course, and not a few advised that since Mr. Langston gave such marked evidences of aptness and power for labor peculiar to the pulpit, he had better turn his attention in that direction. Indeed his old and excellent friend and instructor, Rev. Charles G. Finney, prayed, on closing the exercises of Commencement day, after he had heard the address of his student, imploring the Lord to open the eyes and heart of the young man and teach him his duty as to the choice of his calling for life. Subsequently, as he gave him his parting word of benediction and farewell, the venerable professor said to his student, " My son, you ought to consecrate yourself to the Master's work and preach." But the *high* compliment paid to Mr. Langston on the Commencement day referred to, is found in the words employed by President Finney in his address to him on the presentation of the Master's Degree of the Arts, when on reaching him, as he stood in the central position of fifty other candidates, past graduates of the institution, awaiting like honor, he asked,

"What now shall I say to you? In view of your whole conduct in the college and theological courses of the institution, and especially in view of your conduct this day, had I the power, could the trustees of the institution give me the authority to do so, I would confer upon you two degrees, for you deserve them." This announcement was received by the audience with the wildest applause, and when the young man left the platform upon which the students were ranged, bearing his diploma, he did so the apparent favorite of one of the finest audiences that ever welcomed and greeted an orator on a Commencement occasion at Oberlin.

Mr. Langston did not, however, complete his course in theology till August, 1853, one year after he had received the Master's Degree as mentioned. During his last year of this course, he gave special earnest attention with certain of his classmates and others, members of the department, to the cultivation of the highest possible standard of extemporaneous speaking, adopting the extraordinary and novel method, in connection therewith, of naming the theme—theological, historical, scientific, linguistic, or what not—after those interested had met. The person who had been directed to name the subject, upon the order of a previous meeting, alone had the least knowledge of it till after its announcement. No one was permitted to write a single word upon it, while all were required to deliver addresses as finished as might be in thought, diction, arrangement of matter and illustration, so as to gain the habit of logical, clear, apt, attractive, impressive and perfect extemporaneous address. To the good effects of this exercise Mr. Langston has been wont to attribute much of any success which he may have achieved in addressing public audiences, courts or juries, as well as a large share of any success which may have attended his efforts in training students in law or otherwise, in general or forensic oratory. This training was, above all others, that which the lawyer needed; for he must think and speak often, and sometimes under the heaviest weight of responsibility, in face of solemn emergency, on the spur of the occasion and when he must be correct in his statement of law, and accomplished and effective in his style, manner of utterance and general delivery.

Philemon Bliss was a man of extraordinary character and unusual ability. He had achieved the name and standing of a scholar, lawyer, judge, politician, congressman, anti-slavery agitator, and friend of the colored people of the United States, before he was asked to take a young colored man as a law-student into his office and under his tuition.

The family of Judge Bliss was fortunate in the possession and care of a wife and mother, whose culture and refinement as well as her vigorous sense and sound judgment, were proverbial in the community of its residence. She was kind and considerate of the welfare of any and all persons brought within the limits of her influence and control, and never timid or fearful as to the opinions, even the criticism of others, with respect to her treatment of any one drawn to her by domestic relationships or temporary social intercourse. A family thus constituted, with the persons giving it name and place of the character indicated, must have held exalted and conspicuous position and influence in the society of the community in which it was located. If not the very first family by reason of its circumstances, social, religious, professional and political, in the town of Elyria, the county-seat of Lorain County, Ohio, it would tax any-one acquainted with the society of that place to name one superior to it.

It was to such a man, learned in the law, with such a family, conspicuous and prominent in every way and sense, to whom Mr. Langston made application for a position as a student of law in his office, immediately after his graduation from the theological department of Oberlin College. Fortunately for the young colored man who made this application, both Judge Bliss and his wife had learned of his reputation and promise as a student and lawyer from his best friends, those who knew him well—the instructors of the institution from which he had graduated. He was therefore the more readily accepted by Judge Bliss as his student, and by Mrs. Bliss as a member of their family. This situation proved beneficial as well socially as educationally to the new law-student, and he and his race shall ever stand debtors to the brave man and noble woman who, under the circumstances and in spite of a bitter adverse sentiment then so potent, accorded him such unusual, considerate, humane, just treatment.

Mr. Langston had not been in the office and family of Judge Bliss many days; he certainly had not read over fifty pages of the first law book put into his hands, before an incident transpired worthy of note, calculated to test the feeling and purpose of his preceptor as well as of the community towards him. A clergyman, the agent of the American Colonization Society, had visited Elyria to present to the people in the most popular church of the place the claims of that society upon general favor and patronage. He and his friends had selected Sunday evening as the time, and the great Methodist Church as the place where his address should be delivered. The audience which assembled to hear the address and to give support apparently to the enterprise, was large in numbers and commanding in character. The agent proved to be an orator of unusual ability and eloquence, discovering in his address not only large and varied understanding of his subject, but the very best Christian temper and purpose. He had evidently won the sympathy of his auditors in his treatment of his topic, and had the hope of a large general contribution in behalf of his society upon the close of his remarks. In the spirit and prospect inspired, and sustained by such condition of things, the good man deferred immediate collection from his audience, serving notice upon the people that he would remain in the town during the coming week visiting from house to house, and thus giving everyone an opportunity of contributing according to his pleasure to the philanthropic, patriotic, Christian cause which he represented. Thereupon the usual concluding hymn of the church was announced and sung, when the excellent man who had addressed the people, as

ADMITTED TO THE BAR.

by special invitation, advanced to pronounce the benediction. Mr. Langston, who had heard his address, listening with unflagging attention from the first word uttered to the close, opposing in his own mind everything that had been said, and which he regarded as against the real interests of the colored people, free and slave, with much misgiving and yet under the pressure of the deepest sense of duty, arose and requested the minister to allow him to make a single announcement. Permission was given, and he advertised the people that on the next Tuesday evening at the court house, he would attempt to answer the address to which they had listened, and begged them to make no contributions of the character asked till after they had heard him. Except the surprise produced upon the minds of the people and the anxiety manifested by the orator of the occasion, no feeling was shown as the result of such notice. However, as the audience retired, Mr. Langston with the rest, he began to grow somewhat anxious not only in view of the task which he had taken upon his shoulders, but as to whether Judge Bliss himself would justify or sustain his course, or Mrs. Bliss and the family tolerate it. He had evidently, as he felt, put himself where he must confront and meet in manly proper spirit and manner the prevailing sentiment of the community. All alone in his room, on that memorable Sunday night, in the very court house in which he had promised to speak on the following Tuesday, he wondered and wondered, whether his friends would not condemn him, and he be disgraced by what they might deem ill-advised and foolish conduct.

He had not slept soundly, and was not inclined to tarry long in his quarters the following morning even for his usual early study. A more urgent, weighty and disturbing matter rested upon his mind. He was promptly at the breakfast table, awaiting with no little anxiety any allusion which Judge Bliss himself, or any other person present might make to the occurrence of the preceding evening at the church. He did not have to wait long, and his suspense and anxiety were turned into joy inexpressible when the judge applauded his conduct ; declaring that he would preside at the meeting and introduce him with appropriate approving remarks, and Mrs. Bliss herself asserted that she would be present and would have the speaker's stand graced by her own large and beautiful chandelier. Such influences as indicated made the meeting a great success as to numbers and character, and the support and encouragement given Mr. Langston fitted him in feeling and general knowledge for the effort which the community under the circumstances expected of him. The effect of the meeting, as regarded the cause, was signal and telling against the Colonization Society; while so far as Mr. Langston was concerned, it produced in his favor the happiest results. He succeeded in his speech in not only winning general substantial approval in Elyria, but throughout the county of Lorain, as was fully shown by the several invitations which he received to deliver the speech in different communities, and as his efforts were noticed and commended by the various newspapers published therein. Thus his labors in the interest, as he felt, and in favor of the colored people of the country, were abundantly and satisfactorily rewarded. If he had gained no more than the increased popular favor shown him, his reward would have been all that he could have expected. So far as the Bliss family was concerned, its treatment of him, cordial and kind always, was indeed rendered even more warm and genial.

Inured as Mr. Langston had become to the severe and exacting habits of an earnest student from quite ten years of constant study in the preparatory, collegiate and theological departments of Oberlin College, he was prepared to enter upon the matters of the law, even in an office, with large hope of general unusual success. The lawyer with whom he was to study was a man of such talent, various and special qualifications, with such experience in years of heavy professional labors, with such conspicuous position at the Bar, and such a name as an honest and upright judge, with positive personal interest in his new student, that no one could see anything but inspiring hope and success for him under such favorable circumstances.

This first colored law-student appreciated his position, however, and was not forgetful of the many vexatious conditions underlying and surrounding it. Nor was his excellent preceptor long in emphasizing these conditions to him and advising him as to how they could be overcome and made incentives to give him not only admission to the Bar, but urge him forward in meeting his duty so as to win a proud and honorable standing in his profession. Such conditions will be appreciated when it is understood that this young colored man was a pioneer in legal professional effort; that he was undertaking at a time and in a State to pursue professional study, when the statute books of Ohio were loaded down with Black Laws so-called, which were intended to be, as they were, oppressive of the colored citizen, denying him every opportunity and incentive to self-elevation in the walks of ordinary social, civil, political and professional life; that the public feeling of the State without regard to sect, church or party, fostered and sustained such conditions of sentiment and law. The word "white" was used then, in the Constitution of Ohio, in the clause designating those persons who constituted its voters, in the phrase of such document, "all white male persons."

The young student had advanced but a short distance in study before his preceptor found him anxious and inquisitive as to his admission to the bar. In view of the very language of the Constitution and the Black Laws of the State, he was exercised as to whether upon the completion of his studies and an approved examination, he could be admitted to practise law. When Judge Bliss found that this question seemed to vex and harass him, he bade him to give himself no trouble about it, as he would be prepared to meet any question of color, in his case, when attempt was made to urge it against him so as to prevent or hinder his professional career. He said further and frankly to him, "All that is necessary is for you to so prepare yourself as to pass a first-class examination and thus compel a favorable report as to your general and special qualifications, and to this end I shall be very thorough with you, for we must have no failure."

Thus warned and assured, the first young colored law-student of the United States, studying in a State whose statute books were black with proscriptive acts of inhuman legislation, redoubled his resolution, and pushed forward against the odds indicated upon a sea of professional endeavor unexplored, up to that time, by a single member of his race. Not wanting in hope and purpose, relying upon his individual powers, of which he felt that he possessed reasonable knowledge, and putting due estimate upon the learning and the information which he had already gained at such cost of time, effort and outlay, he treated them all as no other thing than an important and valuable reserved element of strength, to be used as necessity required. Thus favorably situated and encouraged, the colored student applied himself to the subjects of study, made plain and interesting through the efforts of his painstaking, conscientious instructor. Great importance was attached at all times, and as to every subject of the law, to the accuracy, the fulness, and the application, in theory and practice, of all definitions by Judge Bliss;—and that there might be no mistake made here, no inattention and forgetfulness, he cultivated constant reviews, with varied and changing explanations of the law principles, the doctrines and rules occurring in the general and regular lessons of the various text-books pursued. His illustrations were always full, lucid and instructive, being so presented as to command the attention and fix his instructions in the memory. Exercises in writing on law topics, and discussions on such subjects, with all those invaluable advantages connected with the well-organized and skillfully conducted moot court, were wanting. The training which they would have supplied had been furnished in large measure in the present case by the course taken already in the theological school. Besides, Judge Bliss required his student to attend the courts regularly, and often catechized him with regard to the law and the management of suits tried, civil and criminal, involving intricate special principles of law, necessitating wise and skillful manipulation. He was wont

ADMITTED TO THE BAR.

also to dwell to his student on the various apt and effective methods and styles of address proper to be made to the court or the jury, illustrating what he might have to say by reference to the noted lawyers who visited and conducted the more celebrated cases in his judicial district.

Judge Bliss was himself an admirable lawyer, scholarly in his accomplishments, always candid and earnest in his statements of law and fact to judge or jury, bearing himself at all times as master of his cause, cultivating a high and impressive style of forensic utterance which was distinguished for its logical method and its clear, pure English diction. His student never failed to hear him on important occasions, and he was at liberty, even urged to ask any question in regard to the general management of a case, or to inquire why special turn was taken at any point in its conduct. It is not difficult to perceive that a vigilant and intelligent student thus situated and treated would make rapid and advantageous progress in love and knowledge of the subject of his constant thought. Under these circumstances time moved only too rapidly, and the day arrived seemingly too soon when the colored candidate for admission to the Ohio Bar must quit these pleasant places and surroundings for the stern, real and trying things of laborious professional endeavor. So it was!

Two years had passed, and credited with one year's study of the law which he had gained in the last two years of his theological course, Judge Bliss gave Mr. Langston the usual certificate required as to his character and attainments in the law, and moved the court to appoint a special committee to examine him for admission to practice as an attorney and counsellor at law and solicitor in chancery. This action was taken at a term of the District Court of the State of Ohio held at Elyria, Lorain County, September 13, 1854. The committee appointed consisted of three of the best lawyers practicing at that Bar. No one of them was friendly to the new proposition of admitting a colored man to practice law in the courts of Ohio. Two of them were men of age, with fixed principles and feelings, and in politics

Democrats. The third was a younger man, of improving liberal sentiments and a Whig in his politics. The latter finally, as changes were made in national and local political relationships, became an ardent Republican. The committee shortly after its appointment notified Mr. Langston that its meeting would be held at the office of the gentleman last referred to and that his examination would commence without delay. Accordingly he appeared promptly at the place designated, and after the members of the committee had arranged the order of their work the examination began with the question, "What is law?" The examiner who propounded this question occupied himself in full and detailed canvass of all those matters concerning real and personal property as treated in such elementary works as those of Blackstone and Kent, with such special works upon these subjects as he deemed proper. He did not find the candidate making a single hesitation in view of any question put to him, and when he had finished he remarked to him, "I am satisfied," and to his associates, "He has done well." The next examiner according to arrangement took up the subjects of contracts and evidence, and when he had asked all the questions he desired he dismissed the subjects with the remark to the student, "You have read on these topics with great care and thoroughness." The young Whig lawyer then commenced his part of the work, and besides showing an excellent temper he gave evidence of large and critical knowledge of the law to which he confined his examination. He addressed himself to the matter of practice and pleading, and did so with great skill and tact. But here the candidate showed thorough preparation, and the examiner closed with assurance to him that he would be admitted, and that he would see that in the report of the committee his case was duly and fairly treated.

The committee made its report, and so far as the examination and its results were concerned reported truthfully and in favor of the colored candidate. He was found to be a young man of good moral character, twenty-one years of age, qualified to discharge the duties of an attorney and counsellor at law and a solicitor in chancery, and a citizen

124b

THE ADMISSION TO THE OHIO BAR, 1854

of the State of Ohio and of the United States. So far so good! But as they submitted this report the Democratic members of the committee suggested verbally nevertheless that the candidate was a *colored man*.

Five gentlemen, judges, composed the court. The one who acted as chief justice was a member and assistant justice of the Supreme Court of the State, a resident of the southern part of Ohio, where the feeling against the colored citizen was intense and positive. The chief justice in this case was inclined to throw the responsibility of disposing of it upon his associates who resided in the upper part of the State, who would be more apt to meet the colored lawyer in their courts and feel the consequences of his admission. He therefore at once said to them, that they might do as they pleased as to admitting the colored applicant; that he though admitted, would probably never appear before him, and that he was not specially interested in the matter.

It was not until Judge Bliss, and Mr. Gerry Boynton, the Whig examiner already referred to, had invited the attention of the court quietly to the language of the report of the committee, and had suggested that under the law of Ohio Mr. Langston was a "white man," that the court, especially its acting chief justice, seemed determined to give the case serious, just consideration. At this juncture the chief justice inquired of the sheriff, with manifest warmth of feeling, "Where is Mr. Langston?" The officer answered, "He sits within the Bar." Whereupon the judge addressing Mr. Langston, asked him to stand up. As he arose the judge directed him to come forward and be sworn. This he did, and subsequently when in conversation with the same judge he inquired why he was asked to stand, he was told that it was material to know by actual sight what his color was. For in order to his admission to the Bar under the law of Ohio as then expounded, he must be construed into a *white man*, as he was at once upon sight.

The certificate of Mr. Langston's admission to the Bar bears date Sept. 13, 1854.

CHAPTER X.

IMPORTANT OCCURRENCES WHICH AFFECT AND DETERMINE HIS CAREER.

SUCH was the untoward condition of Mr. Langston's health when he had completed his law studies and been admitted to the Bar, that his friends advised and urged him to consult some distinguished and reliable physician as to what he had better do to regain, fortify and sustain it. He did consult an old medical friend, and upon his advice and direction purchased and moved upon a farm located near Lake Erie, in Brownhelm Township, Lorain County, Ohio, nine miles from Oberlin, the most active town in the county and fourteen miles from Elyria, the county-seat. He was to remain upon the farm at least two years, and take regular daily exercise in the open air by working upon it. To all of which he consented and made his arrangements in accordance with such understanding.

The farm which he purchased and was to occupy consisted of fifty acres of the most beautiful fertile soil, with every improvement of buildings, gardens, orchards, ornamental trees and shrubbery, with such woodlands as were necessary to supply fuel and timber for preservation of fences and buildings upon the place. The productions of the farm were various and abundant. The meadows beautiful in their solid timothy, yielded crops of great value and richness; while the fine pasture-lands, well-regulated and thoroughly watered, afforded rich and ample feed for any cattle and sheep brought and supported upon the premises. The orchards were large, consisting of the finest varieties of every kind of fruits, such as apples, cherries and quinces, as well as pears, peaches and plums, and were a source of very considerable revenue. The woods abounded in excellent chestnut and hickory-nut trees, which afforded ample supplies of their fruits every year, and when carefully gathered such nuts not only answered the wants of those residing upon the farm, but many of them were sold to good advantage. The lands used for annual crops were easily cultivated and were unusually productive of corn and Irish potatoes, with such other farm products as were generally grown. Marking the place and seen from great distance all around it, stood a great towering pine-tree, growing near the west corner of the two-storied frame house which constituted the mansion of the farm. The gentleman of whom the place was bought was a farmer of excellent knowledge, wedded to his calling, and who had exhausted his skill and industry in making of his land, located by him and secured of the Government itself, all that his purpose, ingenuity and long years of unremitting diligence could make of it, as a first-class farm and delightful home. He only sold it that he might invest in more capacious landed property of the same sort and because his farm thus improved commanded a very large price.

Mr. Langston was not long after his purchase in locating himself upon this farm. He arranged with an English friend of his, Mr. Thomas Slater, to bring his family, consisting of his wife and son, upon the place and make for its owner such a home as would be mutually agreeable and pleasant. Besides, under the arrangement made with his friend, Mr. Slater was, for his labors and those of his family having to do with the cultivation and care of the property, including all domestic necessary duties, to have an interest in all the products of the place, including those of all lands and orchards as well as the increase of all animals. Mr. Langston was not more fortunate in the place which he bought than he was in the family which he selected and secured to come upon and manage it for him. Mr. Slater and Mrs. Slater proved to be just the persons exactly whom he needed and would have, and their son John, an excellent young man, was in every respect a worthy and congenial companion for him. In such a family, with the pleasant atmosphere which pervaded the household through its influence and direction, Mr. Langston found himself entirely at home, with every want often anticipated and constantly, cheerfully and promptly met. The contract made with Mr. Slater covered the full two years which Mr. Langston had expected to devote to his farming enterprise.

In his purchase of Mr. Ebenezer Jones, Mr. Langston had included all the personal property such as tools, farming implements, wagons and harness, corn and hay, with all maturing crops of every sort. Hence it was necessary, since he was to have immediate possession, that he and his help go at once to work caring for his interests. When Mr. Jones made the sale he advised the purchaser that there was but one single person residing in the neighborhood whose conduct would be likely in any way to render his residence there in any sense disagreeable. The lands of the person referred to adjoined the Jones farm upon the west, and to accommodate Mr. Jones, whose farm lay back from either county road, passing to the eastward and westward thereof, a township road had been opened from the limits of either side of the farm to both county roads mentioned, and the one part of such township road running to the westward crossed the lands of the person named by him. So far as the Jones farm was concerned, though the township road was established for its convenience and benefit, it was not made to constitute any part of such road, nor in anywise disturbed or injured thereby. Nevertheless by common consent anyone desiring to do so was permitted, passing by the draw-bars on one side and the gate on the other, to use the lane running through the Jones farm. And it was well understood when Mr. Langston took possession of it, that no one passed over the lane afoot or by conveyance more frequently than his neighbor, to whom Mr. Jones made allusion. The brother of this man had also ventured to say to Mr. Langston upon an early visit which he had made to him after he had taken possession of his new home, that he feared his brother, the very person referred to, would prove to be a disagreeable and unsatisfactory neighbor. Thus warned, Mr. Langston had determined to do whatever he might to win and conciliate this neighbor. Hence, as he passed down the lane one morning on his way to the post-office, as was his habit, Mr. Langston and Mr. Slater being at work in their potato-field near the lane, the former advised the latter that upon his return he was determined to pay his respects to his neighbor. This neighbor by reason of certain services which he had rendered his country, and certain position which he had won in the days of the "Cornstalk Militia," was known as and called Col. Frank Peck, and was distinguished for the inveteracy of his Hunker Democracy and his unconquerable hatred of abolitionism and the negro. On his return Colonel Peck had reached a point in the lane just opposite Mr. Langston, when the latter addressed him, employing in most respectful manner the words, "Good-morning, Colonel Peck!" No attention whatever was paid to this salutation, until it had been very emphatically repeated. Then reply was made by the colonel in gruff, savage manner, "Who are you?" Whereupon he also came to a halt, and Mr. Langston proceeded in becoming spirit and respectful phrase to introduce himself to this person, who seemed very much chagrined that he should be thus accosted, particularly since such a thing had been done by a colored person, and one who had been educated at the abolition, negro-loving school of Oberlin. He even went so far as to say that he wanted nothing to do with any such person, educated at such an institution. Notwithstanding, Mr. Langston was not easily frightened, and did not fail to hear attentively all that was said and to defend valiantly and soundly the institution from which he had received his education. He even went so far as to advise Colonel Peck that he and his family would find themselves greatly benefited by sending his sons and daughters to Oberlin to be educated, and to be advanced morally and enlightened politically. While this interview had upon the highway did not seem to be wholly satisfactory to Colonel Peck, it was counted a victory by Mr. Langston, and did result finally in such good understanding between them that they became, though differing in politics, agreeable neighbors and real friends.

Mr Langston had not been long upon his farm, not more perhaps than ten days or two weeks, when an attorney living in the neighborhood, doing business in some two or three adjoining counties, especially before the justices of the peace, called to see him. He came to secure his services as his assistant in an important and interesting case, to be tried before the most active and influential justice of Brownhelm Township, who held his court at the center of that town. The case was one which as regarded the parties and the matter in litigation, was well calculated to bring together a large number of persons, and by reason of the fact that it would be tried by a jury of good and true men of the vicinage, offer to an unknown and untried lawyer of tact and talent a fine opportunity to display his ability and skill and thus bring him name and business.

No writer shall ever be able to describe the feelings produced in Mr. Langston's mind by this visit, nor shall any philosopher be able to explain how he was able to contain himself while such feelings held masterhood of his being! He had been told that no one would, in all probability, offer him legal business of any sort, and he had feared that no opportunity would ever come to him, situated as he was, in connection with which he might be able to make any demonstration of talent, learning, skill, or power as a lawyer. A thousand times he had been warned that the fate of the negro was sealed, and in the decree which fixed the destiny of the blackhued son of the race his own position was determined and settled! But now he saw a new light, and his soul was aroused and fired by even a new and better hope!

Mr. Hamilton Perry called upon Mr. Langston, seeking

IMPORTANT EVENTS AFFECTING HIS CAREER.   131

to interest him in the case mentioned to the extent, at least, of securing his assistance, and if not so much, certainly his counsel, with interchange of opinions. Mr Perry was frank and made full statement to Mr. Langston, explaining how he ought not to let this chance pass unimproved, and insisting that if he should take hold in earnest, and do as well as might be expected of a person of his learning, it would give him prestige and influence, resulting it might be in very large professional advantage. After a full consultation, a careful canvass of the facts of the case and the law respecting it to be urged and enforced in order to success at the trial, Mr. Langston engaged to join Mr Perry, and the two resolved to do their best and utmost to win the suit.

One week from the day of this call and conference, the case in question was to be tried. So it was—and so large was the attendance and so great the interest excited by it, that the justice of the peace had to move out of his large office in his house to a more capacious barn-room, where the trial was conducted. The plaintiff in the case was represented by one of the ablest and most noted young lawyers of the county-seat, Mr. Stevenson Burke. To win a suit against him was considered in those days a great achievement, especially when he had brought it, as in this instance. The defendant was represented by Messrs. Hamilton Perry and John M. Langston. When the case was called and the parties had duly answered, a jury was demanded, as of right by the defendant. The jurors selected from the bystanders soon took their seats, and after being sworn to the proper discharge of their duty, heard the statement of the attorney for the plaintiff and that of Mr. Perry for the defendant. The case, as developed in such statements, was one as known in the law of *forcible entry and detainer*, and the question to be settled was whether the plaintiff, the owner of certain premises involved, was entitled to their immediate possession, as against the defendant who held and occupied them. Witnesses were called, sworn and examined in the interest of the plaintiff. Their cross-examination was at first attempted by Mr. Perry; but very soon this work was given Mr. Langston, and he succeeded so well at it that by consent, even the urgent request of his associate, he conducted it to the end. Besides, he examined in chief all the witnesses testifying in behalf of the defendant. The suit commenced at one o'clock in the afternoon, was not submitted for argument to the jury before nine in the evening. The interest in it did not flag, and when it was agreed and announced that two addresses only would be made, one by Mr. Langston and the other by Mr. Burke, the bystanders crowded the barn-room in earnest and deep attention. By arrangement the former person addressed the jury first, commanding the undivided interest of the court, the jury and his auditors, from the beginning to the end of his remarks. Mr. Burke followed in one of his most entertaining, lucid and interesting addresses, everyone present giving him respectful and attentive hearing. Upon the conclusion of his address, the court charged the jury, and without leaving their seats they gave a unanimous verdict in favor of the defendant.

This was a grand closing for Mr. Langston. Never did American lawyer leave a court house with more grateful feelings in his triumph than he did the barn of ·Justice Samuel Curtiss on that ever famous Saturday night of October, 1854, when he had won by verdict of an honest American jury, the first cause which he was permitted to aid in trying. Mr. Perry was happy enough, for he had staked his reputation largely upon the results of this trial. But Mr. Langston felt that his all was staked upon it, and he labored and spoke in it with the earnestness and power of one who would win victory against any and every opposition. On his return to his house, reaching it at midnight, accompanied as he was by Mr. Slater, who had kept near him during all the hours of the trial, ready to rejoice with him should success reward his efforts, they found Mrs. Slater anxious about them both, overjoyed upon their arrival and report as to the great victory which had been won. The good woman had made her best cup of tea, provided

IMPORTANT EVENTS AFFECTING HIS CAREER. 133

her most inviting country supper, and offering all in the very best condition, bade Mr. Langston and her husband to partake with her to their fullest satisfaction. This was a home full now of unalloyed, positive and earnest rejoicing.

The following Sabbath morning, bright and beautiful as it was, bathed in light and happiness a home which, though it contained neither the father, nor mother, nor brother, nor sister, nor other relative of Mr. Langston to rejoice with him, was full of the kindly esteem and regard of those who, though only employed by him and of another and foreign nationality, gave him their sympathy, as they did their care and services. As already intimated, four persons, an aged English gentleman, an aged English woman, their only child and Mr. Langston, were the persons who composed this household. As they sat together about the breakfast table, on the memorable Sabbath morning mentioned, many were the warm earnest words uttered by his friends in commendation of his efforts and success the night before, all speaking as if their glory belonged certainly to the whole family. The old gentleman had just finished telling how one of the neighbors had spoken of the colored lawyer while addressing the jury, and how the crowd generally seemed to be moved by his speech, predicting that great success would follow it, when a knock was made at the door. He stepping forward, opened it to find a person there inquiring for the lawyer. The caller was invited in, and at once on meeting the attorney made known his errand.

The stranger had come to retain Mr. Langston to defend him upon a charge of selling liquor to be drunk, contrary to law, where sold. Full conversation was had with respect to the case, the retainer paid, and the engagement settled for Mr. Langston's services. This person had but just left the door, when another appeared upon a similar mission ; and then followed a third ; and so it continued the whole day, until the lawyer declared that he had been engaged for days in advance, and his pockets were full of retainers. Such was in fact the case. The temperance people living in Lorain and adjoining counties had just commenced proceedings against liquor venders, vulnerable to actions under the anti-whiskey law of Ohio, and the prosecutions were numerous and vigorous, giving special anxiety to those who had been exposed and were being called to judicial account. As Mr. Langston found his services even in such cases in general positive demand, in behalf of a clientage willing to retain and pay him well, he counted himself fortunate indeed in the opportunity which he had enjoyed in connection with the suit tried with Mr. Perry. Often in conversations had with his old colleague, the latter has claimed that he gave the first colored lawyer of Ohio his start in professional life. Whether the statement in such form be true or not, Mr. Langston has ever felt and believed that Mr. Perry did him a great special service when he gave him the privilege of appearing and taking such conspicuous part in the management of the suit in which they were associated.

Mr. Langston's business from this time grew rapidly. Such was the demand for his services in a professional way that he abandoned any further idea of working on his farm. With his improving health following his labors and the excitement connected with them, his determination to make a success of his law business increased and intensified itself. Each case tried by him seemed to multiply his clients and enlarge the circle of his acquaintances and opportunities. He succeeded in a most remarkable manner, his clients including Irishmen, Englishmen and Americans living in the different adjoining counties to that of his residence. In all criminal proceedings he discovered an aptness, skill and success which were certainly unusual. He cleared quite every one charged with crime whose defence he attempted, so that persons in trouble came from distant places to secure his services and paid him therefor large amounts. All his clients were willing as they were able to pay him well and liberally. Within less than one year after his admission to the Bar, and within less than a year after his first suit, his practice had become exacting and lucrative. His clients were all white persons at this time and chiefly those who

IMPORTANT EVENTS AFFECTING HIS CAREER. 135

acted politically with the Democratic party. Such persons did not seem however to fear Mr. Langston's color, nor on account of it to question his ability and skill. They sought him and his services as if they had the largest respect for him personally and full confidence in his learning, ingenuity and fidelity.

The home which Mr. Langston had provided in Brownhelm was an elegant and desirable one for the neighborhood, and as found in his possession and occupation proved to be attractive and inviting to his friends, many of whom spent days and sometimes weeks with him. The buildings upon the place, though of old style, were numerous and convenient for the preservation of all products and the protection and care of all stock, wagons and implements. The dwelling-house was of fair size, with several large rooms above and below, and with a great capacious cellar. Situated as he was it was pleasant for even the most refined who paid visits to Mr. Langston to desire and consent to remain as long as might be in this agreeable rural retreat. Persons of noted character, especially leading reformers, white and colored, frequently came to this home, and were gladly and hospitably entertained.

The town of Brownhelm was a most delightful and agreeable one in all its natural and more prominent artificial features. Five miles square, according to the New England method of limitation and survey, it covered two most beautiful ridges in its site, inclining northward to the lake upon which it was located ; eastward and westward to small streams making their way to the larger body of water and southward to the great prairie lands extending off to the lower parts of Lorain County. There was not a farm in this township which was not cultivated in most approved manner and to the full extent of its area. The population settled there was of New England blood and origin, Puritan in thought, purpose, education and character. Reformatory sentiments, religious, political and anti-slavery, found quick and general growth among its people. Some families located in this community were made famous and conspicuous in the earliest days of the anti-slavery movement for their brave, extreme, radical utterances and professions with respect to the enslaved and freed classes of the negro race. It was in this town and chief among its people, that a noted family coming from Massachusetts settled in a conspicuous place, and at once gave character and name to the whole community. Prominent in the church and controlling in social circles, this family had more to do than any other in directing and sustaining any new sentiment or view, brought into the place by any advocate there, anxious to impress and promote it upon and among the people. It was this family which gave Oberlin College in its early days two of its best and ablest students among the young men, and three of its most efficient and admired students among the young women. The father of this family was Grandison Fairchild, and his two sons to whom reference is made, were Rev. Edward M. Fairchild, late president of Berea College, Kentucky, now dead; and Rev. James H. Fairchild, so long a professor and for twenty odd years the president of Oberlin College, still living at the advanced age of seventy-three years. A third son of this family, an older man than either of his brothers named, but who was not so well known to the public, generally, since he led a less conspicuous and more humble life, was a person of excellent character, brave and outspoken in every conviction and duty. His name was Charles Fairchild. He lived and labored in Brownhelm, where he was carried as a small boy, upon a farm, and yet always conducting himself in such way as to win the respect and confidence of all who knew him.

Against no human being on account of his color, his nationality or his former condition of enslavement, did this family in any one of its members ever discover any other than a just, humane and generous sentiment. Earnest and positive in their opposition to slavery, they held themselves ready, under all circumstances, to do all in their power to elevate, educate and save the poor, ignorant and degraded son or daughter of any class of mankind, however brought to their lowly condition, by action of the tyrant or the

IMPORTANT EVENTS AFFECTING HIS CAREER. 137

slave-holder. Such was the material of which this representative family of the Brownhelm community was composed;—and such, fortunately, was the character of the community itself, mainly, whose best and most valuable elements were of the highest social dignity.

This community was, like the family described, really and truthfully exceptional even in the northern part of Ohio and upon the Western Reserve. At this time the prevailing sentiment upon the Reserve was anti-negro and of positive destestable pro-slavery character in its hatred of such a community and college as those of Oberlin. The following circumstance illustrates and sustains this statement: Discussion of political popular character was just being attempted upon the subject of slavery, as especially to its aggressions upon Northern rights and interests. Feeling against its spread northward was exhibiting itself in more positive political action, and in some localities attempts to elect positively anti-slavery men to Congress were being made. This was true in the Lorain County Congressional District, and Dr. Norton S. Townsend had been nominated and was conducting a spirited and earnest canvass for his election. It was deemed advisable by the congressional executive committee that meetings be held in which Liberty sentiments might be boldly enunciated and defended in every more important place in the district. Among other places a meeting was announced for French Creek, in Avon Township, Lorain County. The gentlemen who were to speak at this meeting were three white persons, Liberty men, and Mr. John M. Langston, a colored man. The last-named gentleman was to make the closing address. Two of the other gentlemen had spoken and the third was making his remarks when a person in the audience propounded to him this question, "Are you in favor of *nigger* social equality?" The young white man addressed showed the greatest embarrassment at once and the greatest possible hesitation, so that the audience, seeing his condition, in claps of the hands, stamping of the feet and other demonstrations of their feelings against him and his sentiments, utterly overpowered him. He was unable to proceed. In this confusion the young orator brought his remarks to a close by announcing that Mr. Langston would follow him and address the people. It was very manifest from all that was said and done at this time that the feeling of the community ran high against the negro and his freedom. It was apparent that the person who had propounded the question presented had sounded the key-note of popular feeling. However, Mr. Langston was at once introduced and attempted in careful though earnest and manly manner to meet such feeling and if possible turn it somewhat if not wholly in favor of his race. He stated first of all the question which had been put to his friend and which had created the confusion, presenting it as strongly against himself and all others similarly interested as possible. Then he proceeded to show what the movement which he advocated had to do with freedom as the birthright of all, and how social equality was a matter dependent upon individual choice, favor or otherwise, and that it was only the enemy of human rights who would undertake to obtrude that subject against reasonable demand in favor equal freedom. At this time Oberlin College because of its fair humane treatment of colored people was the object of intense general hatred, and when appeal was made against one urging the claims of the negro and the opponent would thoroughly and completely vanquish such person, he had the means in his power ordinarily could he charge that he had been educated at Oberlin College. Mr. Langston had closed his comments upon the question asked and had evidently made a very serious and favorable impression upon his hearers, when the gentleman who had offered it in seeming rage and in his last appeal to popular prejudice against him cried out at the top of his voice, even screaming, addressing Mr. Langston, said, "You learned that at Oberlin!" When it was discovered upon Mr. Langston's admission that this statement was true and no great harm had been done, and that he still held the audience, the same individual cried out again, screaming as before, "You learned another thing at Oberlin! You learned to walk with white women there!"

Nothing daunted by the accusation implied in these words, employed even under such trying circumstances, Mr. Langston quickly admitted their truth, and advancing to the very verge of the platform, retorted upon the officious negro-hater who had used them, "If you have in your family any good-looking, intelligent, refined sisters, you would do your family a special service by introducing me to them at once." In the midst of the sudden surprising outburst of popular applause following this remark and in approval of it, an old gray-headed Democrat addressed his vanquished friend, saying, "Joe Ladd, you d—n fool, sit down! That darkey is too smart for you! Sit down!" These last words convulsed the audience, and Mr. Langston retired from the stand in triumph, and Avon Township on election day was carried by a large majority for Dr. Townsend.

It will be perceived that such public feeling as prevailed in Brownhelm Township, giving the colored class recognition and kindly treatment, was fortunate indeed for one situated as Mr. Langston, and it was from the beginning to the end profoundly appreciated and valued by him.

Among the friends who made him visits, and learned of his situation in a country neighborhood so admirably adapted for pleasant business and domestic relationships, he was often asked why he did not marry, and advised to do so as a matter of proper economy and real happiness. Not a few proffered him their good offices in this matter, and some even went so far as to assure him that his early marriage was indispensable to his success and prosperity. He accepted all such wise and kind suggestions, and heard, respectfully, every word of cordial proffer in such regard. About this time, however, Mr Slater and his wife found, that often after what was called a hard day's work, Mr Langston would order his horse and buggy to drive to Oberlin, and often he would not return till early the next morning, giving as apology for his sojourn in that village, that he could not pull himself away from his friends. Finally, one of his most intimate and best friends, a young man whom he always entertained with great pleasure, of whom he had the highest opinion, and in whose judgment he placed the greatest confidence, came to spend three or four days with him. In addition to his business, he had occupied considerable time during the days and the evenings which this friend spent with him, in talking over the most serious change which he contemplated in his domestic relations. He was frank and conscientious in his revelations and expressions of purpose on this subject with his friend. He even went so far as to tell him the name of the young lady to whom he felt that he might present his petition for marriage, to all of which his young friend not only gave his approving judgment, but offered also to bear the letter to the person to whom Mr. Langston would make communication with such petition. The sun was just setting as Mr. Slater, having invited this young gentleman to take a seat in the carriage by his side, was moving off behind two of the finest horses in the neighborhood, when Mr Langston addressing his friend, said to him, "Now, deliver the letter in good style," when the reply was returned, "Ah, indeed!" Mr Slater had not been long in going up to Oberlin and returning, for his horses were fine movers and knew every inch of the ground and how to make the distance quickly and with ease. The first question asked him as he reached the stable and began to unhitch the team, was "Was the letter delivered?" to which he answered, "Yes, sir." Not many days thereafter, the answer to his letter was received, and Mr Langston, indicated to his good friends of the house that it would not be long before he would have to share his home and happiness with one whose stay would be permanent. Preparations for his marriage were at once undertaken, and the young, handsome North Carolina lady, reared in Harveysburg, Ohio, and educated at Oberlin College, to the surprise of many, but to the delight of all their friends, became the wife of Mr. Langston and the mistress of his home.

This marriage was not a hasty one. The parties had known each other well, and were acquainted with their respective circumstances. Mr. Langston had met Miss Caroline M. Wall in 1851, and by an interesting confluence of events he met her again in 1852. The first meeting was at Oberlin, and the second at her own home in Harveysburg. Mr. Langston's visit to Harveysburg at the time referred to, was made in connection with a public mission upon which he had been sent with reference to the education of the colored youth of Ohio. A number of persons, white and colored, students of Oberlin College, had organized in the early fall of 1852, an association whose aim was to create and foster an educational feeling in favor of the class mentioned, and to stimulate and direct any purpose found existing among negro parents to provide such school opportunities for their children as might be practicable, the association holding itself responsible for the supply of teachers of all schools thus established. The association was without funds, and neither able to employ an agent nor to supply needed means of transportation. Mr. Langston being a member of the association, and feeling deeply interested in the object which it had in view, offered his services with conveyance, as indicated, free of all charge to either the association or the public. His offer was gladly accepted, when he entered upon the work, travelling from the lake to the Ohio river, and in various directions across the State, arousing, directing and utilizing public feeling among the colored people for their educational welfare. At this time no public schools were provided in Ohio for its colored citizens, and no public appropriations were made in such behalf. The enterprise which Mr. Langston represented was one of real necessity, and was so regarded and treated by every community to which he presented it in public address or private effort.

Among other places visited by him, and in which he presented the claims and object of this association, was Harveysburg, already named, a Quaker village, where colored persons were treated with great favor, and the members of a single family among them were given superior advantages of education and social contact. Here Mr. Langston met Miss Wall for the second time, finding her family, consisting of three brothers and one sister besides herself, very handsomely located, very kindly treated by the whole community, with all the members of it accorded every educational and social opportunity possible. Indeed, if distinction were made at all with respect to them it was in their favor. The father of this family, Col. Stephen Wall, a very wealthy and influential citizen of Richmond County, North Carolina, had brought his children to this liberal Quaker village, and having thus made them all free, settled them in easy, in fact affluent circumstances, under wise and suitable guardianship, for their education and culture. So great was his constant interest in them, and so ample the provision which he made in their behalf, and so influential were those to whom he committed their business and education, that they were treated everywhere, in church, school and the community, as if they were children of its very best and most prominent family.

Besides finding Miss Wall a talented, refined and pleasant person in appearance and conduct, as he saw her at her own home, in mastery and control of it, with her brothers and younger sister respecting and honoring her authority, while she bore herself with dignity, self-possession and propriety, he discovered in her those elements of genuine womanly character which make the constitution of the true, loving and useful wife. He discovered too, in her conversation and behavior, that she was fully informed as to the condition of the colored people, with whom she was identified in blood in her maternal relationships, and deeply and intelligently interested in their education and elevation. His subsequent association with her only deepened and confirmed this opinion, and when the hour of his proposed marriage came, he had little to do in the way of convincing himself as to the certainty of his future happiness, could he secure her affections and hand. His hopes and expectations are still in progress of happy fruition.

Their wedding occurred October 25, 1854, in Oberlin, at the home of Deacon Samuel Beecher, where Miss Wall was boarding at the time, while she attended the ladies' depart-

IMPORTANT EVENTS AFFECTING HIS CAREER. 143

ment of Oberlin College, of whose senior class she was then a member. Professor John Morgan, their friend and former teacher, by their special desire and choice conducted the ceremony of their marriage. In closing the service, he left with the parties his most earnest, heartfelt benediction, which has ever lingered in their memories, inspiring and blessing their souls. Their wedding-tour consisted of a trip via Cleveland to Cincinnati, where they remained for a few days, as welcomed and entertained by the family of Mr. William W. Watson. During their stay in the city, the respect and consideration shown them in general society were cordial and agreeable. Many entertainments were given them, and their social recognition was pleasant and flattering. Then they visited Harveysburg, where spending several days in the family of Mrs. Dr. Scroggs, a special friend of Mrs. Langston, they were accorded a warm-hearted reception and hospitable treatment. Thence they went to their own country home, to be received with every expression of kindly regard by those who proved to be in every sense their devoted and constant friends.

As showing the sterling moral qualities of the Fairchild family, of which mention has been fully made, their deep sense of justice and their fearlessness in the presence of duty, it is proper to relate here a circumstance in which the son Charles figured as the principal and responsible actor. It was toward the closing days of March, 1855, when the time had come for considering the matter of making nominations for township officers, to name candidates for the trusteeships and the clerkship for the ensuing year, that the Liberty party men of the town had called their caucus and public meeting for such purpose. Mr. Langston had already gained his voting residence, and acting as he did with that party, he proposed to attend its meetings, especially the caucus where the nominations would be made. He was on his way there when he and Mr. Fairchild, going to the same place, met each other and entered into a free and neighborly conversation. As they neared the schoolhouse where the meeting and caucus were held, Mr. Fairchild addressing his companion, said, "Langston, I am intending to nominate you to-night for our township clerk." To this Mr. Langston expressed objection, grounded upon fear that such action would defeat their ticket. He said to Mr. Fairchild, frankly, "My name, I fear, would kill our ticket. We would be beaten by more than a hundred majority. We cannot afford to take such risk. We must nominate men whom we can elect. It is very material that we win our election this spring in our township." "Very well," said Mr. Fairchild; "but you are the best qualified man we have in our town for such a position," he continued, "and no one can deny this. I believe we can elect you, and I am going to insist upon your nomination." The question in Mr. Langston's mind was not one having to do with his qualifications. In regard to that matter he was well satisfied. But no colored man, up to that time, had been named for a public office in any part of this country, and he feared the risk connected then with the experiment, even in Brownhelm Township. He could not dissuade his friend, however, and when after the meeting had been organized and persons had been named as candidates for trusteeships, Mr. Fairchild arose and said many good things about Mr. Langston, dwelling specially upon his fitness for the clerkship, making no allusion to the fact that he was a colored person, and moved his nomination as the candidate for such office, his motion was adopted without the least opposition. As the candidate for the position the name of Mr. Langston appeared upon the Liberty party ticket on election day in the early part of the following April. He received not only the full party vote, but ran sixty votes ahead of his ticket, and he was on the evening of election day declared, upon the count of all the votes cast, duly elected to the office to which he had been nominated. Thus through the influence of the Fairchild family, and especially through the wise, sagacious and fearless action of the son named, the first colored man ever nominated in the United States to an office, and who was elected on a popular vote, had his name brought forward and his nomination and election generously and successfully supported.

This election was of great service to Mr. Langston. Besides giving him, in connection with his office, considerable local prominence and some pay for his services, it aided him in no small degree in his law business. In the first place he was *ex-officio* the attorney of the township, and the public endorsement in this regard did, in the second place, enlarge and strengthen his influence in that capacity among the people.

It was at this juncture and on such endorsement by the vote of *his white fellow-citizens*, not a colored man residing in the town other than himself, that Mr. Langston's official and professional career really took its upward positive shape and character. As he was the first one of his people thus honored with responsible place, he was given at once thereby name and fame all over the country, especially among the Abolitionists, who were making every effort possible to turn the current of popular feeling in favor of the overthrow of slavery and the elevation of the enslaved and nominally free classes of the country. So that no sooner had it become known through the public journals that he had been given place by his election as stated, than he was invited by the American Anti-Slavery Society, at whose head stood such men as William Lloyd Garrison, Wendell Phillips and John G. Whittier, to attend and address their forthcoming May meeting, to be held at Metropolitan Theatre, in New York city. His expenses were all to be paid, and for the first time in his life and experience he was offered pay for his services as an orator. He was asked to speak only thirty minutes, and for that service he was to receive *fifty dollars* in cash. The invitation was immediately accepted, and perhaps no great meeting of any character was ever attended in this country by any one, which paid so largely in its far-reaching results as this one did the young colored man, the recipient of such honorable treatment.

It will not be doubted by any reflecting person that his marriage, his election to the first office accorded to any representative of his race in the United States, and his invitation under the circumstances to address a great audience in a conspicuous place in New York city in favor of human freedom, with all the prospective pleasing results attending such occurrences, must have exerted a potent directing influence upon one commencing his professional and political career. All these circumstances must have been considered by him as facts connected with his life and prospects, signal, rare and significant in the honors and promise which they brought.

CHAPTER XI.

ANNIVERSARY MEETING, AMERICAN ANTI-SLAVERY SOCIETY, MAY, 1855.

MR. LANGSTON constituted no exception to that large class of American youth who had been taught at school and at the hearthstone, that Daniel Webster, Henry Clay and John C. Calhoun were the great representative orators of the United States. He had read their speeches, and many times had been lost in wonder and admiration of the grace, eloquence and power of their best utterances. Especially had this been true of the Massachusetts senator, who in his earlier and more palmy days, cultivated in matchless diction the broadest and most liberal sentiments with respect to free principles and equal rights. He had learned of Lord Chatham, Lord Brougham and Burke, and had often been inspired and delighted by their lofty, finished, masterly periods. He had never hoped to hear the equals of these great American and British orators. They were to him as to the youth generally of his age, ideal characters. But as he confronted in real presence, heard, felt, and was moved by the words of the earnest, brave, inspired men and women who were pleading the cause of humanity and freedom—the cause even of the poor, outraged and degraded slave—in truth, pathos and power, his conception of oratory as modelled after the standards named seemed low and unworthy. These latter made the speeches which realized at last the highest, truest and noblest image of eloquence dedicated to a holy, sacred purpose, when speech alone demonstrates the height and depth, the power and effect of which in its best estate it is capable. When man pleads the cause of justice, liberty, humanity, with his heart earnestly, sincerely, deeply imbued with the conviction of his duty, his soul pure in its consecration thereto, and his understanding illuminated by the light which is divine, he is eloquent. So it was at this great meeting where thousands spell-bound were touched and aroused by the "words which burned and the thoughts which breathed," as they came poured from the devoted hearts and lips of the men and women called to demand as matter of justice to the slave, the immediate and unconditional abolition of his thraldom.

Here it was learned in real life and practice that eloquence, the mysterious influence which convicts, persuades and captivates the human understanding and sensibility, consists in the sentiment, the truth of one's utterance, and not in mere diction, gesticulation, movement, smile or frown, even where accompanied by finished and effective rhetoric. Here the living orators, those upon whom the God of Freedom had breathed his divine afflatus, as upon John or Paul, spoke even for the slave, and the world was compelled to feel and acknowledge their power! Their eloquence came not of words or manner. It was the power made mighty through the truth, which coming from their pure, sincere hearts, carried in conviction and charm the judgment and consciences of their hearers.

The great orators of anti-slavery fame and influence who honored this anniversary occasion by their presence and addresses were William Lloyd Garrison, Wendell Phillips, Theodore Parker, Antoinette Brown, Henry Wilson and Charles Sumner, all of whom took part in the exercises connected with its celebration. To say that the speeches of such orators were master productions worthy of the cause which their authors plead and of the occasion is to use language wholly inadequate to their proper description. The addresses of Senators Wilson and Sumner, one delivered on the preceding and the other on the evening of the anniversary, were marvelous in their conception, power and effect. They spoke indeed as moved by the holy spirit of liberty itself. Perhaps Senator Sumner never reached such moral sublimity and displayed such surprising, matchless power as on this occasion. And even Wendell Phillips, with all the sweetness and charm of his oratory, was too wise, when called by the great audience to follow him in a brief impromptu address, to undertake the task, but said to those who called him, "I know this vast audience is composed of my friends. And since that is so, I feel that you will not attempt to persuade me to open my mouth in this presence after the matchless utterance of our distinguished friend, the senator!" Senator Sumner had selected as the subject of his address, "The importance, the necessity and the dignity of the American anti-slavery movement." He was the complete master of this theme in thought and reading, and observation made at home and abroad. He had been engaged for several weeks in delivering this speech in different parts of New England, and came to New York city in perfect condition of body and mind to make the crowning effort of his life. The occasion was all he could ask, his audience could not have been surpassed in numbers, sympathy and enthusiasm, and thus moved, as well by his surroundings as the deep love of the cause in whose name and behalf he spoke, he displayed the grandest, the most wonderful power. No one who saw and heard him shall ever forget his presence and bearing, his look and manner, his action, the intonation of his voice, his gesticulation, the warmth and splendor of his utterance and power, and last and grandest of all, the closing prophetic declaration in which, his whole soul with all its faith and power displayed, and every nerve and muscle of his body instinct with the life and spirit that moved him, he stirred and thrilled to its very depths the audience in his words, "that the Slave Oligarchy shall die!" In this sentiment of good promise he carried every hearer in his vast audience in wild irresistible admiration and applause of his eloquence.

It is perhaps true that up to this time no such anti-slavery meeting had been held in the United States, one which had brought together so many distinguished persons, on such an important and conspicuous occasion, and one at which such utterances, so impressive and commanding, had been made in the interest of the American slave. The whole city of New York was now moved, and through the press of that city the whole country was reached and affected by the addresses made there in a manner entirely satisfactory to the promoters and friends of abolition. Now the anti-slavery cause appeared to gain new life and hope, while the rank and file of the abolition party found in its leaders a more positive and bold assertion of its purposes and principles.

Mr. Langston spoke on "anniversary day" proper, with Messrs. Garrison, Parker, Phillips and Miss Brown. His speech was novel its general features, and was received with flattering favor by the audience and the public. It was delivered under such favorable circumstances, upon a platform so burdened and distinguished by the presence of the first thinkers, scholars, divines, statesmen, orators and anti-slavery worthies, as Henry Ward Beecher, Dr. E. H. Chapin, Dr. C. H. Cheever, James Mott, Lucretia Mott, Lucy Stone, Gerrit Smith, Henry H. Garnet, William W. Brown, Stephen Foster, Abby Kelly Foster, Henry B. Stanton, Charles L. Remond, Robert Purvis, Dr. James McCune Smith, before an audience of such size and character, that it produced effects which were highly advantageous, personally, to Mr. Langston, and as its friends claimed, of great service to the anti-slavery cause in the United States. As delivered it appeared in the New York dailies in full on the following morning thereafter, and was reproduced in the anti-slavery journals and periodicals of the day. Slavery has been abolished, but as showing the line of thought and prediction adopted by the speaker, young and inexperienced as he was, it is here presented, as found in the annual report of the society for 1855.

AMERICAN ANTI-SLAVERY SOCIETY.

The twenty-second anniversary of the American Anti-Slavery Society was celebrated May 9, 1855, at Metropolitan Theater, New York city. William Lloyd Garrison, the president of the society, presided. He introduced Mr. John Mercer Langston as a graduate of Oberlin College, a colored lawyer who had recently been elected town clerk of Brownhelm Township, Ohio, who would address the meeting.

MR. LANGSTON'S SPEECH.

MR. PRESIDENT, LADIES AND GENTLEMEN:

Some great man has remarked that a nation may lose its liberty in a day, and be a century in finding it out. Does our own nation afford illustration of this statement? There is not, within the length and breadth of this entire country, from Maine to Georgia, from the Atlantic to the Pacific Oceans, a solitary man or woman who is in the possession of his or her full share of civil, religious and political liberty. This is a startling announcement perhaps, made in the heart and center of a country loud in its boasts of its free institutions, its democratic organizations, its equality, its justice and its liberality. We have been in the habit of boasting of our Declaration of Independence, of our Federal Constitution, of the Ordinance of 1787, and various enactments in favor of popular liberty for so long, that we verily believe that we are a free people; and yet I am forced to declare, looking the truth directly in the face and seeing the power of American slavery, that there is not within the bosom of this entire country, a solitary man or woman who can say "I have my full share of liberty." Let the president of this society clothe himself with the panoply of the Constitution of the United States, the Declaration of Independence and the Word of God, and stand up in the presence of the people of South Carolina and say, "I believe in the sentiments contained in the Constitution of my country, in the Declaration of Independence and in the Word of God, respecting the rights of man," and where will be his legal protection? Massachusetts will sit quietly by and see him outraged; the president of the United States will not dare to interfere for his protection; he will be at the mercy of the tyrant slaveholders. Why? Because slavery is the great lord of this country, and there is no power in this nation to-day strong enough to withstand it.

It would afford me great pleasure, Mr. President, to dwell upon the achievements already gained by the anti-slavery movement. I know that they have been great and glorious; I know that this movement has taught the American people who the slave is, and what his rights are—that he is a man and entitled to all the rights of a man; I know that the attention of the public has been called to the consideration of the colored people, and the attention of the colored people themselves has been awakened to their own condition, so that with longing expectations they begin to say in the language of the poet:—

> "O tell me not that I am blessed,
> Nor bid me glory in my lot,
> That plebeian freemen are oppressed
> With wants and woes that you are not.
> Go let a cage, with grates of gold,
> And pearly roof, the eagle hold;

> Let dainty viands be his fare,
> And give the captive tend'rest care;
> But say, in luxury's limits pent,
> Find you the king of birds content?
> No; oft he'll sound the startling shriek,
> And dash those grates with angry beak.
> Precarious freedom's far more dear
> Than all the prison's pampering cheer;
> He longs to seek his eyrie seat—
> Some cliff on Ocean's lonely shore,
> Whose old bare top the tempests beat,
> And round whose base the billows roar;
> When, dashed by gales, they yawn like graves.
> He longs for joy to skim those waves,
> Or rise through tempest-shrouded air
> All thick and dark with wild winds swelling,
> To brave the lightning's lurid glare,
> And talk with thunders in their dwelling."

As the mountain eagle hates the cage; loathes confinement and longs to be free; so the colored man hates chains, loathes his enslavement and longs to shoulder the responsibilities of dignified life. He longs to stand in the Church, in the State, a man; he longs to stand up a man upon the great theater of existence, everywhere a man; for verily he is a man, and may well adopt the sentiment of the Roman Terrence when he said, "*Homo sum, atque nihil humani a me alienum puto*"—I am a man, and there is nothing of humanity as I think, estranged to me! Yes, the anti-slavery movement has done this—and it has done more. It has revolutionized to a great degree, the theology and religion of this country. It has taught the American people that the Bible is not on the side of American slavery. No, it cannot be. It was written in characters of light across the gateway of the old Mosaic system, "He that stealeth a man and selleth him, or if he be found in his hand, he shall surely be put to death." That is the only place in the Scriptures where the matter of chattel slavery is mentioned, and the declaration of the Almighty through Moses is: "He that stealeth a man and selleth him, or if he be found in his hand, he shall surely be put to death."

Theodore D. Weld was right when he said—" The spirit of slavery never takes refuge in the Bible *of its own accord.* The horns of the altar are its last resort. It seizes them if at all, only in desperation, rushing from the terror of the avenger's arm. Like other unclean spirits it hateth the light, neither cometh to the light lest its deeds should be reproved. Goaded to madness in its conflicts with common sense and natural justice, denied all quarter and hunted from every covert, it breaks at last into the sacred enclosure and courses up and down the Bible, seeking rest and finding none. The *Law* of *Love* streaming from every page, flashes around it an omnipresent anguish and despair. It shrinks from the hated light, and howls under the consuming touch, as the demoniacs recoiled from the Son of God and shrieked, "Torment us not." At last it slinks away among the shadows of the Mosaic system, and thinks to burrow out of sight among its types and symbols. Vain is its hope! Its asylum is its sepulcher, its city of refuge, the city of destruction. It rushes from light into the sun; from heat into devouring flame; and from the voice of God into the thickest of His thunders."

Yes, the anti-slavery movement has taught the American people this, and more than this. It has taught them that no political party established on the basis of ignoring the question of slavery, can live and breathe in the North. Where is the Whig party?

> "Gone glimmering through the dream of things that were,
> A school-boy's tale, the wonder of an hour!"

The anti-slavery movement has dug its grave deep; it has buried it and is writing for its epitaph, " It was, but is no more." With Daniel Webster the Whig party breathed its last breath.

And where is the Democratic party? It is in power, but all over it is written—*Mene, mene, tekel upharsin.* Weighed in the balances and found wanting!

I would like to dwell on these results of the anti-slavery movement, but I want to make good before this audience my proposition, that there is not within the length and breadth of this land, a solitary freeman. The American people may be divided into four classes; the slaves, the slaveholders and the non-slaveholding whites, and the free people of color.

I need not undertake to show to this audience that the American slave is deprived of his rights. He has none. He has a body, but it is not his own; he has an intellect, but he cannot think for himself; he has sensibility, but he must feel for another. He can own nothing, all belongs to his master.

Then as to the slaveholder himself, we have all come to think that he has all rights ; that he is wholly independent, in no wise the subject of regulation made even in the interest of slavery itself. Not so; for a slaveholder cannot sit on the bench or stand at the bar, in the forum or in the pulpit, and utter a solitary sentiment that could be construed as tending to create insubordination among the free people of color and insurrection among the slaves. Look at the press in the Southern States; it is muzzled and dare not speak out a sentiment in favor of freedom. Let but a sentiment tending toward abolition escape and what is the consequence? Behold the *Parkville Luminary*, broken to atoms, and the people of that portion of Missouri avowing that that paper never uttered their sentiments or represented their views, and giving thanks to God Almighty that they have had the mob spirit strong enough to destroy that press. Is not this evidence sufficient to show that even slaveholders themselves, are not in possession of their full share of civil, religious and political liberty? If not, consult the statute books of Louisiana and other southern and slaveholding States, burdened with acts forbidding the expression of any sentiment or opinion, tending to the disturbance of their slaves and slaveholding interests.

As to the great mass of the white people at the North, have they their rights? I recollect, when the anti-slavery people held a convention at Cleveland, in 1850, the question came up whether they should hold their next national convention in the city of Washington. The strong political anti-slavery men of the country were there. There were present, Chase and Lewis of Ohio; Cassius M. Clay of Kentucky; Lewis Tappan of New York, and a great many other strong men of the party, and yet when this question came up, how was it decided? Slavery existed in the District of Columbia! And the convention voted that they would not hold the next national meeting at Washington. And what was the reason given? Because the people of that city might use violence! Had the people their full share of liberty, would they have been afraid to go to the capital of the country, and there utter their sentiments on the subject of slavery or any other topic?

But to make the fact more apparent, some two years afterwards, the great National Woman's Rights Convention was held in the same city; and there the very same question came up, whether they should hold their next meeting at Washington or Pittsburg. How was it decided? As the question was about being put, Lucy Stone came forward and said, "I am opposed to going to the city of Washington. They buy and sell women there, and they might outrage us." So the convention voted to hold the next meeting at Pittsburg. Were they in the possession of their full share of liberty? Think of it; our mothers, our wives and our sisters of the North, dare not go to the capital of the country, to hold a meeting to discuss the question of the rights of their own sex. And yet the Constitution declares that the "citizens of each State shall be entitled to all the rights and immunities of citizens in the several States."

I now wish to speak of another class, and more at length—of that class which I have the honor to represent—the free people of color. What is our condition in respect to civil, religious and political liberty? In the State in which I live, (Ohio), they do not enjoy the elective franchise, and why? It is owing to the indirect influence of American slavery. Slavery in Kentucky, the adjoining State, says to the people of Ohio, you must not allow colored people to vote and be elected to office, because our slaves will hear of it and become restless, and directly we shall have an insurrection and our throats will be cut. And so the people of Ohio say to the colored people, that they cannot allow them the privilege of voting, notwithstanding the colored people pay taxes like others, and in the face of the acknowledged principle that taxation and representation should always go together. And I understand that in the State of New York, the colored man is only allowed the elective franchise through a property qualification, which amounts to nothing short of an insult; for it is not the colored man that votes, but the two hundred and fifty dollars that he may possess. It is not his manhood but his money that is represented. But that is the Yankee idea—the dollar and the cent! In the State of Ohio, the colored man has not the privilege of sending his child to the ordinary common schools, certainly not to those provided for white scholars. Nor is he placed, even in the penitentiary on a fair equal footing. If a colored man knocks a white man down, perhaps in defence of his rights, he is sent to the penitentiary; and when he gets there, there is no discrimination made between him and the worst white criminal; but when he marches out to take his meal, he is made to march behind the white criminal, and you may see the prisoners marching, horse thieves in front, colored people behind.

All the prejudice against color that you see in the United States is the fruit of slavery, and is a most effectual barrier to the exercise and enjoyment of the rights of the colored man. In the State of Illinois, they have a law something like this: that if any colored man comes there with the intent to make it his residence, he shall be taken up and fined ten dollars for the first offence; and if he is unable to pay for it, he is put up and sold, and the proceeds of the sale are to go, first towards paying the costs that may accrue in the case, and the residue towards the support and maintenance of a charity fund for the benefit of the *poor whites* of that State. That is a part of the legislation of the State that Stephen A. Douglas has the honor to represent. The public sentiment that is growing up in this country, however, will soon, I hope, be the death of Douglas, and of that sort of legislation.

In the light, therefore, of all the facts, can there be any question that there is no full enjoyment of freedom to anyone in this country? Could John Quincy Adams come forth from his mausoleum, shrouded in his grave clothes, and in the name of the sovereignty of Massachusetts stand up in Charleston and protest against the imprisonment of the citizens of Massachusetts as a violation of their constitutional rights, do you think the people of South Carolina would submit to it? Do you think the reverence due to his name and character, or even the habiliments of the grave about him, would protect him from insult and outrage? So far are the people of this country lost to all sense of shame, that many would laugh at such an outrage.

American slavery has corrupted the whole mass of American society. Its influence has pervaded every crevice and cranny of it. But, Mr. President, I am glad to know that a great change is coming on, and that the American people are beginning to feel that the question of slavery is not one which affects the colored people alone. I am glad to know that they are beginning to feel that it is a National question, in which every man and woman is more or less interested. And when the people of the North shall rise and put on their strength, powerful though slavery is and well-nigh omnipotent, it shall die! It is only for the people to will it, and it is done. But while the Church and the political parties continue to sustain it; while the people bow down at its bloody feet to worship it, it will live and breathe, active and invincible. Now the question comes home to us, and it is a practical question, in the language of Mr. Phillips, "Shall liberty die in this country? Has God Almighty scooped out the Mississippi Valley for its grave? Has He lifted up the Rocky Mountains for its monument? Has He set Niagara to hymn its requiem?" Sir, I hope not. I hope that the Mississippi Valley is to be its cradle; that the Rocky Mountains are to be the stony tablets upon which shall be written its glorious triumphs; and that Niagara has been set not to hymn the death dirge but the triumphal song of our freedom! But, my friends, the question is with us, shall the Declaration of American Independence stand? Shall the Constitution of the United States, if it is anti-slavery, stand? Shall our free institutions triumph, and our country become the asylum of the oppressed of all climes? Shall our government become, in the language of Ex-Senator Allen, "a democracy which asks nothing but what it concedes, and concedes nothing but what it demands, destructive of despotism, it is the sole conservator of Liberty, Labor and Property?" May God help the right!

CHAPTER XII.

HIS PRACTICE AND SUCCESS AS THE COLORED LAWYER OF OHIO.

MR. AND MRS. LANGSTON spent the first two years after their marriage upon their farm in Brownhelm, Ohio. Their first child, a son, was born on the 3rd day of August, 1855. It was was the first child of its nationality and complexion, as already intimated, born in that place. During all this time Mr. Langston gave his constant undivided attention to his law practice, doing business in his own and adjoining counties.

During her confinement Mrs. Langston found in Mrs. Colonel Frank Peck an earnest and constant companion and friend. This good woman could not have given greater attention and care to her own daughter. The new-born babe, through the enthusiastic accounts given of it by this kind neighbor and motherly person and other members of her family, excited no small interest in the community and attracted a large measure of general attention.

He was not many days old when the happy parents and their friends discussed the matter of naming him. His mother, though proud enough of him—large, well-developed, interesting and promising as he was—was quite willing to let his father name him according to his own judgment and pleasure. Not feeling quite equal to the task, grave and important as it seemed to him, the father accepted the assistance of his brother Charles, who happened to be with him at the time

SUCCESSFUL LAW PRACTICE IN OHIO.

and who discovered not a little interest in the child as he bore special affection for both the parents, and would have him bear such name as might promise, in happy augury, good to him. In order that there might be no risk or mishap just here a name was finally agreed upon which represented the two extremes in human character. And hence the boy was at last given two names. The first, as suggested by the father, was one in honor of perhaps the most indifferent and on the whole worthless negro man that he had ever known, and yet one whom he greatly liked and with whom he had passed many pleasant idle moments. While this man was worthless in every exalted important sense, he had not a single bad habit except the one of doing nothing, which seemed to result not so much from faulty disposition as a constitutional want of energy. The boy was named by the father in this respect on the principle that the more worthless the person whose name is taken, the more certain the one to whom it is given might by another turn of disposition and life make it typical of high resolve and important if not splendid achievement. The uncle took the opposite view, and in offering his suggestions as to the second name for the child, brought forward that of the grandest man as he claimed who had ever been known among negroes on this continent. As he pronounced his choice his prayer was that his nephew might become half so great and noted as the one after whom he would have him called. All agreed that the babe should be named Arthur in honor of the indifferent Virginia negro, once his grandfather's slave, and Dessalines, in honor of the great Haytian hero. Accordingly the firstborn boy of the young parents bears the name of Arthur Dessalines Langston.

Pressed by professional engagements and duties, Mr. Langston deemed it advantageous to leave his farm and settle where he might enjoy larger opportunity for the cultivation of the practice of the law. Having disposed of his Brownhelm property, real and personal, he decided to locate with his family in Oberlin. In the spring of 1856 he left Browhelm and took up his residence in the neigboring town named. Though the roads at the time were in the worst condition possible, the morning of the departure from the farm was sunny and cheerful. The beautiful pair of chestnut sorrel horses which had been brought by him upon the Brownhelm farm and used especially for his own driving, had not been disposed of, and were now to be hitched to a two-horse wagon for bearing Mr. and Mrs. Langston to their new home, which had been purchased in the most desirable part of the village of Oberlin. The team had traversed the nine miles' ride a thousand times, but never apparently with so much ease and proudly as driven by their owner now, with the wagon bearing not only wife and child but household goods and products, apples, potatoes, turnips and meats necessary for a new commencement in a new house and upon new premises. Two hours only were required after leaving Brownhelm to bring him with his family team and load to the house and premises which were to be occupied as indicated for the next fifteen years. The horses were just turning their heads in seeming intelligence and apparent joy from a cross street through which they had been driven into East College, near the Langston home, when a resident of this neighborhood, a white man of extremely doubtful Republican feelings and principles, always officious and meddlesome, addressing Mr. Langston, propounded the following interesting but vexatious questions, "Are you coming to live among us aristocrats? Do you think you can maintain yourself among us?" Liberally and fairly interpreted these inquiries were intended to admonish these colored new-comers, the first of their class who had undertaken to purchase and locate a home in that particular section of the most noted Abolition town in America, that it would be necessary for them, according to this man's conception of their condition as to general society, to understand that they would find the usual social barriers erected against their advancement even there.

Mr. Langston was too buoyant and happy, to say nothing about his good breeding, to be in his replies to such unprovoked and unsolicited interference or gratuitous inter-

SUCCESSFUL LAW PRACTICE IN OHIO.

meddling, ungenteel, vulgar or blasphemous. He simply heard; made no reply other than, "We shall see," and drove on. The happiness and the hopes of this young family were greatly stimulated and confirmed by the remarkable attentions and hospitable proffers made them by their nearest neighbors immediately on their arrival. The house was without occupant and since its completion had not been tenanted or heated. It had simply been cleaned and aired, with such arrangements made for warming it and occupation in part, as to make it convenient and comfortable with the least amount of effort for the small family now taking possession. On their arrival the neighbors referred to, witnessing the condition of Mrs. Langston and her babe, came quickly to her relief, insisting that she should consent without the least hesitation to their entertainment of her until her husband could make the hurried necessary arrangements for her comfort at home. Received thus by the excellent leading people of the neighborhood, this family spent the time of their residence there in happy and constant accord, good understanding and cordial neighborly treatment.

This new home was composed of ample grounds, elevated and beautiful; the house was of modern construction, commodious and convenient, with every recent improvement of cellar, kitchen, dining and sitting rooms, halls, parlor and bedrooms, with stairway of easy, graceful ascent. The general finish of the house, inside and out, was all that could be desired to make it attractive and inviting. Besides, its extended veranda, with high windows opening thereupon from the sitting-room and parlor, constituted one of the most comfortable and pleasant features of the structure. It faced in full view East College Street, upon which the premises were located. Of this street it may be said that it was the most popular and desirable for residences of any in Oberlin. Lands upon it for this reason were very valuable and commanded the highest prices. In such a home, with such pleasant environments and in the midst of such agreeable friends and neighbors, Mr. Langston and his family commenced that professional and social life in Oberlin which they can only recollect with feelings of deepest pleasure and gratitude.

One year before Mr. Langston left Brownhelm, Mr. and Mrs. Slater moved with their son John to the far West, where they located in comfortable circumstances upon an unimproved farm, to which they devoted their whole attention and care, making for themselves a fair living, while they enjoyed in their new conditions such opportunities for social, moral and religious improvement as that section of the country then afforded.

The many friends whom Mr. Langston had gained while living in Brownhelm, through his social, professional, political and business relations, did not lose sight of him, nor fail to make frequent calls upon him as they needed his services, nor to bring themselves in social contact with him and his family, after he had located in Oberlin. Colonel Peck and his family, including every member, proved to be constant friends of the Langstons, and often did them the honor to share their hospitality, as they visited Oberlin on business or social errands. Mr. Langston always claimed that he did his excellent friend, Colonel Peck, a special service by directing his attention to the community in Oberlin, which, while it was intelligently considerate of the negro and his welfare, was not in any sense hostile to any white man, whether he held Democratic pro-slavery sentiments or not. And so the good colonel finally admitted.

As intimated, Mr. Langston while upon his farm found his law business steadily increasing in quantity and character. So much was this the case, that he not only abandoned all thought of any other business and devoted himself entirely to the law, but felt confident that his success in such behalf was really assured. He had feared at first that he might not be able to make headway against such opposition in his profession as he felt and expected that he must meet. He knew it was difficult, ordinarily, for a young white person to succeed without great and special encouragement in the practice of law. He had seen several who had failed, because as they claimed, they had no encouragement or sympathy, and had not been able to secure anything like remunerative and self-sustaining business. Among these he had seen one or two very talented persons of the latter class who had given up in utter despair. One of these was a classmate of his own, who seemed to have every promise in his favor, so far as ability, learning and application were concerned, and yet he failed in a profession to whose cultivation he had given time and means, to which he appeared to be devoted, and of whose attractive character, as seen in theory and in the experience of others, he was wont to speak with enthusiasm, often with eloquence. How then was it to be expected that he, without friends in the profession specially interested in him, and but a modicum of encouragement found in the favorable circumstances of his commencement in professional life, thanks to Mr. Perry, could have felt otherwise, constantly, in the beginning, certainly, than that he must fail!

But he was not long in discovering that when one goes upon the market with an article for sale at reasonable rates which is in demand, it matters very little as a rule whether the vendor be Jew or Gentile, white or black. Have you what is in demand and is it of first quality? Is it a trifle better than any other of the sort offered? Here is the secret of success! If one succeed well in defending the liquor-seller or the thief, displaying learning, skill, ability and courage, while he maintains his professional integrity, he need not fear that very soon even the more respectable classes of the community having business requiring such qualifications in the lawyer, will find and employ him. The question after all, as an able and prudent man will always find in life of whatsoever profession he may be, is, can he put upon the market to answer popular demand something superior and individual. A lawyer may even have learning, tact and discretion, and there may be added to these accomplishments personal and professional honor. While, as a rule, these would seem to constitute guarantees of success, failing in the courage which must always come of one's confidence in his own powers and the legal sufficiency of the ground-work of his cause, he would probably never succeed as a great and influential attorney. Indeed it is often the case that such courage even more certainly than the other qualifications mentioned wins success and name for the advocate. Sometimes, too, physical courage is needed, and when this is the case there must be no display of anything like cowardice.

It was not many days after Mr. Langston had located his family in Oberlin, before North Main Street in that village was graced with a new law office, to which the public was directed by a new sign connected therewith, reading—"John M. Langston, Attorney and Counsellor at Law, Solicitor in Chancery and Notary Public." His many friends and patrons in whose behalf he had already served, were not long in finding his new whereabouts, and others in need of his services did not neglect him. The only class in the general population which did not supply him patronage for the first six years of his practice after his location in Oberlin were the colored people. It was not because, probably, of their want of confidence in his ability, skill, courage or success, but because of the constitution of all courts and juries under Ohio law, composed as they were solely of white persons, who as a rule were full of prejudice against the negro, and so easily influenced by any fact or circumstance calculated to stir their feelings against him. It is a fact that every day's labor added to Mr. Langston's reputation, influence and business, and this the class referred to could see and understand. However, they noticed the other significant fact to them, that his clients were all of the white class. They could not understand what the result would be, should a black client appear before the court and jury represented by a colored lawyer. At this time, no black or mulatto witness could testify, under Ohio law, against a white man who objected thereto, and no one of those classes was called to act as juror in any case whatever; nor would it have been regarded as any other than foolhardy, for one of those classes to imagine or attempt to conceive of himself as ever capable of becoming a justice of the peace or judge. The colored people did not employ the colored lawyer because they feared the effects of that course upon their interests, as they were brought under the circumstances to judicial consideration and decision.

Mr. Langston never entertained the least doubt that this explanation was entirely true, nor did he ever entertain the least hard feeling because his own people thus hesitated to give him their patronage. It was just seven years after his admission to the Bar, after his experience as called to practice in Brownhelm and neighboring places, and not less than five years after he had opened his office, that the first colored man called upon him to consult and retain him as his attorney. With this person Mr. Langston was entirely frank and earnest, saying to him that he feared that he was mistaken in his call, that he was the colored lawyer, and that the colored people had not employed him, but appeared in court where they had business by white lawyers. When this man insisted that he knew what he wanted, and told the lawyer that he needed and was willing to pay for his services, having confidence in his ability, his tact, energy and honor, and that he had no fears even before a white judge and a white jury as to the result, Mr. Langston agreed to act as his attorney, and did so to his entire satisfaction in the victory which he achieved in his case, and against a firm of two able and well-known white lawyers. Thereafter Mr. Langston shared fully with his white colleagues of the Bar, even the business of his colored fellow-citizens, winning as many suits for them in proportion to the number tried as for any other class. It is true however that the heavier and more important part of his practice came from the Democratic element of society, and in not a single case to his knowledge was one of such clients disappointed or displeased with the conduct of his business.

As to physical as well as moral and professional courage, Mr. Langston was taught lessons in his experience which it is hoped no other young lawyer, even of the colored class, will ever have to apply in the least sense or manner to protect and sustain themselves in any part of the country, among any class of the people. The facts of each case detailed here will prove to be it is hoped of interest, as serving to show what the public feeling was which the colored lawyer had to encounter and overcome in the early days of his professional career. On several different occasions, in connection with his experience in the less advanced and untried ways of his profession, he was called to meet such displays of ill feeling and bad temper towards him, as to provoke and justify even demonstrations of force within the sacred precincts of the law.

In the first case, he had been engaged and retained to appear in the court of a justice of the peace at Florence Corners, Huron County, Ohio. He was to represent a party, defendant, against whom an action in replevin had been instituted to recover certain creatures—fatted steers. There was more or less popular feeling stirred up against the defendant, a drover living in the adjoining county. It went so far that he was finally notified that neither he nor his lawyer had better make their appearance, especially the latter, in the court on the day of trial, and that if the colored lawyer did appear, he might be compelled to confront even violence. No attention was paid to such threats or the warning, and at the hour precisely for the case to be called, the client and lawyer appeared, and the latter answered promptly for the former. Threatening looks were shown, and menacing words in undertones were whispered against the lawyer, and one brazen-faced person whose words discovered his lack of intelligence and the meanness of his soul, even went so far as to declare as the colored lawyer passed him on the street, that "The community has reached a pitiable condition when a *nigger* lawyer goes in pompous manner about this town." But it was not until the court took a brief recess, awaiting the arrival of six jurors who were being summoned to try the case, that the attorney on the opposite side, a local lawyer, undertook by certain offensive, vulgar language, in accordance with the apparent desire of the rabble, to provoke reply from, and justify assault upon Mr. Langston. He met promptly the insult in such manner and spirit, that at once he turned the popular feeling against his assailant, winning himself the sympathy and applause of the bystanders, and finally the case which he was there to try. If blows were used it was because they were necessary.

In the next case, he had been retained to conduct a cause involving several hundred dollars, consequent upon the breach of a contract made between certain persons residents of Oberlin. The parties had been called and had answered by their attorneys as ready for trial, when Mr. Langston suggested to the court that the opposing lawyers had failed to file an important pleading in the case. This suggestion was received in good part by the court and the attorneys at fault, who upon permission proceeded to draw and file the paper. While such service was occupying the attention of his lawyers, their client, a nervous, excitable man, paced the floor of the court room, moving to and fro, talking apparently to himself. At the time, Mr. Langston stood near by conversing with his client. As the excited gentleman drew near to him, addressing himself, as was supposed, to Mr. Langston, the latter not catching with distinctness the remark, inquired politely of the gentleman, "What did you say?" when in angry voice, with insult in his words and manner, he replied, "I was talking to a *white* man." At the utterance of these words, assuming threatening attitude he came toward and very near Mr. Langston, who, insulted and angered by the insinuations and conduct of this person, immediately struck him with his fist, felling him to the floor. Great excitement of course was produced by this occurrence. The judge sat in his seat, the jurors in their places, the lawyers about the bar, while the by-standers awaited the proceedings of the cause. All were greatly stirred by this exhibition of anger and violence. After the first moment of the surprise thus created had passed, Mr. Langston stepping forward confessed himself as in contempt of the court and ready to accept any punishment, fine or even imprisonment, according to its pleasure; protesting, however, that no man should ever refer to his color, even in a court room and in the presence of the judge and jury engaged in their judicial labors, to insult and degrade him, without prompt and immediate attempt on his part to resent it, with any and every means and method at his command. But the judge would not treat him as in contempt. On the other hand, he held that anyone referring to him, he being a member of the Bar of the State in good and regular standing, in contemptuous, insulting terms and manner, must if even knocked down, take the consequences of his own conduct. And so the grand jury of the county held, when this case had been presented to them upon every circumstance of law and fact, and without a single word of reply or explanation from the colored lawyer. In fact, the foreman of the grand jury told him that its action in his behalf was unanimous and vindicatory of his conduct.

Another matter of interest, in connection with which Mr. Langston felt called upon to defend his professional honor, was that of a very grave charge made against him to one of his clients. He had been employed by the first colored man who had come to his office to secure his legal services. The subject involved was the recovery of a little daughter, who had been taken from the home and custody of her father. The parents having had a misunderstanding had reached mutual agreement and amicable separation. It was understood and agreed that the father should retain control and possession of the daughter. She was, however, wrongfully and stealthily spirited away. To aid him in her recovery the colored father employed his lawyer, as stated. Thereafter, as the client was passing in the street, a white attorney who had enjoyed for a long time the patronage of any colored person having legal business which required professional attention, asked whether he had, really, employed the "*nigger* lawyer" to attend to his case, saying at the same time, "If you have, he will sell you out"; meaning thereby that the colored lawyer would prove treacherous. The colored client in this case was at best a very timid person; however, he was wise enough to come directly to his lawyer and tell him what had been said, and by whom. As between them, the lawyer and client, large mutual esteem and confidence existed, the latter was not disposed to question for a moment the integrity of the former. When Mr. Langston declared that he would see the attorney who had made the statement, at once and with his client, the latter said, "No, do not think of such a thing! You know I have entire confidence in you." His attorney replying said, with great vehemence, "This man must take this whole statement back!" Within a very few minutes, Mr. Langston and his client left his office in company for the court room, where the case was to be heard and determined. On the way they passed the door of the person who had employed the statement as given, so derogatory and unjust to his fellow-member of the Bar. He stood in his own doorway, when Mr. Langston advancing, with his client present, asked him if he had made the statement indicated. He pretended to deny it; but, when his look and manner sustained the colored man's declaration, even beyond the possibility of question, Mr. Langston, deeply moved by indignation and anger, administered to him not only a sound slapping of the face, but a round thorough kicking as he ran crying for help. Preceding Mr. Langston and his client in arrival before the judge, as they entered the court room this attorney with a bloody nose, smarting under the deserved castigation which he had received, was making a very serious and solemn complaint of vexatious and outrageous assault and battery against him by this *nigger* lawyer! But a very brief statement of the facts, without even the most concise explanation, sufficed to satisfy the court that he against whom complaint was made had acted in defence of his honor and should be sustained. This person who had thus outraged a lawyer of standing to his first colored client asked, as he claimed, justice of the court as stated in the first instance and subsequently of the grand jury, against his assailant, as he termed Mr. Langston, but in both cases without effect.

No unseemly or ruffianly conduct is to be tolerated or justified in a lawyer, and yet he must be ready always to defend and protect his professional honor, dignity and standing. If need be, let it be done even with blows!

His residence in Oberlin was not without additional and important advantages to Mr. Langston. Besides giving him improved opportunities for the cultivation of all those weightier matters of his profession, he was placed where he could accomplish more desirable political and official objects. He was at once nominated and elected clerk of Russia Township, and given, *ex-officio*, not only the law business of that town to attend to, but was made secretary of the Board of Education and school visitor. These were important positions in the township, and were of special advantage to a lawyer needing popular endorsement and advertisement in establishing himself in his profession. After Mr. Langston had demonstrated his interest in every enterprise calculated to conserve and promote the common good, the electors of the incorporated village of Oberlin elected him as early as 1857, and repeatedly thereafter, to the City Council, and in 1860 to the Board of Education. He served in this board—an organization provided for the conduct and management of the city union schools—for over ten consecutive years, discovering special fitness and efficiency for the services connected therewith. When, finally, he was compelled by other engagements to resign his position in the board, he had, according to his last election, three years to serve before his term of office expired.

The following letter will show how his fellow-members of the Board of Education, all of them being white persons, regarded and esteemed him. It finds insertion here with profound special pleasure, as coming from those who deserve of him only honorable, grateful mention.

"OFFICE SUPERINTENDENT PUBLIC SCHOOLS
"Oberlin, Ohio, Oct. 6, 1871

"PROF. JOHN M. LANGSTON,

"Dear sir:

"At a meeting of the Board of Education held on the 26th of September *ult.* your resignation as a member thereof, offered on the 16th of the same month, was accepted.

"The undersigned was directed to extend to you an expression of the regard which the board has entertained for you as a member and the regret they feel at the necessity of this separation. Since the organization of the board in March, 1860, you have been continuously a member. You have contributed largely to the commendable progress which the schools have made. Your voice has always been earnest for a greater advancement in the course of study pursued, and in elevating the standard of attainment. In securing this very desirable end, obstacles more or less formidable have been presented from time to time, only to be overcome by a steady and persistent course, imperatively demanded by the best interests of the schools. In the prosecution of this noble work you have enjoyed a long and honorable career, and in retiring from this field, you have the satisfaction of witnessing a grade of schools second to none in throughness and efficiency, in management and good results.

"May you continue to reap in your new field of labor and usefulness the rich harvest which always comes from a determined purpose to do good to your fellows in all the relations of life.

"In behalf of the Board of Education,
(Signed)   "HOMER JOHNSON, *Clerk*."

Such expressions of consideration and confidence, as stated, made as they were in public positive manner by the vote of the people, gave Mr. Langston assured professional standing in the community, and greatly enhanced and extended his influence and business. And he must ever recollect them with pleasing feelings and lasting gratitude.

As to his ability and standing as a lawyer, the following testimony, borne by the late Mr. William Wells Brown, is both interesting and complimentary. It is recorded in his work entitled "The Black Man." He says:

"Being at Oberlin a few years since and learning that a suit was to be tried in which Langston was counsel for the defence, I attended. Two white lawyers, one from Elyria, the other residing at Oberlin, were for the plaintiff. One day was consumed in the examination and cross-questioning of witnesses, in which the colored lawyer showed himself more than a match for his antagonists. The plaintiff's counsel moved an adjournment to the next day. The following morning the court room was full before the arrival of the presiding justice and much interest was manifested on both sides. Langston's oratory was a model for the students at the college and all who could leave their studies or recitations were present. When the trial commenced, it was observed that the plaintiff had introduced a third lawyer on their side. This was an exhibition of weakness on his part, and proved the power of the 'black lawyer,' who stood single-handed and alone. The pleading commenced, and consumed the forenoon; the plaintiff only being heard. An adjournment for an hour occurred, and then began one of the most powerful addresses that I had heard for a long time. In vigor of thought, in imagery of style, in logical connection, in vehemence, in depth, in point and in beauty of language, Langston surpassed his opponents, won the admiration of the jury and the audience, and what is still better for his credit, he gained the suit. Mr. Langston's practice extends to Columbus, the capital of the State, and in the county towns within fifty miles of his home, he is considered the most successful man at the bar.

"An accomplished scholar and a good student, he displays in his speeches an amount of literary acquirements not often found in the mere business lawyer. When pleading he speaks like a man under oath, though without any starched formality of expression. The test of his success is the permanent impression which his speeches leave on the memory. They do not pass away with the excitement of the moment, but remain in the mind, with the lively colors and true proportions of the scenes which they represent. Mr. Langston is of medium size and good figure, high and well-formed forehead, eyes full, but not prominent, mild and amiable countenance, modest deportment, strong, musical voice, and wears the air of a gentleman. He is highly respected by men of the legal profession throughout the State. He is a vigorous writer, and in the political campaigns, contributes both with speech and pen to the liberal cause. Few men in the Southwest have held the black man's standard higher than John Mercer Langston."

CHAPTER XIII.

A RARE AND INTERESTING CASE WHICH TESTED HIS POWERS.

MR. LANGSTON'S practice embraced legal subjects of every character, civil and criminal, which constantly taxed his learning, skill and power. Many noted cases in connection with which he was called to act and made displays of signal ability and tact might be mentioned, but a single one, as presenting an illustration of the laborious and faithful manner in which he did his business, shall answer. The peculiar character of this case, the situation and relations of the parties to it, the remarkable incidents connected with it, the gravity of the charge preferred against the accused, and her past and present position as well as the success and effects of the attorney's efforts, make it one famous and memorable. The names of the parties for prudential reasons may not be given, but the case with all the unique circumstances attending its institution, trial and conclusion, stands here as reported in the judicial records of Lorain County, Ohio. Hundreds who attended the trial and witnessed its conduct are still living, and could were it necessary, bear testimony to the correctness of this statement.

The real parties to this case though it was a criminal one, were two young white ladies on the one part, and a young colored lady on the other. They were friends, sustaining to each other the most intimate and cordial relations. They resided in the same house, though they occupied so far as the colored lady was concerned, different apartments. They met each other daily, exchanged visits regularly and frequently several times each day, and held conversations in free and frank manner upon every conceivable subject of interest to them, confiding to each other even their most important, special and sacred personal affairs. They were students of Oberlin College, and their quarters were located at the home of one of the first families of the town, where like many others of the same class they boarded themselves. The lady of the family, a person of excellent sterling qualities of character, judicious and motherly, took general charge of them. The house was situated in North Main Street, Oberlin, and was several stories in height, capacious in its rooms and halls, and admirably adapted to the purposes for which it was used. Its grounds in front used for garden and yard were ample, with pleasant walks and promenades, and a large field of one or two acres lying in its rear. The fact that these persons were accepted as inmates of the family referred to, would indicate to anyone well advised in the premises, that they were of good social position and possessed of means which enabled them to maintain and support much more than ordinary standing in life. Their presence in such family was to the initiated proof positive that they were ladies against whom no tongue of slander could be used. The white young ladies were representatives of families of wealth and name. And the young colored lady, while without family name or property, was esteemed of the best character, and was supported by a devoted, industrious, thrifty brother, doing business in California, who supplied, even anticipating every want of hers, after the style and manner of a person of ample income.

Thus handsomely and pleasantly located, these young lady students, full of youthful spirit and brightest hope, had advanced far into the winter term of Oberlin College for 1859-60, when the events occurred out of which grew the remarkable suit of which mention shall be made. The three had passed, with several other young lady friends, in

An Interesting Case.

happy, confidential, cordial association, each communicating to the other whatever might be true with respect to her actual health or feelings, the Sunday-evening previous to the Monday morning upon which the crime subsequently charged was said to have been committed. It is to be noted that the young ladies made their personal health, among other special matters, the subject of earnest and protracted conversation. The young white ladies admitted that they were not quite well, and that though they had hoped otherwise, they did not find themselves improving. Notwithstanding, they told their associates that they had been invited by two of their young gentlemen friends to take a sleigh-ride the next day, going as far as nine miles away to the home of one of the ladies in a neighboring town and county, and that they intended to go and take dinner with their escorts and friends at the home at which they would make their visit. These young ladies were not sisters, not even relatives, but friends and room-mates as well as fellow-students.

At ten o'clock, or thereabout on Monday morning, the young colored lady leaving her own room in the second story of the house directly over that of her two friends, made them a call in their own room. After hurried but warm usual salutations, the colored friend inquired of her neighbors as to whether she could serve them in any way. At first the answer was negative. But when on being asked whether they had taken anything warm to drink during the morning to protect them against the cold on their drive, they replied that they had not, their visitor immediately invited and urged them to come to her room, that she might prepare and give them something agreeable and warm. The morning was indeed wintry enough. The snow was deep, solid, and firm, with no prospect of increasing warmth in the frosty condition of the weather. The invitation was accepted and at once the young ladies repaired hurriedly to the room of their friend. The three going together entered her room at the same instant. She asked her friends the question, what they would have, when the answer came, "that which is most convenient and you think best." The little clean tin pan was put upon the stove, wine, with allspice and sugar, was poured into it, and very soon its contents, duly heated apparently, were emptied into three different glasses to be used by each of the three young ladies. The two young white ladies drank theirs at once. But the other declined hers with a mere touch of the lips, declaring that it was not warm enough and was insipid. The two empty glasses were set upon the stand near at hand, and as the young gentlemen with the sleighs were announced at this point, the three young ladies left the room in great haste and together—two to go upon the ride and the other to join the large company of friends who came from their rooms to the yard and street to bid their happy companions good-bye, and to wish them and their escorts a delightful time.

One hour and a quarter had elapsed, as stood the evidence, when the two young ladies upon the ride found themselves deadly sick, both exactly alike, and were both obliged not only to make known their condition to the young men, but to ask of them help. They had travelled over two-thirds of the distance to be gone, and nothing could be done but to drive on, pressing the horses to the utmost of their speed, so as to secure medical aid as soon as possible. Within one hour and a half from the time of starting, the home, where the visit was to be made was reached, and when the young lady who resided there was taken from the sleigh in the arms of her parents, she declared to them that she had been poisoned, naming the person who had done it, and saying that she herself must die. As the other lady was borne from her sleigh, she was found to be sick precisely as her friend. Both were at once put to bed and doctors were immediately called. Upon examination and diagnosis, they pronounced their patients sick of poisoning and in most critical condition, liable to die at any moment. Without the least hesitation, at the home and at the house in Oberlin, as the news of the condition of the young ladies was brought back, with signal

An Interesting Case. 175

unanimity the one who had given the wine, allspice and sugar, was charged with the grave crime of poisoning her associates and friends. The circumstances seemed to justify such feeling and charge.

How two weeks of anxious watching and waiting, with prayers for the recovery of the sick, tarried like some frightful spirit in the household, saddening the hearts of the parents and friends of the two young ladies, now apparently so near unto death! And with the young colored lady and her few staunch friends, as public sentiment grew apace against her and intensified itself, they and she meantime declaring and maintaining her innocence, how slowly and wearily time passed, as they hoped and prayed for favorable results to those who lingered so long as it seemed without change in their condition!

One-half of the two weeks had passed, when the attorney of the accused with his learned assistant, a surgeon deeply read in all those intricacies of medical jurisprudence and poisons, with the legal tests necessary to discover and prove their presence, with their effects, sure and unmistakable, upon the human system, made a visit to the town where the sick were located, to see and converse with their physicians upon their cases, and if possible secure for the surgeon the privilege of a visit to them. The object was entirely accomplished, and as the attorney met the surgeon on his way from the home of the sick, and they talked with each other of the success attending their errand and discussed the impossibility of proof as to the presence of poison in this case, since neither any portion of the contents of the stomach or the bowels had been preserved and analyzed, they were insensible of the imminent danger through which the attorney was passing. They had just reached the hotel at which they were entertained, when a friend, greatly excited, called to advise Mr. Langston that there was a deal of feeling in the community existing against him, in view of the fact that he had been retained to defend the person charged with the poisoning. This person insisted that his protracted stay in the town would doubtless provoke attack upon him, and counselled his immediate departure. He thereupon declared that already the father of the young lady at whose home both of the sick were being cared for, had, as he and the surgeon passed his grocery-store on their way to the hotel, levelled his rifle upon Mr. Langston and taking deadly aim, announcing his purpose to shoot him, fired, being prevented from executing his purpose only by the interference of a by-stander, who, appreciating the situation, touched the gun as fired, throwing the barrel upward, and thus lodged the load in the upper facing of the front door of the store. Thus advised, and wise enough to feel the importance of useless exposure in an excited and irate community, the attorney and surgeon having accomplished their errand, and rejoicing that Mr. Langston had not been shot, in some little hurry left Birmingham with their sprightly team for Oberlin.

And now, at the end of three weeks, the people of Oberlin already profoundly stirred by the reports connected with this case of supposed poisoning, and those connected with the condition of its subjects, were moved to the depths of their feelings by a circumstance which was regarded by all as most remarkable. The party charged with the poisoning had not been arrested. Indeed, no proceedings of a legal character had been instituted against her. Her arrest, however, was expected daily, and she and her friends had taken what they deemed to be in view of such probability, all proper steps with regard to her counsel and defence. One evening, just after dark, as she was passing out of the back door of the house in which she still roomed, she was seized by unknown persons, carried out into the field lying to the rear, and after being severely beaten, with her clothes and jewelry torn from her person and scattered here and there, she was left in a dark, obscure place to die. The moment her absence was discovered, the household and the town were thrown into the deepest excitement and consternation. The bells were tolled! The cry was heard all through the town that —— —— had been kidnapped! This was enough to bring the whole community in its wildest feeling about the house where this young woman lived, and the face of everyone was aglow with anxiety, while the questions were multiplied as they concerned her whereabouts and condition. Finally someone proposed that search with lanterns be made in the open field to the rear, a part of the premises. After long, careful, but at first fruitless quest, she was found in the condition already described. But the whole story of her condition is not told, till it be said that her bodily injuries were very serious, so crippling her that she was confined to her room for several days and then was not able to move about except as she did so on crutches. Her arrest took place within a few days after this occurrence, when Mr. Langston, her attorney, appearing for her, represented her condition, and upon his pledge and guarantee that she should appear according to the demands of the law so soon as able, delay in the trial was granted. And when the case was called, she was carried into court in the arms of her friends.

No case ever tried in Oberlin or originating in that community, had produced such popular feeling as this. The community, deeply stirred as it was, was about equally divided upon the question of innocence or guilt. Many were prejudiced against the accused on account of her color. The major part of the colored people themselves, largely because of her easy and rather unusual social relations to the whites, were ready and did pronounce her guilty in advance. Some of the colored class even went so far as to ask Mr. Langston whether he would defend her, while an aged lady among them expressing their feeling in a general way, told him that he had better not attempt such thing. This counsel however was given to a lawyer who understood too well his duty to a human being who needed defence against a grave charge, even where the community was stirred and excited, to let any such influence disturb or control his professional action. To him the rule stood good—let the world be shaken, but the lawyer shall never neglect nor forsake the performance of that duty which he owes to a client! The attorney of her choice betook himself therefore to the labor of her defence earnestly and faithfully, and on the day when the case was called for hearing, with four of the ablest lawyers of the district appearing to prosecute, with full complement of witnesses to sustain the accusation, popular feeling running high in its favor, before a large, excited concourse of people assembled in the most capacious business-room of the town, the court doubly reinforced, with all things now ready for a judicial contest of matchless character and gravest import to all concerned, Mr. Langston appeared, assisted only by his clerk and accompanied by his surgeon, single-handed and alone so far as professional support was concerned, ready for what was to be the effort of his life. His appearance and bearing showed beyond doubt his willingness, even anxiety to enter the judicial arena and contest without the least fear, in defiance of every danger. The case was called, and his answer for the defence was round, full and commanding. The State had adduced its first witness; she had been examined with all the skill and care which the prosecuting attorney of the county up to his last question could command, when addressing the sole attorney on the part of the defence, he triumphantly said, "*Take the witness.*" He had made a fatal mistake. His last question made it possible for the opposing counsel to enter with the largest liberty a field of defence, in such manner and with such effect as to give him the mastery from the very beginning. He did not fail to seize this advantage and maintain it, not only in the cross-examination of the first witness, but to the very end of the trial, magnifying and emphasizing its effects as bearing upon the question of guilt or innocence, in the light of any rule of law which might be accepted by the court in its decision. Four days had been occupied in the examination and cross-examination of the witnesses testifying for the State, and the learned lawyers representing the Commonwealth had rested. The court suggested to the attorney for the defendant that he might proceed with the examination of his witnesses. But to the surprise of all seemingly in attendance, the attorney instead of intro-

AN INTERESTING CASE.

ducing testimony, moved the court that the proceedings, so far as his client was concerned, be dismissed, since no such evidence as was required by law had been adduced, justifying the holding of the defendant to answer further in that court or before the grand jury. He claimed that the *corpus delicti* had not been proved, and that no such proof of probable guilt had been shown as to justify the detention of the defendant for further investigation or trial. To the question here involved two days were given to earnest and eloquent arguments, pro and con, such as it had not been the good fortune of the court or the people to hear before. The learned attorneys who represented the State displayed all the ability, tact and eloquence of which they were masters, and to say that they were ingenious, able and powerful is only to put the representation of their conduct under the circumstances in too faint colors. Finally, when the State had made its last argument, the prosecuting attorney closing his lengthy, admirable address amid the plaudits of his associates and a large proportion of the people, after an adjournment of thirty minutes Mr. Langston was permitted to make his closing argument in support of his motion. His argument, whose delivery occupied all of six full hours, as his friends and the journals claimed at the time, was replete with learning upon the subjects involved, addressed with the greatest care and skill to the court, clear, forcible and effective, from first to last commanding the closest attention, and at times moving all who heard it to tears, with manifestations, even to outbursts, of the deepest feeling. The end came, and the orphan, friendless young colored woman as many called her, who had been accused, perhaps without reason, and thus outraged without cause, was carried in the arms of her excited associates and fellow-students from the court room, to which she had been brought a criminal in popular esteem, to her home, fully vindicated in her character and name. Now matured in all those qualities of extraordinary genius and power, the young colored woman who was thus represented by the then young colored lawyer of Ohio, has reached such exalted place in American and European consideration, that she has been very justly termed the first artist of the negro race of the Western continent. Her works of art as displayed in marble, tell now how wisely and well her attorney labored in her case to vindicate justice and innocence!

The expressions of admiration, compliment and praise, bestowed verbally and by letter, as well as in the journals of the day, upon Mr. Langston, in view of his conduct of this case and the results following it, were numerous, cordial and flattering. As expressing the change which came over the colored people through the results of the case, it is due that it be stated that the excellent aged colored woman who warned Mr. Langston that he had better not attempt the defence of —— ——, honored him, in view of his fidelity and success, with a dinner in her own home, distinguished as well for the number and character of her guests as the richness and abundance of the repast. Another noteworthy incident, showing the change wrought by the address of Mr. Langston and the acquittal of his client, which may not be omitted here, concerns the conduct of Prof. John Clark, a white gentleman coming from the South, at the time residing with his family in Oberlin. He had given constant and unflagging attention to every movement made and every word uttered during the trial. For the entire time of Mr. Langston's address, he fixed his eyes upon him, being so carried at times by his expositions of the law as to nod his assent thereto; and, at other times, borne on by his flights of eloquence and moved by his appeals, he wept, as if affected to the very center of his being. With the tears suffusing his cheeks as Mr Langston closed his address, deeply excited, he approached him, saying only, "My orator! My orator!" And so thereafter this good man whenever he met the attorney, discovered in his address and conduct his exalted appreciation of him.

CHAPTER XIV.

THOSE SIGNAL OCCURRENCES WHICH WROUGHT FOR FREEDOM.

LOCATED as already described, the family of Mr. Langston increased from one child to five, three sons and two daughters. The boys were Arthur, Ralph and Frank, and the girls Chinque and Nettie. But the family had no sooner settled in Oberlin, than three sons, the children of a Louisiana planter of great wealth, a white father who would educate his colored offspring, were brought to school and placed in Mr. Langston's care and taken into his home. Quickly thereafter, there came a young boy from Africa, who was similarly situated. These children remained thus located, until they had reached young manhood, and completed their respective courses of study. Meantime, his own had reached school age, except sweet little Chinque, who died early when only two and a half years old, and Frank, the youngest of all, too young to be sent to school. The family was also increased in its numbers by the accession of several young ladies, students of Oberlin College, whom Mrs. Langston had consented, to take and care for as her own friends and relatives—in fact her own sister was one of the number. Thus constituted, the family took its place in the society of the town, and as opportunity permitted contributed its full share to its general prosperity, happiness and good name. To say that by reason of its situation and the character of the father and mother it was prominent and influential in the community as respects all classes of the people and all its social interests, is simply to assert the truth. And in the college, in the schools, in the church, everywhere, as regarded every enterprise for the general good, its efforts and means were always given liberally and promptly, according to the full measure of its ability.

During this time Mr. Langston gave diligent care to his business, which constantly increased, becoming more and more important and lucrative. The demands, however, upon his time and services in other directions and for other purposes, multiplied and became more imperative and exacting. The time seemed now to have arrived when the great and wonderful things of the age were to take place, and every man was to be called to his post of responsibility and duty. The time for excuses appeared to have passed, and every real and faithful defender of truth, freedom and the general welfare, was called to bring his best and most sacred offering to the government, whose life must be saved, even though it be done in the death of all else, however valued! Destruction was threatened and the danger was at hand! The frowning, angry face of slavery, its terror-inspiring mien, its words of frightful, horrid wrong and direful woes awaiting all, sent thrills of dismay through every loyal heart, serving under an allwise Providence to nerve every true devoted son for the last desperate contest which must witness the salvation of Amercian liberty, or its utter overthrow, in blood! The struggle came on apace, but only as the public mind was prepared for it through those premonitory, informing and prophetic events, which presaged and preceded its terrible approaching shock. Among such events, with their conspicuous originators and promoters, must be numbered and given chief place, the Oberlin-Wellington Rescue, the Harper's Ferry Movement, and the Declaration of Free Principles, with the organization and institution of a national party to give them practical significance.

Apprehensions and fears had been excited all over the North, especially in Oberlin and upon the Western Reserve, where thousands of fugitive slaves had settled, in view of the enactment of the Fugitive Slave Law of 1850, with its utter demolition of every safeguard of personal liberty, including the *habeas corpus* and the trial by jury. It was not, however, until the spring of 1858, that rumors were heard in Oberlin, the very citadel of human freedom, and alarm was created by the presence of negro-catchers from Kentucky and other neighboring Southern States, who were prowling in stealth and disguise about this holy place in search of their fleeing property. The quick-scented fugitive himself, awake to his danger, was the first to learn and report this condition of things; wisely making himself at the same time attentive to the observance of all the precautions required for his safety, under the circumstances. At once he manifested due care as to his movements in the night-time, and as to any distant trips to be made by him into neighboring country places for work or pleasure. He showed his anxiety, too, in his conversations with his friends, as he sought knowledge of his legal condition; and in his prayers, as he asked God to grant him His protection, with earnestness and faith which were indeed marvelous. He prayed as well for his friends, upon whom he must depend, craving for them such wisdom, courage and cunning as would render them equal to the task of his protection and salvation, without harm to themselves or injury to their households. How earnest, heart-touching and moving were his prayers as they implored the Mighty Jehovah, who had emancipated the Israelites as they believed through Moses, their own son, to save them against all treachery and infidelity of their own numbers. The words of John Ramsey, one of the leading representatives of this class, as he prayed in a public meeting, asking God that there might be found among them *no Judas*, faithless and false, still ring in the ears and stir the feelings of everyone who heard him.

But the spring and summer had passed in Oberlin, with even the first month of the autumn quite half spent, before the expected attack, so greatly feared, was attempted upon any one of the poor, anxious, trembling slaves, who had sought their freedom in flight, and tarried in that goodly town. And, then, this attempt was made, not in bold appropriate execution of the law, but through the treachery of a young white man, who was base enough to betray a fellow-being for pay, into the hands of those who would capture and re-slave him. This base person would do more. He would humiliate and disgrace, if possible, a whole community of good and true people, whose devotion to God, humanity and freedom was proverbial in the highest and best sense. This he would do to the community of his birth, the home of his parents and kin, and in whose midst he might and ought to have sought just title to respect, ability and influence. The thirteenth day of September had come! No day in the calendar shall remain forever, so far as the history of Oberlin is concerned, more memorable. On the one part, in view of the deep darkness of shame which covers it in the betrayal of John Price, it can never be forgotten. On the other hand, in view of the glory which immortalizes it, in the rescue and emancipation of the same man by the noble and brave community which had given him and all his class succor and protection, and now redeemed its principles and professions in a single great deed, whose name and description deserve to be written in the boldest, the brightest characters, it shall live in eternal sunshine!

On this day, among five hundred others, who acting under the impulse of their higher and better nature went out from Oberlin to rescue a human being from negro-catchers, was Mr. Charles H. Langston, who was at the time making a brief visit to the family of his brother. This brother had been called on that very day by a professioual engagement to a neighboring county. At sunset he returned home to find neither life nor stir in or about the village. The whole town seemed to have gone abroad. Upon inquiry he learned that a man had been kidnapped and hurried away to Wellington, where the train could be taken for Columbus, Cincinnati and Kentucky. He further learned that the people, in the purpose and resolution as it were of a single fearless giant, had gone forth to his delivery. He accordingly hurried on to the scene of action, hoping that he might arrive in time to play some humble part in this drama of genuine manhood and courage. He had not gone, however, more than four and a half miles, before he met one of the brave sons of Oberlin returning with the rescued fugitive, John Price, ordinarily so black, but now, as seen under the intensest excitement, in a buggy drawn by the fleetest and most spirited animal of the county, moving at the top of her speed, he was light as ashes. Simeon Bushnell, proud of his triumph, bade Mr. Langston to come back, saying, " John is safe; here he is ; I have him. Come back !" At first Mr. Langston was inclined to obey the order and return, but overcome of a desire to meet the multitude, now victorious, and return with them, he pressed on. But, within a moment or two, he met both his brother and his brother-in-law Mr. O. S. B. Wall, who in blended voices bade him return. Now the roads were crowded with the returning hosts, shouting, singing, rejoicing in the glad results of their brave, defiant, successful enterprise. In the midst of such a company, enthusiastic, happy in a victory won by them in the name of Freedom, it seemed to occupy but a moment to pass five miles, through Pittsfield and Russia Townships, to Oberlin, where a vast concourse of true and patriotic men and women awaited the arrival of their neighbors and fellow-townsmen, to join them in such a meeting in favor of freedom and against slavery, as had never assembled within the limits of that consecrated town. Speeches in denunciation of slavery, the Fugitive Slave Law, slaveholders, and all those who sympathized with and would aid them, were made at this great and wonderful gathering. The pledge of the community was there given, in gravest, most solemn manner, that no fugitive slave should ever be taken from Oberlin and returned to his enslavement. Among other orators heard on this memorable occasion, was Mr. John M. Langston. What he had failed to accomplish in deeds on that eventful day, he attempted to reach and redeem in words, both truthful and wise, while fiery and denunciatory of slavery, its dark and frightful methods and supporters.

The days passed rapidly thereafter, and very soon the grand jury of the United States Court for the Northern District of Ohio had found bills of indictment against thirty-seven prominent and influential citizens, white and colored, of Lorain County, charged with aiding and abetting in the rescue of John Price. A curious fact connected with the *personnel* of this grand jury is found in the circumstance that the father of the white boy who betrayed the fugitive was a member of it. The son betrays, and the father indicts! Shakespear Boynton, the former, and Lewis D. Boynton, the latter, may enjoy, forever, the bad eminence of such conduct. Judas Iscariot betrayed his master, and, in his deep consciousness of guilt and shame, went out and hanged himself! These others betrayed this poor, ignorant, helpless slave, but they found in themselves no sense of guilt or shame, driving them to a deed of self-destruction, in the perpetration of which they might have very properly imitated their great prototype in treachery! Prominent among these rescuers was Mr. Charles H. Langston. No thanks to the authorities that his brother was not, also, indicted and held for trial. The most desperate efforts were made to compass that end, and proved fruitless only in that he was out of the county, engaged in public law business, and not even in Oberlin, certainly not in Wellington, when the rescue was made. At first the thirty-seven accused persons were permitted to make their pleas, and then give their own personal recognizances for their appearance for trial. Subsequently, however, they all by some misunderstanding with the court, to maintain their personal dignity and consciousness of self-respect, and to show the utter tyranical, oppressive operation of the law, refused their recognizances and were confined in the Cleveland jail. Two only were put upon trial. Both, of course, were convicted; for the trial jury was organized and constituted *to convict*, and it did its work according to appointment. Simeon Bushnell was tried first, and then Charles H. Langston. These cases will ever stand among the celebrated noted ones of American judicial history. The arguments made by the learned attorneys representing the defendants, distinguished by the highest moral tone, the spirit of the deepest and broadest sentiments of right, the clearest and the most comprehensive teachings of liberty and law, full of glowing and touching diction, appeal and eloquence, delivered in captivating, attractive style and manner, would alone give name and influence throughout the country to the judicial proceedings of which they constituted so important part, certainly in cases of so much local and national significance. In the trial, however, of Mr. Langston, the remarkable fact stands out in bold relief, that after his conviction, and upon the inquiry of the court whether he or his attorney had anything to say why the sentence of the law should not be pronounced upon him, he offered a reply, a powerful and matchless address, wonderful in the breadth of his views, masterly and unanswerable in his logic and law, and commanding and irresistible in its delivery and effects. This speech carried this case to the ends of the earth, and immortalized not only the name of its author, but impressed his sentiments of liberty, justice, humanity, and sound religious duty, as illustrated in the teachings of Christ, upon every hearer and reader of his words. The lawyers who volunteered their services without remuneration in behalf of the defendants, making masterly efforts in addresses to the jury trying the two cases mentioned, were Messrs. A. G. Riddle, R. P. Spaulding, F. T. Backus and S. O. Griswold. In the cases of the parties as heard in the Supreme Court of the State, upon a writ of *habeas corpus*, the attorney-general, Wolcott, acting in the name of the State, presented an elaborate argument in behalf of the defendants. His brother would have taken public part as one of his attorneys in the trial of Mr. Charles H. Langston, had it not been understood between them that he would make the speech for himself, and in the interest of the Abolition cause, at the time and under the circumstances already described, since he was, without doubt, the best qualified man of his race for such service.

The incarceration and confinement of these thirty-seven citizens on this charge in the prison of the chief city of the Western Reserve, produced great excitement and general comment and adverse criticism throughout the country. After Bushnell's trial and conviction, with Langston similarly situated, except that he had anticipated his sentence by a speech which thrilled the whole country, the great gathering of a hundred thousand stalwart, loyal men of Northern Ohio, brought together through the influence of Joshua R. Giddings and his associates, the worthies of the Anti-Slavery Movement, was a natural, inevitable sequence of the agitation indicated. This great meeting was held to discuss and determine whether the jail which held the noble, brave citizens, rescuers of a human being doomed to slavery, should be torn down and those friends of freedom be themselves set at liberty. The speeches made at this gathering by the celebrated and famous anti-slavery orators moved the nation in such way as to presage to any sagacious person, unmistakably, the early overthrow of American slavery itself. It had in its bloody purposes invaded the sanctity of the rights of white men, and they had determined now that the enemy of their freedom must die. In its death it was easy to discover the approaching life of negro freedom. Among the orators of this occasion Mr. John M. Langston was heard. Of his speech mention was made by a leading journal of Cleveland in the following words:

"On being introduced to the vast audience he said that he hated the Fugitive Slave Law as he did the Democratic party, with a deep, unalterable hatred. He then went on with a clear, noble and bold utterance of sentiments which were clothed in as eloquent language as is ever heard upon the floor of the halls of Congress. The listeners forgot that he was a black man—he spoke a white language, such as few white men can speak. He trampled the Fugitive Slave Law under his feet, for it incarcerated his own brother and his friends and neighbors for disobeying its bloody commands. 'If you hate slavery because it oppresses the black man in the Southern States, for God's sake hate it for its enslavement of white men. Don't say it is confined to the South— here it is on our neighbors and citizens, and shall we say that slavery does not affect us? As we love our friends, as we love our God-given rights, as we love our homes, as we love ourselves, as we love our God, let us this afternoon swear eternal enmity to this law. Exhaust the law first for these men, but if this fail, for God's sake let us fall back upon our own natural rights and say to the prison walls " come down," and set these men at liberty.' " [Cheers.]

No violence was attempted at this meeting; for while the people were deeply moved, they were dominated by just and patriotic convictions and purposes. The governor of the State, Hon. Salmon P. Chase, appeared among them and gave his assurance that by judicial and legal methods the release of the prisoners should be secured within a reasonable time. All placed confidence in that assurance, for they knew the man who made it and felt and believed that his word was worthy of entire confidence. After full, earnest and positive announcement of their feelings, judgment and purposes against the law and all proceedings under it which aimed its deadly blows at American liberty itself, they in orderly, quiet manner returned to their various homes. The moral effects of the meeting remained, working those inevitable results which must be established in the interest of general freedom. The governor kept his promise to the people, and very shortly thereafter the *habeas corpus* proceedings already referred to were instituted and the State Government was heard in such behalf by the learned attorney-general, whose exhaustless argument abounded in the fundamental law doctrines and principles justly invoked in aid of the personal liberty of the citizens against the tyranny and oppression which sought the overthrow of their rights. The Supreme Court of the State failing to sustain these proceedings, it was left for the Common Pleas Court of Lorain County to come to the rescue of its citizens in a charge to the grand jury which, resulting in the indictment of all those concerned in the capture of John Price for kidnapping him, soon brought an end to further proceedings against any one of the citizens still held for trial under the National Act and the release of them all. Thus by a counter proceeding which would open the doors of the state penitentiary to the perpetrators of such kidnapping the proceedings of the United States District Court for Northern Ohio, so far as the Oberlin-Wellington Rescuers were concerned, were brought to a close. All thanks to Judge Carpenter for his sound law and fearless, opportune charge! The counter indictments found in his court upon which arrests would be made and trials instituted against the Kentucky kidnappers, ended the most stupendous, unjustifiable and outrageous proceeding ever presented and prosecuted against any American citizens. At last the Higher Law was triumphant! On the 6th day of July, 1859, the great Oberlin Jubilee meeting was held. The Rescuers were all at home again and their friends and neighbors would join them in grateful celebration of their release finally, through the just vindication of the law. The speeches made on this occasion in the main by those who had been confined, were of a most interesting and inspiring character, full of the warmest sentiments of freedom, with the declared willingness to suffer even greater things to maintain the right. They moved and melted while they nerved with manly purpose every heart of the vast audience which had brought its offerings of praise and thanks to the good men who had thus been deemed worthy of suffering and made victors. Owing to the absence of his brother, Mr. John M. Langston spoke at this time in response to repeated urgent calls. Of his speech a leading journal of that date makes the following comments:

"In his characteristic bold eloquence he spoke fearless and startling words in opposition to the Fugitive Slave Law. He paid a high and proud tribute to the speech of his brother in the United States Court, which was received with loud applause. He thanked his noble friends who had gone up to Cuyahoga County jail—thanked them in his character as a negro—as a white man—as one in whom the blood of both races joined—as a *man*—and as an American citizen. We wished that the wide world could have seen him standing there, pouring forth in clarion notes his noble, manlike and godlike thoughts. No more eloquent speech was made yesterday than his."

It was on the 16th day of October, 1859, that John Brown with a handful of faithful and loyal followers surprised Harper's Ferry by his attack and capture of the Arsenal and Armory. Three days only, prior to this occurrence, Mr.

Langston was visited, at his office and home, in Oberlin, by a person who gave his name as John Thomas. At the time, Mr. Langston was engaged actively in the practice of his profession. This visit did not work, in any wise, special interest or surprise, as strangers were constantly calling for business or other purposes, and as in this case, were always willing to adjust themselves and their demands to his situation. At the moment of this call, the attorney was engaged in a pressing important consultation. Mr. Thomas retired, promising to call again at twelve o'clock, noon, of the same day, saying at the same time that he might accompany Mr. Langston to his house, as he went to dinner. At twelve o'clock, precisely, he returned. He said, " I know this is your dinner hour, according to the rules of this community. If you please, I will walk with you homeward, and we can talk as we go." Setting out, their conversation ran on general matters, until they had gone considerable distance eastward in College Street, when the gentleman, putting his hand gently upon Mr. Langston's shoulder, while he looked him squarely in the face and eyes, inquired, " Am I really addressing John M. Langston?" The reply came at once, and positively, " You are!" " Then," said he, " I will give you my real name. So far, I have not done so. My name is not Thomas. It is John Brown, Jr., and I have called to see you upon matters strictly secret and confidential, and which must not be committed to anyone in whom we may not place the fullest confidence. My father is John Brown of Ossawatomie, who proposes to strike at an early day, a blow which shall shake and destroy American slavery itself. For this purpose we need, and I seek to secure, men of nerve and courage. On this whole subject I desire to talk freely with you, and secure your services at least to the extent of aiding us with your knowledge and advice in securing one or more men." By this time Mr. Brown was entering the gate, having just been invited by Mr. Langston to go into his house, where full and thorough conference might be had after dinner upon the subject named. Ultimately, Mr. Brown retired with his host to his parlor, where full statement of the purposes of his father with regard to the Harper's Ferry Movement and his own mission to Oberlin, was made. He wished to see Mr. Langston, and, if possible, through him find and influence any men willing and ready to join in the enterprise, and, if need be, die in connection therewith, in an attempt to free the American slave. He had visited Mr. Langston, as he said, because it was well understood that he was utterly opposed to slavery; that no fugitive slave had ever come, in search of his freedom, within his reach, who had not received promptly and fully his aid and succor; that his influence among white and colored persons who were earnest in their purposes to promote the Abolition Movement, even in the sacrifice of property and life, was large and positive; that he sympathized with his brother Charles and the thirty-six noble white and colored men who had been imprisoned long weary months in the Cleveland jail, for their disinterested, manly conduct, in the rescue of John Price, his relations to that case having been decided and aggressive; and that he so far enjoyed the respect and confidence of all persons, white or colored, living anywhere in the State of Ohio, that he would be likely to know of anyone of such classes who could be induced by proper representations to leave even home and family, to strike and die for the American bondman. It was at Cleveland, and during the trials of Simeon Bushnell and Charles H. Langston, that Messrs. J. H. Kagi and J. M. Green made the acquaintance and won the friendship of John M. Langston. They had heard and approved his sentiment, as he expressed himself in public and private, in denunciation of slavery and the Fugitive Slave Law. These leading men of John Brown's immortal Spartan band, on their way to Harper's Ferry, had tarried in Cleveland long enough to visit and proffer their services to the thirty-seven good and true citizens there imprisoned. Kagi had even gone so far as to proffer his services to release them all at once. From these men, young John Brown had learned who the person was to whom he made his visit in Oberlin. Under the circumstances, with the knowledge he had gained

Occurrences which Wrought for Freedom. 193

of Mr. Langston from the sources indicated, Mr. Brown's visit was altogether natural, and to one from whom he might expect sympathy, and to some extent, at least, assistance. The conference, somewhat protracted, was interesting enough, and even now, as contemplated after the results of the Harper's Ferry Movement have passed into actual history, has not lost its interest.

In this connection, the names of Sheridan Leary and John Copeland, both natives of North Carolina, but finally residents and citizens, by choice, of the free and famous town of Oberlin, come quickly and unbidden to the memory, and their heroic and manly decision to die, if need be, with John Brown as their leader, challenges the admiration of those who witnessed their conduct and heard their words, as they announced that decision in the parlor and at the conference here referred to, to which they had been in due season invited. The words of Leary shall ring forever in the ears of those who were moved by them when he said, "I am ready to die! I only ask that when I have given my life to free others, my own wife and dear little daughter shall never know want."

How nobly he died, falling in the charge by the side of Kagi, who fell with him in front of the Arsenal at Harper's Ferry, history records. How well John Copeland demeaned himself, as he followed the hero of Ossawatomie to the gallows, after the struggle, and died by his side, history equally records. And the monument which the good people of Oberlin have erected to their memories, shall testify forever how their courage, and their deeds, and their death, are appreciated by those in whose midst they made their homes. The results of the visit and the conference, as here indicated, signify plainly enough how wise and advantageous John Brown, Jr.'s coming to Oberlin proved to be, and that he secured thereby two of the bravest negroes that this country has produced.

It is perhaps, true, that no man of greater physical courage could be found than Leary. No one more fit to take his place by the side of Brown's lieutenant, Kagi, and in unflinching bravery demonstrate the strength and quality of his manhood. Born at Fayetteville, North Carolina, of respectable free colored parents, improved mentally and morally much beyond most of their class, by their industry and thrift placed certainly in comfortable circumstances, he had learned those lessons of freedom by experience, observation and parental instruction which made him at once intelligent with respect to the condition of the American slave, and which inspired him with the manly resolution to do whatever he might in the use of any means which he could control and wield, to overthrow the institution which so thoroughly wronged and ruined the class with which he and his kin were identified. He had married an intelligent and interesting young colored lady, the daughter of a family from North Carolina, also of the same more advanced class of his people. There had been born, at this time, as the fruit of the marriage, a baby-girl now six months of age. For his wife and child he entertained the deepest affection, and only hesitated as to going to Harper's Ferry under John Brown, as he felt that his dear ones might come to want. He said, finally, "Let me be assured that they will be cared for, protected; and if my child shall live, be suitably educated and trained to usefulness; and my life shall be accounted by me of the smallest value, as it is given if need be, to free the slave." He did not have days, he did not have hours, to make up his mind. His conclusions were reached as by a leap, and his eyes moistened with tears only as he thought of the farewell which he must bid his wife and child. His decision, however, was firm and manly! How well he did his duty, the record which is kept of the wonderful, daring, matchless struggle for freedom, made at Harper's Ferry, shall testify! And how nobly he died in the very beginning of that struggle, on the soil of a State cursed by slavery, is written in the intelligence of all those who read its history and admire individual courage as shown in facing death to redeem and save the oppressed.

Of John Copeland, whose father and mother leaving

North Carolina had located in Oberlin, to educate and promote the general interests of their family, the highest and best testimonial may be borne to his character and name, as well as to his devotion to those principles of liberty and equal rights of which he had learned at home, and which had been impressed upon his mind in the teachings which he had received in the school and the church of Oberlin. For many years prior to these occurrences there had been established in Oberlin, what was known as already stated, the Liberty School-house, used by day for school purposes in the interest of the fugitive slaves congregated there, and by night for public meetings, where the same class congregating, told the story of their wrongs and described the outrages which in many cases compelled their flight. At such meetings, John Copeland could always be found, and to the story told by any fugitive slave he always gave the most sympathetic attention, signifying often by the deep scowl of his countenance, the moist condition of his eyes and the quivering of his lips, how deeply he was moved by the recital of wrong and outrage, and how glad he would be to see the institution under which such abuse was tolerated, overthrown and destroyed. With such feelings easily aroused in his soul, the appeal made to him to go out to fight, and maybe to die for those who were enslaved, against whom wrongs were perpetrated too black and barbarous to be described, was not made in vain. As he had honored himself in the company of the thirty-six other true and valiant men who had gone out to rescue John Price, and suffered with them confinement in the Cleveland jail under the Fugitive Slave Law, under the promptings of a manly nature, so now he would honor himself in service to the cause of humanity in a desperate attack upon slavery itself, with John Brown at Harper's Ferry. His name like those of his noble comrades, in both attempts to serve freedom and free principles in his country, even unto imprisonment and death, shall live forever! For they were all martyrs worthy of the faith, whose examples American youth will not despise when emergency comes again to American liberty.

While it is true that in every interview and conference had with any and all persons advocating the Harper's Ferry Movement, or any other such enterprise against any portion of the South, with a view to the abolition of slavery, Mr. Langston held, that the movement would discover such audacity on the part of its promoters and supporters, as to drive the very class—the enslaved—away rather than draw them in needed numbers to it, and thus defeat the ostensible and real object had in view, he maintained always with earnestness of decision and judgment, as a reliable and trustworthy friend of the oppressed, that the movements would at least tend to precipitate a condition of public feeling in the country which would sooner or later create disturbance and finally struggle, which would prove the greatest blessing to the slave and the country. He even predicted publicly that such would be the result. Accordingly, he held that if the indirect but necessary effect of the Harper's Ferry Movement, like the arrest and confinement of thirty-seven intelligent, worthy and influential citizens, white and colored, of Lorain County, Ohio, tended to precipitate the War of the Rebellion, the chief result of which was the overthrow of slavery followed by the enfranchisement of the emancipated classes, all that was done and suffered in such behalf was wisely and well done, and the sacrifices made must ever be considered large moral investments, profitable as well to the people generally, as to those who thus gained their freedom.

It was well, though necessitating to all worthy, sagacious and patriotic citizens, additional labors and sacrifices, that the Republican party was, at this time, thoroughly organized and established for national and state duty. Through it the salvation of the Union, the perpetuity of free institutions, and the general welfare of the people were made actual and permanent facts. To this party Mr. Langston, obeying the call of intelligent patriotism, gave prompt support in every national and local contest and showed himself its sincere and determined advocate and supporter. In this regard, his rank was exalted and his position American, for he followed where Lincoln, Chase, Seward, Sumner, Giddings, Stevens, and the other great leaders and champions of this party of freedom, moved in solemn, manly tread to the accomplishment of those high deeds which make the nation their conscious, perpetual debtor.

CHAPTER XV.

HIS RECRUITMENT OF COLORED TROOPS FOR THE NATIONAL SERVICE.

ABRAHAM LINCOLN had been elected president of the United States! The circumscription, if not the overthrow of slavery, seemed to be at hand. The temper and metal of the South were now to be tested. Would secession, to be followed inevitably by war, be adopted as the only and last source of defence left to an oligarchy of slavery which sought to dominate the country and government? The feelings of the country, gathering strength and intensity under the influence of an agitation rendered serious and affecting by words as well as deeds, calculated to stir and heat the blood, even of a people ordinarily cool and deliberate, ran high as a mighty angry flood about to sweep everything before it. The sagest statesmen were staggered in the presence of the threatening events which threw their black appalling shadows across the republic. They could not speak with authority and reliable forecast as to what of portent and calamity awaited the nation. All could feel, however, the approach of a cruel, deadly storm. That slavery, strong now and defiant in its purposes and designs against the government, would make open war-like assaults upon it, was generally feared. Although few persons in the land seemed prepared to assert the certainty of such procedure, all felt that it must come. The president-elect, the representative of all those republican principles and doctrines which the South loathed and detested, had hardly felt upon his election that such murderous, popular feeling existed in any part of the country as to render his journey from Illinois to Washington city dangerous or difficult. His friends, however, found it necessary to warn him on his arrival at Harrisburg, Pennsylvania, that it would be well for him to move upon his guard in passing through the city of Baltimore to the capital. Early after his inauguration, the South seizing his advent to power as cause for their rebellious proceedings, announced their secession in the thunder of great guns, as they echoed and re-echoed the attack of the insolent, mad oligarchy of despotism upon the nation. The attack at first was treated as an insurrection of small power which might be easily crushed. Soon however the purpose and strength of the insurgent forces were discovered, and instead of seventy-five thousand soldiers called for a brief period of enlistment, the government needed hundreds of thousands of its most valiant men, to go out to make war in earnest and to the end to save the Union, free institutions and the government, as the Fathers of the Republic had bequeathed them to loyal worthy sons. The War of the Rebellion was actually upon the nation!

At its commencement, there was the strongest possible feeling found in all parts of the country, against taking colored men into the army of the nation as soldiers. And it was not until after the famous meeting of loyal governors held at Altoona, Pennsylvania, as late as the early part of 1863, that the purpose was expressed by the late John A. Andrew, governor of Massachusetts, as permitted by his colleagues, and as authorized by the general government, to organize regiments of such persons. His colleagues, the loyal governors present, gave him their consent to that proposition, allowing enlistments from their several States as credited to his own, and expressed the wish that he undertake such work.

There was no man in the United States, all things considered, so well adapted to inaugurate the movement in this behalf, as the man to whom Governor Andrew assigned it. Full of genuine devotion to that freedom and impartiality which knows no color in a human being; wholly alive to the deadly effects of slavery upon every interest of his country; anxious to employ every honorable means to stay its encroachments and to snatch from its bloody clutches any instrument or power which it might wield to the ruin of the government and the country; with full knowledge of the soldierly qualities of the negro troops of the Revolutionary Army and of the War of 1812; Mr. George L. Stearns, an old tried friend of John Brown, a loyal merchant of Boston, wealthy himself and able to secure all the means necessary for the early stages of such work, was the man of all others to be charged with this duty. He was well known in connection with his efforts to prevent slaveholding in Kansas, employing his means largely and his entire influence to accomplish this object. Nor, when questioned even by a committee of Congress with regard to any part he had taken in such work, or any support which he had given John Brown in his raid on Harper's Ferry, did he hesitate to speak frankly and fully on those subjects, telling what he did and what funds he furnished to advance and support either enterprise. New England could not produce a man of higher social position, anti-slavery fame and general influence than Mr. Stearns. He was armed too for this special task by reason of his great knowledge of the leading colored men and their chief white friends of the United States, all of whom he might employ as instruments of the largest importance in promoting the recruitment of the colored troops. It was of the first importance under the circumstances that his knowledge of the colored men of the United States be such that he would understand well how to make selections from among them, so as to secure the largest efficiency with the most desirable results in this service. It was material too that he should have knowledge of such white men in every quarter as might further by counsel and influence any movement which might be made to reach the colored citizen and to secure his enlistment. Accordingly, he had no sooner accepted the responsibility of recruiting the first colored troops from the North to be admitted to the national service, than he did select colored men, who by their ability and influence were capable of doing the most successful work among their own class ; while he organized such committees of white men, in different sections of the country, to aid and support the movement in such general way as seemed to be necessary. To one well advised his efforts in such respects must be deemed of the greatest importance. At the time that he commenced his service, the government supplied neither means nor men for his use. He was compelled to find and furnish both.

As his chief recruiting agent for the western part of the country, Mr. Stearns selected and employed Mr. John M. Langston. The duties which he enjoined upon this agent, in whom he reposed the greatest confidence, were much beyond that of mere recruiting. For he invited him not only to special consultations connected with the service, but expected him to attend and address great popular assemblies, as might seem to be necessary in the great cities and important rural districts, explaining every feature of the national and state laws concerning the recruitment of all troops enlisted and sent to Massachusetts for organization in regiments and service as credited to that State. The questions of monthly pay, allowances generally and bounties were of special importance, and required careful and proper explanation. Besides, the feeling against taking any part as soldiers in the war so far as the colored people were concerned, consequent upon their rejection heretofore, whenever offering to do so, had to be overcome by cautious, truthful statements, made with such candor and appeal as to create after meeting their prejudices, favorable and effective impressions. Mr. Langston's work was largely, almost entirely in the beginning, of such character, and even when Mr. Stearns was himself present at such public meetings he insisted that his agent should do the speaking. He invited Mr. Langston to meet him first at Buffalo, New

York, for consultation. Subsequently, he invited him to meet a large company of friends interested in the work at Philadelphia, Pennsylvania. After this last conference, Mr. Langston entered vigorously, by request of Mr. Stearns and by arrangement made with him, upon the recruitment of the 54th Massachusetts Regiment. His success in this work, especially in the States of Ohio, Indiana and Illinois, was entirely satisfactory, and although a very large number of men—perhaps three thousand or more—was sent to Massachusetts from which to select choice ones for the regiment, its recruitment was soon accomplished. The last seventy-five men taken into Company K, were sent from Xenia, Ohio, where recruited, to Camp Meigs, Massachusetts. Quite immediately upon their enlistment, the regiment was moved to South Carolina, and within a very short time, under its illustrious commanding officer, Colonel Shaw, made its famous charge upon Fort Wagner. Every one of these seventy-five men, young, vigorous, manly, and brave, fell in this charge. They fell with Shaw, and sleep in graves as honorable as his!

A single incident connected with the recruitment of these men is worthy of special mention. The son of an aged black woman living a mile or more out of Xenia upon the public highway, was one of their number. He was her only son, in fact her only child, and she relied upon him for support and protection. This mother called upon Mr. Langston, just after her son had bidden her farewell and left his home. Her heart was evidently moved by the deepest feeling as she thought of him, the dangers which awaited him, and realized that she might not see him again. As she entered the house, inquiring for the man who was inducing and enlisting persons to go to the war, it was feared that she had come, perhaps, to make complaint in violent and untempered language. Her bearing and manner, however, soon removed all such feeling. And, as she opened her mouth, she discovered in the midst of her sadness a temper of remarkable intelligence and good nature. She had not come to make complaint. Instead, she came to say that while she regretted the loss of her son, she wanted him, now that he had gone, to enter the service intelligently, with manly purpose, and to discharge his duty as an American soldier with courage and vigor. She asked that he be, accordingly, fully instructed and disciplined, so that such would be his course. In every word and act she manifested the spirit and devotion of an earnest and worthy American mother. When assured that the greatest care would be taken not only to instruct and discipline, but to protect her son, consistently with the faithful discharge of his duties as a soldier, she expressed full confidence in the statement and the hope that not only all might go well with her child, but that the cause of the government and the welfare of her people might be promoted, if need be, even in his death. "For," said she, "liberty is better than life." As already stated, her son went out to die, making her offering to the country and the cause of her people a precious and costly one. The number of colored mothers who thus gave their only sons, and who might detail in sympathetic words their own similar experiences with those of this one, shall never be known. Fortunately, however, for the country, no one of them is found, even to this day, who would offer any word of complaint. They are all too proud that they were permitted to bear sons, who at last should constitute their richest gifts to the republic.

The 54th Massachusetts Regiment was one composed of selected men. Its *personnel* was of the highest character. Many of the first colored families had representatives in it, and many of the very best young colored men were numbered among its troops. The roster of its commissioned officers showed the names of the very finest representative young white men, chosen and appointed as well with reference to their social position and family connections, as to their qualifications for their several duties. For it was the purpose of the friends of the experiment which this regiment should make in connection with the national service, to wisely and thoroughly furnish it in officers, men and every appointment for the work which it was called to perform. Besides, every care was exercised to put the regiment, while in camp, in the best possible physical, moral and mental condition and discipline for the field. No regiment ever left its camp followed by more hearty anxieties and earnest prayers for its welfare than this one. And no State ever exhibited deeper interest in the success of any portion of its soldiery, than Massachusetts for the troops of its 54th Regiment. Governor Andrew and his agent, Mr. Stearns, appreciated most fully the expectations which were entertained with regard to this enterprise inaugurated by them and the experiences which must await the men of their first regiment. The men were not themselves unconscious of the dignity, responsibility and danger of their position, and yet they advanced to the full discharge of their duties with intelligent American courage. The proof of this is shown in the patriotic, shining record which this regiment made for itself in contests requiring the best soldierly elements and behavior.

Upon the completion of the 54th, Mr. Stearns, with his full force, including of course Mr. Langston, undertook the recruitment of the 55th Massachusetts Regiment. Care was still taken as to the physical condition and make of the men enlisted and forwarded to Camp Meigs, and it is to be said with truth that this was also a regiment of selected men. They were, however, mainly enlisted in and sent from Ohio. At this time denied, especially in that State, the opportunity and privilege of enlistment for the public service on common equal terms, the colored men of Ohio had very generally resolved to leave their own State, and going to Massachusetts, enter the service as citizens of that Commonwealth. More than this, Ohio had provided no bounties for such troops, while Massachusetts had, and the latter had made arrangements through state appropriation for equalizing the pay of colored troops from that State with that of white troops, and all allowances were identical in value and character. It is not difficult to understand how such considerations would operate in determining the action of the colored men. When it is added that they had already come to understand that Governor Andrew and Mr. Stearns were special friends of their race, and would see to it beyond doubt that they had fair treatment in all respects, in the camp and in the field, their action in such regard would seem to be under the circumstances, natural and inevitable. So far as the major portion of the regiment was concerned, it was composed of Ohio men; so much so that Mr. Langston, who supervised and directed its recruitment, determined to have made in his own state and at his own expense, a full stand of regimental colors for it. Accordingly, colors were purchased as ordered and made by Scheilotto & Co., Cincinnati, Ohio. To this arrangement Governor Andrew and Mr. Stearns gave their ready assent and the colors, made of the very finest materials used for such purposes, were on the completion of its recruitment, forwarded by express to Camp Meigs and formally and duly presented. They were borne in pride by the regiment from the camp to the field, in every battle in which it played a part, and returned at last, bearing all the marks of patriotic, brave service, to the capitol of the Commonwealth of Massachusetts, where they can be seen this day, as sacredly kept among the precious relics of the War of the Rebellion.

At first Mr. Langston had intended to deliver the colors in person to the 55th Massachusetts Regiment, and was on his way with them, when on reaching Columbus, Ohio, the governor of the State, the Hon. David Todd, hearing that he was in the city, invited him to call for a special interview. He did so, when to his surprise the governor asked him to engage in the recruitment of colored troops for his state. Heretofore, about one year before this call, Mr. Langston had suggested to Governor Todd that he would be glad, were it agreeable to his feelings and judgment, to recruit and locate a regiment of a thousand and one colored men in Camp Delaware, without expense of a single dollar to the state government, upon the sole condition that they be received, duly organized, officered and employed as regular soldiers in the national service; to all of which the governor made reply of most remarkable character, but what under the circumstances in his State and the country seemed to be altogether natural. This meeting occurred prior of course to the convention of loyal governors, and the answer which he made was a reflection of the general feeling obtaining in the country with respect to the status of the colored American and his relations to the government. His reply was in substance as follows: "Do you not know, Mr. Langston, that this is a *white man's* government; that white men are able to defend and protect it, and that to enlist a negro soldier would be to drive every white man out of the service? When we want you colored men we will notify you." To which Mr. Langston made respectful reply, "Governor, when you need us, send for us." But now a great change had come over the feelings and the judgment of Governor Todd, and he had actually sent for the very man to whom he had made the speech given, and who had made the promise implied in his response. However, Mr. Langston occupied another position than that in which he stood when he tendered his services in connection with the proposed Ohio regiment of the year before. So he explained to the governor and advised him that he could do now no recruiting even in Ohio, without the authority and direction of Mr. Stearns, as he might issue his orders to such effect by command of the secretary of war. He also informed the governor that he had just completed the recruitment of the 55th Massachusetts Regiment, which was composed mainly of Ohio men, and that he was then on his way to Camp Meigs with a stand of regimental colors, purchased as they had been ordered expressly for this regiment. The governor manifested such interest in the matter that he insisted that Mr. Langston allow him to send a porter to his hotel for the box containing the colors, that he might see and examine them. This was done without the least hesitation, and so soon as brought and the governor had seen them, he pronounced them so beautiful and the purpose for which they had been secured so important and interesting, that he wanted them exhibited from the eastern steps of the capitol to a popular gathering, miscellaneous and general, which he offered to call together upon condition that Mr. Langston would make what he called "a war speech." To this proposition the governor was told that it was necessary for the colors to be delivered in Massachusetts at an early day, and that any considerable delay in such respect might work serious embarrassment. However, upon reflection and a little calculation of dates, a hurried meeting was agreed upon and subsequently held. Meantime, in a second visit to Governor Todd, and after he had communicated by telegraph both with Mr. Stearns and Secretary Stanton, it was settled that Mr. Langston should send the colors forward by express and proceed at once to the recruitment of a regiment of colored troops which should be credited to Ohio. The governor accordingly himself had the colors sent forward and he, his private secretary Judge Hoffman, and Mr. Langston made without the least delay all necessary arrangements for the recruitment of the Ohio regiment.

The 5th United States colored troops was the regiment referred to, and it was composed of young Ohio men, in the main of excellent physique, character and courage. Perhaps no braver men ever saw service among any class of people at any period in the history of the world than those who constituted its rank and file. The first three hundred men recruited were deceived by statements with respect to their monthly pay and allowances for clothing. This mistake under the circumstances, was the result of the belief and opinion that the men of Ohio would be treated precisely as those enlisted for Massachusetts, and was wholly natural. In a conference with Judge Hoffman, it was discovered that the rule of law applying to the national service in accordance with which the pay and allowances of the Ohio troops must be regulated, differed from those applied to the Massachusetts troops, in that the national regulations failing in full and equal provision for the colored troops of the lastnamed State, that State made special provision in that behalf. Ohio did no such thing, and hence the error and mistake made as indicated. No sooner had this matter been brought to the attention of the governor than he held and ordered that the men already thus deceived and in rendezvous at Camp Delaware, must have full explanation made to them, and informed that they were all at liberty to return to their homes should they so decide to do, at the expense of the government; that no deception however made could be allowed in their case. At once full explanations were made to the men, the mistakes were pointed out with the greatest care and minuteness, and they advised that they were at liberty should they choose, to leave the camp for their homes. These men had been recruited in different parts of Ohio. About one-third of them came from Washington County, the other two-thirds from Athens and neighboring counties; all of the latter, however, in a single company, as they had been collected through the influence of their leader, who had calculated to enlist them finally for Massachusetts. Indeed, all these men at first had expected to be sent to that State for entry of the service. Their leaders were Messrs. Solomon Grimes of the first one-third mentioned, and Milton M. Holland of the other portion. These two persons, the latter but a mere boy, held their respective companies completely under their influence and control, and either, when the explanations alluded to were given, might have directed his men to leave the camp and they would have gone. However, Mr. Holland and his men were decided and manly at once in their course, thus greatly influencing Mr. Grimes and his men to remain, and so not a single man of the three hundred left the camp. All accepted the explanations as made in good faith, as they concluded the mistakes had been made without intent to do the least injury. Besides, the leaders and every man asserted that he was ready to accept the situation just as it was, and show his patriotism and devotion to his country in efforts and struggles for its defence which might cost him even his life. More beautiful, manly conduct was not exhibited in any camping-ground of the American soldier during the wars of the late Rebellion, than this of these colored troops of Ohio at Camp Delaware. Thereafter, the recruitment of the regiment was conducted with reasonable rapidity and success. Such was the conduct of the men coming to camp, and their reputation for considerate behavior, aptness and attention to drill and soldierly advancement, that all over the State, young colored men were moved to the emulation of their example, and towards the close of its recruitment in many cases sought place in the regiment. On its completion it showed in its *personnel*, a fine body of excellent men, of soldierly qualities and character. Ohio, so far as the rank and file of its best regiments were concerned, could boast of no better material in its representatives collected in any camp, and called as its soldiers to the defence of the government.

Great care was taken to make wise and judicious selections of commissioned officers for these troops. The colonel of the regiment was selected from among the scholars of the State with special reference to his personal respect and consideration of the class of people whose sons he would lead and command in the face of danger. Professor G. W. Shurtliff was a young man of extraordinarily high personal and social character, of strictly Christian principles and habits, with recognized reputation and influence as an abolitionist and friend of the negro race. He was besides a white person, in every sense manly, noble and brave. Every man in the regiment upon making his acquaintance, witnessing his behavior and bearing, became heartily and thoroughly devoted to him as to a faithful, staunch friend, always ready to do whatever he might for the good of his command. The lieutenant-colonel and all the other commissioned officers were white men of great fitness for their special duties and of like high personal and social name and position. The recruitment of the regiment, with the selection and commission of every officer, was completed by the early part of November, 1863. The white inhabitants residing in the neighborhood of Camp Delaware, were at first utterly opposed to having that camp occupied by colored troops. They feared every sort of disorderly, unbecoming conduct on their part, and dreaded them as a host of petty thieves coming among them to commit manifold and frightful depredations. White troops had been in rendezvous there, and it was their bad conduct largely which had superinduced this dread of the presence of the colored ones. However, it is not recorded in the doings of the camp, or remembered by the community, that a single act of vandalism or any conduct unbecoming an American soldier, stands charged against any one of the men composing this regiment, while in camp. It remained there, from the date of the arrival of its first men to that of its departure, for a little over four months. The leading white men of the neighborhood were open and positive in expressions favoring the good conduct of the men. Such record made in camp and by the first regiment of colored men recruited in Ohio, was regarded by all friends of the race as most important and favorable.

Mr. Langston was determined that no regiment going into the service of the government should do so under richer or more beautiful colors than this one. And he was equally determined that they should not leave the camp without suitable and impressive ceremonies in connection with their presentation. He therefore made arrangements with the firm of Scheilotto & Co., of Cincinnati, to make for it a stand of first-class regimental colors. He provided for presenting them at the camp on the day before the regiment was to leave for the field. Governor Todd, ex-Governor William Dennison, with several other leading citizens, prominent in the State, had been invited and were present and took part in the exercises. The principal speech of the occasion was made to the full regiment, with every officer present, by the governor himself. He appreciated fully the real character of the circumstances, and moved in accordance therewith, he made an address of remarkable and peculiar power and effect. It was solemn, earnest, pathetic, impressive and eloquent. He reached the climax however, when in closing he said to the regiment, "My boys, sons of the State, go forth now as you are called to fight for our country and its government! Let your

210a

PRESENTATION OF COLORS TO 5TH U. S. COLORED TROOPS, CAMP DELAWARE, OHIO, 1863

210b

conduct be that of brave, intelligent devoted, American citizens! If such shall be your course, if spared and I can reach you no otherwise, on your return I will come upon my hands and knees to meet and greet you! And my words of commendation and praise shall be prompted by my pride and satisfaction in view of your behavior! But, should your conduct be that of cowards, showing your forgetfulness of the fearful responsibility which now rests upon your shoulders and the supreme dignity of the mission to which your government calls and this State sends you, as you return, I will crawl if need be, away from you, that I may never look again in your faces! I have, however, full confidence in you; and my prayer to Almighty God is that He will protect while He gives you victory in every battle in which you may be called to take part." This address was received in the spirit with which it was delivered, and accepted by the men as the parting counsel of one deeply and cordially interested in their welfare. Every circumstance and feature of this occasion was marked by the happiest, though solemn indications of prospective success. Accepting its colors from the hands of a distinguished ex-governor of the State, who above all others present could employ words befitting that service, tender, generous and affecting, the regiment discovered in its deep emotion and intelligent expression of its feelings, as shown in the response of Colonel Shurtliff, its appreciation and value of the honor done it in their presentation. The record which the regiment made in the desperate and deadly struggles in which it played important conspicuous part under those colors about Richmond and Petersburgh, shall tell whether they bore them bravely in glory to the end!

No state bounty had been provided by the government of Ohio for these troops. Massachusetts had done her duty in such behalf for her colored troops in generous provision. Mr. Langston, therefore, undertook to raise by voluntary contribution, at least money enough to make a small purse, to be presented to every man of the regiment on the day that the colors were given. He succeeded in collecting only enough to give each soldier two dollars and a half. This sum, in view of the very kind treatment which the commandant of the post, Colonel McCoy, had shown the regiment, and in view of its very great respect and love of him, was used to purchase presents for himself and his wife. The gift to him was a fine gold watch, and that to his wife a rich, costly and elegant ring. Mr. Langston presented the gifts in the name of the regiment to the commandant. This officer was so deeply moved and affected by this unexpected proceeding, that he was compelled, in the midst of his tears even, to ask ex-Governer Dennison to thank the regiment for himself and Mrs. McCoy.

The regiment leaving Camp Delaware in the early part of November, 1863, went directly to Portsmouth, Virginia, taking its place in the Army of the James, in that Department of that State. Very shortly it was ordered into active service, and figured with unsurpassed courage and brilliancy in at least ten battles about Richmond and Petersburgh, winning special distinction in its charge upon New Market Heights. Its courage, gallantry and endurance were put to the test, indeed, in this charge which gave it such note. The names of several young men connected with this regiment, especially certain of its non-commissioned officers, who, by reason of the sad havoc made among its commissioned ones in killed and wounded, were permitted to and did make honorable records in hot, deadly battle, might be mentioned. Indeed, their names shall be written here, because of the merits and deserts of those who bear them, and because they represent a great class whose highest aspiration is discovered in their desire and determination to serve, even unto death, their country and its government. Milton M. Holland, Powhatan Beatty, Robert A. Pinn, James S. Tyler, James Bronson, not to mention others, constitute a galaxy of heroes, who by exemplary, manly, and daring conduct, as officers and men of the 5th United States colored troops, are entitled to signal fame and renown.

An incident connected with the recruitment of Milton M.

Holland and the men whom he held under his command, when Mr. Langston commenced his work in connection with the enlistment of troops for this regiment, is worthy of special note here. Mr. Stearns had sent to Ohio a young white gentleman to assist in the recruitment of the regiment, who while active and energetic, was a person of unusual moderation and wisdom. He was especially successful, as a rule, in all errands of business upon which he might be sent to any given person or place. Of amiable disposition and pleasing manners, he soon won favor with men wherever found, who were inclined to enter the United States service. Such was his kindly treatment of every colored person, that he was not long, when he had opportunity, in bringing such one to clear and decided sense of his duty in the matter of his enlistment. Learning of Holland and his men as situated in a temporary unofficial camp in the Fair Grounds of Athens County, near the city of Athens, Ohio, Mr. Langston, desirous to secure their enlistment for the Ohio regiment, sent the gentleman spoken of, his assistant, Captain Dunlop, to Athens to meet, confer with, recruit and bring them at once to Camp Delaware. The men were found in camp as stated; but so determined to go to Massachusetts, there enlist and be credited to that State as the men of the 54th and 55th Regiments had been, that they would not allow him, or any other person to enter their camp grounds to talk with them of their enlistment in Ohio. Captain Dunlop was compelled to telegraph these facts to Mr. Langston, and he was compelled himself to go to Athens and seek approach to Mr. Holland and his men through special white friends in whom they had great confidence. No man could reach the men except as he did it through their captain, as they called Mr. Holland. He was a young colored Texan, sent North and located as a student at that time in the Albany Colored School, prominent in that part of Ohio. He was by nature a soldier. He smelt battle from afar, and was ready at the shortest warning to engage in deadly conflict. At the time he was really a lad of about nineteen years of age, with all the fire of such youthful, daring nature as he possessed in blood and by inheritance. He was a young person of remarkable native intelligence, good name, bearing himself constantly, even among his men, so as to win the largest respect and confidence. The promise of manly life and endeavor were apparent in his case on the most casual observation and contact.

Mr. Langston took the precaution on reaching Athens, having learned somewhat of this young man and of those by whom he was regarded and treated with special consideration, to call upon the chief business man of the town, the leading banker, Mr. Moore, a person well known and of the greatest respectability, to ascertain what he might with respect to him and the men generally under his control, and whether the community favored the recruitment of the state regiment of colored men. He found that Mr. Moore was exactly the man to answer every question respecting such matters with intelligence. He was so entirely acquainted with Mr. Holland and the men controlled by him, and had such influence and entertained such feelings, that he was able and did bring Mr. Langston at once into such relations to all concerned, that the work in view was accomplished very speedily and with the least possible difficulty. He even went so far as to put his fine saddle-horse at the disposal of Mr. Langston, to ride to the camp grounds, a mile away, and to give him a note of introduction which proved wholly satisfactory in securing the attention and confidence of those to be reached. It was about five o'clock in the afternoon on a beautiful day in June, and in a section of the country famous for its richness and delightsome conditions, that Mr. Langston, armed as indicated, approached the gate of the Fair Grounds where he would find the men whom he sought. A sentinel was on guard, and it was very apparent that he must be treated with becoming consideration and respect by any one who would through him secure communication with the commanding officer. Such etiquette was duly observed, and it was not long before the visitor was confronted at the gate by the student-officer in command.

The note of introduction was at once presented, when formal salutations and compliments were passed, and the two persons up to that time utter strangers, seemed to be wholly at home with each other. The errand of the visitor was made known with careful detail, and information given that no colored troops would be sent from that date to Massachusetts from Ohio, while a regiment would be at once recruited of such men and duly credited to Ohio. Upon this statement, with the request that he might bring the subject of their enlistment for the regiment to the attention of his men and take their decision in the premises, Mr. Holland replied that he would at once consult with them, and if he found them willing to do so he would make all the necessary arrangements to that end without the least delay. He retired, going to his headquarters, and within a very few minutes the fife and drum were heard and the gathering of the men near headquarters was immediately witnessed. Not tarrying in his movements, the young man returned, and inviting Mr. Langston in most polite manner to enter the camp, directed his sentinel to let him pass. Dismounting, as conducted by Mr. Holland, Mr. Langston went directly to the headquarters, where the men all drawn up in hollow-square awaited his arrival, and his statements and explanations. The manner and behavior of the young colored officer during this whole affair was that of a youthful, brave American, hopeful of an early opportunity to display any courage which he might possess in a battle the results of which would work the salvation of his country. It is enough to say here that in less than an hour and a half from the time he and Mr. Langston exchanged salutations, through his good offices he and his one hundred and forty-nine men had signed the recruitment rolls, and had promised to leave the Athens County Fair Grounds for Camp Delaware the next day at ten o'clock in the morning.

During the night the good banker, Mr. E. H. Moore, to whose great kindness so much was due for any success attending this transaction, sent in great haste to Cincinnati, to purchase a beautiful silk company flag, to be presented early on the following morning to the men as they left their camp grounds, passing through the city on the way to the depot to take the train, via Chillicothe, to Camp Delaware. The flag arrived in due season, and was formally presented with no little *éclat*. The men had left the Fair Grounds in good spirit and in fair general condition, and it is not saying too much to state that they made a fine impression in their parade and conduct, in the city and upon the community. The presentation speech was made by a young gentleman, the son of the donor of the flag, Colonel Moore. His address was full of stirring sentiments, highly ornate and affecting. The response on behalf of the men was made by Mr. Langston himself, in such spirit and manner as to gain not only the favor and applause of those in whose name he spoke, but the sympathy and good will of the vast concourse of loyal citizens who heard him. From Athens through Chillicothe and Columbus to Camp Delaware, such were the bearing and behavior of these men, that they constantly won popular admiration and applause. Throughout their camp experiences, labors and struggles, they maintained, however tried and tested, unsullied reputations.

In the charge at New Market Heights, the young Texan student who figured as described in the Athens County Fair Grounds, now become a veteran in service if not in years, the color-sergeant of the regiment, when he had discovered how his troops had lost in the early stages of the charge, well-nigh all its commissioned officers, including especially the colonel and lieutenant-colonel, under the pressure of the deepest excitement and in the purpose to achieve victory or die, passing his colors to another soldier of the regiment, took himself command of Company C, of which he had been made at first the orderly-sergeant, and with it led the charge, winning a victory which brought not only large favorable results to the government, but additional and signal glory to American arms. It was in this charge, requiring the best elements of the genuine brave American soldier, indifferent to danger and determined to snatch success from desperate odds, that the young colored men whose names have been recorded, won as well their distinction as their medals of bronze and silver.

In a conversation had with Gen. B. F. Butler, just after the war and his election to the House of Representatives, in speaking of the 5th United States colored troops, its colonel and its behavior during its service, especially its charge at New Market Heights, he said in warm emphatic manner to Mr. Langston, " I had only to command and Shurtliff with his regiment would attempt and perform any feat of daring and danger. He and his men constituted the very best soldierly material—their morale was of the highest and best character. The regiment was one of the very best of the national service." Continuing, he said, " This regiment made its celebrated charge under my observation, and while every man performed his duty with courage and devotion, those to whom I awarded medals demeaned themselves with such heroism as to merit at once the commendation of their commanding officers and the praise and gratitude of the country. So far as the conduct of the color-sergeant, Holland, was concerned, in the charge at New Market Heights, had it been within my power I would have conferred upon him in view of it, a brigadier-generalship for gallantry on the field."

Recruited for three years, or until the close of the war, this regiment having gained and occupied conspicuous rank among the best that had fought to maintain the Union, preserve and sustain free institutions, with slavery everywhere abolished, returned, with victory perching on every banner of the national government, the Rebellion fully suppressed, without a blemish on name or character, distinguished for the glory which its patriotism and courage had won. It went to Camp Chase, Ohio, where with seven hundred of its original recruits, it was mustered out of the service, October 5th, 1865.

CHAPTER XVI.

HIS FIRST OFFICIAL ERRAND TO THE NATIONAL CAPITAL.

ABRAHAM LINCOLN had been elected president of the United States for the second time. Andrew Johnson had been elected vice-president. Both had been inaugurated and had entered upon the duties of their respective offices. Grant, the great Captain of the century, the commanding officer of the American army, still confronted the leader of the Confederate forces, and not even the matchless secretary of war, Stanton himself, could say that the close of the bloody contest was at hand, and peace must soon be declared, with victory gained by the national soldiery. To the common observer it seemed as if war must still be waged. Notwithstanding two years and more had passed, since on the first day of January, 1863, the Emancipation Proclamation had been issued, the forces of the Confederacy continued their defiance of the government, and in numbers, purpose and courage, seemed far from defeat and general surrender.

It was under such circumstances that Mr. Langston, after he had completed his services in the recruitment of colored troops for the regiments of Massachusetts and Ohio, made his first official visit to Washington city. It is to be added, that wherever opportunity had been given, all along the lines of battle, the colored troops, in whatsoever service they were engaged, had demonstrated their possession of all those elements of obedience, endurance, fortitude, loyalty, enthusiasm and devotion, always deemed necessary in the highest and best type of the reliable and worthy soldier. Up to this time, two colored men only, had been given commissions as regular officers of the national army. Martin R. Delaney and Orindatus S. B. Wall were the persons who had thus been signally honored. The first bore the commission of major, the second that of captain. Both had been given duty in connection with the recruitment of colored troops. They had not at this time been assigned to service, either in a company or regiment, according to their official designations. It is true, too, that the large number of non-commissioned officers found in the various regiments of colored troops, had not only demonstrated excellent military capacity and aptness, but great general warlike knowledge, coolness and decision in the midst of emergency and danger, as well as readiness and alacrity in the discharge of their duties, however manifold and trying. The government had discovered, certainly, that they composed a loyal military corps, worthy of every confidence, in view of their intelligence, patriotism and devotion, and that their instruction, drill and experience must have fitted them for any official position or duty to which they might be called. This, without doubt, was true of a very considerable number, at least, of such officers.

Mr. Langston's errand was indeed official; but he had not made a journey to the capital to ask for an ordinary place under the new administration. Nor was he seeking a position free from responsibility and danger. The civil service may have been inviting to persons far more intelligent, patriotic and worthy; but his attention and desires were not directed to anything connected therewith. He had come at his own expense, moved by patriotic considerations, to say to President Lincoln and Secretary Stanton that the time had arrived, in view of the intelligence, experience, loyalty and service of the colored troops, for the commission of a colored man to a colonelcy in the national service, with authority to recruit his own regiment and to officer it with colored men taken from regiments already in the service and who had given evidence of high soldierly qualities on the field of battle. Upon his visit with this mission in view, he being well acquainted with and the friend of Gen. James A. Garfield, then a member of Congress, having left the field to serve his constituents and the people generally in that capacity, Mr. Langston went directly to him to seek his good offices in introducing him properly to the secretary of war, and his counsel and advice with respect to and approval of his plan. He found the young, magnificent representative of Ohio, and the brilliant general who had won such enviable note and name through his masterly deeds upon the field, not only willing to do what he asked, but patient to hear and counsel him with respect to his novel but important proposition. He was prompt, earnest and enthusiastic in his approval, and without the least hesitation conducted his colored Ohio friend, with whom he seemed specially pleased, for introduction to the prince of military secretaries, whose frown or approval had dismayed or delighted so many aspirants for high martial position and responsibility. Indeed, such were the appearance, manner, address and bearing of this great secretary to the ordinary visitor, that even the bravest of his fellow-citizens approached him with anxiety and manifestations of timidity. Not so, however, with Garfield. He was a brave and fearless man; always bold, clear and positive in the advocacy of any measure or individual in whose promotion and interest he desired to exercise his judgment and efforts.

General Garfield, in the introduction which he made of his friend to Secretary Stanton, did not hesitate to speak of him in most favorable terms, dwelling in warmest approval upon his character, his ability, his loyalty, and his valuable services rendered in the recruitment of troops for the 54th and 55th Massachusetts regiments, the 5th United States colored troops; his employment of a substitute for himself for the service, when in no wise exposed to draft, or any enforced military duty, and other evidences furnished in his conduct, showing his devotion to the government and its support. He also dwelt in earnest, intelligent, patriotic words upon the wisdom, dignity, propriety and advantage which characterized and would be the natural results following the adoption of the proposition submitted for the recruitment and organization of an entirely colored regiment. He did not hesitate to affirm that the government might expect on the part of such a regiment, conduct of the highest soldierlike character, with the largest measure of advantageous signal effects. Upon this representation, in connection with such favorable introduction to the secretary, who was himself a citizen of Ohio, it was under the circumstances entirely natural that both the originator of the proposition and the proposition itself should secure favorable consideration. The secretary even went so far as to express his own pleasure in view of what might be made, under wise direction and management, important results of the enterprise suggested, and was pleased to request General Garfield to go directly with Mr. Langston to Colonel Foster, who was at the time in charge of the recruitment of all colored troops, and explain to him upon introduction of his friend the measure proposed. He assured General Garfield that if upon thorough examination of the matter by the proper officer of his department, it was found to be feasible and probably advantageous, he should approve it. The visit to Colonel Foster was in no sense less agreeable than that to his chief officer, and his appreciation of the proposition and its author, with whom he seemed to be well acquainted by report, was not less hearty and cordial. So soon as Colonel Foster had the matter suitably explained, he promised that it should have his serious, prompt attention, and without delay he would present his conclusions and decision in due form to the secretary, so that General Garfield and Mr. Langston could hear from the department upon the subject without any unnecessary delay. Pleased with their visits and interviews with these distinguished military officials, General Garfield and Mr. Langston separated, with the belief firmly settled in their minds that this new proposition for the military advancement of the colored troops, which must give them ample opportunity for the display of any military genius and original prowess which they possessed, led and commanded by officers of their own nationality and complexion, would receive the sanction and approval of the authorities.

Mr. Langston remained in the city of Washington while this matter was held under consideration. He was in the city when Gen. Robert E. Lee made his surrender on the ninth of April, 1865, and the Rebellion was thus brought to a hurried overthrow and its armies to utter defeat. Other and additional troops were no longer needed. Those in the service must be soon mustered out and return to their homes. For this reason the department very properly concluded not to adopt the measure suggested, and accordingly communicated its decision to that effect, shortly after the surrender, to those concerned.

Perhaps no proposition of any character whatever so deeply and thoroughly interested Mr. Langston as this one. He always felt that in it he saw the complete redemption of the colored American from every proscription, legal and social ; as he might make, upon his own original force of character and courage, a record thereby on the field of battle and in the shedding of his own blood in defence of the government and the country, which would emancipate him from every distinction felt and made against him. It was an opportunity of rare good fortune for him to be called, to the number of one hundred and eighty thousand, to fight with his fellow-citizens the battles of the country, though commanded by officers of another nationality and color. It would have been, however, immensely more advantageous to him, redounding to his lasting good, in a more just and considerate appreciation of his character and deeds, could he have engaged in battle for the country, led and commanded by those who bore his own lineage and image. Another great fearful emergency of the government may bring him such opportunity. If so his salvation, as indicated, need not be despaired of, for it shall come, thus, certainly, even though greatly delayed. The experiences of this, like

FIRST OFFICIAL VISIT TO WASHINGTON.

all other governments which have been established by man, are signalized throughout their existence by urgent and pressing occasions of trial and struggle, which require the devotion and service of all good citizens, and in view of duty well and thoroughly done under such circumstances, the loyal and true who demonstrate ability and worth may make sure of their reward, in equal impartial justice and fair equitable treatment.

It was during Mr. Langston's sojourn in the capital at this time, that the horror of horrors took place. Two nights before, he had stood with the multitude looking into the face and listening to the words of the president, who while he spoke like a prophet, reminding one of the ancient Samuel as he called the people to witness his integrity, little dreamed that any man in the whole land could be found base and cowardly enough to do him harm. His words seem now in view of his assassination so soon to follow, those of warning, admonition and counsel, grave and thrilling to his countrymen. How, without the least suspicion of danger to her husband, sat his good wife near him, apparently conscious in highest and profoundest sense of the estimate and value put by the people upon his services. For he was now a statesman without an equal; a leader, as grand in the immense proportions of his individuality as Moses himself; an emancipator of a race redeemed through the wise and sagacious adjustment of those moral and legal forces which constitute the glory of American Christian civilization, and the savior of a country which shall be at last the theater where shall be displayed the golden, precious drama of man's truest and noblest life and triumphs in freedom as conserved, promoted and sustained by impartial law. But the evil hour made haste, and the great city of his presidential residence, as well as the whole country, was startled and shocked with the announcement of the assassination of the immortal Abraham Lincoln.

Mr. Wade Hickman of Nashville, Tennessee, in Washington city at the time as the body-servant of Vice-president Andrew Johnson, brought the sad tidings of the occurrence to Mr. Langston. Coming to his hotel he called upon him, not only to bring that information, but to declare his purpose to allow no human being inimical to, or having designs upon, his life, to reach the vice-president, except as he did so over his dead body. The night of the terrible tragedy in Washington city was full of awful terrors, well-calculated to inspire one of the natural courage and devotion of Hickman to make this resolution and express it in his emphatic, positive terms. Besides, there was danger, as it seemed to him, that he might that night, in his attempt to protect and defend the vice-president, lose his own life. Hence he expressed the earnest request to Mr. Langston that should he fall in this work, which was to him serious and imperative, that he would make known to his family and his friends in Tennessee that he had fallen in meeting attack against a man who was then regarded as the friend of every negro in his State. Mr. Langston made faithful promise to his friend that he would discharge the duty enjoined, should there come necessity for so doing, with fidelity and truth. Fortunately however for the country, the vice-president was spared, and the brave negro who was at once his servant and his friend, though faithful as devoted, was not called to die in defence of the successor of the murdered president.

Mr. Langston, as early as November, 1864, had been invited by the colored people of Nashville, Tennessee, to visit and address them on the second day of January, 1865, when they with their fellow-citizens would celebrate the anniversary of the Proclamation of Emancipation, issued by President Lincoln, January 1st, 1863. Now, for the first time in the history of the race so far as the South was concerned, the colored people were to hold their meeting in the hall of the House of Representatives of the state capitol. Such high privilege had been accorded them through the influence of Hon. Andrew Johnson, who was then military governor of the State. Just before this time, in addressing this class of his fellow-citizens, he had declared could they find no other he would be their Moses; and accordingly he treated them with such consideration and kindness, as to win their respect and confidence. When, therefore, Mr. Langston debated the question as to his safety should he accept the invitation given and speak as requested, on making known his fears in such regard to his friends in Nashville, they secured and sent him a letter from Governor Johnson, in which he was assured of complete and entire protection, with the opportunity and privilege of the largest freedom of expression. Accordingly the invitation was accepted, and on the last day of December, 1864, Mr. Langston arrived in Nashville, where he was met by a committee of leading colored men, among whom was found Mr. Wade Hickman, here mentioned. His reception was, though formal, distinguished by every mark of high personal consideration and was most cordial and agreeable. He was at once presented to the governor, who welcomed him in kind terms, and bade him to rest assured of entire protection and freedom from the least molestation. At the same time he bade him to exercise in his address the largest freedom of sentiment and expression. More ; he added that he should be at the meeting himself, and expected to hear a speech which would justify the high hopes of those who were the promoters of and specially interested in the meeting.

At this time Nashville, so soon after the memorable battle had there between Generals Thomas and Hood, was full of troops, with their officers, a gallant dashing set of men, making even the community brilliant as well as lively by their presence. In a great audience, filling a hall like that of the House of Representatives, their attendance, as they came attired in full military dress, gave a striking impression and dazzling appearance to the assembly. The meeting was large and imposing, and besides being honored by a conspicuous array of military characters, was made noteworthy by the presence of the governor himself. No more interested and attentive auditor gave the orator of the occasion his respectful consideration. The whole day had been spent in public exercises, including a grand, enthusiastic parade, which so impressed the whole community as to give great popular *éclat* to the immense gathering which took place as described, in the evening at the capitol. Mr. Langston was greatly flattered by the attentions paid him by the governor, and was moved with special gratitude towards him, when after he had thanked him for and congratulated him upon his address, he invited him urgently to call at his office the next morning, saying as he did so, he had a service which he desired that he should perform. Before the one addressed could make reply, the great committee composed of Henry Harding, James Sumner, Buck Lewis, Abraham Smith, William C. Napier, Wade Hickman and others, answered through their chairman, "He shall call according to your request and we know he will be glad to do your bidding." Accordingly, as conducted by the committee, at eleven o'clock on the morning of the third day of January, Mr. Langston visited the governor to learn that he did really have a service of the most interesting and remarkable character, which he asked him to perform. Delicate and peculiar as the service was, Mr. Langston suggested respectfully that there was so much that seemed to him to be official connected with the matter, that he felt that no one could take the place of the governor in its performance. To which he answered, saying that while he appreciated the suggestion, he was not so far the master of his feelings as to trust himself in any attempt to perform it, and hence begged Mr. Langston to render him the help which he needed. This appeal secured the expected assent.

Thereupon Governor Johnson proceeded to inform Mr. Langston and the committee in substance how in the late fight between Thomas and Hood, thirty thousand raw negro recruits had been employed on the part of the government; that they were so located in the line of battle that it was possible for the Confederate general to bring to bear upon them his heaviest guns, and that he did so, feeling doubtless, that they constituted the weak point in the line, which if carried by him would certainly bring him victory and make his march through Tennessee and Kentucky to Ohio, a practicable result. He added that charge after charge was made upon these men, who reformed and took their places in firm position after each one, until in the last when victory was brought though indescribable slaughter to the forces of the government. They fought in many cases standing upon their comrades, wounded, dying and dead, in heaps. The exhibition of courage, fortitude, coolness and determination on their part, he claimed had not been surpassed by Roman, French, English, or American troops, under any circumstances, however well drilled and fitted for service. Continuing, he said he had wept, as in anxious, fearful mind, he witnessed their conduct, praying meantime, that in the manly stand which they might maintain, they would prove themselves the saviors of their country. Leaving the field in victory ten thousand only survived this terrible shock of arms. He said, "The ten thousand survivors are in camp upon the outskirts of this city. I want you, Mr. Langston, to go to their camp, and in the name of the government and the country, as I request you, to thank those men for their matchless services. Tell them that I do not come myself, because I could not face them without such feelings as would render me wholly incapable of addressing them. My feelings would entirely overcome me."

Arrangements were duly made, under the direction of Major Dewey, of one of the colored regiments referred to, and Mr. Langston in obedience to the request indicated, addressed the ten thousand colored troops with their officers. No attempt shall be made to describe the sight and impression afforded and made in the presence of these black heroes, who had won such distinction in the service of their country. It is enough to say that Mr. Langston used from the United States wagon which constituted his platform, as he stood before them gathered in hollow-square after military fashion, such words and expressions as seemed under the circumstances to be befitting. And yet all that he said seemed tame and lifeless in the presence of the manly deeds and achievements of the soldiers, who had served in such signal manner the government and the country. As he closed and was conducted and supported upon the tongue of the wagon to the ground, among others, officers and men, who saluted him in cordial complimentary terms, was an aged black man, clothed in the garb of a corporal. He was a person far advanced in years, with hair as white as the snow which slightly covered the earth. There was however no bend in his body and no dimness in his eye. Erect, quick and easy in his bearing, he looked the perfection of the soldier. His address to Mr. Langston was of familiar fatherly sort. For he employed towards him these words: "John, how are you?" To which reply was made: "You have the advantage of me." "Oh, yes," said he, "greatly the advantage. For when you did not weigh ten pounds, I held you in the hollow of this hand. I knew your mother when she first came upon Quarle's plantation, in Louisa County, Virginia. I knew your half-brother William and his two sisters, and your brothers, Gideon and Charles. Yes, I have the advantage of you." These words came to Mr. Langston as if from the "vasty deep," and from one who had known him as he had never known himself. To them all, astonished as he was to find a man of such age in the service, he inquired, "What, sir, are you doing here?" He answered, "John, I have entered the service to fight until there is no more slavery in this land." To this the statement came, "You never were a slave!" He quickly answered, "Always a slave, John, always a slave; but always a fugitive slave!" His look and manner showed this to be true. For his air and address were those of full consciousness of the dignity of his manhood. Mr. Langston bade him good-bye, and as he turned away, Major Dewey said to his companion, "That is the greatest man and the most influential of all the troops and the officers gathered here. His words inspirited and encouraged the men in the late great fight, making them firm, cool and reliable." The fugitive slave of Louisa County, once so feared, whose visit so terrified Uncle Billy, had thus become a leader and hero of his race and his country!

ADDRESSING THE COLORED TROOPS AT NASHVILLE, TENN., 1864

228b

The report of this wonderful proceeding characterized by flattering words of Major Dewey, with respect to Mr. Langston's address made in the name of the President of the United States and the Governor of Tennessee specially, proved to be wholly satisfactory and agreeable to Governor Johnson.

Having made the acquaintance, personally, of the distinguished military governor of Tennessee, under such unusual and agreeable circumstances, and having found Mr. Hickman, as indicated, near to him, in the intimate and responsible relations of his trusted servant and friend, it was entirely natural that Mr. Langston, who had supported Andrew Johnson upon the National Republican ticket for the vice-presidency, should have been greatly pleased at his meeting both such persons, as described, at the national capital. The circumstances, as the same concerned the assassination of the president, were grievous beyond expression, and moved by sentiments of the most exalted consideration and the deepest sorrow, he delayed his sojourn in the capital to witness the funeral ceremonies of a citizen whose name, though he be dead, is more synomymous and typical of the great principles of American civilization, as illustrated in great names and great moral, heroic deeds, than any other, save perhaps that of Washington himself. With respect to his funeral cortege, a single occurrence was witnessed which bore the most profound and interesting signification. Entire preparation had been made, even to the location of all troops to take part on this occasion in the parade, which, if ever surpassed in numbers, was never in dignity, conduct and effect. At the last moment, however, a negro regiment arrived, coming to the capital from tidewater Virginia. Its arrival was barely in season to be given place at the head of the procession, to do, in fact, the honor and sacred service of bearing the coffin of the great emancipator from the hearse to the catafalque, the temporary resting-place in the rotunda of the capitol. Such services, so honorable and sacred, were to have been performed by others. An Allwise Providence, however, so adjusted the order of affairs, as to give this high privilege to the representatives of the four millions whom he had emancipated. If ever fitness, moral propriety was seen under like circumstances, it was here fully realized, and can but be duly appreciated. Mr. Langston's heart was big with gratitude, his soul filled with thanksgiving, as standing near the southwest corner of the capitol, he saw the proud negro regiment leading the line of march down Pennsylvania Avenue, up Capitol Hill, to the east door of the building, where, as the procession halted, its representatives were permitted to bear, with tenderest care and silent affection, the mighty dead to his resting-place in state.

He prolonged his stay in Washington even a little longer that he might witness the results of the change in the government connected with the induction of the vice-president to the presidency of the United States. The orderly, peaceful accomplishment of this result was regarded with profound anxiety and interest by every intelligent citizen. This is always the case even in ordinary times. But under the circumstances, so unusual and stirring, popular and individual solicitude was excited profoundly and generally. However, all was done without the least disturbance or jar in the government machinery, complicated and delicate as it is, and all moved on smoothly and harmoniously, accomplishing naturally the usual important interests of the country. Before President Johnson had taken possession of the White House, while he occupied for official purposes quarters in the Treasury Building, Mr. Langston as chairman of a committee of colored men duly appointed and organized, waited upon the new president, and, in behalf of the colored people of the nation, expressed their hope that in him they would find a ruler, who like his predecessor, would see to it that every law which concerned their welfare was duly executed, and they protected and supported in the full measure of all those rights and privileges which pertain to American citizenship. In his answer to this address the president was earnest and positive in the promise that his colored fellow-citizens should find in him a friend mindful always of their welfare, and vigilant and vigorous in the execution of every law which had been enacted in their behalf. Besides, he assured the committee that to the extent of his ability and influence as the chief executive of the national government, he should exert himself to fix and entrench the abolition of slavery with the general enfranchisement of the colored citizen in suitable amendment of the Constitution of the United States. The impressions made by this meeting upon the minds of the committee were entirely favorable to President Johnson, and all left him with expressions of sincere, hearty good wishes for the success of his administration.

CHAPTER XVII.

HIS EARLY LABORS AND OBSERVATIONS AMONG THE FREED PEOPLE.

THE colored American had hardly been made free, the War of the Rebellion had not been closed, when Mr. Langston commenced his travels among the freed people. Thus, he gained broad and minute observation at once of their actual condition and probable future. On his visit to Nashville, Tennessee, made in the last days of 1864, he had reached Louisville, Kentucky, where his friends were outspoken and positive in their belief and assertion that it would be impossible for him to go in safety by train from that city to the former, to which he had been invited, and urged him not to attempt the trip. Up to the day on which he proposed to make that journey, few trains of cars had passed over the road going southward which had not been interrupted by Bushwackers, and in many cases thrown from the track, while the passengers were generally robbed and not infrequently treated in violent, abusive manner. He was not intimidated nor discouraged by these representations and facts, although they did create in his mind great anxiety and some fear. When it was found that he was fully decided to go, a friend of his, a colored man, well acquainted with that section of the country, and, hence, a person fully conscious of the danger about to be incurred, determined to take the train with him, carrying his carpet-sack, with all his papers, into the smoking car, while Mr. Langston should take his seat in the regular car provided for ladies and gentlemen. Leaving Louisville accordingly, the journey was made from city to city on the usual time, with all necessary stops made on the way and without any disturbance to the train. Numberless wrecks of great trains, passenger and freight, were seen in passing, thrown from the track. The train bearing Mr. Langston and his brave Kentucky negro friend, as indicated, arrived for the first time for months, as due at the depot in Nashville. Both were roundly congratulated by their friends upon this fortunate, though then uncommon result. The courageous conduct of Mr. William Howard in this case, merits special grateful mention, and shall never be forgotten nor neglected by the one whose interest he sought to protect and sustain at such danger and risk to himself. No example is furnished in the history of the colored people of the country, where one of their own number, moved by considerations respecting the welfare of another, shows larger manly, heroic behavior. Let the name of that person be written in enduring golden characters.

It was at this time and in this manner that Mr. Langston made his first general trip of observation of the colored people of the South, just now coming out of slavery and entering upon their new life of freedom in this country. Perhaps no better arrangement could have been made to secure from the very beginning for him, survey and contact of great bodies of such people, now in early movement, searching for a spot upon which to place their feet for life and its achievements. Now the army was near these people, and they felt its presence, as the emancipating and protecting power which the government had sent them. Even colored regiments, great bodies of colored troops, were seen, as they moved among them, by their presence and influence inspiring and encouraging the newly emancipated to earnest and manly effort in the hope of their improvement and progress. The sight of a people large in numbers, and peculiarly marked in nationality and experience, now just made free, was thrillingly interesting; and in spite of one's faith in God, as holding their destiny in His hands, and confidence in them to meet any duty and trial whereunto they were called, the question came spontaneously and irresistibly, What shall they do? Their condition was not promising; and yet, they moved at once and promptly, in intelligent, earnest and considerate activity, as if impelled and directed by an Allwise Supreme Power. Hungry, they seemed to know that they would be fed. Thirsty, they seemed to feel that they would be given springs of water. Naked, they seemed to be assured of abundant raiment. Houseless and homeless, they seemed to move in faith and confidence of certain provision. Such feelings did not beget idleness nor inattention to duty. Their reliance in an overruling Providence gave them earnestness, sobriety and wisdom of life. Their thoughts were easily directed and their purposes aroused to those duties which respected their education, the accumulation of property, the cultivation of all those virtues and habits which are indispensable in a country and under a government where they must build their homes and win their standing, commingling in ordinary enterprises of business, trade and labor, with the native and foreign elements which compose the population of the country.

In Kentucky and Tennessee, as well as other Southern States lying more nearly upon the border-line of freedom, were located then many colored people who had been free for a long time, born so or emancipated. Their presence was of incalculable advantage to those who were just leaving their slavery. They had, notwithstanding their hard condition socially, made some progress in earnest life. They had built for themselves churches; in some communities they had established schools for their children; they had in some cases accumulated considerable property and made for themselves small but desirable homes. Such families as the Alexanders, the Seals, the Goens, the Adamses, the Trabues and the Taylors represented this class in the first-named State, while the Napiers, the Hardings, the

Sumners, the Lowerys, the Smiths and the Churches represented it in the latter. The goodly example exhibited in the earnest and intelligent conduct and success of these persons, born and reared in their own midst and among the very class which once held them as slaves, did much toward influencing and directing those just made free, in the ways of improving and advancing manhood. Indeed, those who had started and made some little progress in those ways could, in their words, bid the others to follow; while their lives and good fortune, humble and small, offered a stern command as well as a lively impulse and motive to press forward with decision and courage. It is true that the government was represented even then among the freed people by its great Bureau with its numberless agents, but mainly to give a modicum of protection with its too small provision for food of rough and coarsest sort, in limited measure for the extremely needy. It is time, too, that the boundless and matchless charity of the North was represented by its great associations and devoted workers, discovering zeal and high purpose with respect to the good of these people. But no influence, however important, imposing and sustained, was from the beginning so potent as that of the free colored class, which, emancipated first and suitably prepared by its experience therefor, wrought now in example and effort to elevate and direct the thoughts and purposes of the millions just passing the gateways of liberty. While due recognition shall be made of all those charitable, philanthropical and Christian endeavors of good men and true women coming from all over the country, even those services of the government performed through Gen. O. O. Howard and the Freedman's Bureau, no failure must be had in the proper estimate and appreciation of God's providence, as shown in the gradual freedom of such numbers of the colored class as He would use in promoting the welfare of the great body of the people whom He would so soon and in such miraculous manner speak into freedom! Nor shall there be failure in the right estimate and appreciation of the happy and effective results of the wise and judicious behavior of these forerunners of the emancipated hosts.

What is here stated and claimed was illustrated and sustained in admirable manner by the colored men who managed and conducted the first great meeting which they held at Nashville, in the second year of the general emancipation. There was no white member of their executive committee. There was no white person called to assist with counsel or means. The colored men alone contributed the knowledge, skill and funds needed to make that meeting in every detail a wonderful success.

Of the women of the emancipated classes a fact must be mentioned, which was discoverable at once, and which is worthy of special and emphatic note. Allusion is made to the business understanding and tact of the average colored woman, who proved herself in every practical sense and way to be the leader in all moral and material enterprises adopted and undertaken for the advancement and promotion of their people, newly emancipated or other. They were foremost in designs and efforts for school, church and general industrial work for the race; always self-sacrificing and laborious; while they were not less apt and ready to accept in their own individual case, any proffered aid or support in such behalf, coming from the government, or any good people of the North or other quarter, through church or special association. In all such matters these women seemed to be guided by a high and extraordinary moral or spiritual instinct. Through all phases of his advancement, from his emancipation to his present position of social, political, educational, moral, religious and material status, the colored American is greatly indebted to the women of his race, who have wrought with wisdom and earnestness in his interest. This fact with respect to them and the inevitable results which must follow, was patent to the intelligent observer in the earliest days of emancipation. No history can be written of those early days of American freedom, with justice accorded to all who have played from the beginning a noteworthy part, without large place and truthful mention of the women of the freed classes. They have in their conduct and labors, so far as their race is concerned, emulated, largely, the "virtuous woman" of the Scriptures.

With his observation of the race commencing in such States as those named, including another of the border slave-holding States, Missouri, neighbor to the great northwestern Commonwealth made the theater by John Brown for his matchless deeds in favor of freedom, it may be very properly claimed for Mr. Langston, that his opportunities for early survey of the condition and probable prospects of the emancipated classes were of the most advantageous character. Many incidents connected with his travels and efforts among these people, under such circumstances, possess rare interest and significance.

It was on the fourth day of July, 1865, that Gen. John M. Palmer, then in command of the government forces in the State of Kentucky, and in general military control and management of public affairs, especially those which respected the negro classes, which, under his *régime*, were being rapidly emancipated, after due consultation with the president of the United States, called and addressed a vast assembly of such people in the suburbs of the city of Louisville. The meeting was immense in its numbers and remarkable in all its conditions. Three negro regiments, still in the service, with a great unbroken negro artillery company, were thrown about to guard and protect this gathering of a hundred thousand men and women, brought together to hear the welcome words of their freedom. They had never seen before the sun so bright, the skies so lovely, the breezes so balmy, and nature so charming, as now, on the memorable anniversary day of American independence. Sweeter, prouder and happier words were now to come to them than any they had ever heard. They were to be spoken by one whose words should not be like those of the Scribes and Pharisees, without authority. The orator of this grandest of all occasions to them, would speak in the name of American law and by authority of the most potent commanding force of the government. The people would hear proclamation, made by the military commanding officer in the name of the national government, of the utter overthrow of slavery in the State, and the full and complete freedom of the slave, so that he might not return at the command of anyone claiming to be his owner and master, to any service which was not the subject of his own choice, according to an honest and fair contract made with him. This step was to be taken in accordance with the judgment and approval of the president of the United States, Hon. Andrew Johnson, and would serve to answer and determine forever, all charges made against General Palmer by Kentucky slaveholders, who complained that he was engaged to their great annoyance and injury in freeing contrary to law, by a curious system of passes, all their slaves. It was apparent that the thousands who gathered, composing a vast, immense, expectant assembly, felt and realized the importance of the occasion. The arrival of General Palmer, in his carriage drawn by four horses, preceded by his band of music and followed by his imposing array of military and popular characters, was signalized by such a storm and flood of applause as has seldom greeted the ears and gladdened the heart of the most triumphant honored hero. The general had just returned from Washington, where he seemed to have gained special inspiration for his matchless task, and, as he rode in his carriage with two colored men seated therein near him, Rev. Henry Adams and John M. Langston, through the streets of the proud city of Louisville, he displayed no other feelings than those of confidence and satisfaction. He was now to perform his part in the work of general emancipation. He seemed conscious of the dignity and glory of the task. Well he might! All honor to him, he did it well! His speech to the people, brief as it was, was full of the deepest, the most far-reaching consequence, and the eloquence of its meaning and its happy effects could only be measured by the movement which it produced in the hearts and minds, in the feelings and purposes of his vast audience, whose response in applause came like the dashings of contending floods, in hottest, wildest contest. He concluded his wonderful utterance with the statement that: "*Now, by the Declaration of Independence, by the Constitution of the United States, by that law of our country which makes all of its inhabitants free, since our government is a democracy; as commanding officer of this Commonwealth, by the power and authority invested in me and upon the instruction and approval of the president of the United States, I do declare slavery forever abolished in this State.*" No speech heretofore made by any orator in the United States of America, had ever had such close and climax. No audience such as this had ever been addressed within the vast limits of the Union. And the fourth day of July, on which the American people are wont to magnify the blessings of liberty, as guaranteed to them in the free institutions established by the Fathers of the Republic, had never been honored by such expressions of high sentiments, fraught with the blessings of unconditional liberty to the poorest classes of the community. How the words of the general were received by those who with upturned faces and grateful hearts heard and rejoiced in them!

On this occasion, in the midst of such interesting, thrilling, patriotic circumstances, Mr. Langston, as specially invited, was introduced by General Palmer as he closed his address, as a representative of the American negro who could speak of the blessings and advantages which the people might expect to enjoy in their freedom as regulated and sustained by law. He must deliver a speech which would in no wise tend to abate the enthusiasm, disturb the happiness, lessen the gratitude or fail to inspire with the hope of a glad future, all those, however conditioned, who were for the first time then his auditors. How well he performed his task was shown in the deafening applause which followed its close, and in the graceful, apt and charming words of the prayer made by the noted colored Baptist minister, Mr. Adams, who, in thanking God for what was then and there witnessed and felt by the people, complimented Mr. Langston as he dwelt with emphasis in his thank-offering upon what he pleased to term, "the matchless, eloquent address of the young colored orator who had been permitted in such truth and power to instruct this vast gathering of former slaves, just now made free."

This constituted the second peculiarly interesting and unparalleled gathering of freed people, seen and addressed by Mr. Langston upon the very soil and in the midst of the very circumstances of their emancipation. And in such observation as he was able to make in public, and of the people in their private and domestic relations, he was so entirely delighted with all he witnessed as to be thoroughly persuaded in his feelings and judgment of the good future which, on the whole, must await the newly emancipated classes.

Occupied upon various occasions during the intervening and closing months of 1865, in addressing the freed people located in several of the chief cities of the border Southern States, early in 1866 Mr. Langston was invited to visit the city of St. Louis and there address his third great meeting of such people. They had arranged to celebrate their state emancipation, and upon special effort to that end brought together an immense, imposing meeting. The people came from every part of the State to its chief city, in response to private and public invitations, so that the vast audience chamber of Veranda Hall of that city lacked capacity for the accommodation of those who crowded it, occupying only standing room, after all seats had been removed, and even upon an admission fee of one dollar for each person in attendance. Immense and various as this assembly proved to be, it was representative, at least only of the upper and middling classes of the colored people, who were able to pay the charge indicated. As such, it was a remarkably fine one, unsurpassed in its appearance, its attention and general behavior. The address on this occasion was one in which the orator attempted to impress those lessons with respect to education, labor, thrift, forecast, economy, temperance and morality, which are indispensable to fair and permanent progress in freedom. It was received with the deepest earnestness and the most profound appreciation, being interrupted only from time to time by the approval of the people, as demonstrated in the outbursts of their applause.

At this time the Constitutional Convention of the State of Missouri was in session, and had reached that part of its work which concerned the consideration and adoption of a provision, which, while it secured the freedom, gave equal civil rights to the freed people. This subject was pending before the convention, but grave doubt was felt very generally by the class immediately interested, especially the more intelligent among them and their friends, that the full measure of civil rights might not be given them. Invitation, therefore, was extended to Mr. Langston to address the Constitutional Convention in favor of the colored people of the State, urging in their behalf such just and legal consideration as to lead to the gift of full, equal civil rights at least, under the new Constitution. This invitation, with the duty which it implied, was accepted, and on the next night, after he had delivered the address already mentioned, upon due and ample preparations, he did address the Constitutional Convention. Every member of the convention was present and heard him with solemn, serious attention, in Veranda Hall, and in the midst of a vast concourse of colored people who were directly and deeply interested in the proceedings of the meeting. Though the address was lengthy, it was heard from beginning to end with great patience. At the great dinner given the members of the Constitutional Convention and the distinguished guests who were present, Mr. Langston was not only given a seat of special honor, but his speech was made the subject of many flattering expressions with respect to the law, the logic, the morality, the learning, the justice and the humanity which it embodied. The late Hon. Charles D. Drake, perhaps the foremost member of the Convention, subsequently a member of the United States Senate and more latterly chief justice of the United States Court of Claims, was peculiarly kind and pleasant in his expressions with regard to it. And it is a very delightful matter of record, that the Constitution was so framed and ratified as to provide for the colored people of the State their full measure and equality of civil rights.

In connection with these meetings other names deserve special mention, some as exerting great influence in their promotion and success, and others, younger, as inspired and impelled to exalted resolve and effort. All these last, the promoters of the meetings and those specially blessed thereby, now referred to, were of the emancipated class. Rev. M. M. Clarke, a leading minister of the A. M. E. Church; Revs. J. W. White and W. P. Brooks, ministers of the Baptist; and Messrs. P. G. Wells and Alfred White, were all full of zeal and energy at this time in promoting the common cause of the people. The last two had won, even at that time, enviable names, as earnest and laborious business men. Messrs. William Gray and J. Milton Turner, both young men without name, inspired and impelled by the influences then exerted upon their susceptible and aspiring minds, have become since, by earnest and persistent efforts, orators of rare ability, and have won high place among the foremost of their race. Clarke, Wells and Gray sleep among the dead! The remembrance and influence of their goodly lives still survive. Messrs. White, Brooks and Turner are still active and earnest in labors for the good of the people. Mr. Turner has within the past few years added to his name and standing, by filling with distinction and success a position of great dignity and responsibility, as the minister resident and consul-general of this government near that of Liberia.

Upon the close of his labors connected with these meetings, Mr. Langston was engaged by the same executive committee through whose influence and patronage he had visited St. Louis, to make a canvass of the States of Missouri and Kansas, with special reference to visits and addresses in the larger cities of those States to the colored people. Their enlightenment and inspiration with respect to their life in freedom, the obligations and duties which it imposed and the future of blessing and reward which they might hope for should they meet such duties and obliga-

EARLY LABORS AMONG THE FREED PEOPLE. 243

tions with intelligence and vigor, were to constitute the themes to be explained and enforced. Besides general meetings as indicated, Mr. Langston was to address the Legislatures, respectively of Kansas and Missouri, at Topeka and Jefferson City. It was deemed necessary and proper to address thus the legislators of these States upon the law concerning the status of the colored American, now set free, in order that in any attempts which might be made to legislate specially in his case they might be guided in such efforts with wisdom and good understanding.

Arrangements having been completed, Mr. Langston entered without delay upon his work, making speeches in St. Louis, at Macon City, at Hannibal, at Chillicothe, and at St. Joseph, in the State of Missouri; and at Atchison, Leavenworth, Wyandotte, Lawrence and Topeka, in Kansas. The meetings at all these places were large and enthusiastic. The white as well as the colored people turned out at every point in large numbers, and the journals of the various cities made free, full, and for the most part favorable comments upon the addresses delivered. The meeting at Topeka, where the Legislature as prearranged was addressed, proved to be a very great success. The Hall of Representatives was greatly wanting in capacity to accommodate the large number of people anxious to hear the speech. The attention and consideration given the speaker both by the law-makers of the State and the people, were entirely satisfactory and augured well for the colored citizen of the State in its future legislation. At this time the newly emancipated classes of Missouri and Arkansas were found moving in large numbers to Kansas. Many of them were so situated as to indicate plainly their former condition of enslavement. In their present one of freedom, in too many cases they were without even the merest necessary indispensable articles which one must feel would make life even with the largest liberty tolerable.

Returning from Topeka, on his way to St. Louis, Mr. Langston visited for the second time the city of Lawrence, addressing once more a great assembly there convened.

Thence returning, he attended meetings at Kansas City, Sedalia, Jefferson City and St. Louis. In all these cities the meetings were large, orderly and successful. The one at Jefferson City, held as that at Topeka, in the hall of the House of Representatives, with all the members of the Legislature present, and a vast general audience, was successful, impressive and imposing beyond the most sanguine hope of its promoters. Here Mr. Langston was treated in princely style. Besides being received by a large respectable local committee of prominent well-known colored gentlemen with peculiar *éclat*, entertained at the first hotel in the city, with every want anticipated and supplied, with the state officers, including the governor, General Fletcher, treating him with marked attention, the senators and members of the Legislature making him cordial and considerate visits, his sojourn in the city was made thoroughly agreeable by the general popular favor shown him. In due season he was conducted into the hall of the House of Representatives, with the great band employed for the occasion playing in most lively, stirring strains, "Hail to the Chief." He was introduced to the brilliant, crowded audience in most felicitous style, by a prominent member of the House of Representatives, the Hon. Enos Clark of St. Louis. The address on this occasion proved to be thoroughly acceptable to the colored people and the Republican and liberally-minded portion of the great audience. The members of the Legislature, who were specially addressed, gave constant unflagging attention to the whole utterance; and those who did not accept its sentiments, treated the speaker with great respect and cordial consideration. The Democratic and conservative, illiberal classes were not pleased with the great distinction that marked Mr. Langston's reception, his entertainment, and his treatment by the Legislature and the people. The consequence was that the Democratic papers of the capital and State, including the Democratic metropolitan journals, were filled for weeks with badly-tempered, ill-advised and untruthful, disparaging comments upon the whole affair. The Republican journals, on the other hand, throughout the State, were firm, earnest and manly in their notices, speaking always in favorable, even flattering terms of the orator.

The manner in which Mr. Langston was received in this mission of earnest effort in behalf of the freed people in all parts of the States named, is abundantly illustrated in certain sample notices of himself and his work here given, taken from newspapers, published in several of the different places which he visited, and where he spoke. Of the object which he had in view, one journal speaks as follows:

"Mr. Langston, we understand, will present to our citizens the cause of his race—their rights, duties and responsibilities, and the claims they make upon the community and the State. We do not understand, however, that he will do this arrogantly or in any unbecoming terms. Reason and truth will be his instruments.

"We bespeak for this gentleman a candid hearing. The arguments he may present will be no more nor less powerful because proceeding from the lips of a colored man. Let them be judged of from the standpoint of sound reason and good sense, regardless of extrinsic influences."

The same paper, the "Daily Courier" of Hannibal, Missouri, December 18, 1865, after Mr. Langston had spoken, employed with respect to his address upon "Education, Money and Character," the following words:

"We could not help wondering as we listened to the eloquent utterances of John M. Langston, where was that terrific iron heel of pro-slavery despotism that five years ago would have crushed in its incipiency as if it had been an egg shell, such a demonstration. Gone down with the institution which it supported and which supported it ; gone calling on the rocks and the mountains to fall on it and hide it from the wrath to come; crumbled to pieces beneath the very earthquake which itself invoked to topple down the glorious fabric of our Union ! Thanks be to God, that Union is emblazoned with a new glory and cemented a hundred-fold stronger by the best blood of its noble patriots ! But where are the men who opened the gates of Janus and unloosed the furies of war? Consumed—perished ingloriously and ignominiously and forever. And triumphing over their downfall, Freedom now holds its jubilee !

"Such was the triumph last Saturday night, when a former slave addressed his former fellow-slaves, now citizens, on the great subjects connected with their duties and responsibilities to their country and themselves and their privileges as American citizens, while there were none to molest, but many to cheer.

"We cannot attempt to follow the eloquent speaker in his train of remarks. Those who did not hear him, could gain no adequate idea of the rare excellence of the address from our poor and meager jottings. Suffice to say that his words were full of appositeness to the audience and the occasion. To the colored men he said, 'Above all other things, get education! Get money! Get character!'

"When the Missouri State Convention on the 11th of January last, abolished slavery throughout this State, he was telegraphed to come to St. Louis to help the colored people of that city thank God and the Convention for making them free. He went and electrified St. Louis with his eloquent words.

"He now comes again to Missouri, this time to canvass the State for the benefit of the freedmen—to assist them up and help them on with words of cheer and with good advice. May God speed him and bless his noble efforts."

The meeting at St. Joseph, Missouri, was one that produced such effect upon the public mind, as to stir to its very depths the pro-slavery sentiment. This was shown in a letter which Mr. Langston received on the following day after his speech. The journals of the city characterized the author and the letter in becoming truthful phrase. In speaking on this subject the leading paper used these words in an editorial entitled "The Spirit of Slavery:"

"It is well known that Mr. John M. Langston, a colored man, has been in this city for some days past, pleading in the most eloquent and able terms for the rights of his own race, and as an orator and close thinker, will compare favorably with any man who has addressed a St. Joseph audience for months. Mr. Langston came among us well endorsed as a courteous man and Christian gentleman, and while here was the guest of G. C. Barton, Esq., of this city, who has long been acquainted with him, and knew Mr. Langston when he was in college and will endorse all that we say of him in this article."

Speaking of the scurrilous anonymous letter which he received, this journal says:

"Its contents show that the writer is a mean, cowardly rebel and sympathizer with treason, and chooses to show his courage, not by going into an assembly in a manly way and meeting argument with argument, but by an assault from behind, just where he has been during the four years of the war, and sending to Mr. Langston an anonymous letter. And well may he *conceal his name*, he dare not make it known in this city. The spirit manifested in this letter is the real spirit of slavery, that institution which is abhorred of God and man, and which, thank God! the Constitution of these United States tolerates *no more forever*. But read the letter."

"'*Saint Joe*, Dec. 23, 1865.
"'Mr. J. M. LANGSTON:
 "'Sir:
  "'Feeling an interest in the philanthropic object you have in view,

which you so ably represent and eloquently advocate, I cannot know danger threatening you without giving timely warning.

"'It has been ascertained that an organized band of horse thieves have visited this city for the purpose of operating and it is believed that you are an accomplice, if not the president of the party. So firmly is this the conviction of some, that threats of personal violence have been made, and actuated by a purely humane motive I would earnestly advise your immediate departure.

"'Respectfully,
"'A FRIEND.'"

This letter had no effect upon Mr. Langston's movements, except as it may have aroused and quickened the purposes of his friends to give him the largest possible opportunity to plead with efficiency the cause of the negro.

The meeting held at Topeka, the capital of Kansas, was concluded by the remarkable expression found in the following resolution, as offered by Gen. John Ritchey and adopted without a dissenting voice:

"Resolved, that as the right of self-government is one of the natural, essential, and inherent rights of man, we will extend the right of suffrage to citizens of African descent."

The paper in which this resolution was published, in speaking of the speech and the meeting, uses the following terms:

"Long before the hour for speaking the hall of the House Representatives was filled to overflowing with eager listeners, to hear that distinguished orator of Ohio, Mr. John M. Langston. When the hour arrived the meeting was organized by calling Mr. Charles H. Langston, a brother of the speaker, to the chair, who made a short and pertinent explanation of the objects of the meeting, closing with the introduction of the orator to the vast multitude before him."

Of the speech, after presenting it, substantially, the paper concludes by saying:

"Taking this speech altogether, it was an able, eloquent and logical effort, made at the right time, and in the right place, and in the right direction."

The St. Louis "Missouri Democrat," on the eleventh day of January, 1866, referred to the meeting held at Jefferson City, with the head line, "Langston before the Legislature," followed by this special dispatch:

> "This week is furnishing us with occurrences of unusual interest; the least to be forgotten among them is that John M. Langston, the colored orator from Ohio, who has recently been addressing mass meetings of colored people in various parts of the State, addressed a large audience in the hall of the House of Representatives a night or two since. It was a strange spectacle in the capital of Missouri. The hall was filled to its utmost capacity. The members of the General Assembly turned out in a body. The east half of the hall was exclusively appropriated by the colored people, while the west half was reserved for *white* persons.
>
> "Mr. Langston was introduced to the assembly by a talented and leading young member of the House, Enos Clark, Esq., of St. Louis, in a few well-chosen remarks. On opening the orator said: That the Representatives of Missouri permitted the use of their hall for the occasion, he could with difficulty realize, and that they did extend this courtesy, really, is a fact deserving the prominent mention he gave it, as pointing to the principle of equal rights carried to the ascendant through the red sea of revolution. He spoke eloquently and well. His plea in behalf of his race for the simple award of justice and human rights addresses itself with irresistible force to the better judgment of men. Even conservatives, many of whom were present and listened with marked attention, admitted the vanquishing force of his logic, and acknowledged frankly the fairness and justness of his argument."

This trip thoroughly completed, embracing four great States, gave Mr. Langston such full, general observation of the freed people with whom he was brought in association, as greatly to broaden, improve and strengthen his ideas of and faith in the ability, promise and final elevation and standing which they would gain, as wisely directed, in this country. He has not been mistaken in the views which he then formed, expressed and defended, with respect to that result. He rejoices, as do all its friends, in the progress and success with which the negro race has been blessed in the cultivation of education, the accumulation of property, and the development and growth of all the cardinal virtues of human character, without which no people can ever reach permanent good, greatness, or even desirable name.

CHAPTER XVIII.

HIS FIRST PROFESSIONAL CALL TO WASHINGTON AND HIS APPOINTMENT AS GENERAL INSPECTOR OF THE BUREAU OF REFUGEES, FREEDMEN AND ABANDONED LANDS.

THE intensity of popular feeling in favor of the government in the early days of the Rebellion, when calls were made to all concerned for their noblest and truest sons, was manifested in nothing so completely as in the readiness with which often the last son and the only one, was given to defend and maintain the Union. A family consisting of three persons, an aged father, an afflicted daughter and a son, residing in Pittsfield Township, Lorain County, Ohio, owning a small farm which they cultivated for their support, was separated in one of the earliest calls of the government by the enlistment of the young man. He was the pillar and prop of a household that seemed helpless, desolate and forlorn without his presence. He had enlisted and served his first term with honor and distinction. He had re-enlisted, and entered with vigor and earnestness upon a second term of service. His absence from home seemed quite enough for his father and sister to endure, loyal and patriotic as they were, loving their country and government in such sincerity and truth as to be willing to give him up for its defence, who would otherwise at once protect and support them. Indeed, so much they were glad to do in making what was to them a serious and important sacrifice. But a great affliction had overtaken them. For, in an evil hour, influenced by untoward associates, the son, the young soldier who bore the hope of their name and household, had gone astray.

The father and sister, with hearts full of the deepest anxiety and grief, in the last weeks of 1866, came to the office of Mr. Langston to make known to him the story of the arrest, trial, conviction and confinement of the son and brother in a military prison. They had gone to their neighbors and friends, seeking counsel and support in any efforts which might be made to alleviate his condition or to secure his release. As directed, they had now come with their hope well-nigh gone, to ask the professional aid of the lawyer, to whom they made known the facts reported. As inquired of they were glad to bear testimony to the previous good character of the soldier, and offered in proof of his good conduct the honorable discharge which had been given him. They told, too, how all the neighbors would substantiate all their declarations in favor of him, as he was known by them before he entered the service.

Their earnest, anxious solicitude was thoroughly expressed in the questions, "Can anything be done for him? Can you secure his release?" Letters from him were then produced, in which he directed his father and sister to employ the attorney upon whom they had called and of whom he had some knowledge, advising that if employed, he might prove to be specially serviceable. In his letters, he assured his friends also that he had not had a fair and just trial; that upon a due examination of the proceedings of the court before which his case had been tried, errors and irregularities would appear, and also insufficiencies of evidence and law would be found, of such character and such number as to justify prompt and energetic efforts in his behalf. Besides expressing his confidence in Mr. Langston's ability and skill to find all such defects and faults in the proceedings of the court, he urged his belief that his influence with the authorities was such as to secure for him favorable action in view of them. Upon the urgent request of all concerned, especially in view of the pathetic appeal of the sister, Mr. Langston agreed to do what he might for the relief and reinstatement of the son in the service. On investigation, he found that he was able to make for the young man an excellent name. He was able, too, to show that his record as a soldier was good ; that he had done good service, and without a single exception, had always demeaned himself so as to gain and retain the respect and confidence of his officers and comrades. This was the first offence ever charged against him. It was a grave one, to be sure—robbery of certain property from a poor man who had refused to comply with demands of a number of soldiers, partially in liquor, in whose company this one at the time was found. The regiment to which this soldier belonged was in camp at the time of this occurrence at Nashville, Tennessee, and it was after a visit to the city, on their way back to the camp, that this crime was said to have been committed.

Fortified in the plea of his prior uniform good conduct, advised as to the haste and irregularity of his trial, with several informalities marking the proceedings of the court, and persuaded that his conviction was not sustained by evidence duly adduced, Mr. Langston resolved to present the case upon a carefully prepared statement of all such facts and considerations to the president of the United States and ask his action in behalf of the soldier. At first it was decided to bring and conduct the case so far as such application was concerned, by correspondence. Subsequently, however, upon further reflection and consideration, it was determined to have it done personally, even if the expenses connected with the proceedings should be greatly increased. This course necessitated a trip to Washington city and a visit to the White House. The friends of the young man were fully convinced of the wisdom of this course and were positive and hearty in advising and urging it. Accordingly, fully armed and confident of success, in the early part of January, 1867, the attorney found himself in the national capital upon his first professional call to that city.

No one can tell what patience and perseverance are, till

he makes his first tour from a distant State to Washington to see the chief executive of the nation. Not to say one word of an office-seeker, how hard it is for a worthy citizen, moved by every sacred and holy consideration and motive, often to see that high officer of the State! How, day after day till the days make weeks, that person may have to go and wait, and leave and return again, repeating his visits before he can gain sight of the executive and take a single step in any business which he may have in hand! So the Ohio lawyer passed the first week after his arrival at the capital in visiting and waiting without avail at the Executive Mansion. How many times in that week daily, he heard the kind voice of the door-keeper as he announced to the multitude of waiting American citizens, each anxious to make known his wants, that the president would see no one until the next day! How often during that time he went away anxious about his client, wondering whether he would be able the following day to do anything for him! So the days came and went, till late in the afternoon on Saturday preceding the Sunday on which General Grant called at the White House to read to the president his celebrated address to the retiring army. On the memorable Saturday afternoon to which reference is made, Mr. Langston grown desperate in his solicitude for his client, when the door-keeper had announced that the president would see no one until the next Tuesday, advanced upon that person, presuming to inquire whether he might not under the circumstances crave and secure his good offices to gain for him a brief interview with President Johnson. At first the door-keeper shook his head and declared that the president was so occupied that he could not think of disturbing him with any such matter as that suggested. However, upon recognition of the person addressing him as an old friend whom he had known in Ohio and whom he knew to be favorably regarded by the person whom he sought to see, Mr. William Slade, then acting as the door-keeper of the White House, agreed and promised to bring his case at once to the attention of the president.

After conducting his friend into the library, where he left him, saying that as soon as it became convenient he would present his name to the president and make known the result, he bade him to be patient and remain as situated until his return. Two long hours had passed, when an attaché of the mansion came to the library, lighted the gas and delivered a message from Mr. Slade, to the effect that Mr. Langston must be patient, for all would be right. Not long thereafter the excellent door-keeper, entering the room and calling to his friend, said, "Come now, Langston, the president will see you." The desired moment had arrived, and as Mr. Langston entered his office the president on receiving gave him a cordial welcome and greeting. Quickly and in few words he made known the object of his visit. He was greatly surprised when the president, after hearing him attentively, said that it would be impossible for him to give personal and immediate consideration to the case which he presented. "There are," he said, "a thousand and more such cases awaiting consideration and decision before this one. I cannot promise," he continued, "to do more than to refer it to the officer charged with such matters." He did, however, permit Mr. Langston to add a few words to those already employed, in making a vigorous appeal to him in behalf of the soldier; dwelling upon the anxiety and solicitude of the aged father and dutiful and loving sister, in whose name he came as well as that of the young man involved; when the president, seeming to be specially moved, asked whether Mr. Langston's name appeared upon the papers as the attorney in the case, he adding that he would see what he could do and saying to him that he might call again within two or three days. On leaving President Johnson, meeting Mr. Slade at the door, he tarried to thank him specially for his kind valuable services. Now exhibiting no little cordial interest in Mr. Langston, Mr. Slade asked him how he would spend his Sabbath, the next day. When told that he had no special engagement he invited him to attend, sitting with him and his family, public worship at the 15th Street Presbyterian church, and at its close dine with him, to all which ready assent was given, with suitable acknowledgment of the honor conferred. At the appointed time, on Sunday morning, Mr. Langston repaired to the church indicated, and finding Mr. Slade's family pew very near the pulpit, he took a seat back, which was more agreeable to him, since from that seat he could see and hear the minister to greater satisfaction and advantage.

On that day the pulpit was filled by the Rev. Jonathan Gibbs, of Florida, who discoursed upon a clear conscience from the Pauline standpoint. His sermon, full of learning and eloquence, occupied only about half an hour, when at the close Mr. Slade, with other officers of the church, circulated baskets for the usual collection. He, on reaching the pew in which Mr. Langston sat, immediately notified him that the president desired to see him, and that he would do well to go at once to the White House. Handing his basket to a person near at hand and taking leave of his family in hurried manner, he accompanied Mr. Langston. They had just reached the door entering the library of the White House, when General Grant came out, and the president, calling Mr. Slade, asked if he had found Mr. Langston. The latter answering for himself, paid his respects to the president, who said to him, "I am on the mercy-seat to-day, and I have concluded to take your case up and dispose of it at once." Continuing, he said, "I suppose you have been to church. If so, you are in good frame of mind for impartial honest judgment. Now, sir, from what you know of this case, were you president and I the attorney, is there enough of justice and merit in it to justify your petition for the release of the young man and his restoration to position in his regiment?" A positive affirmative answer was made, when his military secretary was called and ordered to make entry upon the papers of the case, according to the petition which they contained, and directed to transmit them to the honorable secretary of war, who would make order for the release and reinstatement of the soldier.

No report of any proceeding ending happily as this did

was ever made to an aged parent and affectionate sister, which gave greater joy and occasioned greater happiness in a humble household! They had given their son and brother to the government with patriotic satisfaction. They had received him again to honor and the service of the government, with thanksgiving and gratitude which no pen may describe.

Other incidents connected with this visit to Washington city are noted here with interest. The president had completed the service to which he had been asked to address himself in the release and restoration of the young white soldier, when he engaged in general conversation with Mr. Langston as to politics and his profession, inquiring in connection with the latter, whether he had been admitted to the Supreme Court, and whether he was acquainted with Chief Justice Chase, to whom he offered to give him a letter of introduction. Of course, a letter from such exalted source was accepted and used, notwithstanding the chief justice had known the bearer of it for many years in Ohio. It was presented the next morning, when the distinguished recipient welcomed in most cordial manner his acknowledged friend. He had not forgotten how in every political contest in which he had appeared as the chief figure, whether in effort for election to the Senate of the United States or the governorship of Ohio, as an earnest and loyal Republican this friend had always given him his sympathy, influence and support. Nor did he put low estimate upon the services which his visitor had rendered in such behalf. He therefore received and treated him with marked consideration. After quite protracted conversation upon political matters, with special emphasis and stress put upon the probable use, ultimately, of the ballot by the colored American, the chief justice suggested to Mr. Langston that he would do well to visit and make the acquaintance of Gen. O. O. Howard, Commissioner of the Freedmen's Bureau, offering at the same time to give him a line of introduction to that person. His introduction, encouched in warm graceful terms, was accepted. The visit to General Howard was in every sense interesting and profitable. He had known of the commissioner, of course, by reputation for many years, as one of the leading officers of the army, a friend of the negro race, and a man of sterling Christian character and worth. His desire therefore to see and know him from actual observation and contact was natural. He found the general wholly occupied in feeling and thought with the great philanthropic work to which he had been appointed by President Lincoln, and which he would carry forward, if possible, to the utmost success, in the name of the principles and purposes of patriotism and Christianity, which he professed and maintained. He was not a little surprised, however, when the general, after dwelling upon the educational work which he hoped to accomplish among the freed people, suggested to him that at an early day he might need his assistance in that special department of his service. He took his post-office address, saying that he should, according to his necessities, communicate with him. To this, however, Mr. Langston replied that he desired to adhere closely to his law business, more so than he had been doing for some little time. On leaving General Howard, with pleasant grateful feelings for the consideration shown him, he agreed to answer promptly any communication which he might see fit to make him. Then, after a hurried introduction to General Ketchum and Rev. John W. Alvord, both conspicuous officers of the Bureau, the latter being in charge of its educational work, Mr. Langston took his departure, in the belief that President Lincoln had not only served the negro well in his emancipation, but in the appointment of an able officer and noble man to take care of his interests, as he left slavery for freedom.

Not least among the interesting incidents of this visit to the capital, stands the double occurrence of Mr. Langston's admission to the Supreme Court of the United States and his mishap with Hon. Jeremiah S. Black, one of its most prominent and noted members. Gen. James A. Garfield had known Mr. Langston as an Ohio lawyer for many years. He was also his friend. He had now the opportunity of serving and honoring him, and he did not hesitate for a single moment, but acted promptly and in obedience to the impulses of his great, generous heart. He was a member of the Supreme Court, conspicuous for his large ability and professional success. Accompanying his friend to the court, vouching for his learning, his experience and character as a practicing attorney and counsellor at law and solicitor in chancery of Ohio, he moved his admission to that court;—and Mr. Langston's certificate of admission bears date January 17, 1867. He had passed from the court room proper, having thanked General Garfield for the kind service which he had rendered him, and but just entered the clerk's office across the hall-way, to pay for and secure his certificate of admission to the court, as the Hon. Jeremiah S. Black entered hurriedly to ask the clerk, Mr. D. W. Middleton, to give him small bills for a twenty-dollar note. When he found that Mr. Middleton could not accommodate him, turning to Mr. Langston, he inquired whether he had small bills and would serve him. Taking his money from his pocket, he was in the act of granting his request, when he asked, "Have I the honor of addressing the Hon. Thaddeus Stevens?" to which Mr. Black —extending one hand for the change and the other with which he would pass the twenty-dollar bill, greatly agitated and meantime backing, as if he would leave the office by such movement, so that Mr. Langston was compelled to advance towards him—with frowns and oaths answered, "No, sir! No, sir! You have not!"

As Mr. Langston turned to the clerk, he found him shaking with laughter, as he declared, "That is the best joke of the season. Black would not have had you call him Stevens for the largest fee he has received for the past ten years." These two great Pennsylvanians, lawyers of acknowledged talent and power, politicians ranking as the leaders of their respective parties, extremely ultra in sentiment and feeling, were opposed to each other for reasons which may be easily imagined, and accordingly entertained towards each other personal animosity of deep and unyielding character.

Not only in the professional success which attended this call to Washington was Mr. Langston specially favored, but by the occurrences detailed, which added not a little to his subsequent advancement and interest.

Shortly after his return to his home and business in Oberlin, Ohio, in April, 1867, Mr. Langston was made the recipient of several telegrams in a single day, calling him to duty under the national government. It seemed to him that he had barely had time to report his professional success to his venerable client and his daughter, who were so solicitous for the soldier son and brother. He, certainly, had not been able to do more than to tell his friends, imperfectly however, with enthusiasm of the sights and scenes which he had observed in Washington city, and of the great men met there, whose words and influence he still retained and felt, as they moved him.

He inclined to accept the call, yet he loved his profession and its pleasant duties. He was devoted to his home, and was always anxious to discharge every obligation to his family. He was indisposed, in fact it was with the greatest difficulty that he could think with the least degree of allowance, of breaking, even for a season, those tender local and neighborly ties which connected him with the community in which he lived. He had been educated in Oberlin, and he had been honored by frequent popular expressions in his favor, even elected to office upon the generous vote of its friendly considerate citizens. Now he was called to debate seriously, and at first he doubted whether it would be wise for him to leave his actual position, so agreeable and promising in every way, for one whose cares, responsibilities and dangers he did not and could not fully understand and appreciate. And yet the call of duty seemed to have reached him.

It was not easy for him to make decision in this matter. Not until his wife suggested to him that it might be well to return to the national capital and confer with those who sought his services before he reached final conclusion in the premises, could he bring himself to the serious entertainment of the proposition to quit even temporarily his profession for any service of the government. Finally, he accepted this suggestion. He promised his friends and several clients that he would certainly return to his business again in a short time. He made all arrangements for his return to the capital, having set in order everything at his office and made engagements for the care and prosecution of all business in his hands requiring immediate attention. He turned sadly and mechanically, as a friend said, from his office door, after locking it, and made his way homeward. On entering the house, as the family had gathered for its usual mid-day meal, the questions met him from all sides, "Are you going? Have you concluded to leave? When will you return?" To none of these questions, whether addressed by child or adult, under the affecting circumstances, was he able to make ready positive answer. He did reply, "I think I will go." The subject was a serious one and solemn enough ; and the response, whatever its character, came from a heart full of doubt, burdened with the deepest anxiety. And yet decision had really been made and the purpose to leave for Washington directed every step and arrangement to such end.

The real cause that produced hesitation and indecision in this case after all, was found in the apprehension that Mr. Langston might not return to those old ways of the law along which he had been passing for so many years, in pleasant, delightful occupation. It did really seem to him that he stood at the mouth of the grave, in which he was consigning to mother earth the remains of that which he would not, and yet must leave; whose presence gone, he seemed to have met his greatest loss! Then came the fear, intensified through the kind offices of the imagination, that the new task upon which he was about to enter might not be agreeable; might prove to be difficult and unpromising; and in his attempts to perform it according to any expectations which he or others may have formed, he might fail, and he be compensated, not in success and honor, but in failure and disappointment.

At last, the spirit of his manhood asserted itself, and in defiance of real obstacles, prospective, imaginary difficulties, his purpose became fixed to meet any duty before him with reasonable courage, and a few days only had elapsed before he was for the second time in the presence of Gen. O. O. Howard. After greetings had been exchanged, he was told that his arrival was opportune, giving satisfaction. The general said, in substance: " We need you, and shall proceed without delay to explain the work which we desire you to undertake. It will be difficult enough, taxing all the ability, all the learning, all the eloquence, with all the wisdom, discretion and self-sacrifice which you may possess. You will be appointed and commissioned as General Inspector of the Bureau of Refugees, Freedmen and Abandoned Lands. As such officer, you will address yourself in all parts of the country to which you shall be sent, to arousing, inspiring and encouraging the freed people, especially in earnest and intelligent effort to cultivate and sustain among themselves, all those things which pertain to dignified, useful American life; to impress upon them the importance of educating themselves and their children, of laboring intelligently and diligently to accumulate and save those means indispensable to their location in comfortable necessary homes, and of so demeaning themselves in all their new relations to the community, that while prejudices and feelings of hatred against them are allayed and removed, they may win the respect and gain the confidence even of those who formerly held them in bondage. To accomplish this object," the general continued, "in all your efforts, and especially in your set addresses, while you are plain and honest in your utterances to the freed people, you must be so cautious and discreet as not to provoke the ill-will of those, who, chagrined at their defeat in the field, were opposed not only to the emancipation of the slaves, but to all efforts on the part of the general government having in view their education and the amelioration of their material, moral, religious and political condition. Your field of labor," he said, " will be the whole South, including the District of Columbia, Maryland, Kentucky, Tennessee and Missouri. You will be ordered here and there, as the exigencies of the service may require, and wherever you go, putting yourself in communication with the officers and agents of the Bureau, you will discover and report any short-comings or omissions of duty on their part, while you may ask of them any service calculated to advance the interests of the people through your own instrumentality and labors. It is the purpose of this Bureau, and its management must tend constantly to that end, to accomplish in the largest practicable manner, the objects of its creation." Moved now by the enthusiasm of a genuine philanthropist, the general stated that among those objects the general improvement of the freed people, as they are found making such headway as seems to be possible to them among the classes constituting their former owners, must be regarded and treated as of the first importance, and he emphasized and impressed this consideration according to his judgment and feeling of its necessity and dignity. Above all things the importance and necessity of education, economy, industry and virtue should be impressed upon them. Intemperance, the inordinate and expensive use of tobacco, with all those extravagant habits of ordinary life among the more ignorant classes of society, should as rapidly as possible be removed so far as they are concerned, and the bad effects of such outlays and habits upon body, soul and fortune, be carefully and wisely explained to them. They must be made if possible, an intelligent, thrifty, valuable class of the population. Rising from his seat at this point, and raising his left hand with emphatic gesture of the same, he said, "Mr. Langston, this is your work; here is your field; do you accept this mission? You may not say no, for your duty to your country and your race, not less than that to your Heavenly Father, who has so signally blessed you, commands it! From this moment, we shall count you our officer and agent, and at an early day your commission as the General Inspector of the Bureau, with carefully prepared instructions, embodying, substantially, my explanations, shall be draughted, duly signed and conveyed to you. Until then you may make such survey of the school work under the Bureau, in this city and Alexandria, as may be convenient and agreeable to you, reporting from day to day at these headquarters. Your pay will begin at once."

Thus Mr. Langston was given, in earnest, emphatic statement, explanation of the great work to which he had been called. Its dignity, importance and necessity were fully appreciated; so much so that he was led to question his ability to meet the expectations which were entertained with respect to the results of his labors. He felt that he had been honored exceedingly, and did not fail to realize that his appointment to such a duty was an exalted expression of confidence as to his fitness therefor. He commenced his work accordingly in the cities of Washington and Alexandria.

He was not permitted to remain in Washington city long without his commission, formal instructions and first order to duty. He made his first tour through the State of Maryland, embracing visits specially to Baltimore and Frederick. At the latter place he met and addressed an immense concourse of freed people, with Gen. O. O. Howard, Gen. Charles H. Howard and Judge Bond present. He delivered the principal address, although the other persons named followed in appropriate, pertinent remarks. They all gave the newly appointed inspector special attention, and upon the conclusion of his address, paid him many compliments. On returning to the capital within a very few days thereafter, he received his second order to another field of duty.

He was directed to make a tour of the State of Virginia, visiting Alexandria, Leesburg, Culpepper Court House, Orange Court House, Charlottsville, Gordonsville, Louisa Court House, Richmond, Petersburg, and thence returning, Fredericksburg. At all these places the schools of the freed people were duly and thoroughly examined, and the scholars carefully instructed as to the necessity and advantage of diligence and care in the performance of their duties, and the obligation which rested upon them to so demean themselves in general ordinary life as to win the respect and the consideration of those in whose midst they lived. Besides, great concourses of the people were addressed upon all those subjects—educational, moral, political, industrial, and social—which concerned their highest good and most enduring welfare.

To say that this trip was interesting to the inspector who thus visited the schools and addressed the scholars and the people, is only to describe his feelings in the faintest manner. Here time can only be given to hurried accounts of the meetings and any incidents connected therewith, addressed at Leesburg, Louisa Court House and Richmond ; and those at such places are specially referred to with their incidents, because of their importance, representative character and interest.

That Mr. Langston's position with respect to the Republican party and the advocacy of its principles, measures and men at the great meetings which he addressed may be properly understood, it should be stated that from the time he entered upon his duties as general inspector of the Bureau, he acted by special engagement as the representative and duly accredited advocate of that party. Nowhere, therefore, as he traveled and spoke, did he fail to present and defend in moderate, wise manner, its claims upon the support of the newly emancipated classes and their friends.

Sometimes, and at special places, he met distinguished advocates of Republicanism, particularly upon his tour through Virginia, when such advocates made bold and positive assertion and defence of the past action and prospective measures of the party, urging their hearers to give it their sympathy and support by influence and vote. On such occasions, Mr. Langston was not behind the boldest in earnest and decided utterance or action in favor of the distinctive doctrines of that party. The meeting at Leesburg was one at which distinguished Republican orators made their appearance and delivered speeches in its favor.

On the second day of June, 1867, accompanied by Mr.

William B. Downey, Generals Farnsworth and Pierce, and Col. L. Edwin Dudley, Mr. Langston left Washington city for Leesburg, where all the persons named were announced to speak at a mass-meeting of Republicans to be held that day at that place. And on the next day, as the Leesburg meeting would be, in fact, continued, they would speak at the beautiful Quaker town, Hamilton, situated at the foot of the mountains, twelve miles away. The company reached Leesburg a few minutes before midday, and took quarters at the only Republican hotel in the place. Dinner was served at one o'clock, and the meeting had been called to be opened an hour later. When dinner was announced, Mr. Langston, as had been his custom always, answered the bell by walking at once to the dining-room, to take his meal with his friends at the first table. At the dining-room door, he was met by the landlord himself, who told him that he could not go in, that he could not eat at the table. At this moment, General Farnsworth came up and inquired, "What is the matter?" To this question the landlord replied, "This man wants to go in the dining-room and take his dinner at my first table with my white boarders. He shall not do it." General Farnsworth replied, saying, "He will do so, if he wishes, for he is with us, and we propose to stand by him." Colonel Dudley appearing and hearing this remark of the general, said, "Yes, we do!" Mr. Langston said, then, "Mr. Landlord, I shall eat my dinner now, with my friends, if there is no good reason why I should not." Whereupon the landlord answered, "If I should let you go in and eat now, my hotel and all the property I own would be burned up as soon as you left this town, and I beg you, Mr. Langston, to let me arrange your dinner in your room. You shall have waiters and everything which the hotel can furnish, to your taste and desire." "Mr. Landlord," Mr. Langston asked seriously, "will they burn your hotel?" "Yes," he said, "they will! That I fear, and for that reason only, I object to your taking your place with your friends at the table." "Then," said Mr. Langston, "you may arrange my dinner in my room, and

GENERAL INSPECTOR, BUREAU OF REFUGEES.

Colonel Dudley and I will dine there together, so prepare for two." This was done, and the landlord was relieved of every apprehension.

The meeting was in all respects a great success. In numbers, in good order, in the attention paid the speakers and in the promise of good and lasting results it could not have been surpassed. It made such impression even upon the minds of the leading white men of the place, that the mayor, who had been invited to act as its presiding officer and who had declined that honor, after witnessing the character of the gathering and listening to the admirable addresses delivered, expressed the deepest regret that he had foregone the distinction which had been proffered him.

Upon the close of this branch of the meeting at Leesburg, the gentlemen named, including Mr. Langston, took carriages late in the evening and drove by a most picturesque route to Hamilton. At this place they spent the night in Quaker families of the neighborhood, where all was genuine happiness and pleasure. Early the next morning, by special invitation, the whole company went upon a most exhilarating horseback ride across a branch of the Alleghany mountains, when upon their return they partook of a general breakfast of the most inviting and relishing character, prepared and offered by the most wealthy and prominent Quaker of the neighborhood. At ten o'clock an immense meeting had convened, when the exercises for the day were opened. This meeting was a great, impressive picnic gathering held in the midst of a grove naturally beautiful beyond possibility of just description. A sight interesting and delightful was furnished at midday, when a recess was taken and the vast assembly broke itself up into groups of friends and neighbors to partake of their respective bountiful delicious lunches. Nothing could have appeared more neighborly, more cordial and delightful. It may not be inappropriate to state here, that it was during this time that the beauty and gallantry of the occasion manifested themselves in their most signal, striking manner. Even the staid orators of the occasion were moved to such displays of genteel behavior, as to win many a kindly expression of the handsome, cultured Virginia ladies who gave *élat* to the meeting by their presence.

It was not until the day had passed far on toward sunset that this meeting was brought to a close, and all concluded that the one held at Leesburg and this one at Hamilton, constituted, taken together, a grand, magnificent display for Loudoun County, in favor of Republican principles. Leaving this beautiful Quaker neighborhood with feelings of special gratitude and pleasure, the company, composed as already described, came directly back to Leesburg to take the train for Washington city. However, having an hour or more to wait for the train, the gentlemen all went to the hotel at which they had stopped the day before, to get supper. To their surprise they were refused entertainment, "because they had with them the negro orator, Langston," who had insisted the day before upon eating in the dining-room and at the first table. Leaving this hotel, with its Republican landlord, they went directly across the street to a house kept by a Democrat and an ex-rebel, who received them kindly, giving them every attention, not changing his conduct toward them even after he had read, in looking over his register, upon which the strangers had each written his name, in bold, firm hand—

JOHN MERCER LANGSTON,
Negro, Oberlin,
Lorain County,
Ohio.

Shortly after this occurrence, the hotel of the Republican landlord was burned to the ground; and that of his Democratic neighbor, who would not abuse a colored wayfarer, who, tired, worn and hungry, knocked at the door of his house, became the popular one of the town, its business greatly improving and its revenues materially increasing, through the patronage of those who turned from the former because of his unhandsome conduct, and to the latter because of his unexpected, generous and manly behavior.

This feeling and result had manifested themselves before the hotel was burned, and thus the Republican landlord lost more than he gained by his illegal and unseemly conduct. He sowed the wind; he reaped the whirlwind!

At noon, on the fifteenth day of June, 1867, Mr. Langston reached Louisa Court House, Virginia, this being his first visit to that place since his departure therefrom, a mere child, in 1834. He was accompanied by several friends, officers of the Bureau and others, prominent citizens of Louisa County. He had spoken at Gordonsville the day before, and had been met there by parties who had accompanied him, as stated. He was welcomed at the depot and conducted to his hotel by a club of colored men numbering fifteen hundred. It divided itself into two sections of seven hundred and fifty each, and Mr. Langston, leaning upon the arm of its president, a white man, Captain McCracken, walked between these sections to the Louisa Hotel, where rooms had been taken for him and where with his friends he was to be entertained. As he was about entering the door of the hotel, tarrying for a moment to observe the vast concourse of people, white and black, convening, he caught sight of a large, fine looking, intelligent, influential man, apparently white, who seemed to be greatly angered at what was taking place. He immediately asked the gentleman who was conducting him to his rooms, who this was and what was the matter with him, to which reply was made that, "The person is General Gordon, the meanest rebel in the country. He is mad because we are having this meeting and you are to address us. He would break it up if he could. But, thank God, he cannot do it." These words of the president of the club stirred a little bit the anxiety of Mr. Langston. However, he became at once reassured when informed that the whole county had come out, so far as the whites were concerned, to see and hear "Quarles' boy"; and so far as the colored people were concerned, they had all come to see and hear "Lucy's son," and that there would be no disturbance of the meeting.

Mr. Langston had reached his rooms and his friends had just left him, when a young white man, entering without the least ceremony, put to him the following question: "Are you one of us?" Mr. Langston hesitating, said he did not quite understand the question, when the young man repeating himself, inquired, "Are you one of *us?*" Still hesitating, and begging his pardon for any obtuseness he might show, he said to the young man, "Please explain yourself," when he asked, "Are you a Virginian? And were you born in our county?" To both these questions, Mr. Langston answering, said, "Yes, I was born in this county, three miles from this court house; and if the facts that my father and mother are buried here; that the record of my birth, settlement and status are kept in the archives of this county, and that I am interested in everything that pertains to the welfare of this old Commonwealth, would make me a Virginian, then I am one." Thereupon the young man said, "Then you must speak from my porch, for all distinguished Virginians who speak here always speak from it." At this point Captain McCracken entered the room to introduce Mr. Langston to the owner and proprietor of the hotel, the gentleman in conversation with him. When he disclosed what had been said, the captain asked the hotel-keeper whether he was in earnest and was willing to have his porch used by the meeting. He replied promptly, "Yes, I want Mr. Langston to speak from it." Arrangements had been made for speaking from the steps of the court house, but a change was immediately made, and at two o'clock the speaker was conducted to the porch of the hotel, in front of which he found an immense concourse of people, white and black. His reception was of the most cordial sort, every person present seeming to be in good nature and pleased, except General Gordon, who was seen standing upon the extreme right of the audience, full of spite and anger.

On being introduced by Captain McCracken, Mr. Langston found himself confronting an audience composed of sons and daughters of Virginia, men and women, those high in official place and those pursuing the humbler walks of life, aggregating a vast concourse of thousands of persons with whose names he had been familiar from his childhood. Although he had left them and their neighborhood many years before, such was their spontaneous greeting that he felt in their presence as if he had returned to the bosom of those who were his friends. All were attentive, and as he opened his remarks, demonstrated in appearance and behavior their deep interest in him. His speech was commenced with kindly affectionate allusions to his father and mother; his birthplace and old home; the death and burial of his parents; their resting-place, side by side upon the plantation a short distance away, where they had lived together so many years; the executors, Nathaniel Mills, Quarles Thomson, John R. Quarles and William D. Gooch, influential, prominent Virginia gentlemen who had so wisely and efficiently settled his father's estate to the satisfaction of all concerned, securing to certain emancipated persons named in the will of his father, their freedom and their bequests. He told how after so many years had passed and the great war had ground the shackles of the enslaved to dust, and all were free, white and black, and all were at peace, uniting in a common purpose to make the country great, prosperous and happy, he rejoiced to stand before such an audience in the county of his nativity, in the Commonwealth of the Old Dominion, in whose welfare he could not be otherwise than deeply interested as a loyal and devoted son. These introductory remarks occupied his attention for quite fifteen minutes, when turning to his right to address the presiding officer, as he would enter upon the formal address to be delivered, he found General Gordon occupying a chair upon the porch—the platform of the meeting, upon which were seated the gray-headed venerable men prominent in society and influential in the community—placed very near the spot which he occupied. The general adjusting himself in his seat, fastened his eyes and attention upon the speaker, to whom he gave the strictest audience for over two hours and a half. Upon the close of the speech, advancing, he offered the speaker his hand, which was at once taken, while he exclaimed, "Langston, you are one of us, and we are proud of you!"

Then followed a scene which can never be forgotten. The vast assembly, moving in thousands across the porch, greeted Mr. Langston, as he stood, with kind words and expressions calculated to touch and move his feelings. The venerable white men, besides expressing to him their kindly sentiments, assured him that they had known his father and were sincerely and profoundly considerate of his welfare. The aged negroes, burdened with cares and many of them broken by the tasks of their former lives, extending their hands, said to him, "God bless you! God bless you! We knew your mother! We never expected to see this day! Thank God! Thank God! We are glad to see and hear you."

Exhausted by his effort and such kindly, yet taxing treatment, Mr. Langston was compelled to ask his friends to let him repair to his rooms, where perhaps, after a brief rest, he might be somewhat restored to his wonted strength and vigor. As he left the porch, he was surprised to find that General Gordon, who had stood near him during every second of the time occupied with the closing scenes of the meeting, now assisted him, with Captain McCracken, to his rooms. On reaching them, as he was about to lie down, the general, adjusting the pillows upon the bed, said to him, "Before you go to sleep, let me beg your pardon for the many blasphemous, vulgar expressions which I have made against you and against your coming here to address our people. I trust you will forgive me. So much I desired to say to you myself, and to bid you now the heartiest welcome to the community. We are all proud of you! Your wonderful speech will do us incalculable service." With such expressions of changed kindly feeling, General Gordon left the rooms, leaving Mr. Langston to wonder in amazement and yet in delight, at the altered and improved sentiments which he had just employed.

After resting perhaps an hour, on rising Mr. Langston

AFTER THE SPEECH AT LOUISA COURT HOUSE, VIRGINIA, 1867.

270b

having made his toilet, with due reference thereto, went with his friends to the house and home of Captain McCracken, to dine with him and certain Republicans of local note who had been invited. Dinner had just been announced and company was moving toward the dining-room, when a knock was heard at the front door, which was answered by Captain McCracken himself. On opening it, he found to the astonishment of all present, that General Gordon with a friend had come to invite Mr. Langston, in the name of the white ladies of Louisa Court House and its neighborhood, to address them that evening in the Baptist church of the place. At first his friends objected, fearing that some difficulty might result. On the assurance of General Gordon that the invitation was sincere, that the ladies desired to hear him, and that he should be not only well treated but entirely protected, with full liberty to speak in the freest manner, the invitation was accepted. General Gordon declared himself ready to preside at the meeting, to introduce the speaker, and to guarantee him the fullest protection. Certainly, Louisa Court House has never witnessed a more beautiful, orderly, enthusiastic female assembly than that which greeted Mr. Langston on the evening of the fourteenth of June, 1867, in the church mentioned. The beautiful Virginia daughters of Louisa County gave him a royal, memorable reception. He addressed them on "The duty of the American woman in this hour of our reconstruction." Upon the close of his remarks, General Gordon, who had been called to act as the presiding officer of the meeting, delivered in endorsement of the address of the afternoon and the speech of the evening, an utterance which was no less characterized by its learning and eloquence than its cordial courtesy and profound friendly sentiments. He was really learned; he was enthusiastic and eloquent, in the most exalted and captivating sense; his periods were radiant with the jewels of the most elegant, luminous rhetoric. His was the speech of a generous, noble Virginian, containing the fervor and charm of the most soul-stirring utterance. He showed himself an orator of large and commanding power. At the conclusion of the meeting, Mr. Langston was made the subject of the most cordial, flattering congratulations. At the reception, so spontaneously and enthusiastically improvised in his honor, hundreds of the ladies tendered him a hearty shake of the hand, with generous expressions of ardent favor of his address.

Quitting the meeting in company of General Gordon and his friends, Mr. Langston was making his way to his hotel, when to his great surprise the general extended to him an invitation to breakfast with him the next morning. So surprised was he at this proceeding that he answered the general by saying, "You do not mean what you say! I never ate at a second table in my life, nor did I ever eat at a table where discrimination was made against me on account of my color. I could not breakfast with you otherwise than as I did so as your friend and equal, and with you and your family," to which General Gordon promptly and earnestly replied, saying, "That is just exactly the invitation which I give you; only for the sake of convenience we will breakfast at the hotel, where I can accommodate you and your friends." Continuing, he asked, "What hour will meet your pleasure?" Seven o'clock was agreed, and at that very moment General Gordon himself called for and conducted Mr. Langston to the dining-room and the table, giving him the seat of honor next to and upon his right, facing his excellent, interesting and agreeable wife. Such attention and consideration had never up to that time been accorded a person of negro extraction in that place, and it created great comment while it received the approval of the community generally.

The breakfast completed at half-past eight o'clock, General Gordon with a large number of Virginia friends and relatives of Mr. Langston, some taking carriages and others going on horseback, accompanied him to a plantation three miles away belonging then to Mr. William Kent, where the graves of his father and mother were located. About these graves many pleasant things were said to the son, of his father and his peculiar character; and of his mother, with

VISITING THE GRAVES OF HIS PARENTS.

272b

her deep devotion to every one of her children, especially of her interest in the young baby boy who could barely call to mind her death-bed scene as he stood beside her grave with his soul quickened by feelings of love, veneration and respect for those parents whose sleep had already been so long, secure and undisturbed.

Leaving this sacred spot, the place of his birth and the home of his earliest childhood, at the suggestion of General Gordon, Mr. Langston and his friends, on their return to the court house, paid a hurried visit to Mrs. Nathaniel Mills, who surviving her venerable husband by several years, was now quite one hundred years old. Her faculties were all intact; her mind was clear, and she was deeply affected by the honor as she styled it, which was paid her in this call. She said many pleasant things to Mr. Langston; told how deeply interested her husband had been in his education and general welfare; and declared, were he living, that he would be glad to join the neighbors and friends of Captain Ralph Quarles in welcoming his son, of whom he could not be under the circumstances otherwise than proud, back to the neighborhood, even if it be for only a passing visit. Perhaps Virginia has not produced a woman who more entirely realized in her life and influence, it may be in a limited way, upon the community and its interest, a higher ideal of womanhood than this good one of whom these words are written.

Returning to the court house, where a hasty lunch was taken, at twelve-thirty o'clock, Mr. Langston, after thanking his friends for the kindness shown him and bidding them farewell, took the train for Richmond, the capital of the State, where he spoke at three o'clock in the afternoon. He was received at the capital with every display of marked popular respect, and there assembled at the hour appointed for his meeting on the public grounds about the statuary, which give grace and honor thereto, thousands of people, white and black, to hear his speech. His platform was historic and unique, calculated to inspire in him lofty and commanding thoughts; for the great and the good, as immortalized in marble, looked down upon him, and in their silent but expressive faces and mien, seemed to challenge while they prompted his best, most patriotic utterance. Never before had such an audience convened on those grounds, about those masterpieces of art, to hear such an orator under such circumstances! In that vast gathering stood a man, near the speaker as he occupied position upon the base of the statuary, of remarkable character and name, a noted ex-governor of the Commonwealth. He gave considerate, respectful attention to the address, and when it was finished he was among the first to congratulate the speaker and thank him for the moderation, wisdom and eloquence which distinguished his effort. This man was the famous Henry A. Wise, the governor of Virginia when that State dealt with John Brown and his companions, finally executing the hero of the Harper's Ferry raid. This meeting, promoted and sustained by such persons as General Brown, chief agent of the Bureau at the capital of the State, Messrs. Hunnycut, Manley, Taylor, Brooks and others, white and colored, prominent citizens of the place, was pronounced a great success. Of Mr. Langston himself and his address, the leading daily paper held the following words:

"At the square on the east side of the monument a very large meeting was convened yesterday afternoon, to hear Mr. John M. Langston, the colored lawyer from Ohio. His style was highly oratorical, his language choice, and altogether the radical party have few speakers as good as he. His speech was confined to an argumentative discussion of those subjects which pertain to the freedom of the colored American and his natural right of citizenship. From his standpoint, we have never heard the subject more intelligently handled."

After extended inspection of freedmen's affairs, with meetings and addresses as stated, Mr. Langston returning to Washington city, after preparing and presenting his reports to his superior officer, was very soon thereafter ordered to a more distant Southern field of labor.

CHAPTER XIX.

HIS LABORS IN THE SOUTH, THEIR INFLUENCE AND EFFECT.

MR. LANGSTON, after an extended and successful trip through Mississippi and Alabama, on his journey northward learned through the newspapers that President Johnson had in contemplation a change in the commissionership of the Bureau of Refugees, Freedmen and Abandoned Lands, and that his own name had been mentioned in connection with the place. After his arrival at the national capital, he visited the Executive Mansion, and there had a full and free talk with the president on the subject. President Johnson was outspoken and positive in his opposition to General Howard, and did not hesitate to declare his purpose to relieve him of his position. His expressions with regard to him and his management of the Bureau were extremely severe, sometimes blasphemous. Throughout his conversation he indulged in most harsh and offensive criticism of him, insisting that he should be relieved. He stated that he would be exceedingly glad if the colored people could agree upon some able and efficient man of their own number for that position. He declared his readiness to appoint him, and intimated his willingness to give the place to Mr. Langston. Finally, he went so far as to give him time to consider the matter. However, Mr. Langston insisted that the highest interests of the colored people and the efficiency of this service instituted in their behalf, seemed to him to require the continuance of General Howard at the head of the Bureau. From his observation of the service, with close inspection of the results already accomplished, Mr. Langston claimed that President Lincoln had made no mistake in calling General Howard to the commissionership, for he appeared to be in every way sagacious, wise and efficient. Besides, he had already won the confidence of the liberal people of the country, whose great church, missionary and charitable organizations were supplementing in outlays and labor the enterprises so much needed to further the work of the Bureau among the emancipated and impoverished classes of the South.

In this same interview with the president, as he discovered that Mr. Langston did not incline to accept the commissionership of the Bureau, he suggested to him that he would appoint him, if he preferred, as United States Minister to Hayti. But Mr. Langston showed no disposition whatever to accept this foreign place.

On leaving the president however, Mr. Langston did promise to call upon him again at an early day, to give him his conclusions fully and decidedly in regard to these matters. Upon consultation with friends well advised and in whom he had special confidence, he took another course entirely. He called upon General Howard, his chief, and made bold as he conceived it to be his duty, to make known to him the purposes of President Johnson, as stated. He advised General Howard also that he had no doubt that General Grant, who was then acting as secretary of war *ad interim*, standing firmly for his continuance in his position, would succeed even as against the president, in keeping him there. He further stated what he had said to the president on the subject and that he would be glad to say even more in the same direction to the secretary of war. Accordingly a call was arranged, and Mr. Langston accompanied by Col. L. Edwin Dudley, a white friend of his and a special admirer and friend of General Howard, and Mr. John T. Johnson, a prominent colored citizen of Washington city, a friend also of General Howard, fully alive to his

LABORS IN THE SOUTH.

great services to his race and deeply conscious of his worth, visited General Grant for the purposes indicated. The secretary, after being fully advised by Mr. Langston as to the intentions of the president with respect to a change in the commissionership of the Bureau, and after listening attentively to what he had to say in favor of the continuance of General Howard as commissioner, in view of the work which he had inaugurated and which he was accomplishing with such signal and important results, expressed himself in bold, earnest and positive manner against the change which the president suggested. In the course of his reply he not only spoke in comprehensive, liberal, wise terms of the Bureau, its institution and work, telling how he had himself in his management of the colored people, flocking to his army along the Mississippi River, been compelled to adopt the policy and plans of its construction and management, but praised the action of President Lincoln in the appointment of General Howard, and dwelt upon those distinctive and peculiar qualities of his character which fitted him pre-eminently for the work which he had in hand. He declared that he would sustain him to the full extent of his ability. However, he said he had no influence with the president, and would only be able to sustain General Howard, as he did so in his official capacity. Besides, he added that he did not know that he would be kept in his place for the next twenty-four hours. He did not hesitate to speak in severe and earnest terms against the policy which seemed to be actuating the president generally, nor did he hesitate to express his views in emphatic and eloquent manner with regard to what the negro had a right to expect of the government in the way of protection and support, even to the extent of the bestowal of full citizenship, including the ballot. It was when he had completed these utterances that Mr. Langston, in the presence of his friends, full of excitement, moved by the sentiments of the great secretary and matchless general, rushing to him and thanking him for what he had said, declared that such words and such opinions would make him the next president of the United States, and that in the name of the negroes of the country, their friends and the loyal masses, he would then and there nominate him. His friends not only bore intelligent and emphatic testimonies in favor of General Howard and his retention as chief of the Bureau, but being moved as Mr. Langston himself was by the words of General Grant, expressed their enthusiastic approval of his suggestion to make the secretary president of the United States. General Grant knew full well that President Johnson's objections to General Howard were personal, political and partizan, and he met them accordingly with severe biting criticism. Perhaps he never was so severe in criticism upon any man as he was at that time upon the president, in view of his proposed action and the reasons which he understood actuated him thereto. He could not have been more earnest and eloquent in any words of commendation of any person than he was in those employed in behalf of General Howard and his efficiency as an officer, especially as the commissioner of the Bureau. It is with the largest degree of satisfaction and pleasure, that it may be recorded here that General Howard held his position to the end; and while his success in all the labors connected with the Bureau depended mainly upon his own personal ability and wisdom, it may not be forgotten that his retention and support were due in large measure as indicated to the action of General Grant, than whom he never had a more intelligent nor a more loyal friend, so far as his endeavors respecting the material, educational, political, moral and religious advancement of the newly emancipated classes were concerned.

For the entire two years and a half of his service in the Bureau, Mr. Langston made repeated visits to the former slaveholding States, in labors connected with the general advancement of the freed people. It is wholly impracticable under the circumstances, to give here anything like full accounts, with even limited details, of the tour made by him through each State visited. As illustrating the general work and the advantageous results connected therewith, it is not convenient to do more than refer to special visits made to several different States, and not more than one of the great meetings held and addressed by him in each. The States to which reference shall be made, since they are by reason of their location and character representative, are North Carolina, South Carolina, Louisiana, Alabama and Georgia, with such general allusion to the educational work in others as may seem to be pertinent and proper ; for great schools, colleges and universities were founded in several, with which the general inspector had certain relations and duties of such character and importance as to make it but just to him that special though brief mention be made of them.

On the twenty-sixth day of October, 1867, he made his first visit to Raleigh, North Carolina. He had heard much of the colored people of the Old North State, both free and slave ; how that the former down to 1835, had enjoyed, measurably, the advantages of public schools and the elective franchise ; and that the older persons of that class exhibited in conduct and life, mentally and morally, the good effects implied in that social condition. He had also heard that in that State special pains had been taken by slaveholders for a long time, with respect to their slaves, to put many of them to trades ; and that in that Commonwealth more than any other of the South, it would be found that colored persons were in large numbers master-workmen in the different mechanical callings. In his early life, he had made the acquaintance of a young black man of North Carolina, who, having mastered in that State all that was merely mechanical in the trade of the gunsmith, so that he manipulated in the most skillful manner, every material used in his art, even from its crudest condition to its most improved and polished state, but had however, been given no real knowledge of the science of his calling. His case was, indeed, characteristic ; the use of the hands simply was improved, with adequate exercise of the memory ; and there the negro mechanic, as the young man claimed, was left to struggle as best he might. And yet, so much of merely mechanical instruction had its beneficial results in moral and material advantage.

Going into North Carolina with such impressions as to the more improved condition of the colored people, and to the capital of the State of which he had heard also many pleasant things, he expected to find not only a large colored population, but one of unusual improvement, advanced in material circumstances. He expected to find schools and churches among them, well-ordered, of large membership and attendance. He expected to find among them too leading men of their own color, prepared really to direct and encourage them in the cultivation of the useful things of freedom. In all these respects he found no evidences of unworthy life and thriftlessness calculated to disappoint him. Far otherwise. For the homes of the people indicated on their part the possession of industrial wisdom and prosperity. The large attendance of orderly, comparatively well-dressed children in the schools, indicated the popular estimate put upon education; and the several large churches of varying denominational character discovered the general appreciation of morality and religion prevailing among the people. The leading man at that time found among these people, residing in Raleigh, enjoying the respect and confidence of all classes, prominent in politics and influential in the work of education and general improvement, was the Hon. James H. Harris. Active as he was at this time, manifesting constant interest in everything that concerned the welfare of the people, it is not surprising that subsequently he became both a conspicuous figure in state affairs and in Republican national conventions, wielding such influence as to win national name. He was repeatedly elected to the state Legislature, and was honored with a seat in the State Constitutional Convention. After serving thus his fellow-citizens and enjoying their confidence to the very last, Mr. Harris died only about one year ago. This gentleman, with others of like prominence, white and colored, including the governor of the State, composed the committee which received and entertained Mr. Langston on his first visit to Raleigh; and it was he who introduced him when he made his first speech there in the African Methodist Episcopal church on "The education and elevation of the colored people."

The meeting was characterized as a very large one, the most attentive and orderly that ever assembled in the city. Prominent white persons, such as Gen. Nelson A. Miles, Col. J. V. Bomford; the superintendent of education, Mr. Fiske, and the governor of the State, Mr. Holden; Hon. C. L. Harris and others attended. Mr. Langston, accompanied from his quarters in a carriage by Messrs. James H. Harris and John R. Caswell, was received by the audience as he entered the church with enthusiastic applause. Mr. Harris' address of introduction was brief but eloquent, concluding with the words, "I have now the honor of introducing to you the orator of the evening, the colored Edward Everett of America." "The Raleigh Weekly Standard," the leading newspaper of the State, in speaking of Mr. Langston's address in an editorial notice, employed the following words:

"This distinguished colored orator addressed a very large audience in the African Methodist Church in this city, on Wednesday night last, and for more than two hours held them spellbound by his genius and eloquence. We give to-day only a brief sketch of this magnificent speech.

"Mr. Langston is now in North Carolina, as an officer of the Freedmen's Bureau. His address on Wednesday night was confined mainly to the subject of education. He occupied a wide field in the course of his address, and said very many things, which, if heeded and practiced by the colored race, will prove of the utmost advantage to them. The whole address was lofty and generous in its tone, and contained nothing objectionable in matter or manner to the white race. Such a man by constantly traversing the country and addressing the people of both races, would do an incalculable amount of good."

As early as November 5th, 1867, Mr. Langston visited Raleigh for the second time, and addressed in Tucker's Hall one of the largest and most enthusiastic mixed meetings ever held in the capital. Of his speech on this occasion, the "Weekly Standard" made the following comment:

"Mr. Langston spoke for more than an hour with unsurpassed ability and eloquence, laying before his audience the best exposition and defence of Republican principles to which we have ever listened. His speech produced a fine effect, and cannot fail to be productive of good among our people of all classes."

Here it is proper to state, that in his visits to North Carolina, Mr. Langston did not confine himself in his labors to the capital. He visited, inspected the school work and addressed large meetings of the people at Goldsborough, Tarborough, Wilmington, Fayetteville, Greensborough, New Berne, Elizabeth City, Charlotte and Salisbury, and wherever he went he was heard patiently and attentively by all classes.

Going subsequently into South Carolina, Mr. Langston visited Columbia, the capital, and Charleston, the principal cities of the State. In the Palmetto State he was received and treated with marked consideration and kindness. His principal meeting was held at Charleston on the Battery, in sight of Fort Sumter, upon which the first gun of the Rebellion was fired. No one shall ever describe the beauty of the city, the sea and the sky, as they appeared on the evening on which the whole city seemed to turn out to hear the colored orator from the North; and no pen can record in sufficiently just and truthful manner, the sober and considerate behavior with which the vast concourse of white and colored people of this Southern city heard him. He discoursed of those means of education, property and character, with loyal devotion to the government, which were essential to the elevation of the colored American, formerly enslaved, and the reconciliation and happiness of the white American, formerly the owner and master of the slaves. For two hours and a half, in the glory of a moonlight unsurpassed in that region, with the attention and respect of an audience only disturbed as it applauded the words of the speaker, Mr. Langston dwelt in effective manner upon the themes indicated. As he closed his speech in the prediction of a future to South Carolina and the nation in which all shall forget past differences of condition and nationality in the consciousness of their unity and happiness in being simply American citizens, the applause which greeted that utterance was full, cheering, enthusiastic and deafening.

He left the city of Charleston feeling that the work of education and improvement of the black and white races would go rapidly on, resulting not more in the complete renovation and exaltation of the former than the happiness and prosperity of the latter.

After his return from South Carolina, and during the presidential canvass of 1868, Mr. Langston received a communication from the leading Republicans of the State bearing upon his late visit and asking his return, which shows how profoundly and generally his labors had affected the people, and how they were appreciated. This communication is inserted here, in justice as well to those who wrote, signed and transmitted it, as to him of whom it speaks and whose efforts were sought.

"*Columbia, S. C.*, September 25, 1868.

" JOHN M. LANGSTON, ESQ.,
"Dear Sir:

"The undersigned, members of the Republican party, having heard your recent addresses in this State, and being convinced that your services as an orator and public speaker would be of the utmost advantage to the friends of justice and equal rights in this State, respectfully and earnestly urge and solicit you to return to our State during the present campaign and join in the great work of carrying South Carolina by a decisive majority for Grant and Colfax.

" Without intending any personal flattery, we say to you that we believe your superior education and powers as a speaker will command a hearing and consequent enlightenment of mind on the part of our white fellow-citizens, which they would accord to no other man within our acquaintance.

" Pray endeavor to so arrange your duties as to allow you to be with us during the month of October.

" We remain, dear sir, very respectfully, your obedient servants,

(Signed.) ROBERT C. DELARGE, Rep. from Charleston.
J. A. SWAILS, Senator from Williamsburg.
W. R. HOYT, Senator from Colleton.
T. J. MOSES, JR., Speaker of House of Reps.
C. H. PETTINGILL, Rep., Williamsburg.
A. J. RANSIER, Rep. from Charleston.
R. H. CAIN, Senator from Charleston.
REUBEN TOMLINSON, Rep. from Charleston.
H. W. PURVIS, Rep. from Lexington.
CHARLES D. HAYNE, Rep. from Barnwell.
D. E. CORBIN, Senator from Charleston.
JONATHAN J. WRIGHT, Senator from Beaufort.
JAMES M. ALLEN, Senator from Greenville.
W. E. ROSE, Senator from York.
Y. J. P. OWENS, Senator from Laurens.
J. K. JILLSON, Senator from Kershaw.

W. B. NASH, Senator.
L. WIMBUSH, Senator, Chester.
H. J. MAXWELL.
H. H. JENKS.
JOHN B. DENNIS.
WM. W. H. GRAY, Rep. from Charleston.
BENJ. F. JACKSON, Rep. from Charleston.
J. H. RAINEY, Senator from Georgetown.
R. J. DONALDSON, Senator, Chesterfield."

However anxious Mr. Langston was to comply with this very cordial and flattering invitation, he was so situated by reason of prior engagements, that he was unable to do so. He therefore made this reply:

"*Oberlin, Ohio*, October 1, 1868.

"Dear Sirs:

"Your welcome letter of September 25, has been received. I thank you for the kind invitation which it conveys to return to your State to aid you, according to the measure of my ability, in carrying the election therein by a majority as large as possible for Grant and Colfax, the nominees of the Republican party, and the representatives of Law and Order, Peace and Liberty. I am only too sorry that prior engagements, connected with my official duties and the canvass, render it impracticable for me to accept your invitation.

"You will permit me in this connection to thank you for the grateful words in which your approval of my course when in your State recently are expressed.

"With sentiments of profound gratitude and with high consideration for each one of you personally,

"I have the honor to be, yours very respectfully,

"JOHN MERCER LANGSTON."

Mr. Langston made his first visit to Louisiana, reaching New Orleans, December 31, 1867. His arrival in that city and State was heralded by the "New Orleans Republican," in an editorial which reads as follows:

"It is with no common pleasure we announce the arrival in our city of the Honorable J. M. Langston, of Ohio, one of the ablest lawyers and most eloquent orators the colored race in this country has produced. Mr. Langston, we understand, visits the South in the capacity of general inspector of schools for colored children, under instructions from Major-General Howard, commissioner of the Freedmen's Bureau, and not as many may suppose, purely in the interest of any political party, although to say that he is no partizan would be doing him an injustice. All the readers of the Republican will remember

LABORS IN THE SOUTH. 285

the eloquent speeches delivered by him in Mississippi and published in our columns last summer. It is but truth to say that no speeches comparable with them have been in our columns since. We know of but two or three men in our national legislature who can approach him in natural gifts of speech and cultivated graces of oratory. He is an able, honest and loyal man, loyal to his country, loyal to his race, and not ashamed to stand up before the whole world and in himself prove that while a negro's blood is in his veins, a more than white man's eloquence is on his tongue, a more than white man's loyalty is in his heart.

"On New Year's day Mr. Langston's voice will be heard in Mechanic's hall. Let the loyal people of New Orleans crowd it to its utmost capacity. No worthier man has stood upon its platform, no abler man has reasoned with the people who are there wont to assemble. Go early, and you will need no further inducement to remain late."

Mr. Langston remained in the city in connection with his labors there for some two or more weeks, during that time visiting several places in the State, especially the capital, Baton Rouge. Besides visiting every colored school, inspecting and addressing them all, he made seven stated speeches in different sections of the city, beginning with the one delivered in the hall of Mechanic's Institute, and closing with the one delivered at the St. James African Methodist Episcopal church. At this time, the Constitutional Convention of the State of Louisiana was in session in its chief city, and the leading men of the State of both classes and all parties were in New Orleans, each full of enthusiasm and purpose with regard to what he conceived to be the organic law needed for the State. A large number of the members of the convention and those in attendance upon it, honored Mr. Langston by attending his meetings. Among the gentlemen who gave special attention to him, doing all in their power to make his visit and labors pleasant and profitable, were, of the colored class, Captains P. B. S. Pinchback and James H. Ingraham, Dr. Roudenez and Major Dumas, Hons. Oscar J. Dunn and George Y. Kelso; and of the white class, leaders of the Republican party, Messrs. H. C. Warmoth and M. A. Southworth, Thomas J. Durant and J. H. Sypher, J. S. Harris and W. L. McMillen. Nearly all of these gentlemen were members of the committee which received and entertained Mr. Langston, displaying in that regard the most generous hospitality, with exalted personal consideration. The manner in which he was treated is fully evidenced in the fact that through the kindness of this committee, his trip to Baton Rouge was made upon the beautiful steamer, the "Wild Wagoner," as put at his disposal for the trip by its owner, General Mansfield, with such outfit for his accommodation in every way as could be called only princely.

At the meeting held at Mechanic's Institute, Capt. P. B. S. Pinchback was made president, assisted by a large number of vice-presidents. The audience was an immense one, bright and brilliant by reason of the presence of so large number of beautifully dressed ladies, and distinguished by the attendance of many persons of note and character. Perhaps no meeting held in any one of the great cities of the Union among the colored citizens, was ever honored by the presence of so many men of their own class noted for their wealth, intelligence and social position. This will not be doubted when one calls to mind the names of those who composed the committee of reception just now given. The speech of the occasion was given respectful, attentive audience for the full two hours occupied in its delivery, and the applause which accompanied its utterance, as well as the congratulations which were given the speaker at its close, testified of the good impression which had been made and the favor which he had won.

In its issue of January 2nd, 1868, the "New Orleans Republican," among other things contained the following complimentary notice:

"The hall of Mechanic's Institute was crowded almost to suffocation last night to hear the eloquent orator from Ohio, Mr. John M. Langston. He disappointed no one. All who went expecting to hear an able man heard one. His speech would have filled the gallery of the House of Representatives or the Senate chamber in Washington had it been delivered in either of them, and would have both gratified and enlightened learned senators and members of Congress and the people generally.

"His speech last night satisfied us who for the first time heard him, that he is destined to wield an immense influence with the colored people of this country, and that influence, we rejoice to say, in every sense of the word, will be that of a wise, sagacious, Christian statesman. We use the words Christian statesman, knowing that they mean much and should never be thoughtlessly applied. Mr. Langston is the first man we have heard in a long while to whom we have thought we could honestly apply them. In his speech last evening he confined himself to an elaborate argument to prove that the negro had always been a citizen of the United States, had fought in every war in its history in defense of the nation, had voted in almost every State and had never once raised the standard of rebellion. He maintained that the Constitution recognized no distinctions of race or color; that the word *white* was not to be found in any important public document until the cupidity of white men placed it there, and that the prosecution of the war against the rebellion which resulted in the emancipation of every slave in the land and the Reconstruction Acts of Congress were all done and passed in and not out of constitutional limits.

"This argument was the burden of the speech, and although logical throughout, it was interspersed with wit and eloquence and sarcasm which swayed the audience as if by the wand of an enchanter. Men applauded in spite of themselves; laughed in spite of themselves; frowned in spite of themselves. We were entirely satisfied with Mr. Langston and sincerely hope he can be prevailed upon to remain with us during the approaching campaign. We want his voice heard in every parish in the State and we want every white and black man in every parish to hear it. With him in the field we shall dismiss all fears about the ratification of any constitution our convention may pass."

The following letter addressed to Mr. Langston on the twentieth day of January, 1868, indicates in emphatic manner the estimate put upon his services by the thoughtful, patriotic leading men of Louisiana:

"*New Orleans, La.,* January 20th, 1868.

"MR. J. M. LANGSTON,

"Dear sir:

"We cannot allow you to leave New Orleans without expressing our gratitude for the services you have rendered the Republican cause during your brief visit. Your speeches have had the effect to destroy prejudice and build up a good feeling between the two races. Our greatest regret is that you have to leave us so soon. The zeal you have manifested in the cause of our State induces us to intrude a few requests.

"You have seen enough here to show you that our canvass must be conducted almost entirely by speakers. Public documents and printed speeches are much needed to aid us with those whose education is such that they can read; but the great masses of our people are illiterate and can only be instructed by speakers and canvassers. We therefore hope you will call upon the Executive Committee at Washington and impress this upon its members.

"We need about six good speakers, two or three of whom should be colored men, and money enough to send them with about twenty others into the country parishes. We have but few railroads and off the river communication our expenses will be very large. We will be able to raise among us here from eight to ten thousand dollars. We need aid of our friends in the North to the amount of ten thousand dollars more. With this we feel sure we can reach every voter in the State and carry the Constitution.

"We wish to invite your aid in this matter and feel sure that you will meet with success.

"May we hope to have you return and aid us in the campaign. If so, we will be profoundly grateful.

"Very truly your friends,

(Signed.) W. L. McMILLEN, H. C. WARMOTH,
GEORGE Y. KELSO, JAMES H. LANDERS,
JAMES H. INGREHAM, GEORGE W. DEARING, JR.,
J. S. HARRIS, SIMON JONES,
M. A. SOUTHWORTH, HUGH J. CAMPBELL,
T. A. RAYNALS, J. H. SYPHER.

However willing to serve his friends of Louisiana and do what he might to promote and sustain Republican principles and measures in that State, as manifested in the election of candidates of the Republican party and the ratification of the State Constitution, Mr. Langston was not able to return thereto, as requested and urged in the above letter. He had to content himself with advising the National Executive Committee as to the necessities of the Republicans of the State, and pressing the importance of generous action in such regard.

Justice requires that emphatic mention be made in this connection of five colored men, leaders of their race and prominent and conspicuous members of the Republican party, residents of Louisiana, upon whose influence and assistance Mr. Langston relied largely when visiting that State. Messrs. P. B. S. Pinchback, Oscar J. Dunn, George Y. Kelso, Dr. Roudanez and Major Dumas, were all persons actively engaged in reconstructing their state government and in the inauguration and promotion of such good social enterprise as tended to the improvement of their race in every substantial way. The name of each is recorded here with feelings of gratitude as well as admiration. The record which each has made in his own way, upon his own intelligence and efforts, proves how wisely and correctly any discreet observer discovered at once in their conduct the brilliant future which lay before him.

It was while Mr. Langston was in Louisiana at this time that General Warmoth and Oscar J. Dunn were put in nomination for the governorship and lieutenant-governorship of the State by the Republican party. It was largely through his influence that the Constitutional Convention, then in session, was brought to change a provision of the document, upon which it had already acted, reducing the age of the governor from thirty years to twenty-five, so as to make General Warmorth eligible. It was through his influence largely, also, that Mr. Dunn finally accepted the nomination to the lieutenant-governorship. At first, such was the feeling among certain of his most reliable friends with regard to the nomination, that fears were entertained by them as to the final results. Besides, several of such friends, knowing his great influence and the preponderating effect which it would likely produce in favor of the ticket nominated, and who favored a colored person at its head, exerted themselves to the extent of their power to prevent his acceptance. These considerations at first seemed to have great weight with Mr. Dunn. More than this, without political and official experience of any sort, he felt misgivings as to his ability to discharge in acceptable manner the duties which might be enjoined upon him. The prospect was that they might be numerous, difficult and responsible. It was not until Mr. Langston had spent four full hours in serious earnest appeal to Mr. Dunn, as they walked up and down Canal Street upon the night of his nomination, and at last when they were about separating at four o'clock in the morning at his house, in the presence of his wife, Mr. Langston made a moving, persistent, final entreaty to him, in the name of his race, to accept the high honor and responsibility tendered him ; and not then, until Mrs. Dunn, inclining to the views presented by Mr. Langston, said, " My husband, you must do your duty," that he gave the least evidence of his purpose to yield his judgment and accept the nomination.

Subsequently, after General Warmoth had been elected governor and Mr. Dunn lieutenant-governor, the latter finding himself at home in his new position, honored by his fellow-citizens as few men had ever been on a memorial occasion of mutual interest and pleasure, he thanked Mr. Langston for the manner in which he had insisted upon his acceptance of the nomination of his party to the high office which he held. It is a fact, too, that Mrs. Dunn never met Mr. Langston, at home or abroad, that she did not in cordial terms thank him for his conduct and treatment of her husband, as described. And it is matter of congratulation that Oscar J. Dunn, the first lieutenant-governor of the colored race duly elected by the voters of any State of the Union, proved to be in all his conduct an official without spot upon his good name, of large and commanding influence, honored and respected by his fellow-citizens of every class and political faith.

It is perhaps true that in no part of the South was Mr. Langston received with greater consideration and heard by larger audiences than in Alabama on the various visits which he made to that State. He visited Montgomery, and spoke there at the capitol on the third day of Feburary, 1868. His address delivered at that time before an immense concourse of people, was published in the papers of the State, although it was extremely lengthy, covering ten columns in the "Daily State Sentinel." Comments upon it were favorable, generally, and in some instances flattering. The editorial notice of the "Sentinel" read as follows:

"We have great pleasure in laying before our readers to-day a report of the masterly speech of the Hon. John M. Langston of Ohio, delivered on Thursday last to the public meeting held at the capitol. No report could do justice to the orator, and we have been reluctantly compelled, for want of space, to omit the many racy illustrations which made the performance sparkle. Those who had the privilege of listening to his address will long remember it, and we are assured that our readers will enjoy the perusal even of the meager report in our columns."

It was at the close of this speech that the governor of the State (Parsons), who had given respectful, considerate attention to it throughout, taking from his own shoulders in the presence of the retiring masses of the people his cloak, threw it about Mr. Langston as he hurried him from the steps of the building from which he had spoken, by his own kindly assistance into the executive office, where he found fire, with warmth and protection against cold. Such considerate treatment under the circumstances, made deep impression upon the heart of its recipient, and even to this day it is recalled with feelings of profound gratitude.

It was at Montgomery during one of his visits that Mr. Langston witnessed the first general election of a Southern State in which the newly emancipated class was permitted to take part. At this time he had been in the city several days, prosecuting his work as general inspector, visiting and examining the schools of the freed people and directing as to their general interests during the day, and at night attending Republican league clubs, holding meetings and arranging for the forthcoming election, being thus detained and occupied in useful service. Such devotion to principle and party as was shown by the new voters can never be effaced from his memory. Their patience, their endurance of insult, threats, and in some cases even violence, were marvelous; while it did really appear from the extended, crowded lines of persons pressing forward to vote, that not a single colored man had been left at home. Everyone as a rule voted the Republican ticket, even those who knew full well that to cast such a vote was certain sure dismissal from the service of those in whose employment they gained their daily support for all dependent upon their labors.

Besides visiting places of less importance while in Alabama, Mr. Langston gave special attention to the condition of the freed people in the greater cities of Montgomery, Selma, Demopolis and Mobile. And wherever he went he found them industrious, diligent, and often thrifty; all of whatsoever condition exhibiting especial interest in education.

About the middle of February, 1868, Mr. Langston made his first visit to the State of Georgia. He went directly to Atlanta, where he made his home with the teachers engaged at the time in the conduct and management of the colored schools of that city. He was received by them in cordial hospitable manner, and through the good offices of Mr. Ware, who was at once the principal of the schools and a subordinate agent of the Freedmen's Bureau, he was enabled to make a general and thorough inspection of the educational work among the freed people throughout the State; visiting such places as Savannah, Macon, Griffin, Columbus, Brunswick, Augusta, Americus, Albany and Andersonville. At each of these places, he not only did the special school work with which he was charged, but addressed on their educational and material improvement, large popular audiences. It was at Albany, when speaking in the evening in the Baptist church of the place, and while urging the young colored men who composed in part his audience, to educate themselves as thoroughly as might be and as speedily, in view of the special responsibilities which awaited them in the early future, that he predicted that some of them might be called to high national official place; whereupon, an aged Southern man, seated upon the platform and near the speaker, having his prejudices deeply aroused, cried out at the top of his voice, "Never! Never, in the United States of America!" It was not long, however, before Mr. Langston's prediction was verified in the nomination and election of Mr. Jefferson Long to Congress from the Macon district of the State.

Among the most interesting and largely attended of all these meetings, was that held Sunday afternoon at Andersonville, near the old Rebel prison, where at that time the work of educating the freed children was conducted by two most efficient white lady teachers, one from Ohio and the other from California. All classes of the people turned out to hear the address on this occasion, and everyone gave attentive, serious, respectful audience. In fact, wherever he went in the State, he found the people of both classes ready to receive him with marked consideration, and hence his tour of the State was not only interesting but remarkably pleasant.

At Atlanta, Mr. Langston found on his arrival the State Constitutional Convention in session. The city was overflowing with distinguished orators, politicians and statesmen of the Commonwealth. He was himself specially honored by an invitation of thirty members of the convention to speak in their hall at such time as might suit his convenience. The correspondence between these gentlemen, members of the convention and Mr. Langston, was as follows:

"*Hall Georgia Constitutional Convention.*
"Atlanta, Ga., Feb. 11th, 1868.

"JOHN M. LANGSTON, ESQ.,
"Dear sir:

"The undersigned members of the Georgia Constitutional Convention will be pleased to have you speak in their hall at such time as you may find it convenient to do so.

(Signed.)

JAS. G. MAUL,	O. H. WALTON,
A. A. BRADLEY,	G. W. ASHBURN,
D. G. COTLING,	T. G. CAMPBELL,
S. W. BEAIRD,	J. H. CALDWELL,
W. H. ROZAR,	G. W. CHATTERS,
L. G. W. MINOR,	R. ALEXANDER,
P. B. BEDFORD,	J. E. BRYANT,
JOHN MURPHY,	B. CONLEY,
ALFRED BOWDOIN,	W. L. CLIFT,
FLOYD WOOTEN,	ISAAC SEELEY,
GEORGE HARLAN,	W. N. NOBLE,
WM. C. CARSON,	J. A. JACKSON,
JOHN T. COSTIN,	JAMES STEWART,
J. C. CASEY,	C. H. PRINCE,
H. M. TURNER,	J. M. RICE."

Mr. Langston replied:

"*Atlanta, Ga.*, Feb. 11th, 1868.

"MESSRS. J. E. BRYANT, H. M. TURNER, B. CONLEY, J. H. CALDWELL, and others, members of the Constitutional Convention of Georgia:

"Gentlemen:

"Your letter of this date, in which you invite me to speak in the hall of your convention, is before me. I thank you for this kind invitation, and the expression of confidence which it indicates.

"It will meet my convenience to speak to-morrow night. The subject of my remarks will be. The status of the Colored American.

"With sentiments of high consideration, I have the honor to be,

"Your most obedient servant,

"JOHN MERCER LANGSTON."

A very large and beautiful audience assembled to hear the address delivered on this occasion, and the "Atlanta Daily New Era," of the thirteenth of February, expressed its estimate of the speaker and his effort in the following language:

> "A large and attentive audience of both races assembled at the hall of the convention last evening to listen to the address of Mr. Langston, the celebrated colored orator from Ohio. The theme was the right of the colored race to American citizenship, and it was discussed in a manner that fully established the reputation the orator has gained throughout the country."

The extent and importance of Mr. Langston's labors in connection with the schools, the educational and general advancement of the emancipated classes of the country, deserve here special emphasis. He labored assiduously and wisely in every State and city which he visited to those ends, always doing his utmost to inspire both parents and children with the necessity, would they achieve proper standing in the community and win success and happiness in life, to do all in their power to cultivate those sacred, valuable advantages of education and improvement, without which no race could be elevated. He reached and impressed thus thousands of children found in the schools, while through his influence hundreds of the most interesting, intelligent, worthy young boys and girls of the race were stimulated to earnest and persistent efforts for their advancement. Thousands of parents who otherwise would have hesitated and faltered in their duty, were stirred and encouraged by the words and counsels impressed by Mr. Langston in his addresses. Wherever he addressed the freed people, he was fortunate in the attention given him and the goodly impressions which he was able to make upon the minds of his hearers. Besides, he was often able to so advise principals and teachers of the schools as to add greatly to their efficiency and success in their work.

Of the great number of state educational conventions, the large gatherings convening in connection with the laying of cornerstones of universities, colleges and schools, as at

Atlanta, Nashville and other places, and meetings held upon commencement occasions, where the services of Mr. Langston were asked and had, mention only may be made, without details which would prove without doubt interesting and pleasing. Reports, however, of all labors made in such behalf through the Bureau and its officers, attest the value as well as the earnestness and efficiency of their performance.

Among the most agreeable things connected with his tours, his labors and his experiences under the Freedmen's Bureau in the South, was the cordial welcome which he received everywhere from the devoted, laborious, self-sacrificing workers, mostly white persons, who having left pleasant Northern homes and families, had gone among the emancipated classes, where they gave their services generally upon the most limited remuneration, sometimes without pay, to the education and elevation of the ex-slaves. But the consideration above all others which renders him satisfaction in largest measure in connection with his labors is found in the fact that so many of the young boys and young girls whom he found in the schools of the freed people of the Southern States, have since by diligence, perseverance, industry and good conduct, won for themselves respectability, influence, usefulness and name in the community. One of this class of representative young colored men, having reached exalted useful position and won national name for himself as an educator and orator, has recently died and been buried, amid universal regret and sorrow, in the soil of his own native State of North Carolina. Dr. John C. Price, the president of Livingstone College, so active, energetic and useful in life, shall not be forgotten nor lose his influence in death!

CHAPTER XX.

HE FOUNDS AND ORGANIZES THE LAW DEPARTMENT OF HOWARD UNIVERSITY AND IS MADE ITS VICE AND ACTING PRESIDENT.

As an educational instrumentality, crowning the work which had been done in that behalf in the interest of the freed people by the government through the Freedmen's Bureau, with Gen. O. O. Howard as its commissioner, Howard University had been founded and located at Washington city, the capital of the nation. Very properly it bore the name of the man who projected it and mainly contributed to the possibility and fact of its erection. If he could be personally honored in having his name used thus and the memory of his efforts in behalf of the freed people perpetuated, it was all well, for his conduct and success in this respect merited signal, conspicuous commemoration.

It was well, too, that a great liberal university, proposing to embrace and offer in its comprehensive curriculum all those subjects of education necessary to a complete and finished classical and professional training, should have established in connection with it and under its control a law department whose course of study should offer every opportunity and means according to the best and most varied standard for legal preparatory accomplishment. That necessity was met in the establishment of the law department of Howard University in 1868. After this decision, the question naturally arose as to who should be called to the high dignity and responsibility of organizing this department—the first law school known in the world for the special education of colored youth, male and female. And yet this school was to be so conducted that there should be no exclusion of any person seeking its advantages. Indeed, it was the hope of all concerned that its wise, efficient management would offer inducements calculated to bring at least a respectable number of white students to its membership and instruction.

It is apparent upon the least reflection that the person called to manage the enterprise ought to bring to his work large and various general scholarship; ought to be master of extended, minute and accurate knowledge of the law, with easy and effective methods of imparting instruction in it; with such business experience and habits as would make him successful, while moderate and sagacious in the management of the undertaking. The whole country was open to the Board of Trustees. They might make any selection they saw fit. They were not limited even by the want of means, and they might have with great propriety under the circumstances, since they were not circumscribed by any considerations of complexion or nationality, honored in their choice some distinguished white lawyer. At this time there was but a single limitation, according to the rules and regulations of the university, governing the trustees and restricting them in the choice of their teachers and professors. This limitation was found in a provision of the by-laws requiring that all persons in order to be eligible to professorships, must be members of some evangelical church in good and regular standing.

According to this rule Mr. Langston was ineligible, and when General Howard, in accordance with the action of the Board of Trustees and by their direction, notified him by written communication in which he inclosed marked copy of the by-laws, inviting his attention to the provision named, he was compelled to return reply to the effect that he could not accept the position of professor of law, to which according to his letter he had been elected, since he was not a member of any church and had not concluded to join one. Thereupon, however, the Board of Trustees abrogated that regulation, and thus made Mr. Langston eligible by their action to the professorship which they tendered him, and he was unanimously elected thereto on the twelfth day of October, 1868. Within a reasonable time after this action, he proceeded to the organization of the department; not however until as late as September, 1869, after he had terminated his relations with the Freedman's Bureau.

In the regular organization of the department there were appointed as his assistant professors, Hon. A. G. Riddle and Judge Charles C. Nott, and as instructor, Mr. Henry D. Beam, all these persons being white lawyers of excellent name and standing, bringing to the department, therefore, large and commanding influence. The department was successful in the numbers, the character and the conditions of its students from the beginning. Its first class numbered ten persons, one lady and nine gentlemen. All completing the course regularly, according to requirement, after a thorough examination upon every branch of the law, were graduated and admitted to practice in the Supreme Court of the District of Columbia. The course embraced three years of time, and the students were required to pursue with diligence and regularity, under their several lecturers, professors and instructor, all branches of the law, with exercises in a well-organized and thoroughly conducted moot court, held every two weeks. The forensic exercises, consisting of disserations, addresses and debates, with what was known in the department as "the extemporaneous oration" on law topics, held weekly under the direction of the dean, were calculated really to fit a student in thorough and complete manner for the duties and labors in the office and the court house, of an attorney and counsellor at law and solicitor in chancery.

So far as the recitations, the exercises of the moot court and the extemporaneous oration were concerned, special effort was employed to make each most thorough and advantageous. The extemporaneous oration was employed to develop in the students ease, grace and effect in what might be termed impromptu forensic address, and to cultivate in them readiness and accuracy of thought, with immediate command and control of their knowledge bearing upon any subject put in issue and debate. This exercise was found to be in the beginning exceedingly difficult, and from it students as a rule drew back, preferring to write and commit to memory. However, after they had contracted the habit, to some extent, of excogitation, or of calling to mind their information and learning, holding all in memory, fitting the dress to the thought and presenting the same in natural, graceful manner, according to the occasion and its requirements, this exercise became altogether acceptable, and discovered in many cases the greatest possible versatility and power of address. It was found to be true as a result of this exercise, that very soon the young man who could not extemporize as required for the shortest possible period in his exercises, became finally often a steady, effective speaker, as easy and natural as a born orator. It would be difficult to find a single student trained by this method, who was not according to the ordinary standards of oratory an effective speaker.

The exercises of the moot court, including the draft of all papers, the management of every sort of suit involving the principles and rules of law, both civil and criminal, with the practice of the courts, fitted one, in the mastery of himself, his general knowledge as well as that of the law and its practice, for active, earnest work in his profession. These exercises were conducted under the immediate supervision and direction of the instructor, Mr. Beam, who besides his large natural interest therein, was admirably fitted for their conduct by his extended and various knowledge of ordinary legal practice.

Besides such exercises, calculated to work the results indicated, the lecture system of instruction was diligently and thoroughly cultivated. It would be found difficult, indeed, to offer any students lecturers more acceptable and efficient in a class-room than Mr. Riddle and Judge Nott, both possessing great aptness in the art of imparting instruction, with such agreeable manner as to gain and hold the attention of the most indifferent student. With the recitation system as thoroughly and diligently cultivated, it would be quite impossible for any student with average ability and ordinary learning, to pursue the course for the time required with only tolerably fair diligence, without mastering its various branches of study. Careful examination at the opening of every recitation and lecture was made with the class upon such portion of study as had been considered at a former meeting, so that it was quite difficult for any one of the students to pass any class duty in his studies unimproved.

All recitations, lectures and other exercises of the department, except the Sunday morning lecture, were had in the evening, after five o'clock. Such was the good understanding with President Grant and his cabinet officers, during both his terms of the presidency, so far as Howard University and its educational work were concerned, that Mr. Langston was able to secure for his students of the law department, clerical and other positions of service under the government. Thus, by working during the day, they could earn fully all means required for their support and education, including all text-books which they might need. Indeed, some of the students received such monthly remuneration as to enable them to save means for future use, after they had met every ordinary necessary outlay. At times Mr. Langston had as many as a hundred persons, male and female, colored and white, thus located, while pursuing their studies as his law students. General Grant was especially interested in the education of colored youth, and in more than a hundred ways showed his deep concern for the success of Howard University and the work of its law department.

As the faculty of the department was organized with Mr. Langston as its dean, as already intimated, and Mr. Beam its secretary, it became the duty of the former to deliver a course of lectures to the students upon professional ethics. These lectures, involving full exposition of those branches of intellectual and moral philosophy so essential to strong, firm basis even in a thorough understanding of the law, were prepared and delivered with great care. The wise comprehension of the ethics of the profession was calculated to inspire a high ideal of its dignity and aim in the student, with such sense of honor and courteous, considerate conduct as to give him favor and influence finally, with the client, the court and the jury. And this the lecturer appreciating, sought to impress upon the students. The lectures were delivered during each term from nine to ten o'clock every Sunday morning, in the principal lecture room of the department. All the law students were required to attend, and it was in no sense an irksome duty for a single one. Besides, it was common for large miscellaneous attendance of the university generally, and their friends, to manifest their interest in the exercises.

Not infrequently this Sunday lecture of the dean, like the forensic exercises and the moot court, was visited by distinguished, scholarly persons; sometimes those learned in the law, as well as at others those conspicuous among leading thinkers; who often by their words as well as their presence, complimented and honored the school. Sometimes these Sabbath morning exercises were made great occasions of note and influence when some distinguished philosopher or lawyer addressed the students.

The friends of the university will not forget how memorable these exercises were made on a certain Sabbath morning, when on the invitation of the dean, Ralph Waldo Emerson visited the department and upon an urgent appeal made to him, addressed the students, telling them as no other man could do what books they should read. This lecture, reported by a sort of providence, without any special arrangement therefor, carried the school in name and influence around the world. For how could Emerson speak under such circumstances, before such an audience, without sending his words as on the wings of the wind to the uttermost parts of creation! So his address appearing in the "New York Tribune" the following Monday morning, went on its mission, to be read as it moved in every language, by every student who would improve himself as he purified and elevated his soul, through those impalpable though real agencies whose lasting influence in their immortal presence forever attract and win the spirit of those who find companionship with great authors in their written printed teachings. But this lecture was worth more to the student than the lessons taught in its illustration of sentiment and doctrine. It was a practical enforcement and exposition beyond all comparison as to the admirable condition in which one finds himself when forced to summon all his thoughts and learning for a pressing occasion, and when he is compelled, standing upon his feet or seated in the lecturer's chair, to dress his thoughts, the creations of his imagination and his learning, presenting the whole in such logical order and scholarly method as to charm and impress those who hear, admire and applaud. Here was forceful illustration of the good effects of the "extemporaneous oration," seen in its golden fruits as employed by the philosopher and scholar *par excellence* of the country.

On this occasion, in hesitating to address the class when first asked to do so by the dean, Mr. Emerson stated that it was not his habit as a rule to speak without careful preparation. Consenting however, finally, his performance demonstrated how easily one, the master of himself and his powers, thoughts and knowledge, can use even upon the spur of the moment, in impressive, winning style, with grace of diction and effective imagination, those commanding ideas, principles and maxims which constitute the rules of education and moral growth. No exercise was ever permitted in the law department of Howard University on Sunday morning, the lesson of which, with the impressions made, did not tend to the highest professional, ethical instruction of the students. And, perhaps, no address ever exerted larger influence for good to the students than this one of the noted philosopher of New England.

Mr. Langston, with his associates, professors and instructor in this department, served for seven years, and in every sense and particular there was sustained among them absolute harmony of purpose and effort. To speak of Hon. A. G. Riddle as a lawyer of first-class ability, accomplishment and influence, possessing national name, and as being a lecturer of rare qualities of learning and effective address, is not to compliment him specially, only to do him simple justice in unvarnished phrase. To speak of Judge Nott as a lawyer occupied constantly with those matters of professional thought and effort of exalted and intricate character, and thus made familiar with the law in its science and letter by experience as well as study; and rendered the more competent to impart instruction with regard thereto, in reliable, impressive manner; expert and apt as he was, naturally, in teaching, is to use such language with respect to him as would indicate but poorly his merit. As a conscientious and faithful instructor, earnest and painstaking, well read in the law and enthusiastic in his efforts to impart a knowledge of it to his students from the text-books and otherwise, and as laborious in the skillful and efficient management of the moot court, Mr. Henry D. Beam won the respect, the confidence and the admiration of his colleagues of the faculty and the students of the department. Thus organized and constituted, the special instructions and exercises of the department were conducted for the whole time during which Mr. Langston acted as professor and dean. The results accomplished were, all things considered, entirely satisfactory.

It was in the law department of Howard University that the first class of colored law students ever known in the United States was organized, and for the first time in the history of the world a young lady was found in the class, sustaining full membership, who graduated with her associates in June, 1872. Miss Charlotte B. Ray, leading all her sisters in that course of study and with the full purpose of professional labor, graduated with high honor. In all her examinations and in the public exercises occurring in connection with the graduation of the class, in which she took part, reading a paper on *Equity*, as she had prepared it, this young lady from New York city, the daughter of Rev. Charles B. Ray, a person well and favorably known, showed herself thoroughly fitted for service in her profession.

The students of the department were not only required to pursue with care and master its curriculum, but to subject themselves upon the close of the course in order to graduation to a final rigid written examination upon one hundred carefully prepared questions covering the whole body of the law in its theory and practice, in test of their qualifications for admission to the Bar upon the diploma which might be awarded them ; and to prepare to the approval of the dean, commit to memory and deliver or read on Commencement Day a dissertation upon some subject of the law selected by the student. These commencement exercises were of a very high order, and drew large audiences of the very best people, white and colored, of Washington city to the First Congregational church, where they were always held. It was the uniform rule at their close to have the graduating class addressed by some learned member of the profession. The first class was addressed by Hon. Charles Sumner. He had been engaged already to address on the same evening the graduating class of the Columbia Law School, and his remuneration had been fixed at a very large sum, when he was invited by the dean to address this first class of colored law graduates. However, when the invitation was presented and the circumstances of the case were explained, especially those features impressed that this was the first class of young colored lawyers ever graduating in the world ; that no man could so fitly address them as himself, and that no other man should have the honor, Mr. Sumner forewent the other engagement and consented to perform this duty. His address was one of the finest, as it was one of the most appropriate orations that it had ever been the privilege of any graduating law class to hear. It was model and matchless in sentiment, doctrine and diction, conveying to the students such counsels and directions as they needed, about to enter as they were upon untried ways to them and their kindred, in a country where prejudice existed against them on every hand, and yet where the great principles of law in the light of which they must be elevated, if at all, were to be discussed, expounded and enforced by legislative enactment and judicial construction and application.

After the graduation of the first class, others followed in due course annually thereafter during Mr. Langston's continuance in charge of the department. It was at this time that the very ablest young colored lawyers studied and graduated under his tuition. A large number of young white persons also pursued their course of professional study under his direction, graduating according to the circumstances of their several cases with the ordinary classes of the department. Among those who pursued the course of study now settled in business in various sections of the country, may be mentioned Messrs. James C. Napier and Josiah T. Settle, residing respectively at Nashville and Memphis, Tennessee; James H. O'Hara, Winston, North Carolina; Joseph E. Lee, Jacksonville, Florida; D. A. Straker, Detroit, Michigan; E. H. Belcher, Atlanta, Georgia; M. M. Holland, John A. Moss, Thomas B. Warwick, J. W. Cromwell, William E. Matthews, John C. Rock, James H. Smith, Will. H. Cole, Washington City, D. C.; A. N. Gage, G. W. Boyden, Chicago, Illinois; James Rouse, Bedford, Pennsylvania, and D. W. Stevens, Oberlin, Ohio. Others might be named as having succeeded well in their profession within the first ten or fifteen years after their graduation, but who too prematurely sickened and died, in some cases from exposure and overwork in their inhospitable situations in the South; while one or two were killed because of their earnest and manly defense of dark-hued clients, whom they sought to protect in the use of such legal professional means as they deemed just and proper. Among those of the first class referred to, all able as young lawyers, well educated and promising, who had made their mark before passing away, were Messrs. O. S. B. Wall, John F. Quarles, John H. Cook, Charles N. Thomas, George E. Johnson, George H. Mitchell, Abram W. Shadd, R. P. Brooks, John H. Blanheim, William C. Roane, Edwin Belcher, Charles N. Otey, H. O. Wagoner, Jr., Mary Shadd Carey and James M. Adams, whose names and characters are held in honorable memory by those who knew them; while among those whose lives were brought to violent close in outrage and wrong must be recorded the name of Mr. Nathaniel G. Wynn. He was engaged at the time of his murder, in Lake Village, Chicot County, Arkansas, where he had located, in defending a negro client against whom public sentiment was unduly aroused and whose defence, requiring earnest and vigorous effort, brought him in contact and conflict with a baser class of society whose leaders did not hesitate to plan and execute his assassination. He was a student of rare native and acquired ability, of moderate though energetic habits of life, forceful and eloquent in his utterances to the court and jury. He made display always, of such skill and capacity in the management of a cause, as seemed to promise from the very beginning success in its conduct.

The circumstances connected with the death of Captain O. S. B. Wall were such as to justify special comment upon his case. He had been practicing at the Bar regularly for some years, winning not only a good name as a practitioner, but making large gains by diligent and honorable management of his business. It was while standing before the court arguing a cause that he was stricken with paralysis. He lingered for one year, broken in body and shattered in intellect, most of the time helpless, with his reason gone, dying in 1891, profoundly mourned by his relatives, friends and patrons. Naturally a man of sterling qualities of character, improved greatly in all respects by his professional education and training, he not only became a person of broad general influence, but won the highest respect and consideration of those who employed him as their attorney and of those who knew him as a citizen, neighbor and member of society.

Mr. John H. Cook, who died two years before Captain Wall, his classmate, had won before his death high consideration among the lawyers of the Washington Bar. In all his efforts he displayed careful study, accurate knowledge, with unusual tact and ability. While he was not eloquent he possessed talent, application, industry and perseverance, with such abundant fidelity to duty that he was recognized by all as a most worthy, reliable and efficient attorney.

John F. Quarles, by appointment of Gen. U. S. Grant, president of the United States, was in 1872, at the request of Mr. Langston sent as United States consul to Barcelona. He was continued in that service, as transferred by reappointment of President Hayes subsequently to Malaga. He served in this capacity in all seven years. Quitting the service, on returning to this country he located as an attorney and counsellor at law in New York city. When he was taken sick and suddenly died, he had been located in the metropolis, doing a large lucrative business meantime, for five years. He had made such impression upon his associates at the Bar and the court before which he chiefly practiced, that honorable special action and notice were made of his death, with record thereof placed upon the records of the court. He was a young man of rare scholarly accomplishment and promise, and his death has caused a void which will be filled if at all, with greatest difficulty from the ranks of his race.

Mr. James M. Adams, who died within the year 1892, was a young white man of such sterling qualities of individual character and devotion to his duty as a Republican, fearless in the advocacy of the broadest liberal principles of social equality, even as embracing all persons without distinction of complexion or nationality, that he is worthy of emphatic, favorable mention here. Besides, he became a lawyer of mark in the region of country where he lived and died, and thus rendered himself a noted illustration of earnest and successful professional achievement.

Indeed the graduates of this department while under the management of Mr. Langston, discovered in their practice wherever situated such preparation for service and such appreciation of professional obligation and duty that they, so far as attempts were made by them to perform the services of the attorney and counsellor at law, won marked and influential positions as members of the Bar.

As the name and character of the law department of the university became known and the results of its training were made manifest, an increasing number of white students joined it and pursued, with their colored associates, its regular courses of study, many of them graduating with honor and satisfaction to their friends. Several such persons in different parts of the country are now occupying conspicuous and desirable positions in the profession.

No class graduated without a parting word from the dean delivered immediately after he had presented the diplomas, and it was always one of counsel and encouragement. Every State of the South had its representatives in the law department; several of the North were also represented, and quite a number of persons from the West Indies attended upon its instructions.

All the students of the department entertained and manifested uniformly toward their dean special respect and affection. They not only yielded ready obedience to every rule and regulation prescribed, but every request and suggestion of his was accepted by them in the spirit of real docility, with cheerfulness and gratitude. He was regarded and treated by them as a parent and benefactor. On a noted and memorable occasion in February, 1870, the students of the department provided, at large outlay to them, certain articles of silverware, jewelry, cane and books, copies of Shakespeare's works, constituting a gift of rare richness and value, which with considerable and becoming circumstance and ceremony they presented to the dean, in expression of their high esteem and appreciation of him. The presentation, made in the presence of an imposing audience of their friends in the lecture hall of the department, was an impressive and brilliant affair. The articles were greatly admired, selected as they were with taste and judgment. They are valued and preserved as sacred heirlooms, and the donors are remembered with sentiments of profound regard and gratitude.

Perhaps no instructor ever found his students more thoroughly devoted to him, or more appreciative of his services rendered in their interest. All of them were cared for so far as necessary, not only in matters of study and scholarly culture, but in those material needed wants connected with their daily life and labors. Mr. Langston counts that his happiest days of professional labor were those spent by him in service in the law department of Howard University, and he counts them useful and honorable as he was permitted to start the foremost colored youth of the country upon those lofty dignified ways of the law, of which they and their fathers had known nothing in their experience. The results of his labors in this behalf are grateful and pleasing to him as he marks and considers the high standing already gained by the young lawyers, white and colored, who studying under his tuition and taking their diplomas of graduation from his hands, have won distinction and standing at the American Bar.

As Gen. O. O. Howard had given Mr. Langston the position of general inspector of the Bureau of Refugees, Freedmen and Abandoned Lands, so he had been instrumental in bringing him to the high scholarly, professional place in the institution of learning which bore his name. There seemed to be very little left in honorable promotion, with opportunity for dignified useful labor, which this friend could accomplish through his further efforts in this direction. But the time came in 1873, when his circumstances and duties were such that change and readjustment must be made in the presidency of the university. It seemed to be absolutely necessary that General Howard should retire altogether therefrom and a successor be provided for the place; or provision be made should he remain president in name, for a vice-president who should be in fact the acting president of the university.

It was entirely natural under the circumstances that that course in the premises be pursued and that such person be selected for duty as the projector and chief patron of the university might suggest and recommend. General

Howard had been in management of the university for some time, and in that capacity had manifested in his work such conscientiousness and sincerity, with such sagacity and moderation as from his experience and reputation might have been expected. Who then could be so well qualified to advise, counsel and direct those in authority, as this friend of the university and this person so entirely acquainted with its condition and necessities? His words were very properly considered to be those of an impartial and well-informed promoter of an enterprise which was perhaps in his estimation, above all others important and sacred.

The trustees had convened in regular meeting, with an unusually large attendance. The deans of the several departments of the university, according to a well-established regulation, were also present. The president in opening the meeting, had offered one of his most solemn, earnest prayers, asking the Lord to enlarge the understandings and enlighten the minds of those in authority, so that they might meet and discharge with due wisdom any duty which might be imposed upon them in furtherance of the university whose interests they held in their control. It was not known, nor did anyone imagine why General Howard should, under the circumstances, thus invoke with such peculiar feeling the influences of the Spirit. No one understood that he was about to make a communication as to himself, his relations to the university and his prospective movements, which would affect so deeply and seriously every person present. No one could have believed in advance of his own statement, that he could entertain and propose any change in his attitude to the presidency of the university. His position therein seemed to be from fitness and propriety, permanent and unchangeable.

However, so soon as the ordinary pressing business of the meeting had been disposed of, General Howard made known formally his purpose of leaving Washington city within a short time, for duty in connection with the army in a distant part of the country. He also submitted in the same statement, that under the rules and regulations established by the trustees he would be compelled to resign the presidency of the university. This announcement was both surprising and affecting. However, recovering somewhat from its immediate effect, while they fully appreciated the results to follow the separation, the Board of Trustees and the friends present entered, as in duty bound, promptly upon the consideration of what should be done.

At once, in anxious profound attention, all gave audience as they ought to have done to General Howard, who in clear concise manner described his circumstances, with explanation of the causes which necessitated the action proposed. He indicated, also, what might be done in the way of provision for filling the vacancy which must occur upon his resignation. If his resignation should be accepted, to take effect at once, a successor might be elected and inaugurated without delay. Should he be permitted to absent himself for an indefinite period, while holding the presidency nominally, a vice-presidency might be established and filled, the person called to that place serving from his inauguration as the acting president of the university.

So far explanations and suggestions had been made and the Board of Trustees were giving attention to them, when Mr. Langston, the dean of the law department, and Professor Westcott, the dean of the college department, were requested by the president himself to retire from the meeting for a few moments; but they were asked at the same time, not to go beyond the quick and easy reach of the meeting, as they might be needed. These gentlemen retired. Why they were asked to do so, neither understood; nor did it occur to either, that any question with respect to change in his relations to the university was to be discussed. Certainly, the dean of the law department could not have thought that his name would be in any wise considered with respect to the executiveship of the university. It was true that at the time the law department was in a most flourishing condition, with large attendance and increasing promise. However, its dean did not, in view of these facts, connect his name with such promotion as was implied in an election to the vice-presidency of the university.

About one hour had elapsed when Professors Westcott and Langston were invited to return. They had but taken their seats in the Board, when the president addressing Professor Langston, made to him what was a most surprising and unexpected announcement. It was that he had not been permitted to resign; that he had been given by the trustees an indefinite leave of absence; that provision had been made for the establishment of a vice-presidency, and that on the recommendation and request of himself, he (Professor Langston) had been elected unaminously to fill the position. He further explained that under the circumstances the vice-president would take immediate, uninterrupted charge of the university; that he would adopt his own policy as to its management, and that the president would not interfere with him, other than as he sustained and promoted him in his work. He added that so far as the salary connected with the vice-presidency was concerned, it had been fixed at fifteen hundred dollars per annum, and that there should be no interruption or disturbance of Professor Langston's relations to the law department, it being understood that he should continue his services as professor and dean therein.

Urged to decide and make known his acceptance of the vice-presidency at once, since Professor Langston questioned in his own mind his ability and fitness for such high place, with its various and trying responsiblities, he asked under the circumstances to be given a few hours, until the next morning, to accept or decline it. Upon the adjournment of the meeting he had a full, free talk with General Howard, who assured him that he would render every assistance practicable to make his administration agreeable and successful; that he personally desired very much that Professor Langston should take charge of the university, and that he had accordingly recommended him. He also said to him, "You must not decline this honor, although it brings grave resonsibilities and arduous duties."

"Your success," he continued, "in the management and direction of the law department, shows that you possess all those qualities of character, learning and experience, necessary to make an efficient and honorable record in this higher and more responsible scholarly capacity." Thus assured and encouraged, Professor Langston accepted the vice and acting presidency of the university. He was duly inducted into office and entered at once upon the discharge of its duties.

While there was deep general regret that General Howard found it necessary for him to practically resign his connection with the presidency of the university and put its management in other hands, it is a fact that Mr. Langston's appointment, as indicated, was received with great favor and popular approval. Whatever changes he found it necessary to make in any of the departments, and whatever regulations he deemed it proper to adopt for the general good of the university, were kindly and cordially approved by the authorities. Students increased in numbers; the university grew in favor, and the professors as well as the patrons were pleased with the evidences discovered on all sides of the success which was promised in the new and vigorous administration. The business condition of the university was not disturbed; really it was improved by close and economical financial management. Indigent students found themselves provided for and their interests wisely conserved. The encouraging and fostering influence of the new executive was felt no more in the law department, which he loved as the child of his own creation, than in the collegiate, the normal, the medical and the theological. Very soon there was no student under his control who did not recognize him as his friend, interested alike in his progress as a student and general prosperity and happiness. All confided in him, and without hesitation brought all matters of anxiety, trouble and disappointment to him, feeling assured that in him they would find a willing sympathizing counsellor. The professors and teachers in all the departments sustained him in every effort made to promote any special interest, and in every one of general character, concerning the whole university. In all public exercises, as in all the duties of the various faculties, as they respected ordinary instruction and discipline, he enjoyed constantly the encouragement and the support of all called to authority. Indeed, the harmony obtaining throughout the university among professors and students, as far as the acting president was concerned, with cordial good understanding, was most unusual and signal.

The first year of his administration was closing when the Board of Trustees convened in their regular annual meeting and Mr. Langston was called to preside for the first time. This meeting was held in June and about the commencement time. It found the vice-president in the midst of those duties which were naturally connected with the closing scenes of the academical year of the university, and such exercises as were usual at that time. Everything had moved smoothly as indicated, and the prosperity of the university as well as its good order was apparent. In this meeting, held June 17, 1874, the Board of Trustees adopted unanimously and transmitted to Mr. Langston its action as follows:

"Rev. George Whipple moved that the Board of Trustees express their thanks to Prof. John M. Langston for the manner in which he has discharged the duties of acting president, and we will give him our hearty support in all his efforts to sustain and carry out the policy of this Board as developed at this annual meeting."

Subsequently, on the 30th day of June of the same year, as Mr. Langston was opening the public exercises of the normal department in the college chapel in the evening of that day, General Howard, in attendance upon the meeting of the Board of Trustees then in session and as commissioned by such body, entering the chapel, asked permission to interrupt the exercises at their very beginning for a few minutes. Attention was given him accordingly, when stepping upon the platform, he delivered to the acting president in the presence of the crowded audience of students and friends of the university, a most remarkable though brief address, complimenting him upon his successful management of the affairs of the university up to that time, and stating that the trustees had found themselves so pleased therewith that they had directed him to present the follow-resolution, which had just been unanimously adopted by the board.

"Resolved: That the Degree of Doctor of Laws be and is hereby conferred on Prof. John M. Langston, Vice-President of this Board of Trustees."

This resolution, afterward duly engrossed, was presented in formal communication. It is needless to state that the address of General Howard with the action of the Board of Trustees, as explained by him, was received with the liveliest demonstrations of approval and applause by all who heard him. It was difficult indeed for Mr. Langston to even express his thanks in the simplest manner, by reason of the popular protracted exhibition of general favor showing itself for many minutes, even in uncontrollable outbursts.

Among other testimonials which may be adduced to show how, even in his rigid and thorough discipline had in the management of the university, Mr. Langston succeeded, the following extracts taken from an article written by Mr. Yardley Warner and published in "The Freedmen's Monitor" for the month of November, 1874, after a visit paid to it and a careful examination of each of its departments, are presented:

"The institution (Howard University) has just become erect and solid. The piles of her fabric have just been driven down to the hard pan prepared to bear the superstructure which the industry of the freedmen and the liberality of their friends will soon lay upon them. The local administration is the true and the vigorous; the right man has come to the front at last—John M. Langston, acting president. Talk to Mr. Langston closely; inspect everything and everywhere. See a moral standard higher and upborne more faithfully than that of any college in the South, if not than any in the North. No smoking nor spitting of any sort in the chapel nor in any of the rooms; the most thorough and easy discipline and a very happy social temper pervading the whole community inside the walls."

During the entire time of his administration called to

make no compromise with student, professor, or officer of the university calculated to disturb or lower his standard of authority and discipline, Mr. Langston maintained with equanimity and moderation the good order and prosperity of the entire institution. During this time, as acting president, he addressed the graduating class of each department, holding such views, if addressing one graduating from the normal department, or one from the college, or one from the theological, or the law or the medical, as seemed calculated to elevate and sustain the ethics of the profession to be pursued, and to stimulate active and earnest purpose in the cultivation of those sacred, holy things of learning and science, to be gained and mastered would one succeed in the highest and truest sense in the calling of his choice.

Having served the institution as professor of law and dean of the law department for seven full years, and as vice and acting president for two years of such term, after he had attended to every duty connected with the commencement exercises, presided at the annual meeting of the Board of Trustees, and had presented to them his annual report, showing the general and financial condition of the university, in June, 1876, Mr. Langston feeling that the time had arrived when a president should be provided by due election and inauguration for the institution, tendered his resignation. He felt that the time had come, with the conditions of the school, then, in every sense good and its prospect for usefulness promising, for the trustees to elect a president, who entering upon his duties with earnestness and vigor, assured of hearty support, with means, might make the university an educational power representative of the highest style of American scholarship, morality and Christian influence. In order to this end, he believed that a president of marked individual personal character, large and general reputation as a scholar and educator, and acknowledged efficiency in general business, should be elected. He held that such distinct individual character and power, with ample knowledge of and sympathy with the great body of persons to be educated at the university, were indispensable to its success. His resignation was accepted, but his name was mentioned with no little emphasis in connection with the presidency now to be filled, by the colored members especially, of the Board of Trustees. Finally, however, the Rev. George Whipple, the leading member of the Board of Trustees, and at the time the secretary of the American Missionary Association, was elected to fill the vacancy. It is due all concerned that it be stated that every colored trustee voted for Mr. Langston, while every white one voted for Mr. Whipple. However, Mr. Whipple did not accept the position, and when Mr. Langston left, his associates of the law department left also, and the university was for some time without a president. In no sense or manner was any objection or criticism made by any trustee or officer of the university, at any time during Mr. Langston's administration, of his conduct or management of its affairs. And to this day no words of censure or faultfinding have been heard in such regard, against him. In the seven years of service as professor of law and dean of the law department, and vice and acting president of Howard University, the record which he made is one of which he may not be at all ashamed, but the rather satisfied and proud.

CHAPTER XXI.

PRESIDENT GRANT APPOINTS HIM A MEMBER OF THE BOARD OF HEALTH OF THE DISTRICT OF COLUMBIA.

ON the fifteenth day of March, 1871, President U. S. Grant, "resposing special trust and confidence in the integrity, diligence and discretion of" John M. Langston, appointed him a member of the Board of Health for the District of Columbia. Such responsibility and honor had never been conferred upon a colored man before in the United States, either in connection with the national or any state government. He was the first and perhaps the only sanitarian that his race had produced so far as this country was concerned. The honor and the responsibility came without solicitation, and to the surprise of the one who was dignified by it. He had not supposed that in the creation of this sanitary organ any one of his particular class would be considered, even by a Republican administration, in the appointment and commission of those who should compose its membership; especially, since no representative of that class had claimed such technical knowledge, or gained such experience as to make his case one warranting that action in his behalf. It is true, however, that Mr. Langston was given the appointment in view of the fact that he was a lawyer by profession, and the Board of Health would, in addition to the services of learned and distinguished doctors, and an able lay member taken from

DR. D. W. BLISS.   JOHN MARBURY JR.

JOHN M. LANGSTON.

DR. T. S. VERDI.   DR. C. C. COX.

BOARD OF HEALTH OF THE DISTRICT OF COLUMBIA.

318b

the more advanced and active business class, need those of an efficient and vigorous attorney.

Created for special and well-defined objects having concern for the public health of the national capital and the District of Columbia, under a law passed by Congress February 21st, 1871, providing for and conferring authority and power in that regard, new indeed to all the people of the United States, and needing exact construction in order to its wise enforcement, it might be supposed very properly that persons eminent in their professions, noted for their technical knowledge, resulting as well from their experience and observation as reading and study, would be called to constitute the *personnel* of such Board. And, indeed, the rule indicated seems to have been the one which the president followed in the selection of the persons who should direct and control the service about to be inaugurated. Provision was made for the appointment of five persons, with salaries, each, at the rate of three thousand dollars per year.

Since all that broad field of science which had to do with all those nuisances troublesome and destructive to the public health must be explored, it was proper that at least three of the five persons to be named should be gentlemen of the medical profession, well and thoroughly read generally in their calling, and specially, if possible, with respect to the subjects implied as falling within the purview and scope of their authority and of their control. It was, too, proper under the circumstances, that the great branches of the medical profession, Allopathic and Homœopathic, should each be represented in a national health organ located as this was, finding its jurisdiction within the District of Columbia. Accordingly, the president selected Drs. C. C. Cox and D. W. Bliss as the representatives of the first, and Dr. T. S. Verdi of the second, the latter standing among the first members of his school.

Grave questions of business importance would necessarily arise with respect to the application and enforcement of those provisions of the law which respected the prevention of domestic animals from running at large within the cities of Washington and Georgetown; the establishment of one or more pounds therein; the collection and removal of offals therefrom, and the expenditure of all funds appropriated for those purposes. Hence the propriety of appointing a man of broad business knowledge and understanding, competent to the wise and effective discharge of any duty which might be involved in any action taken under the law. The Hon. John Marbury, Jr. was appointed, therefore, such member of the Board. But if doctors were needed and a business man to secure, according to the learning and ability of each, the wise and efficient enforcement of a law whose provisions were comparatively new and whose purposes had not been attempted hitherto in the District of Columbia, where more than a hundred thousand people were found, many of them persons of wealth and influence, and a large proportion of them utterly opposed to that law and any effort at its execution, how could the Board hope to succeed without the learning, skill and labors of a lawyer? Hence the appointment of John M. Langston as the lawyer of the Board by President Grant, to whom he was debtor for many marks of exalted consideration during his administration of the government. The expression of confidence and esteem made by the president in this appointment has always been profoundly and gratefully regarded.

The first meeting of the members of the Board was informal, and held at the office of the then governor of the District of Columbia just after each one had received his commission and taken the oath of office. The object in meeting at this time and at that place was to make the acquaintance of each other and to gain, so far as practicable, full understanding from Gov. H. D. Cooke as to his expectations of service from the Board, under the law establishing it and prescribing its powers and duties. At this time Mr. Langston had not met one of his future colleagues, nor had he made the acquaintance of the governor. Hence he entered the office and the presence of the meeting unheralded and without introduction, to take his seat apart and to receive no recognition until after the gentlemen other than himself, members of the Board, had been fully addressed by the governor in answer to such questions as they had seen fit to ask him, and such suggestions with respect to the enforcement of the law concerning the sanitary service as they had deemed it prudent and agreeable to make. In fact, the governor was ready to retire and the gentlemen to separate, when Mr. Langston begged of Governor Cooke the privilege of putting to him with a little more precision and definiteness two or three questions upon as many provisions of the organic law creating the Board and defining its authority. It was apparent from the appearance of the governor and the look of the members present, that it was necessary for Mr. Langston to give the authority at once by which he appeared in that gathering and essayed to catechise his excellency. Perceiving this, he made haste, taking his commission out of his pocket, to state that he had been appointed a member of the Board; that he had just taken the oath of office before the secretary of the District, and by him had been directed to appear at once at this meeting. Thereupon he was recognized, and was permitted to present his inquiries accordingly. In view of the questions put, it is but just to say that two very distinct things were discovered by all present. One was that Mr. Langston, who now engaged in conversation with the governor, putting questions to him which, when he did not seem to be quite at home in answering, so assisted him by his skillful suggestions and insinuations as to show himself fairly informed, even as a lawyer, as to the subjects upon which the conversation was had. The second was that the knowledge already shown by the governor and other members of the Board and the information imparted were neither full nor exhaustive; not even sufficient for wise and comprehensive action under the law.

Mr. Langston so soon as advised of his appointment had not only read and studied with care the provisions of the act creating the Board, but he had secured and read diligently the sanitary reports and proceedings of the Boards of

Health of Massachusetts and New York, and his questions and answers in his interview with Governor Cooke were largely founded upon and reflected such information as he had gained from those sources. It served however to put him immediately in new and pleasant relations, personally, with the members of the Board, who from that time treated him in all respects with kindly, impartial consideration. The governor thereafter, too, always displayed the most cordial, considerate respect for him.

Shortly after this occurrence the members of the Board held their first formal meeting in rooms provided for that purpose, to organize and constitute the various committees necessary for the proper discharge of its service. Dr. C. C. Cox was elected president; Dr. D. W. Bliss, secretary; John Marbury, Jr., treasurer; John M. Langston, attorney, and Dr. T. S. Verdi, health officer. The several committees were duly constituted, and the different persons selected for each were named according to their respective rank and position thereon. Mr. Langston was made chairman of the Committee on Ordinances, with Dr. Bliss as his associate member; and Mr. John Marbury, Jr. was made chairman of the Committee on Finance, with Mr. Langston as his associate. Mr. Langston's position as chairman of the Committee on Ordinances made him in fact, *ex-officio*, the attorney of the Board. As thus constituted, the standing committees remained for the entire period of Mr. Langston's membership of the Board. It was the especial duty of the Committee on Ordinances to draw all ordinances, rules and regulations needed for the government of the Board in its service, under the law of its creation. It was its further duty to pass upon all questions connected with the service involving any legal question to be decided by the Board. Its plan and order of business was to prepare and report its opinions and other matters in writing, where forms of regulation or blanks merely were required, submitting the forms in either case with the report to be approved and adopted by the Board itself. It is not difficult, in view of this statement, to apprehend and appreciate at once the dignity and responsibility of this committee, and particularly the importance and necessity of large intelligence and knowledge, with sagacity and moderation on the part of its chairman, who in the very nature of the case must handle its laboring oar. It is true, however, that in this instance Dr. Bliss was a ready, able and efficient associate, without whose aid in many cases the chairman of the committee would have found himself taxed even beyond his knowledge and ability.

No sanitary organ has been created in any part of the country composed of material as furnished in its members, prepared to enter more wisely, courageously and enthusiastically upon its duties than this one. No such organ ever accomplished more far-reaching and important results for any community than this one for the national capital and the District. Though the three physicians were gentlemen in regular practice, each with a large and rich patronage, no business duty or interest was ever permitted to interfere with their obligations as members of the Board to the public. Nor was any private engagement of Mr. Marbury, though he was an active, laborious merchant, ever permitted to disturb his duties in that respect. And though Mr. Langston was engaged in professional duties which commanded his constant attention and efforts, he never neglected the sanitary interest of the community. Meetings of the Board were held regularly once, at least, every week; when necessary, as was often the case in times of epidemics, daily. It is a fact, too, that no important subject was ever presented or considered by the Board when the learning, judgment and vote of each member, pro or con, were not taxed and given. Indeed, the members of the Board prided themselves upon such persistent purpose to consider thoroughly every proposition of business commanding their attention, that they established public meetings where free and open debate was cultivated, and where untrammelled individual vote was cast. The proceedings of such meetings were published regularly, as reported by the representatives of the press in the daily papers of the capital. Often extended addresses involving elaborate statement of facts and figures as presented by different members taking part in the debates, were published. The proceedings of the Board were always public, therefore, and conducted in such way as to challenge comment or criticism.

So far as the law was concerned, whether its enforcement respected the condemnation and abatement of those things which were declared public nuisances injurious to the general health ; or the condemnation of products, vegetable, animal or marine, unfit for use; or the collection and removal of offals, including the collection and removal of dead animals; or the prevention of domestic animals from running at large within the limits of Washington and Georgetown, care was had, while guarding scrupulously and protecting the rights of all concerned, to maintain its provisions so as to secure the highest real good of the community. It is matter of congratulation to be able to record the fact that so wisely and efficiently was every step taken in such behalf, that in no single case judicially investigated on charge made against the health officer of the Board or any other subordinate, did the Board ever leave such investigation with damage awarded against it, its officer or agent, or with detriment to the public.

It is just to state here that through the kindness and considerate action of the Board Mr. Langston was given in his assistant attorney, Mr. Henry D. Beam, such conscientious devotion to duty, ability and skill, that he was always strongly, firmly and successfully supported in the courts, whatever the question involved in any trial had against any exercise of apparently undue authority or power by the Board of Health. And Mr. Langston has never seen the time when he was not fully sensible of the great service rendered by his associate, often under circumstances which required tact, learning and persistent effort.

Within less than two years after its organization it was deemed wise by the Board of Health to appoint a health officer, not one of its members, who should give his entire time to the superintendence and direction of the service.

APPOINTED A MEMBER OF THE BOARD OF HEALTH.

Accordingly, after considerable effort to secure an efficient appointee to that place, Dr. P. T. Keene of New York city was selected for the position. He was found to be not only a gentleman of rare professional culture, with large knowledge of sanitary affairs, but an officer of great wisdom, energy and efficiency. Besides, he soon won as well the respect and confidence of the members of the Board as the favor and fidelity of the large number of inspectors and subordinates directed and controlled by him in obedience to the rules and regulations made for that purpose. During his entire association with this officer, with whom he was brought in daily official intercourse, Mr. Langston never found him at fault in apprehension of any law or regulation to be enforced through his agency; nor in want of devotion and sincerity of purpose to execute it up to the full measure intended to promote the general welfare. Such was his study of all the rules and regulations of the Board as well as the organic law, that he soon became intelligent as to his whole duty, and so fully fortified for any attempt made to meet and maintain it. It is apparent that the execution of the law in its wisest and best manner must have depended, at last, largely upon this officer, and Mr. Langston is only too glad to bear this testimony to one whose friendship and whose assistance he has always valued.

A testimony which the excellent president of the Board of Health, Dr. C. C. Cox, bore to the labors and efficiency of the Committee on Ordinances in his annual report for the year 1873, is presented here with no little satisfaction. It reads as follows:

"The report of the Committee on Ordinances presents a faithful exhibit of the enactments, regulations and blanks adopted by the board during the past year. These relate to the running at large of domestic animals in the cities of Washington and Georgetown; foul privies and water-closets; the removal of dead animals; the prevention of the spread of small pox and other epidemic, infectious and contagious diseases; disposition of garbage; the drainage of lots, etc., etc. The ordinances, prepared with great care by J. M. Langston, Esq., the distinguished chairman of the committee, will be found to embrace provisions in connection with a large variety of sanitary subjects. The best evidence of the manner in which this duty has been performed is found in the fact that, although so frequently tested in the courts, the ordinances, rules and regulations have been invariably sustained."

An agreeable experience connected with Mr. Langston's membership of the Board of Health and sanitary service, was found in an extended inspection tour, embracing several of the largest cities of the country, to gain a more comprehensive and accurate understanding of the sanitary law, the regulations, the service and its efficiency, in those cities. The Committee on Ordinances composed the commission sent on that errand; and such cities as Baltimore, Philadelphia, New York and Boston were those which were to be visited, and whose service was to be carefully and thoroughly studied in all its branches and operations, with reference to full and complete report of the results thereof to the Board. This mission was undertaken by that committee, and Dr. Bliss and Mr. Langston went abroad upon an errand which not only proved serviceable to each of them as sanitarians, but in large measure profitable to the Board itself, as the report which they made upon the completion of their inspections will show. But this tour was marked by many very amusing and agreeable incidents. One connected with their visit and experiences in Boston is especially worthy of note. It is due both gentlemen that it be stated here that Dr. Bliss and Mr. Langston were friends in the largest, best possible sense; and that understanding each other exactly and appreciating always each other's sympathies and feelings as well as each other's temper and toleration even of jest, though curious and unexpected often, they were always free and natural in their conduct when together. Hence, as both were of decidedly marked complexions—Dr. Bliss dark, for a white man, and Mr. Langston light, for a colored one—they often joked with each other as to which one constituted the negro member of the Board of Health. And it was not infrequently the case that such jokes on this subject passed between them as to stir the amusing and ridiculous in human nature to its very depth.

In order to full appreciation of the incident about to be

given, it is necessary to know who and what Dr. Bliss was. Physically a man of the handsomest possible endowment, possessing a well-formed person from head to foot and a face and head expressive of the largest native intelligence, his bearing was that of one conscious of his power and capability. He did not possess by reason of the nobility of his nature a single envious or jealous feeling. And an Abolitionist as he was in sentiment, in favor of fair and equal treatment of the colored man as respects every right, privilege and opportunity, his feelings and judgment were the result more of the promptings of his own being than the deductions and consequences of reading, thought, or abstract opinion. Hence often Mr. Langston told him that there was no special virtue to be ascribed to him because of his ultra sentiments in favor of freedom and equal rights. He told him that he was constitutionally right on all such subjects—that the Lord had made him so. But, as intimated already, he was in his complexion very dark; quite as much as if he had in his composition and blood a large infusion of the Indian. He was a person of remarkable accomplishment in his profession; a sanitarian of large various reading, extensive observation and unusual experience. His protracted services as a surgeon of the army, handling in the various hospitals thousands of patients brought under his management and control, in connection with whose treatment and care it was necessary to apply all the principles of science and the teachings of medico-sanitary art, furnished him opportunity for knowledge and improvement which developed in him a love of sanitary service, rendering him a veritable enthusiast in that respect. He allowed no opportunity furnishing addition to his stock of information of such character to pass unimproved, and no subject of moment in such behalf was treated by him as of small and useless consideration.

In the department of vital statistics, it is probably true that this country has not furnished a person more deeply read or more entirely scientific. He cultivated the literature of that subject most diligently, and constantly added to improvement upon it as discussed even in standard works, by his own various and accurate thought and observation. Besides, he was fruitful in original thought and study upon all matters of sanitation, often displaying in private conversation with his associates, or public address before the Board, enthusiasm and eloquence in the presentation, exposition and defence of any views, theory or belief which he might entertain upon the subject. He was, too, always an agreeable companion and gentleman ; full of kindly feeling ; indulgent to his friends, and fond in unusual measure of any dignified proper pleasantry. He always appeared to great advantage in society, winning by his appearance and bearing, even when in silence, the attention and respect of any who might be near him.

Dr. Bliss and Mr. Langston had been in close communication with the Board of Health of Boston, called together for such purpose, all the members being present, for quite two hours, asking questions as to the organization and conduct of the sanitary service of that city in its various branches. Careful, considerate, elaborate answers had been made thereto, with full and exact explanations as to the rules and regulations governing the service, embracing all blanks and the methods of enforcement with the checks and balances held upon its employes to secure the largest and most profitable results to the community. The promise had just been made to the members of the Washington Board of Health that at an early hour the next day they should be taken in carriages about the city and by boat to the dumping grounds for offals, to witness the practical operation and results of the service. At this point there came a lull in the conversation upon sanitary matters proper, and the president of the Boston Board of Health, Mr. Alonzo W. Boardman, inquired as to the *personnel* of the Board of Health of the District of Columbia and the style of its composition. Answers were made to his questions with considerable display of satisfaction by Mr. Langston as he spoke of the three learned doctors, a business man of high name and broad influence, and a lawyer, as constituting its membership. It came very naturally under the circum-

APPOINTED A MEMBER OF THE BOARD OF HEALTH. 329

stances for Mr. Boardman, a Boston man, to suggest by way of inquiry, "I believe you have a colored member of your Board." To this Mr. Langston replied, "Yes, we have. He is a man of great ability. He is very learned, and his accomplishments are comprehensive and various. He occupies deservedly high place in his profession, for he is complete master of everything pertaining to it. Of rare scholarly attainments, he is a sanitarian that it would be quite difficult to match anywhere in our country. And it is not certain that he has an equal in Europe. He is an eloquent man, and submits no measure as he advocates no proposition, without display of learning, eloquence and power. He is held in the very highest esteem by his fellow members of our Board, and heard by them as a sort of sanitary oracle."

While Mr. Langston was engaged in this apparently very remarkable statement about the colored member of the Board of Health of the District of Columbia, as Dr. Bliss knew him, his own dark face bore in livid colors the anxiety which moved his soul and excited his seemingly outraged sense of propriety, as the questions stood pictured in his eyes and trembling on his lips, "What does Langston mean? What is he going to say? Is he going to make a fool of himself here?" when Mr. Langston turning, with his eyes full on this matchless man—the thoughtful, expert member, indeed, of the Board of Health of the District of Columbia, worthy of all that had been said of him—addressing Mr. Boardman, said, " Mr. President, our colored member is here ; and I have now the honor to present to you my distinguished friend, Dr. D. W. Bliss!" Thereupon, Dr. Bliss, relieved by the turn given to this procedure, said, "Gentlemen, it is true, we have a colored member; and it is true that he is here. But it has not yet been determined whether my friend Langston, or myself, is that person. I am darker than he ; but his hair curls more than mine." Here a general laugh occurred, and the conference closing in cheerful pleasant feeling, all went to the restaurant for something both to eat and to drink, after Boston's generous method and style. The *actual colored member* of the Washington Board was, thereafter, as well as before, treated by all concerned in liberal, hospitable manner.

Mr. Langston was treated, always, in kindly, respectful manner by his associates in the sanitary service of the District. He was given prominence at all great gatherings convened by the Board for national or local purposes having in view the advancement and promotion of the service which it controlled. Upon all banqueting occasions, even where distinquished and foremost sanitarians even from the South were present and took conspicuous places at the tables and prominent part in the exercises, his presence and his influence were noted and emphasized ordinarily by the respectful, and often flattering mention of him and his labors by the president of the Board. It was not however until he had been called to a foreign position in the national diplomatic service, in 1877, and tendering his resignation, had come to take his leave of his associates in the service, that the Board expressing its opinion and estimate of him and his service, formulated and adopted by unanimous vote the following complimentary resolutions as its most exalted and appreciative testimonial of his worth:

DISTRICT OF COLUMBIA, BOARD OF HEALTH.

Washington, Oct. 2, 1877.

"The following resolutions presented by Dr. C. C. Cox at the meeting of the Board held this evening were unanimously adopted: Resolved, That in accepting the resignation of Professor J. M. Langston as member and attorney of the Board of Health, it is both a privilege and pleasure to express, as we do, our appreciation of his eminent personal worth, his rare intellectual endowment, his valuable services in the department of public hygiene, and especially his useful and unremitting labors in promoting the sanitary interest of this District.

"Resolved: That in his long association with this Board, its members have ever found in him an agreeable gentleman, a true friend, and a faithful collaborator in the cause of public health.

"Resolved: That while sensible of the personal and public loss sustained by us in the severance of our friend and colleague from the arduous position with which he has been so long and laboriously associated, we congratulate the Government upon securing for a distinguished diplomatic relation abroad a gentleman so eminently qualified to do honor to his country in the office to which he has been assigned.

"Resolved: That Professor Langston be furnished by the secretary with a copy of these resolutions, suitably engrossed, and signed by the officers of the board."

These resolutions, beautifully and elaborately engrossed, duly signed by the officers of the Board and appropriately framed, were sent on the nineteenth day of October, 1877, to Mr. Langston, and can be seen hanging upon the walls of his house at Hillside Cottage, among other valuable documents and pictures which are prized and preserved by him as of rare and sacred worth.

In addition to this expression of personal esteem and official estimate, the Board increased Mr. Langston's obligation to it by a dinner and reception given him upon his retirement. On this occasion many pleasant and flattering things were said of him and his services by the members of the Board and others present interested in their work, which are remembered with feelings of special obligation and thankfulness.

More than this, the health officer and the subordinate employes of the Board would not allow Mr. Langston, whose care, consideration and efforts as the attorney of the Board had been constantly exercised in their behalf, and without the least detriment to any one of them, leave them without a cordial, honorable manifestation of their appreciation of him and his labors, and their regret that they could no longer enjoy the association and protection of their friend and officer. Hence, they prepared and presented to him, at the rooms of the Board of Health, on the adjournment of the last meeting which he attended, a formal address, expressive of their feelings and kind wishes, accompanying the same with the gift of a most rare, beautiful and valuable diplomatic ring, upon which in richest precious stones are represented the gods of Wisdom and War, Minerva and Mars. The present, typical and emblematical of the service upon which he was about to enter, was especially significant and appropriate. The address presented through Dr. P. T. Keene, the health officer, chaste and elegant in sentiment and diction, reads as follows:

"PROFESSOR LANGSTON:

"Six years and more, we the employes of the Board of Health of the District of Columbia, have enjoyed your official relationship. Remembering with pleasure and pride mutual labors and successes in a common cause, and realizing that our pathways are now diverging, we earnestly desire that you accept at our hands and keep always with you, a pledge of the respect and esteem we shall cherish for you wherever may be your future home, whatever your field of labor.

"You go, now, the chosen, honored representative of the United States Government, upon one of her most important foreign missions. In the midst of the dignity and applause which will attend your diplomatic triumph, and in all the future years they unfold before you, the victories, the honors, the rewards—yes! (and they needs must come) the disappointments, griefs and sacrifices of life—we trust this simple golden circlet will constantly remind you of our parting prayer; that the blessings of health and happiness and Heaven's gracious approbation may attend your steps, even to the gates of eternity, whose emblem, with your permission, we now place upon your finger, and reluctantly say, Our excellent friend, good-bye!"

The following day, the daily papers of the city of Washington made notice of the proceedings mentioned in the following manner, with full publication of the address and minute description of the ring:

"Last evening upon adjournment of the Board of Health, the president stated that the employes of the Board had an affair of their own on hand which they invited the members to stay and witness. He moved that the council room of the Board be placed at their disposal. This being done Mr. D. S. Jones, the chief clerk, rose and stated that the employes desired to present to Professor Langston, who was present, a parting gift, a token of their esteem and regard. He introduced Dr. P. T. Keene, the health officer, who he said had been selected by the employes to make the presentation." Then followed the address, as already presented, "which visibly affected the professor," as stated in the papers, "who made a brief feeling reply." Of the gift the papers gave this account: "The present consists of a handsome gold ring with very rare cameo settings, it being a double side face bust of 'Mars and Minerva,' the stone being seemingly of two layers, the under, on which the face of Minerva is carved, being pure white, while the upper, bearing the head of Mars, is a mag-

APPOINTED A MEMBER OF THE BOARD OF HEALTH.

nificent lava color. It was purchased from Messrs. Galt & Bro. and bears the inscription, 'J. M. Langston, from employes, Board of Health, D. C.'"

This ring, worn as directed on every great diplomatic occasion during his years of service in that behalf, has always been treasured as a thing which possesses even more than magical power. It has seemed to be from the hour of its presentation the very talisman of Mr. Langston's good fortune. As a memento of the kind sentiments which its donors entertained for him it is invaluable.

It is a matter of real satisfaction to Mr. Langston that after he had left the Board of Health, Congress, upon careful consideration of the subject, enacted the ordinances, rules and regulations which he had drawn and presented as stated, and which the Board had adopted and published as regulating its sanitary service, into a formal sanitary code, as the law applicable to the District of Columbia, and to be enforced therein. That law is still in existence and is enforced, though the Board of Health as such has been abolished, through a health officer and his inspectors and subordinates. Another high honor paid to Mr. Langston and the Committee on Ordinances even before he left the Board, consisted in the fact that a Commission of the Japanese government sent abroad in search of a sanitary code of laws to be used in Japan, after visiting the large cities of other countries and several of the United States, chose as most applicable to their condition and as embodying the principles of law which might be and which ought to be enforced in conservation and promotion of the public health, the ordinances, rules and regulations of the Board of Health of the District of Columbia; and the same were adopted as the legal provisions accepted for that purpose by that government.

While it is true that during the entire time that Mr. Langston was connected with Howard University as professor and vice and acting-president, he was an active and laborious member of the Board of Health, as stated, he allowed no clash in his duties to prevent his prompt and efficient discharge of them all. And if he found special pleasure in his labors connected with the professional education of the colored youth of the country, he did not value less the pleasant and profitable associations had with the members of the Board of Health, offering opportunities such as could not be otherwise found for improvement in all those matters of science which pertain to public hygiene.

Of the five members of the Board of Health as originally constituted, Dr. Verdi and Mr. John Marbury, Jr. as well as Mr. Langston are still alive and active in business. Drs. Cox and Bliss, however, after long service in their profession and great usefulness to the community, like many to whom they administered so tenderly and sympathetically, passed some years ago to their long sleep and silent home. Their professional names and influence retained their brightness and power to the close of their lives; indeed, each won additional and increasing honors in the higher and more exalted walks of scientific, medical and political endeavor in the very last days of his career. Dr. Cox gave the government his final efforts, as appointed to a high and honorable position in its foreign service; while Dr. Bliss, as the chief surgeon in the celebrated case of the late President Garfield, won by his skillful and devoted care of his distinguished patient deserved fame and honor.

CHAPTER XXII.

THREE GREAT ENTERPRISES WHICH COMMANDED HIS SPECIAL ATTENTION.

CHARLOTTE SCOTT, a freed woman from Virginia, deserves the credit of having proposed the erection of a monument in honor of Abraham Lincoln as the emancipator of the American slave. She resided at service in Marietta, Ohio, at the time of his assassination, and so soon as she heard of it, on the 15th of April, 1865, she brought five dollars, the first money she had earned in freedom, and giving it to her employer, asked him to communicate her proposition to some person whose influence and action might result in the accomplishment of that important design. The subject was at once brought with the gift, the first contribution made to the enterprise, to the attention of Mr. James E. Yeatman and the Western Sanitary Commission of St. Louis, Missouri. Placed in these hands, the work in that behalf assumed form and direction of such character as to give it promise of early success. Through Mr. Yeatman and the commission, Mr. Langston became interested in it, and as requested by them, brought the subject to the attention and patronage of the freed people of the South as he travelled among them, especially to the consideration of any colored troops still retained in the United States service. The soldiers were easily moved by appeals made to them and gave freely and liberally. All funds were sent directly to Mr. Yeatman, without the least deduction of any sort or for any purpose. By reason of the efficient and liberal management of the commission, the whole sum necessary to provide the work of art suited to the purpose, and to pay all expenses found due, was soon raised, and as early as the fourteenth day of April, 1876, the monument, completed in every particular, was ready for unveiling.

The whole country finally seemed interested in this enterprise, and when Mr. Yeatman wrote Mr. Langston, directing him to make full arrangements for the unveiling exercises, the latter did not find it difficult to secure even official and government aid to further in the highest and most important way that purpose. The leading officials of the municipal administration of the District and the members of the general government, including its executive, judicial and legislative departments, as well as the citizens generally of the national capital and many from various sections of the country, gave evidence in large and liberal measure of their deep interest in the work. In every way contribution was made by them in generous and considerate action to make the occasion one worthy of the man and the cause which were to be honored in the dignified offering of an emancipated race. Congress ordered that the day appointed for the unveiling should be, so far as the capital was concerned, a national holiday, and adjourned itself to attend in a body the exercises; the Supreme Court, moved by the same feelings, also adjourned and attended, the chief justice and his associates all being present, while President Grant and all the members of the Cabinet gave, in their presence, the highest possible testimony of their appreciation of the great name and illustrious example of the immortal Lincoln, whose virtues endeared him as well to every white as every black man—for he was the benefactor of all. Such being the case, it was not strange that an audience, perhaps the largest and most remarkable that had ever assembled in this or any other country on like occasion, was brought together. The vast concourse numbering over a hundred thousand persons, composed of distinguished officers, civil and military, of every grade and character known to the government, senators, representatives, with the great body of the employes of the government and a multitude of the people, honored the occasion with a presence, attention and orderly conduct calculated to give the largest possible *éclat* to the proceedings.

It had been intended and arranged that Mr. Langston, who had been made the presiding officer of the occasion, should not only receive the work in the name of the emancipated classes, as presented by Mr. James E. Yeatman from the Western Sanitary Commission, but that he should unveil the monument to the gaze of the assembled throng. However, Mr. Langston, at the last moment, finding President Grant seated upon his right on the great platform erected for the occasion, and moved by a deep sense of the fitness of such action, requested him to manipulate the cord which drawn never so slightly would cause the fall of the drapery which covered and concealed the monument. On being introduced, with suitable apology made by the presiding officer, President Grant by touching the cord as indicated, unveiled the monument, consisting of a bronze group of figures of colossal size, which at once produced a grand and enthusiastic outburst of appreciation and applause. The roar of cannon, the strains of martial music, the shouts, the huzzas and cheers of the people, discovered the joy and gladness with which they would honor the emancipator of the continent. The popular demonstrations of approbation continued repeating themselves for many minutes, and in their participation there seemed to be no difference between the most exalted and the humblest member of the great gathering. All rejoiced together in the wildest, most unmeasured enthusiasm.

The monument, as described, stands on a granite pedestal ten feet high. The martyred president, in bronze, stands beside a monolith upon which is a bust of Washington, in *bas relief*. In his right hand he holds the Proclamation, while his left is stretched over a slave upon whom his eyes are bent, who is just rising, and from whose limbs the shackles have just burst. The figure of the slave is that of a man worn by toil, with muscles hardened and rigid. He is represented as just rising from the earth, while his face is lighted with joy as he anticipates the full manhood of freedom. Upon the base of the monument is cut the word "Emancipation."

As stated, the figures are colossal, and the effect impressive. On the front, in bronze letters one finds the following inscription:

"FREEDOM'S MEMORIAL.

"In grateful memory of ABRAHAM LINCOLN, this monument was erected by the Western Sanitary Commission of St. Louis, Mo., with funds contributed solely by emancipated citizens of the United States, declared free by his proclamation January 1, A. D. 1863.

"The first contribution of five dollars was made by Charlotte Scott, a freed woman of Virginia, being her first earnings in freedom and consecrated by her suggestion and request, on the day she heard of President Lincoln's death, to build a monument to his memory."

On the reverse side is the following:

"And upon this act, sincerely believed to be an act of justice warranted by the Constitution, upon military necessity, I invoke the considerate judgment of mankind and the gracious favor of Almighty God."

In closing his address made in connection with the delivery of the monument Mr. Yeatman employed the following statements:

"The amount paid Mr. Ball for the bronze group was $17,000, every cent of which has been remitted to him. So you have a finished monument all paid for. The government appropriated $3,000 for the foundation and pedestal upon which the bronze group stands, making the cost in all $20,000. I have thus given you a brief history of the Freedmen's Memorial Monument and how and why the Western Sanitary Commission came to have anything to do with it. To them it has been a labor of love. In the execution of the work they have exercised their best judgment—done the best that could be done with the limited means they had to do it with. It remains with you and those who will follow you to say how wisely or how well it has been done. Whatever of honor, whatever of glory belongs to this work, should be given to Charlotte Scott, the poor slave woman. Her offering of gratitude and love, like that of the widow's mite, will be remembered in heaven when the gifts of those rich in this world's goods shall have passed away and been forgotten."

Mr. Langston, in receiving the statue, addressing Mr. Yeatman and the audience, employed these words:

"In behalf of our entire nation, in behalf especially of the donors of the fund with whose investment you and your associates of the Western Sanitary Commission have been charged, I tender to you, Sir, and through you to the commission, our sincere thanks for the prompt and wise performance of the trust and duty committed to your care. The finished and appropriate work of art presented by you we accept and dedicate, through the ages, in memory and honor of him who is to be forever known in the records of the World's history as the emancipator of the enslaved of our country. We unveil it to the gaze, the admiration of mankind. Fellow-citizens, according to the arrangement of the order of exercises of this occasion, it had fallen to my lot to unveil the statue which we dedicate to-day; but we have with us the president of the United States, and it strikes me that it is altogether fit and proper to ask him to take part in the exercises so far as to unveil the monument."

Others who took part in the exercises were Bishop John M. Brown, who offered prayer; Hon. J. Henri Burch of Louisiana, who read the Proclamation of Emancipation; Mr. William E. Mathews, who read the poem written for the occasion by Miss Cordelia Ray, of New York city; and Hon. Frederick Douglass, who delivered the oration.

In every way and sense the exercises were of high and impressive character and the incidents of the occasion must be remembered with gratitude and pleasure.

The Freedmen's Savings and Trust Company was an institution created for the financial and business education of the freed people, in whose branches located in the different States of the South it was believed these people might make their deposits with advantage and safety. Assured by those who composed its Board of Trustees as well as those who had its official duties in hand, that the institution was entirely reliable and that its affairs were conducted with wisdom and efficiency in the interest solely of its depositors, Mr. Langston, after its organization, wherever he went in the South spoke of it in commendatory terms, and advised the emancipated classes whenever they had occasion to deposit their accumulations to patronize and support that banking institution. It was not, however, until 1872, upon the retirement of Messrs. W. S. Huntington and H. D. Cooke from the Board of Trustees of the company that Mr. Langston had any direct official responsible connection with it. Then he was invited and pressed to accept place in its Board of Trustees by his friend, the vice-president of the institution at the time, Dr. Charles B. Purvis. It was represented to him that there was not only need of services such as he might render in the Board itself, but that by reason of the retirement of the gentlemen named there had been made a vacancy in the Finance Committee of the institution which he might fill with great advantage to the company and doubtless with pleasure to himself. He became a trustee accordingly through the kindness and courtesy of the gentlemen composing the Board, and was subsequently made a member of the Finance Committee, in 1872.

On entering upon his duties in that capacity, Mr. Langston found himself in association in the Board of Trustees with many friends of the freed people, distinguished in their general reputation and influence as successful business men as well as in their devotion to the cause of such people. Mr. J. W. Alvord was president; Dr. Charles B. Purvis, vice-president; and Mr. Daniel L. Eaton, actuary, with an assistant, Mr. George W. Stickney. Among the Board of Trustees he found besides Dr. Purvis, several colored men of note and influence; among the latter class Mr. Frederick Douglass, who had been a member of the Board for several years. Mr. W. J. Wilson, a colored man, well-known in the country, and Major Fleetwood, were employed, as well as other colored persons, in subordinate places, as cashier and book-keepers. Apparently the institution, so far as the Board of Trustees was concerned, and the officers and employes as well as the standing committees, was in prosperous and promising condition. However, Mr. Langston's attention was very soon called, in meetings of the Finance Committee, to the real condition of the institution, which he found to be anything other than satisfactory, by reason of the fact that unwise manipulation of the funds had been had, especially in connection with many bad loans which aggregated large sums of money, the collection of which was hard and difficult. Besides, the institution had been brought in such relations to the community, and had reached such a condition in public estimate, that "runs" were quickly made upon it; and often they worked considerable losses, in sacrifices which were necessitated frequently in the sale of securities. At all events, Mr. Langston found that his position was one of trying responsibility, delicacy and labor. So deeply interested was he, however, in the bank, its various branches, found all over the South, the work which it proposed to accomplish in the interest of the newly emancipated people, and the importance and necessity of maintaining its life and good name in order to the support of its promises and the payment of its indebtedness to such people, that he resolved to do all in his power to save it against all odds and every adverse circumstance.

It is matter of great satisfaction to him to be able to state, that every considerable poor and doubtful loan of the bank was made before he became a member of the Board of Trustees, and every practice calculated to work its ruin had been made a part of its management without his knowledge or participation, before he had any concern in its control. The greatest care was exercised, every means practicable was exhausted in the Finance Committee, of which he was a member for the two years during which he held connection with the institution, in every case of loan asked, to determine the situation and value of any real property offered as security, and the probability and certainty of securing upon forced sale of it, the whole amount loaned, with all expenses made necessary in the transaction. In all respects, from the time he was made a trustee and a member of the committee named, he exercised every diligence and care to save and perpetuate the company. He was not slow to oppose any proposition or measure whose adoption in his judgment would disturb or injure the bank, as he was prompt and positive in accepting and urging the adoption of any proposed action calculated to promote its interest and prolong and extend its life and usefulness. To all this, were it necessary, the officers of the institution as well as the committee with which he acted so laboriously, and as he trusts and believes, intelligently, could testify.

The first year of his service, as indicated, was passed with such experiences and such improving knowledge of the company and its affairs as to show in very clear and striking manner every feature of its weakness and strength. The weakness of its organization, especially so far as the establishment of branches in distant states was concerned, used mainly for the collection and transmission of funds to the chief banking house, located at the national capital, where all moneys and securities were handled and controlled, and the general business of the institution transacted, became, in experience, sensibly manifest. And when the rule was brought to mind which had been adopted, that all loans must be made from Washington city, even to persons residing in States in which branches were established and large amounts of deposits made, the weakness of the organization in such behalf, in a business point of view, became strikingly apparent. It is only necessary to consider the inconvenience of this rule, its expensive and impracticable character, to discover and appreciate the truth of this statement. Besides, it so operated, practically, that a depositor having large transactions with the institution through a local branch did not gain, by such condition of things, where he would avail himself of it, the credit to which his bank account entitled him. Much inconvenience was experienced from this condition of things; and yet by careful management the objections indicated were reasonably overcome.

During this time it was easy to discover how the least thing, false rumor even, of political significance, would produce a movement against the bank. The rumor that the institution was specially interested in the last election of General Grant to the presidency of the United States, and that it was contributing largely to that end, produced a movement against it which cost it a considerable amount in sacrifice of valuable securities. Notwithstanding all objections however, coming from whatever source and caused by whatever influence, on the whole the institution was one calculated to accomplish great good in demonstrating in its large deposits the intelligence, industry, economy and thrift of the emancipated classes, and in its educating effects upon them in every business way. Every friend of the freed people could have desired only its prosperity and life. With such feelings actuating him, Mr. Langston, with full knowledge upon the subject, did all he could to conserve and promote its interests.

Two things unfortunate, as he believed, occurred during his connection with the Board of Trustees of this institution, to which he interposed what seemed to him to be important and insuperable objections. At the annual meeting of the Board of Trustees, held in March, 1874, the proposition was made to supersede Mr. John W. Alvord, the founder of the institution and its president, by the election to its presidency of Mr. Frederick Douglass. The subject was discussed with large freedom in the board meeting, and the most liberal and kindly feeling was expressed by all. The only question which weighed specially with those who would maintain the bank in its very best conditions as to public feeling with regard to it and its general business success, concerned the effect of that change. Mr. Langston was open and positive in the opinion that any change under the circumstances was ill-advised and would prove injurious to the bank. Besides, he claimed as openly and positively, that Mr. Douglass would find the presidency of the institution difficult, trying and disappointing to him. But nevertheless, he was frank and earnest in his avowal, that if the friends of Mr. Douglass in the Board were determined to press his case, and he desired and would accept the office mentioned, feeling that he was willing and capable to discharge its duties, he should, having spoken freely and made known his fears, vote for him. However, the results have demonstrated fully that Mr. Langston's judgment in this matter was entirely correct. For it is true that Mr. Douglass had not been president many days before he discovered and expressed his disappointment, and not long thereafter the condition of the bank was found to be such that the proposition to close it was gravely and seriously considered. The famous saying of Mr. Douglass that, "his friends had married him to a corpse," in speaking of his election to the presidency of the bank, may be recalled here with profit to all concerned.

But as early as the month of June, 1874, the bank was closed. To the manner of winding up its business by three commissioners, at large outlay to the patrons of the institution, Mr. Langston was with several other trustees entirely opposed, believing and maintaining that its concerns should all remain in the hands and under the control of the trustees, who should be required to close all up in due orderly business-like manner, and pay to every depositor the amount found to be due him, so far as the same could be done from the proceeds of the property, securities and funds of the institution; while he maintained also that not a single dollar should be paid for any service connected with the settlement to any trustee, and that should there be any indebtedness found to exist in favor of any depositor, representation in such regard should be made to the general government and appropriation be asked to pay the same. However, upon the day on which the bank was closed it had assets, with cash on hand, which if wisely manipulated were abundant to pay upon Mr. Langston's plan within a reasonable time every dollar of the bank's obligations. His plan was not sustained, and to this day the honest, confiding, patient depositors of the institution are waiting for and needing balances due them. At no time in the history of the transactions here recorded did Mr. Langston advise the conduct of the affairs of the institution by the trustees for any other purpose than to secure, finally, the results suggested. He opposed the closing of the bank and settlement of its affairs through commissioners because of the great expense attending the transaction, and the final inability of the commissioners to make appeal to Congress, in case of default of funds to pay depositors, in such a way as to secure the needed appropriation. He believed that the trustees alone could accomplish that object; and if the institution, with all its affairs, was to be controlled and settled by any other agency than its Board of Trustees, he was of the opinion that it might be done by a single person even with greater efficiency and far less expense than by three such agents as the commissioners.

Here no word is offered against any one of the persons named as the commissioners; for Mr. Langston assisted in the selection and approval of them all, under the law providing for their appointment. Besides, they were gentlemen well known to him, as they were to the entire country, as persons of high social position, excellent business reputation and commanding influence. Indeed it would be difficult enough to find three more worthy gentlemen than Messrs. Creswell, Purvis and Leopold, who were designated by the Board of Trustees itself as the three commissioners. The objection, as already stated, clearly was not to the commissioners in their individual or official character, but to the method, cumbersome and expensive, implied in their appointment and as sustained by the results which followed.

Perhaps the failure of no institution in the country, however extended its relations, however generally it enjoyed popular confidence and popular patronage, has ever wrought larger disappointment and more disastrous results to those interested in its creation, management and support than that of the Freedmen's Savings and Trust Company. Nor was there ever found in the population of any country, at any time, under any circumstances, persons who could so ill afford to be thus disappointed in the failure and dissolution of any institution than the freed people in those of this company. The day is distant even now when they will lose entirely their sense of disappointment and their consciousness of loss in its failure. Of course, in proportion to the deep sense of the advantage and profit of the institution, as realized by the freed people themselves, they would feel its shipwreck and ruin. The sentiment therefore that no depositor of the class indicated should be allowed to lose a single dollar of his deposits, although the government itself might be compelled to make appropriation to prevent that result, is not without just foundation in popular conviction and judgment. This feeling must be increased largely, too, and sustained in popular decision, when it is recollected that the name of the government was too often called in that way in connection with this bank, as to give the uninitiated and credulous reason to believe that the government would guarantee and sustain it in all its liabilities. The people had full faith in the government which had emancipated them, and could not doubt for a moment the sincerity of its purpose and power, so far as the support and maintenance of their welfare were concerned.

It will forever remain matter of the profoundest regret that after this company found it necessary, by reason of unwise management, ill-advised investments of its funds, with injudicious manipulation of its securities and unfortunate change of its executive officers at a critical juncture in its history, upon its suspension, instead of continuing it in the hands and under the control of its Board of Trustees, who could make no charge of any kind for their services, it was committed to three commissioners, whose salaries aggregating nine thousand dollars per year, made, besides other outlays occasioned under the law of their creation, a very large draft upon the funds of the bank which otherwise might have been paid, as they ought to have been, to the depositors.

The history of banking institutions in this country will fail to furnish any examples of such want of wisdom and judgment, to say nothing about the utter disregard of the interests of those immediately and most seriously concerned, as the plan described, adopted for the close and settlement finally of the affairs of this company. It is to be recorded in favor of the trustees, generally, that they were willing, maintaining their positions as unpaid officers of the bank, to undertake the prompt and complete adjustment and payment of all claims to the extent of the last dollar of property and money to every depositor and creditor. If that course had been pursued, a large saving would have been made and the trustees themselves would have been given the opportunity of making good, at the least possible outlay, their promises and obligations to the freed people, who constituted the great bulk of the depositors.

Mr. Langston gave two years of prompt, diligent, and as he believes, wise service to the company, advising and pressing in every practicable way, not only the collection of every doubtful debt due, but counselling and sustaining the judicious, faithful control and management, under the law, of all its affairs. It is entirely agreeable to him that, as he has been informed and believes, there was not a single dollar loaned by vote of the Finance Committee after he became a member of it, as approved by the Board of Trustees, which was subject of loss to the company. His labors in behalf of this institution were those of one not seeking his own good, but that of those who, just entering upon the new ways of freedom, needed guidance and just direction so as to meet the new responsibilities, obligations and hopes of their lives.

In nothing connected with the welfare of the freed people of the United States has Mr. Langston been so profoundly interested as their education. In nothing has he deemed it so much a privilege and pleasure to labor as in its interest and to promote its advantage. It was far back in 1853 when he met Miss Matilda Minor, a young white lady of rare scholarly attainment and culture, engaged at the time in the conduct of a school for young colored girls in Washington city. At this time she was at Oberlin College, upon a visit made in the interest of the education of colored youth. Her account of her work even then, small as it was, was of the deepest and most thrilling interest to all who heard her as she described it; while her enthusiasm as shown in her conversations led every one to applaud, while he admired her devotion and heroism. Little did Mr. Langston realize the pleasure that was in store for him in the coming future, not distant, when with slavery abolished in the District of Columbia and throughout the United States, he would be called with others when Miss Minor was dead, having served well her day and generation, to care for and invest in further and larger operations for the education of colored youth, the property which she had accumulated and dedicated during her life to that purpose. Here is another case of man's short-sightedness. Here another instance of heroic devotion of one's self to a good cause so grandly and wisely that one builds for herself a monument in good works, more enduring than brass or granite.

In the northwestern section of the city of Washington, when property in that locality was not estimated at large figures, Miss Minor, without knowing how well and wisely she would invest, purchased a square of unpromising ground, upon which she hoped at some convenient time to erect a commodious appropriate structure which she would dedicate to the education of the more promising young colored girls of the capital. She died, however, before her plans in that behalf could be consummated. Slavery was abolished; a new impulse was given to the education of the colored youth of the country; and the old Board of Trustees having in charge the property described, as appointed and constituted during her life, was called to fill vacancies in its numbers, when Mr. Langston with one or two others was honored in a call in that direction. He found himself as agreeably situated with his colaborers as he was pleased with the object upon which he was called so expend his efforts.

After careful consideration, in 1874, the property referred to—the city meantime having been greatly improved in the particular section where it was located—was sold with reference to reinvestment of the proceeds of the sale so as to enlarge and render effective the purposes of Miss Minor with regard to the education of the colored youth. Accordingly reasonable sale having been made, a site was purchased and the Minor Normal School building, large and imposing, convenient and model in its construction, located on Seventeenth Street Northwest, well known now throughout the city of Washington, was erected and dedicated to educational purposes in the fall of 1877. The last public duty performed by Mr. Langston before he left the United States upon a foreign mission, to which he had been appointed, was to preside at the dedicatory exercises of this building.

In severing his connection with his kind associates of the Board of Trustees of the Minor Fund, Mr. Langston recollected with sentiments of the liveliest gratitude how cordially and considerately he had always been treated by them, and how harmonious and pleasant their meetings had uniformly been, since every member was moved solely by an earnest intelligent purpose to secure the highest and most lasting good of those concerned most deeply in his labors.

At the time Mr. Langston was called to the positions and the performance of the duties here described, his time was fully and pressingly occupied by daily labors connected with professional and official responsibilities. And yet he was more than compensated in the satisfaction which he gained and enjoyed in the consciousness that he was laboring in either capacity, doing that which tended to the permanent promotion and advantage of those who, newly emancipated, needed counsel and support.

CHAPTER XXIII.

HIS APPOINTMENT AS MINISTER-RESIDENT AND CONSUL-GENERAL TO HAITI AND HIS ARRIVAL AND RECEPTION AT PORT-AU-PRINCE.

A RESIDENT of the State of Ohio, youthful and ardent, at the very beginning of his practice as a lawyer, thoroughly imbued by study, reading and association with the importance and necessity of maintaining and applying republican principles, through every practicable method, to save the government, preserve the Union, and conserve the general welfare, Mr. Langston found himself ready as early as 1856, at the very birth of the Republican party, to enter with his profoundest earnestness and sympathy upon its advocacy and support. From that time on, in voice, vote and labor, this party had in him, according to the full measure of his ability, ardent and constant defence. In his judgment, all that was hopeful to the oppressed classes of the country, of whatever condition or complexion, must come through its agency. He believed that American liberty itself, fast losing its footing by reason of the encroachments of slavery, must depend upon it alone for its ultimate salvation and perpetuity. Only through its instrumentality, as he held, confronting and overcoming the Democratic and Whig parties, could the people save the Declaration of Independence and the Constitution intact, so as to perpetuate those free institutions provided and established under those great

Appointed Minister to Haiti.

state papers of matchless merit and power, by the fathers and founders of the republic. Moved by these considerations and exercising this political faith, his devotion to republican principles and the party which sought to maintain them was natural, and to one of his constitutional temper inevitable and whole-hearted.

Beginning with the very first nominees of this party to the presidency and vice-presidency of the United States, he spoke and voted for every single one;—deeming it his duty to pursue this course, not merely as a colored man, shorn largely of his liberty and rights, thus seeking to regain and enjoy them; but with a large purpose, the patriotic, commanding motive of saving American freedom itself, in the interest of all the people and their posterity. Having voted to that purpose for Lincoln, Grant, and those worthies who had preceded them as leaders of the party, and yet who were not elected to the high offices to which they were named, when he was not able with many others who desired and sought the nomination of the Hon. James G. Blaine to secure that end, he was ready to enter with vigor and confidence upon the support of Ohio's ablest and most available representative at the time, the Hon. Rutherford B. Hayes.

Full of admiration for the great ability, magnetic, dashing and charming qualities of character possessed by the foremost statesman of Maine and New England, notwithstanding his opposition to the "force bill," so-called, in the early part of the year 1875, quite twelve months before the Cincinnati Republican nominating convention, Mr. Langston ventured in conversation with Mr. Blaine to urge his acceptance of the nomination to the presidency of the United States, assuring him that the support of the colored American could be brought to him. Repeated conversations were had upon the same subject subsequently, and in connection with others interested in the same political result, he spared no pains while he made every effort practicable to accomplish it. Among other things he proposed an informal, though remarkable and important gathering at Mr. Blaine's own house, who lived at the time on Fifteenth Street, near H, Washington, D. C., and who was the chief figure in the House of Representatives, and the most commanding, attractive, popular leader among Republican statesmen.

The *personnel* of the gathering referred to was as remarkable, peculiar and interesting as the gathering itself. Those present were Mr. Blaine himself, his wife, and Gail Hamilton; Messrs. James A. Garfield, George F. Hoar, Colonel L. Edwin Dudley, six bishops of the A. M. E. Church, Rev. H. M. Turner and John M. Langston. A lunch of rare excellence was given by Mr. Blaine, at which he of course presided, displaying as much charm and skill in his behavior at his own table and on this occasion as he had ever shown elsewhere. Everyone present was delighted with his cordial, hospitable conduct, feeling as he listened to his attractive, marvelous conversation with his worthy colleagues and compeers of the House—Garfield and Hoar— and the negro worthies present, representatives of both piety and learning, that of all men in the nation he was the fittest for the exalted chair of state. On coming away after taking appropriate leave of the ladies present, who had also demeaned themselves in such happy, agreeable manner, winning thereby the favor certainly of every colored guest for Mr. Blaine and his household, tarrying upon the doorsteps of his residence Mr. Langston, anxious to know how his colored friends felt in view of their treatment and Mr. Blaine's explanations of his purposes as a Republican with respect to national affairs, inquired of them how they were impressed and whether they were pleased with the great statesman. The answer was unanimous, earnest and positive that he was the man who should be made president. All agreed to a united and vigorous support of him, and accordingly while Mr. Langston did with his friends everything he could do to secure that object, even going to Cincinnati and laboring with all his might for days in that behalf, and the Rev. Mr. Turner was honored with the privilege of following Colonel Ingersoll in seconding the nomination of Mr. Blaine, they were defeated. No one attending this select, memorable gathering failed to give Mr. Blaine so far as possible his earnest and active support as opportunity permitted, for the presidency of the United States. So sure did the result in this case seem to be even in advance, that arrangements were made for Mr. Langston to speak at several places in Ohio—among others at Athens—in confirmation of the action of the convention and in favor of the election of its nominee as expected, the Hon. James G. Blaine. The competitors and rivals for that honor, Bristow, Morton and Conkling, were too numerous and too powerful to render that result possible; and hence as already stated, Governor Hayes received the nomination. Instead of addressing the meetings referred to in favor of Blaine, Mr. Langston addressed them in favor of Hayes. Beginning thus at once, he continued his labors, speaking for the Republican nominees for president and vice-president, until at the close of election day the people had recorded their judgment by their vote in favor of Hayes and Wheeler.

The last speech which Mr. Langston made during this canvass was that delivered by him from the west steps of the state capitol of Ohio, when Governor Hayes and his excellent wife, seated indoors where they could hear every word which he uttered, gave him their undivided attention for over two hours. And when he had closed his speech, invited by the governor himself into the executive office, he was introduced to Mrs. Hayes and given a reception which for cordiality and high personal consideration could not be surpassed.

Upon his election and inauguration President Hayes, by reason of the conspicuous and important part which he had played in connection with the former, in distributing honors and offices in the foreign service tendered Mr. Langston one of five different diplomatic and consular positions. The manner of conveying his purpose in this behalf was no less flattering than surprising. For although President Hayes had assured him within a few weeks after his inauguration that he did not intend to forget him in the distribution of his official patronage, he had no thought that he would appoint him to a foreign place, or convey to him his purpose in that regard by the most prominent member of his Cabinet, with the offer that he might make choice as indicated. He was not without full knowledge that he had served the party and its nominees during the past campaign with fidelity and efficiency, but he inclined to the belief that should anything be done in his case in the way of advancement in his position, it could only be to some more prominent and lucrative place at home.

Although often urged by Senator Sumner to fit himself specially for diplomatic service, with the offer even of assistance in the study of the French language, of which the senator was a master, and in international law, as applied particularly and practically to that service and of which the senator had large knowledge, Mr. Langston had always treated the possibility of such high honor being conferred upon him as wholly chimerical and without the least prospect of realization. But here it was, in fact, upon him; with appointment to a country and near a government employing as its vernacular the French language; for advised as to the character, the health, and the probable duties at the capital in which he might be located, he selected his place as minister-resident and consul-general in the historic negro republic of Haïti. So soon as he had received his appointment he entered upon such preparation as seemed to be practicable within the very brief period elapsing before he must take his departure.

Though educated according to the very best methods of the schools of his country, with large experience of general business in his own profession and otherwise, Mr. Langston found himself now in want of that special knowledge in too great measure indispensable to the easy and effective performance of the new service upon which he was about to enter. The hurried and imperfect instructions, verbal and written, given at the State Department, did not prove at all adequate for those necessities which confront one situated as he was, upon the very threshold of his mission. Choosing a place of great importance, connected with which grave responsibilities were numerous and urgent, involving not only a comprehensive, delicate understanding of international law doctrines and usages, but a mastery at least of the French language, Mr. Langston felt himself fairly well off in his knowledge of the former, while wholly at fault in his understanding of the latter. For the benefit of any who may contemplate a residence abroad as a representative of the American government, in a French speaking country, in a capital where it is necessary in order to make social and business progress to speak French, that person would do well to fit himself by diligent, faithful mastery of that tongue before he leaves his own home.

Mr. Langston was largely influenced in the choice of the government near which he would represent his own, by considerations of peculiar and special character. He had thought much, as he had read of this government built and supported by negro genius and power. He had familiarized himself in youth with the history of the people who, emancipating themselves under Toussaint, had under Dessalines declared and established their sovereignty, founding for themselves a republican form of government. He had learned how for more than seventy years, in spite of frequent revolutions, destructive often of thousands of lives and incalculable amounts of property, this people had maintained their nationality and independence. He had heard, too, that many of their leading men were scholarly and accomplished, and that so far as the medical profession, the bar, and commerce were concerned, men of large ability and business knowledge exercised controlling and directing influence. He had also been advised that a standing army, sometimes reaching in its numbers many thousands, and embracing all males over eighteen and under forty-five years of age, did not disturb, materially, the general education of the people as conducted in parochial schools, supported by the government and under the guidance and management of the Church. He also understood that upon a concordat made with the Roman Catholic Church by the government of the country, the Roman Catholic religion was made national and supported by national appropriation; and yet freedom of thought and religion was tolerated everywhere and by all classes; so that even there, the dominant moral influence was held and exercised by the Masonic Order, which is in its numbers as comprehensive well-nigh as the entire adult male population. He had further learned that in this condition of affairs considerable progress had been made under the various noted rulers of the country, in all those things which pertained to well-ordered national life. In short, he was impressed that in all such respects as well as others not specially named, but which concern a progressive nation, he would find in this negro country, with its Black Republic, a condition of life which, while it realized, would justify the dream of his youth with respect to an actual negro nationality. He therefore chose above all others within his reach the Haytian Government as the one near which he would make his residence as the diplomatic and consular representative of the United States.

More than this, upon special representations made to him by an old sea captain distinguished in the American navy, he had been led to believe that the country, mountainous, abounding in beautiful forests and limpid streams, was simply delightful, offering in its productions of flowers, fruits and vegetation generally, rare beauty and excellence, with health and comfort in its salubrious, charming climate, especially upon the mountains, with its ever-changing but famous land and sea breezes, the sources of constant bodily vigor and ordinarily, great longevity. Of its skies, its sunrisings and sunsettings, its scenery of land and sea, all exquisite in beauty and charm, he had read and heard from his very boyhood; and now that he could see all these matchless things for himself the seeming pleasure of doing so became irresistible, and he concluded to locate at Port-au-Prince, in many respects really a tropical, handsome city, situated upon a bay whose magnificence is unsurpassed and fascinating. He was not, when finally located in that country, disappointed in a single particular.

In addition to such information as he had gained by reading and from the person specially to whom allusion has been made, when Mr. Langston had reached, really, his conclusion and yet hesitated a little about going to Haïti, in view of the reports always circulated as to the inhospitable deadly effects of the climate in and about its capital, Port-au-Prince, another person, also high in the American navy, wholly familiar with the country and the conditions of life there, called upon him and advised, for his own sake, personally, and that of his country as well as that of the Haytian people themselves, that he accept and go upon the mission, assuring him that however high his expectations might be, the actual results would compensate him in such measure and in such way that he would be, finally, happy and proud of his decision and course. He has always felt under special obligation to Captain Brown, to-day librarian of the Navy Department, for his good services rendered him in this regard.

Mr. Langston was thus thoroughly confirmed in his judgment and determination when he received from the president, through the State Department, his appointment and instructions as the minister-resident and consul-general of the United States near the government of Haïti. However surprising at first this appointment was to him, it became at last a genuine inspiration and matter of pride. What other feelings would an intelligent American, patriotic and loyal, expect to have seize and control his being? Sixty-five millions of people; the fairest, the richest, the most beautiful country of the earth; a government stronger and more enduring than the foundations of the mountains, steady and firm, as resting in the affections, the intelligence and virtue of the community, compose and constitute the constituency and power which the American diplomat must feel he represents. Conscious of these facts, how could he be otherwise than inspired; how else than have his soul moved by the feelings of earnest, patriotic, manly pride! And then the representative of the United States government in this case, was going to a country where he might hope to witness inspiring scenes and accomplishments in connection with a nation and people in whom he must have special and ardent interest. He was to represent the great Republic of the North, the matchless government of the Anglo-Saxon race, near that of the Black Republic of the South, whose people had from slavery asserted and maintained their freedom; and thus emancipated had declared and supported their independence and sovereignty, as led and directed by their own sons, the gifted Toussaint and the valiant Dessalines. He would behold now for the first time, in actual realization, negro nationality in harmonious, honored activity, in a country (though an island in its dimensions) second to none in its beauty and richness—fit to be the very Garden of Eden!

Mr. Langston's appointment bore date September 28th, 1877, to take effect on the first day of October; and immediately thereafter, necessary arrangements having been completed, with the usual allowance of time for instructions given him, he took his departure, reaching New York city in time to take passage upon the steamer "Andes" of the Atlas Steamship Company, an English line, sailing at the time between New York city and the open ports of Haiti, including Cape Haytian and Port-au-Prince. This was his first voyage at sea. After three days of rather severe seasickness, with Hatteras left behind and the more difficult parts of the Crooked Island passage coming in view, so as to discover many of the beauties of that section of the continent to a novice in sea-faring life, rallying and becoming firm of foot as of health on shipboard, he enjoyed the trip thereafter with a zest and pleasure real and inspiriting.

On the Sabbath which intervened, Captain Hughes, in command of the ship, insisted after a late breakfast that religious exercises, including the reading of a Scripture lesson with appropriate remarks, be conducted, all the passengers being invited to be present, and so far as any one or more of them might be inclined to do so, take part, according to desire and choice therein. Special respect was shown the American minister, who was not only invited to preside and conduct the reading, but to make such remarks as might please him, pertinent to the occasion and circumstances. This he did and thereby won great favor with the officers as well as the passengers on the ship. Indeed, the captain complimented him by declaring that he would make a most excellent chaplain. Several times, in fact, after he had been heard at this meeting, he was invited by all on board to make addresses. And when nearing the close of the voyage it was proposed to honor the captain by opening a bottle of champagne and drinking his health, Mr. Langston was, by unanimous call and applause, made the orator *par excellence*.

The ship made her first stop in the outer harbor of Cape Haytian—not however coming to anchor—to await the arrival, first of the health officer of the port, and secondly the pilot, who were not long in making their appearance and coming on board. The doctor arrived first, and was welcomed by the captain as a person of character and authority. Calling for the ship's bill of health he made quick work of its examination, and declared that all was right. He had not quitted the ship however before the pilot came aboard, and welcomed by Captain Hughes, after the usual salutations, went directly upon the bridge of the ship, and taking full command, issued his first order, in obedience to which, at once, the vessel was put under way and carried to her place of anchorage within the harbor.

These officers both were extremely black men ; and yet, appearing in uniforms of official character and demeaning themselves with intelligence and propriety, they made a remarkably good impression. As they arrived in small boats, mounted the great ship by a rope ladder, approached its officers, performed their respective official duties and then retired, paying their respects to the captain and replying to any questions put by any passenger to either of them, they were made subjects of close scrutiny and observation by everyone who saw them. They were indeed objects of the liveliest interest to Mr. Langston. He had never seen up to that time men of their complexion holding such positions and performing such duties. His curiosity therefore was profoundly excited, so that he inquired of the captain who they were and what they came aboard of the ship for? To these questions he replied in full explanation, adding at the same time, "You are now, Mr. Minister, in a negro country, and as I intend to invite you to go ashore with me, I will show you sights which shall be new, and perhaps a little surprising."

It was early in the morning, about eight o'clock, on the sixth day after the ship had sailed from New York city, that it reached Cape Haytian. At ten o'clock, having gone ashore with the captain and his own private secretary, Mr. Adrian H. Lazare, Mr. Langston was occupied in a most interesting, strange and novel way, as these gentlemen, each with no little enthusiasm and emphasis, pointed out to him the wonders of this ancient city of the Black Republic, where marvelous things had occurred formerly, as well in earthquakes of awful effects as in the doings of those chiefs of the country, Dessalines, Christophe and others, whose deeds of valor and triumph are remembered as recorded in the history of this part of Haïti, with the liveliest interest and pride. This introduction to Haïti and the Haytians was in every sense a new revelation to Mr. Langston. He had hitherto only seen the negro in his best estate at home, in nominal freedom and dependence. Now he beholds him the owner of a great country, the founder and builder of a great government, with a national sovereignty and power respected and honored by all the great Christian civilized powers of the earth. And yet the Haytian appeared to be liberal, generous and cordial to any foreigner, of whatsoever nationality or complexion; while on every hand he exhibited upon this first view of his country and life, as shown in the large business interests and activities of this first city of the North, that his success and prosperity depended not only upon his intelligence, but the vigor and energy which he cultivated. This first view of the country and people thus accorded Mr. Langston, though but a mere glimpse of what he was to see, was most favorable and excited in him an earnest desire to reach the capital, where he would find the very best conditions of Haytian life and society.

Having landed any passengers aboard for Cape Haytian, and having discharged all freight brought to that port, the good "Andes" weighed anchor and went to sea, bound for Port-au-Prince, at seven o'clock on the evening of the same day of her arrival at the cape. As they were leaving this port the captain promised his passengers two things—that they should have a trip to the capital of such speed that at seven o'clock the next morning the ship should be at anchor in the harbor of Port-au-Prince; and that he would carry them over a portion of the sea, the Northern Channel so-called, within easy view of the coast, whose scenery was unsurpassed by anything, even on the Hudson, closing with a sunrise over the Tuyeaux mountains, lying about the city of Port-au-Prince, which in radiance and splendor could not be surpassed in the world. He kept his promise in both respects, and by nine o'clock, after he had held a reception of distinguished friends who awaited his arrival, on shipboard, the American minister, having bade Captain Hughes, with other friends made within the seven days of his seafaring experience, farewell, left the ship by a small boat for the shore. Once there, the vision and reality of absolute, positive negro nationality presented itself to him, in boldest, most striking features, and yet without such disagreeable and unpleasant circumstances as to cause the least anxiety or regret that he was at last in the capital of the country, near whose government he should reside.

Even the ride from the great ship by small boat to the shore, as Mr. Langston landed in the harbor of Port-au-Prince, was full of novelty and interest. He was in fact accompanied by a sort of convoy of small craft, all in the hands and under the management of skillful accommodating Haytians, who give constant attention to that service. The honorable representative of the British government and the American minister, who had for so many years represented their respective governments near that of Haïti, paid their respects to Mr. Langston on shipboard and conducted him ashore. Each had his carriage in waiting and subject to the desires of Mr. Langston, to be used by him for his conveyance to the hotel, the legation of the United States, or according to invitations extended him, to the home of either of the gentlemen referred to. On reaching the shore he found large representation from the American colony awaiting his arrival, and from it he received a most cordial and flattering welcome. After kindly greetings, with introductions to several prominent Haytian officials connected with the custom house and port, his baggage meantime having been put in order and forwarded to the residence of Hon. E. D. Bassett, the retiring American minister, Mr. Langston took carriage and was, in company with his host, conveyed to the American Legation. Here he and his secretary, Mr. Adrian H. Lazare, were accorded the heartiest possible reception, and after a short but delightful stay went to the house of the American minister, three miles away in the country. Here he found a pleasant home, fit for the repose and rest of one who had just come from a fatiguing trip upon the sea. The consideration and hospitality with which Mr. and Mrs. Bassett received and treated Mr. Langston and his secretary, remembered with such lively sentiments of gratitude, are profoundly appreciated. Nor shall it be forgotten that in connection with this family, the near neighbors, the household of Gen. Joseph Lubin, did much to render their stay at Sans Souci entirely agreeable and profitable. Several days thus spent with these companions gave Mr. Langston the best possible opportunity for making rapid progress in the study of all those things which respected Haïti and the Haytians. The subjects were comparatively new and interesting, and were studied with no little ardor. Daily visits were made to the city and full observations were taken of life and activity, business and other, therein. Nothing was allowed to escape notice and inquiry. Even the different conditions of the population were noted, so that whether American,

English, German, French or Danish—for all these diverse elements were found among the people of this city—presented themselves, they were at once recognized by their marked difference from the Haytian. The Haytian nationality, like the Haytian speech and manner, was peculiar and distinct. His habits as well as his manifestations of kindly regard were his own. While the very best conditions of Haytian life and society are seen in Port-au-Prince, it never loses its individuality and identity. As a class the people are hospitable, considerate and kind to strangers, especially Americans, and in no act or exhibition of feeling on their part ever discover any inclination to discriminate against one on account of his color except in the purchase and possession of real estate. Mr. Langston was well pleased with all he saw in Port-au-Prince, in the main, and was especially delighted with the evidences of wealth and culture which he found among the people generally. Their educational and religious condition, though both were dominated by Roman Catholic influences, pleased him much. He recognized his ability within a very short time after his arrival, to locate himself, so far as the people, the government, the city and the neighboring country were concerned, in very agreeable circumstances. He was especially delighted—charmed in fact—with the generosity manifested by every Haytian with whom he was brought into social or other relations. General Lubin illustrated all that is here referred to in his kind offer made both Mr. Langston and his secretary, to use, according to their desire and necessities, his horses, bridles and saddles during their sojourn with Mr. Bassett, without the least cost and at any time. Besides, he not only invited the new minister to pleasant quarters and entertainment at his own house, but gave him free use of his valuable library, offering daily such information with respect to his country and countrymen as he felt the minister might need in entering upon his diplomatic duties.

Port-au-Prince is located upon a harbor of great capacity, accommodating shipping of large proportions, as it represents every flag and nationality. Surrounded as this city is by mountains which lift themselves thousands of feet above the level of the sea, its situation is one of remarkable natural strength and defence. All shipping in this harbor is entirely protected against every violence of the ocean and every ship rides at ease as anchored therein. Upon the summit of the loftiest mountain range, lying back and east of the city, is located the famous national fort, which is supposed to be quite sufficient to defend it and all shipping of the harbor against attack from the sea. The views seaward from the city are extended and commanding. The approach of any craft, warlike or other, is easily detected at great distance away, as it arrives either by the northern or southern channel leading into the harbor. The Island of Gonave lying off in the sea, to the west of the city, dividing the ocean and thus creating such channels flowing about it, and at the same time so closing in the harbor as to make it a safe and delightful retreat for all shipping, presents to everyone looking upon it a mountainous, rugged, picturesque prospect of marvelous and striking sublimity. At sunset, ordinarily, it is a thing of indescribable radiance and glory, with the twilight lingering and playing about it often till far into the evening. To say that a city thus situated and surrounded must be beautiful in its site as well as quite impregnably fortified by nature, is to make an assertion with respect to Port-au-Prince which will be accepted without question.

Such considerations will all be appreciated when it is recollected that this city is the capital of the nation; that here the national palace is located; that here the national assembly, composed of the Senate and House of Deputies, holds its stated meetings; that here the executive officers as well as the judicial, military and naval, have their homes; and that here the retired distinguished statesmen of the country make their residences; while here also the chief and most valuable commerce of the country is conducted. The further consideration that the nation is one distinguished for its revolutionary movements, which are sometimes very severe, protracted and destructive as well of life as property, must enhance especially in general estimation the fortified condition of the capital as indicated.

The city is so situated that it is of easy access from all parts of the island by sea, and can be reached without serious difficulty from any point inland by the ordinary citizen coming on horseback or on foot. Its situation is central; it is the metropolis of the island, and the business of the republic—political, official and commercial—is mainly done there. Whatever may be the general view which one gains in travel in or about the island; however he may catch glimpses of its great mountains, their rich, productive sides and slopes; the plains, fertile and fruitful, as the Cul-de-Sac; it is only as he sees the products themselves garnered and collected there, the coffee, the logwood, the hides, the honey, the sugar, the cotton, the domestic animals, horses, cattle, sheep and poultry of every sort, grown in the country, that he realizes and may estimate justly the fertility and productive power of its soil. It is as the stranger finds these products accumulated in the markets and storehouses of Port-au-Prince, that he can understand the quantity and value of them. So far as the fruits of the island are concerned, the orange, the lemon, the banana, the cocoanut, the mango, with others of tropical character and name, he must travel about the island to appreciate these, since little account is made of them as articles of commerce. These fruits however are of excellent quality, and as articles of diet of the greatest importance, as will be discovered at once by such association with the people of the country as to bring one to their tables.

The most imperfect observation of the country in its great leading features impresses the stranger with its exceeding natural beauty. Nor is any part of this impression lost as one is brought face to face with its great mountains and their streams, the latter losing themselves finally in the sea; and the plains, whose productiveness discovers itself so generally in sugar-cane, which seems to be inexhaustible in quantity, excellent in quality, not requiring resetting, in many cases, for great periods of time—as long sometimes as fifty or more years. It is hardly necessary to state that the American minister, surveying the harbor, the city and the surrounding country under the agreeable circumstances pictured, from the deck of the goodly ship which had borne him across the Atlantic; then landing in the metropolis of Port-au-Prince at an hour of stir and activity in its business, with the streets alive with its energetic driving multitude, was profoundly and favorably impressed with the scenes which he witnessed.

The business activity of Port-au-Prince is very remarkable, and it is there that one is impressed with the extent as well as the value of the commerce of even this small territory, with ill advised and insufficient cultivation. And when one witnesses the character of the shipping of its harbor, its capacity and nationality, he can but be impressed with the fact that the leading nations value its commerce in such manner and to such extent as to be determined to seeks its division, if it be impossible for any one of them to gain it wholly. The great ships that fly the British, the French, the German, the Russian, the Austrian, the Danish, the Norwegian and the American flags, not to mention others, are often found anchored in this chief harbor of the nation, each bent on vying with every other, though in friendly competition, for cargoes calculated to supply its home markets. The chief staples of the country are logwood, hides, sugar, cotton, honey and coffee. The former is mainly exported to the United States, and the latter sold principally in European markets.

No one may infer from anything already stated, even in view of the accumulated products found in Port-au-Prince, that there is anything like a well-regulated, progressive agricultural system of industry in Haïti. Whatever is produced there now seems to be rather the fruit of natural, spontaneous growth. No such cultivation of the soil is found as in the earlier and more prosperous conditions of the island. Were the people to adopt a system of wise and efficient agriculture it would be difficult to limit the extent, quantity and value of the rich products which would repay their industry. The coffee-orchards properly cared for would yield fabulous quantities of this valuable staple, and the sugar-plantations as well-attended would prove to be sources of incalculable wealth. The cultivation of cotton and logwood, made subjects of wise industrial management, would also add largely to the general wealth of the island.

It is a matter of surprise that a country of such easy cultivation, and so productive even in its neglect, belonging to a people who know its value and capability and who ought to be able to appreciate their own condition, is not cultivated with greater wisdom and thoroughness, so as to make it produce in fair if not abundant measure those things which in the markets of the world are highly estimated, because in constant demand. This condition of things can be accounted for only in one of three ways. First, that the people dislike the labor needed in the cultivation of the soil. Or, secondly, that they are so occupied with other things that they cannot give attention to such labor. Or, finally, that they do not value and appreciate the results connected with the wise and intelligent cultivation of their lands. All these reasons are given at different times, by different persons acquainted with the subject, in explanation of the condition of agricultural affairs in the country. Whatever may be the cause it is a fact that the Haytian, as a rule, does not turn his attention to the cultivation of the soil. And it is also a fact that no president of the republic, however anxious he may have been; however willing to secure large special government appropriations to that end, has been able to induce any considerable number of his countrymen to turn their attention to agriculture and its benefits, so as to lead them to cultivate with anything like large advantage their own plantations.

It was Jeffrad, the president of the republic succeeding Soulouque, noted no more for his patriotism than for his general knowledge of the best interests of his country, who undertook to demonstrate to his people the great importance and profit of improving their industrial pursuits as regarded their agriculture. To do this he established in the plains of the Cul-de-Sac, three miles from the capital, a model national plantation, where all necessary buildings, machinery, implements and improved methods of cultivation were adopted by him and his advisers. He spared in this enterprise no needed outlay, and besides employing a skillful superintendent, gave constant attention to it himself. He had no sooner however been deposed and driven from his country than his countrymen, who ought to have taken interest in this movement and aided to the extent of their ability in giving it success, began the work of its utter destruction. And before Jeffrad had died, while in exile at Kingston, Jamaica, the destruction had been made so complete that there was hardly any evidence in building, machinery, or otherwise, left to tell of any good results which had come of that enterprise. The canals, even, established for irrigating purposes, conducting the water from neighboring mountain streams across the plantation, had been entirely destroyed and all left in utter and frightful ruin.

Nor is the Haytian connected, in large numbers, with the heavier, more important conditions of the commerce of his country. Many of them are engaged in small mercantile business. Now and then one finds a large Haytian house doing a good trade. Often Haytian women are found engaged in trade even of considerable character and profit. The heavier parts of Haytian commerce and trade are found, however, in the hands of foreigners and under their control, chiefly of Frenchmen, Germans, Englishmen and Americans. The Haytian seems rather to be given to matters of political, official, military and professional character, particularly medical and legal. For ordinary purposes it would be found quite difficult to secure the services of any Haytian, youth or adult. Haytians are wont to employ for menial and domestic duties foreigners who come to their country from the neighboring islands—chiefly men and women from Jamaica and St. Thomas. This condition of things is quite apparent as one reaches and moves about Port-au-Prince. One exception to this statement, touching domestic service, of remarkable and striking character, should be noted. It is that washing and ironing, done in the most primitive though often most excellent manner, are confined quite entirely to Haytian women. The washing, which consumes fabulous quantities of soap, is always done in a stream of running water, and by rubbing the clothing in the hands ordinarily; but when heavy and more thoroughly soiled, the washerwomen often place the pieces upon a stone, in the stream, and pound them with a wooden paddle. While this process may be wearing upon the clothes, washing in Haïti is pronounced by all acquainted with the subject as being well done. Of course, women who seat themselves in the streams to do this work dress in scantiest possible attire. They never do any ironing lest they take cold. Others, who never wash, attend to and do that service. Perhaps nothing strikes the stranger, particularly the American, arousing his curiosity and interest more thoroughly than the sight of a large company of Haytian women seated in a stream of water, one above the other, at reasonable distances apart, as far as the eye can reach, scantily dressed, with the limbs and sometimes other portions of the body exposed, hard at work upon their tasks. It was in passing to and fro from his residence to the city, that Mr. Langston was wont to witness this curious and remarkable spectacle.

The population of Port-au-Prince is between thirty and forty thousand. The residences are many of them well built for a tropical city. The business-houses, many of them are large, constructed of substantial materials and made fire-proof. The streets, crossing each other at right-angles, running north and south and east and west, are, in many respects, while without the regular pavement so well known in the cities of the United States, of fair width, well drained and kept in such condition as to make them easy of passage for pedestrian or teams. Some of the streets too are made beautiful by ornamental shade-trees, which in a hot climate and city are often found very grateful. The breezes, land and sea, which in a normal condition of the atmosphere prevail with great regularity in Haïti, are particularly felt and enjoyed at Port-au-Prince. Indeed, nothing so quickly attracts the attention and commands the admiration and gratitude of the stranger as these breezes. The land breeze prevailing for the first twelve hours of the day, cool and refreshing as it always is, is succeeded, beginning at twelve o'clock precisely in the day, by the sea-breeze, which while it proves to be a perfect disinfectant, is stimulating and strengthing to every one in most sensible and affecting manner.

The highest and best society of the country is found at the capital; for besides the government officials, the judges and prominent members of the Bar, together with the distinguished professors and instructors of the schools, the archbishop and chief officers of the church, and the representatives of all foreign governments reside there. Into this society the new American minister was very shortly introduced through the kindness of his friends, and found his experiences in that behalf congenial and agreeable. While he was unable in the beginning to speak the language of the country, he found the society of the city composed of so many foreign elements using the English language, that he was able to make himself quite at home even from the very first. Furthermore, his secretary was so much the master of the French and Spanish languages and was so attentive to the minister, that he found little embarrassment in even social life, for Mr. Lazare was always present and ready to translate and interpret for him. It is hardly necessary to state here that the inhabitants of Haïti, so far as the Haytians themselves are concerned, are chiefly black people. They are of delicate and refined physical as well as mental make; not ashamed of their complexion, nor apprehensive of their equal ability with any other class of people. Perhaps in no negro population, numbering between six hundred thousand and one million souls, can one find as few mixed bloods as in Haïti. While the French people supplied them language, religion, law, and many ordinary habits and customs, they did not succeed to anything like a large degree in mixing their blood.

When Mr. Langston arrived at Port-au-Prince, in November, 1877, Boirond-Canal was president of the republic, with the Hon. H. Carrié his secretary of state of foreign relations. The reception given him by these officers of the government at the national palace, very shortly after his arrival, in the presence of the whole cabinet and other noted officials, was cordial, being characterized by marks of unusual considation. The National Band with a detachment of the National Guards affording appropriate music and doing military duty on the occasion, in honor of the new American minister and his government, signalized and distinguished his official recognition. The president gave the new minister upon his introduction by his retiring predecessor, the warmest and most respectful audience, and upon the conclusion of his remarks, such welcome to the confidence and consideration of the government and the people in his capacity as representative of the American Republic, as to insure him a happy and useful residence in the Black Republic of the West Indies. Thus it was rendered possible and practicable for him to secure just attention and determination of every matter which he might have to present to the government, in the name of any American citizen; while he maintained good understanding and amicable relations with the nation to which he was accredited.

An incident of rare character and interest which marked the reception given Mr. Langston by President Canal deserves special note. The minister had observed the portraits of John Brown and Charles Sumner hanging upon the walls of the palace, in the large and beautifully decorated audience chamber, and he very well understood how the negro patriots and the people of Haïti generally esteemed them both. The likeness of the latter was life-size and a painting of striking excellence and beauty. The senator was himself truthfully portrayed in it; so aptly that the very words which he was wont to employ in defence of negro liberty seemed ling'ring upon his tongue and lips. The picture had been purchased by the Haytian government of the American artist whose creation it was, at unusual expense, and it was greatly prized. In his address Mr. Langston had made allusion to Senator Sumner, assuring the president that the friendship of that person, which he possessed, was one of the pledges which he offered of his amicable feelings and purpose toward the Haytian government, at the same time directing attention to the likeness by his gesture. Whereupon the president, leaving his seat upon a raised platform arranged for the occasion, as surrounded by his full cabinet and supported by a large company of distinguished officers, civil and military, approaching Mr. Langston and feelingly offering him his right hand, kissed him upon either cheek, while he declared "that his government and his people would ever treat the friend of Sumner with the kindest and most abiding consideration." This salutation and treatment were justly considered a manifestation of the most profound and affecting expression of exalted personal esteem, so far as the minister was concerned, and special friendly, even fraternal respect for his government. As the American minister left the palace the National Band played in his honor the air of the famous "John Brown song." The Haytian people loved John Brown because he stuck, against every odds, for the freedom of the slaves of the United States. They would immortalize the name of Charles Sumner, because, besides being the bold, fearless, eloquent champion of negro liberty, he opposed the annexation of Santo Domingo to the United States, thus maintaining as they believed in important sense and manner the integrity of their territory and the perpetuity of their government.

Among the noted men met almost immediately on his arrival in Port-au-Prince, certainly within a very few days after his recognition by President Canal, were several leaders of the country distinguished either in connection with its business, its politics, its professions, its scholarship, its learning or its religion. Conspicuous among these characters were Messrs. Bazlais, Paul, Price, Manigat, Lespinasse, Lubin, Miott, Montasse, Audain, Pradine, Thébeau, Délorme,

Ethéart, Ludecke, Keitel, Tweedy, Peters, Weymann, Bishop James T. Holly, Rev. C. M. Mossell, Captain Cutts and Dr. John B. Terres. In addition to these gentlemen, representative in the sense indicated, the diplomatic and consular corps, with Major Stewart as its dean, composed such elements of general interest and influence in the social life of the capital as to make even a stranger feel quite at home among them, especially one who must now join them in the consideration and decision of important and exalted matters of international character. Of the Haytian gentlemen who deserve in this connection special notice by reason of their conspicuous positions respectively, and their commanding influence, must be mentioned Boyer, Bazlais, Linstant, Pradine, J. J. Audain, and M. Délorme. The first of these persons was recognized by all among well-informed Haytians as a political leader of great ability, of unwonted magnetism and power, as brave as he was eloquent, learned in the English as well as the French language, who had won as a parlimentary orator a name of renown and fame. The second was noted as being the ablest and most successful lawyer of the Haytian Bar. His opinion on professional matters as expressed in addresses to the court or otherwise was regarded by his fellow attorneys as authoritative and final. A man of extended European travel and large information of American affairs, with general knowledge of the United States, its laws and institutions, he was liberal as well as cultured, discovering always great admiration for the progress and advancement of the American people, in whose government he entertained profound and constant interest. The third person, Mr. Audain, was a representative of the business capacity, perseverance and success of the Haytian himself. He always maintained high position in credit, influence and name among the business men of his own country, and the merchants with whom he had relations in Europe and the United States of America. Mr. Délorme occupied high place among the people of his country as the representative of letters and science. In that regard he had won, at home and abroad, an enviable prominence. Indeed, it would be difficult to find among any class of persons speaking the French language many who had not read several of the works, fictitious or scientific, of this famous Haytian author. It was through the very kind considerate offices of the Hon. E. D. Bassett that Mr. Langston was so promptly introduced to these famous Haytian celebrities and won their lasting friendship.

The institutions of the capital, the great churches, Catholic and Protestant, the schools and colleges, parochial and other, the Masonic and charitable organizations, the government buildings, including the palace, with conveniences for movement about the city in public conveyances, carriages and tramway, with hotel accommodations and market facilities, were found to be ample and suitable. In this capital, with such friends and associates of character and culture, in a tropical country of great richness and beauty, and in the midst of a black nationality, the American minister, newly arrived and recognized, entered upon his duties with no little *éclat*.

CHAPTER XXIV.

THE LEGATION AND RESIDENCE OF THE AMERICAN MINISTER AND HIS DIPLOMATIC AND CONSULAR SERVICES AND ACHIEVEMENTS.

ON his arrival at Port-au-Prince Mr. Langston found that the American Legation, as located, established and furnished, was neither in appearance nor dignity what he felt it ought to be. He proceeded therefore, at once, to make other and improved arrangements in this respect. He realized that a great government like his own should find its sovereignty, power and glory housed in quarters worthy of its character and name, and to that end he exerted himself in prompt and special effort.

Such a property, situated upon the Rue Pavé, in the central portion of the city and belonging to an American citizen, commanded a view of the surrounding country and was in such near neighborhood of the palace, the residence of the president, the government offices, the main business part of the city, the custom house and the port, as to make it in every sense more desirable than any other in the capital.

It was at *Sans Souci*—the place whose name is so unique and expressive—"without care"—that the American minister at once established and spent the greater part of his time while he remained in the beautiful Island Republic. There at his own home, which was enjoyed as it was appreciated by all concerned, he received and entertained not only his own citizens, resident of the republic, or sojourning there on errands of pleasure or business, but all visitors, Haytian or other, who honored him with calls, for the most part social merely, occasionally ceremonious. It was here too that he gave several of his earlier receptions, when his associates of the diplomatic and consular corps, with distinguished officials of the government, including the president of the republic, honored him by their presence in acceptance of his hospitality and entertainment.

On the fourth day of July, 1878, the first anniversary of American Independence following his arrival in the country, Mr. Langston had that occurrence noted and signalized in a reception given by him at his residence. Every member of the diplomatic and consular corps was invited and attended, together with a large number of the most prominent government officials, including the president and the members of his cabinet. The dinner given was American in every feature—improved somewhat by the large use of tropical additions in meats, vegetables and fruits—and discovered in the generous provision made in connection with it the cordial and liberal hospitality with which the distinguished guests were received and treated. According to special arrangement there followed the dinner sentiments upon which remarks pertinent to the occasion and circumstances were made by several of the more prominent persons present, including the president of the republic and the representatives of the German, the French, the Spanish, the Dominican and the British governments.

The company was large and representative; and the expressions had, whatever the sentiment upon which remarks were made or the person speaking, were friendly and eulogistic of the United States government, the progress of the nation, its free institutions and its people. The remarks of the representative of the British Government reflected in apt and striking manner the feelings of everyone present, and received upon their delivery enthusiastic approval and applause. The address, in view of this fact, is here given. The American minister had proposed the sentiment "The

Queen of England, Empress of India," when Major Stewart, her Britannic majesty's minister, dean of the diplomatic corps, responding, spoke as follows:

"I have listened with heart-felt gratification to the gracious words just uttered by the honorable gentleman, my American colleague, at whose hospitable board we are now, under such happy circumstances, met, and right glad I am that there are so many present who understand the language in which he has spoken, for depend upon it, his words will somehow or other find their echo far beyond the precincts of the gallery where we are sitting.

"In common we must all have admired the dignified and poetic eloquence of our host; but you could not all have felt as I do, and as my compatriots at the table feel, the impressive force of what he has said respecting our Queen, our countrymen, and—suppose a long drawn interval—respecting myself, Her Majesty's agent in these parts, and the organ of Her Majesty's Government.

"Nature has not bestowed on me, nor have I acquired by study, such eloquence as we have just been listening to, eloquence that, like eolian music, charms the ear and would often lead captive the reason. I am not going to make the vain attempt of imitating such eloquence; but I would ask you to lend me your ears for a few minutes while I try, in a homely way, to return thanks for the toast so handsomely proposed and so cordially accepted by you all. Believe me when I tell you that my words will express my own genuine sentiments, and, if I am not strangely mistaken, those of my countrymen in general.

"First then, let me affirm that Her Britannic Majesty fully deserves the high eulogiums of our eloquent host. In the eyes of her subjects that distinguished Lady possesses all the qualities of a great Sovereign, and, what they do not less prize, all the graces and virtues that adorn woman in the social and domestic circles.

"Yes, the English do love and reverence their Queen, although to most of them she is but an ideal personage, an unseen abstraction of exalted greatness. But that greatness,—and herein lies a strong principle—is felt to be their greatness too: the Queen, in fact, is the crowning point of the pyramid of our institutions and social system, the material center, to use another simile, towards which all our feelings of nationality converge. Queen Victoria has already been forty years our Sovereign; I think we have done pretty well under her; and our prayer is that she may still live long to reign over us.

"God save the Queen.

"But it is not of their Queen alone that the English are proud. Speaking figuratively, nations, like individuals, sometimes beget their like. England is very prolific in that way, as may be seen by the number of her colonies established in different parts of the world. Her eldest colony is now the great Republic of the United States, and this day we commemorate, not the birth of the colony, but the birth of the free and independent state into which that colony by natural development was changed as the butterfly is from the chrysalis.

"The birth was perhaps somewhat painful and forced; but no birth is without pain and many births require force. However that may be, England, like the mother of Scripture, now rejoices that a man child was born—I still speak figuratively—and again rejoices to see that man child grown to giant proportions and Herculean strength.

"The bantling state numbered some three millions when, one hundred and two years ago this day, it proclaimed its independent individuality. It now numbers forty-six millions, and it is increasing at the rate of a million a year.

"If the United States are now great, and great they are, what will they be a few score years hence—but we must leave it to the future to tell its own story.

"It must be noted that the numerical statistics of a people exhibit only the raw material of that people's force: for we know that the primitive force expressed by numbers, may be almost indefinitely multiplied by the applications of science. See, for instance, to what degree a man's effective strength is increased by the use of a pulley. Well, in no country in the world, is science more effectively or generally employed in multiplying human force than in the United States. So that a million of Americans are worth much more than a million of some other nations; and we all know that they are every day improving in practical value. Now, these are the people with whom we English are in close family relationship. On our side the relationship is commonly designated cousinship. I do not know how it is designated on their side; but leaving that apart, I believe our common wish is, to live in reciprocal good fellowship, working out together in noble rivalry the great ends of human progress and intellectual development. It would indeed be a sad thing for the world if we were to follow hostile and conflicting courses; for a difference between England and the United States carried out to the bitter end, would not cause less disorder and confusion in the world than the displacement of the equator or the uprooting of the poles—while, on the other hand, England and the United States, resolutely marching forward hand in hand, in the way of peace, may do much to prepare the world for that blessed time when, as we are taught to hope, wars shall cease, the sword shall be turned into a ploughshare, and the lion shall lie down with the lamb."

The service which was organized in the legation under Mr. Langston's direction, as the minister-resident and consul-general of the United States, was as his official designation indicates, diplomatic and consular. As a consular officer he was required to supervise, direct and perform two branches of service, the one as consul-general, his district in such respect embracing all the open ports of the republic in which his government had established agencies; and as consul, having charge of all those matters which pertain to that officer in the port of Port-au-Prince. In fact he was required to do the work of the diplomat, the consul-general, and the consul of his government. When established in his new quarters he organized and adjusted his forces to that state of the service. In addition to the force of which he found himself possessed, as respected himself and his private secretary, he secured the appointment of Dr. John B. Terres as vice consul-general of the United States, and in that character had him recognized by the Haytian government.

Besides organizing his service in this manner for efficient work, Mr. Langston at once put himself in such relations and communication with his subordinate consular officers as to improve and facilitate his business beyond any degree hitherto attained. The result was that very many defects therein were soon discovered and correction and improvement adopted. In some instances, for example, a wrong construction and interpretation had been put upon certain provisions of Haytian law with respect to navigation, and under this misunderstanding the enforcement thereof was had to the serious annoyance and wrong of American shipmasters and owners. More than this, in one or two cases laws had been passed providing for the levy and collection of duties in United States ports, as well as others, upon exports destined to Haïti; which regulations, wholly illegal, wrought in important sense obstruction and hindrance in trade and navigation. To illustrate the first condition of things mentioned, not many months after Mr. Langston had entered upon his duties he had reported to him five American sailing vessels recently arrived from several foreign ports to that of Miragoâne, and that each was fined fifty dollars for what was termed a breach of the law, in that they had not had their papers properly certified by a Haytian consular officer in the foreign port from which they had come; when as a matter of fact there was no Haytian consular officer residing in that port and the captain of the ship had done all that was required in having his papers certified by a notary public. These ships had been fined under an old view of the law and under a perverted custom, neither of which would bear the test of proper knowledge, or sound judgment; and when the attention of the proper officer of the Haytian government was called to the subject in intelligent, vigorous manner, correction was promptly made, with the fines returned, and the correct rule thereafter pursued.

As illustrating more fully the other condition of things referred to, the Haytian law provided that when a bill of merchandise was purchased in New York, or any other place in the United States, to be shipped to Port-au-Prince or other open port, for sale in Haïti, or otherwise, before such merchandise could be shipped the consular officer of the Haytian government residing in the place of purchase should collect one per cent. of the value of the goods, a portion of which he was allowed to retain for his services, while he made credit of the balance to his government. The United States consul-general addressed himself with vigor and purpose to the matter of securing the repeal of this law; and after bringing the subject fully both to the attention of his own government and that of Haïti, by the combined influence and power which he was able to exert under the instructions of his own government as a diplomat and consular officer, he accomplished the repeal of the law and freed American trade and shipping from its illegal and unjust exactions.

Up to the time that the United States consular service in Haïti was thus reorganized and rendered efficient, it appeared to be, as it was, utterly lifeless. Not even had an annual consular commercial report ever been made, of consequence and value, from that country to the United States government. In presenting formally to the United States Congress the commercial conditions of its own and foreign countries as related to each other in their trade, in speaking of Mr. Langston's commercial report for 1878, under the title of Haïti, the secretary of state, the Hon. William M. Evarts, employs the following expressions:

"A very interesting report, and all the more interesting as being the first of any consequence received from that republic, is herewith submitted from Consul-General Langston, at Port-au-Prince, on the natural features, laws, religion, population, agriculture and general trade, of Hayti.

"According to this report the importations of Hayti, for the year ending June 30, 1878, amounted to $8,007,321, and the exports to $8,234,687, showing a small balance of trade in favor of the republic.

"The importations consist of dry goods, ready-made clothing, soaps, implements of industry (such as hoes, axes, machetes, picks) ordinary hardware, drugs, medicines, crockery, lumber, marble, coal, carriages, brick, butter, cheese, lard, flour, sugar, groceries, codfish, provisions, and liquors. The importations are chiefly from the United States, France, England and Germany. The consul-general notes the introduction of certain articles of dry goods from the United States and their growing popularity.

"The trade with the United States for the year under review, was as follows:

"Importations, $2,608,000; exportations, $2,785,000; being almost one-third of the total trade of Hayti.

"The principal articles of import from the United States consist of the following articles, of which it may be said that they almost monopolize the market: provisions, tobacco, soap, and hardware (such as nails, axes, shovels, hoes, and printing materials).

"With the introduction of cotton manufactures and other articles of merchandise, and their growing popularity, it is thought that our trade with Hayti can be very much increased."

It is true that by the wise management of the consular officers of the United States government, under the direction of the consul-general as located in the the open ports of the republic, special impulse was given to trade with their country and its importance and value greatly enhanced. In illustration of this statement reference may be had to the introduction of American blue denims, which brought into the Haytian trade proved to be so acceptable, though manufactured without the least reference to the demands of trade in that country as to quantity in each piece, with color or other peculiarity, that they took possession of the market, driving out even English manufacturers of that character, causing the merchants, who had invested largely in that grade of goods from that source, to admit in many cases very considerable loss. On one occasion, in connection with this subject, a German merchant who had lost quite heavily upon his investments in the English goods, said to the American consul-general, "The Haytians have gone crazy on American blue denims," to which the officer replied, "Their frenzy is the perfection of wisdom."

On the next Sabbath following this conversation, when the American consul-general attending the great monthly dress parade of the army, sixteen thousand in number, clothed in pants and coats all made of American blue denim, and in addition thereto found most of the ordinary classes, men and women, attired in the same material, it did really seem that the good German merchant had fair cause for his complaint. However, this trade went on and other American cotton goods of important and valuable character were added gradually to the importations of that country.

During his entire term of office Mr. Langston gave due attention to every commercial interest of his citizens at home and in Haïti. So far as practicable he urged the development of trade in that behalf, and the protection and advancement of every interest pertaining to American shipping; at no time neglecting either the captain or the sailor, whose rights, privileges or welfare seemed to be in anywise endangered or disturbed. As he exercised wise discretion and earnest effort to that end himself, he required diligence and exertion to the same purpose of the consular officers and agents who were under his direction. The largest, most desirable results rewarded these labors.

So far as his services in his diplomatic capacity were concerned, such was the situation of affairs in Haïti on his arrival that Mr. Langston was called immediately to duty. Indeed he was introduced to the major part of the members of the diplomatic corps at a meeting held by that body within at most the second day after his recognition by President Canal. The matter in contention respected an important claim urged by the Spanish government against the Haytian, and involved such elements of intricacy and delicacy as to necessitate grave and elaborate consideration by the corps. The papers in the case were written in the Spanish language, while the debates had upon the matter involved were conducted in French. In the sequel, the judgment of the corps embodied in its advice to the government duly formulated, was drawn by the new American member. Subsequently, in all matters brought to the attention of the corps, whether they respected the obligations of the Haytian government to foreign powers or concerned differences between that government and revolutionary leaders and movements of domestic character, he was made both as regarded his judgment, counsel and labors, a member of conspicuous influence and effort.

So far as his own citizens and their claims were concerned he was confronted by many grave and serious matters, some standing for even more than twenty years, requiring consideration and settlement at the earliest practicable moment. One case especially, involving over a million of dollars in the claim preferred—a reclamation which had commanded the close thought and exercised the great learning of Secretary Seward, which had its origin in violent and unjustifiable treatment accorded an American citizen, even before the late rebellion—was early presented to Mr. Langston for full investigation and report to his own government, with reference to the preparation and presentation of instructions to him for its consideration and settlement by the Haytian government as the same might be brought to and urged upon its attention. Another case which was of long standing, involving a very large amount as the measure of damages for the nonfulfilment of a contract made by the Haytian government with an American citizen, which case had already commanded the serious attention of the United States government but which had not been settled because of diverse points of law and fact about which there were contrarieties of belief and opinion, was brought also at an early day to his notice for investigation and report. Upon his report the honorable secretary of state instructed him to proceed in the latter, as in the former case, to press the claims of his citizens. Still other matters of great importance and moment of quite too long standing, in which American citizens were deeply concerned, aggregating a very considerable sum of money, against the Haytian government, were pressed upon his attention and commanded his efforts. Upon the consideration of these matters and their settlement he was early instructed, and entered with earnestness and decision upon such efforts in regard to them as seemed to him to be wise and advantageous.

In every case, either by settlement with the Haytian government directly, or by some arrangement of arbitration and reference, he brought all these matters to reasonable, amicable conclusion and adjustment; maintaining always all the rights, privileges and immunities which his citizens might claim under the Treaty of 1864, made by his own with the Haytian government, and under those regulations and usages justified and sustained by all civilized powers according to accepted international law.

So far as he had obligations and duties as a member of the diplomatic corps, growing out of his relations to the Haytian government on the one part, or any foreign power on the other, whose representative was associated with him in that body, and who was entitled by the demands of law or acknowledged usages to his sympathy and support in connection with any question of significance resulting from any act or omission on the part of the Haytian authorities, he acted promptly, but always with becoming caution and moderation. To one unacquainted with the real condition of the country near whose government he was accredited— often disturbed by revolutions threatening its very existence, involving and working too frequently immense destruction of property and life and at times the property and lives of citizens of other governments residing therein, thus causing reclamations, presenting vexed questions of liability of international character for discussion and adjustment— the difficulty of his situation and the responsibility which he was compelled to carry constantly will not appear in their full gravity, nor in anything like full measure, upon any other than the most serious careful reflection. This would be true of him in his simple individual representative capacity, since the voice and the judgment of the United States of America must be heard and accepted as he presented them. And no one was ever more conscious of the dignity and responsibility of his position, nor more appreciative of his duty and the necessity and propriety of its wise and judicious performance than the person who at this time was called to speak for the most intelligent, worthy and free nation on the globe, while he was permitted to formulate and express the judgment and purpose of the best and most powerful government known to man.

But when it is recollected that he was during his entire term, the only lawyer a member of the diplomatic corps, and that for the whole time of his service, after the first two years, he was dean of that body, his position may be thoroughly and justly appreciated. As dean of the corps in the country of his residence and in the midst of the circumstances so peculiar and unusual which surrounded him, he was held to specially trying and difficult responsibilities and duties. Besides, as the American minister he maintained what was regarded as new and debatable ideas as to the obligations of his legation in times of revolution, as affording refuge therein to rebels overtaken in defeat. His conduct in refusing shelter and protection to such persons was novel, and put him in such relations to every other legation and consulate exercising diplomatic functions, as to impose upon him additional responsibility and explanation. Besides, prior to his arrival and control of the United States Legation, his predecessors had, without a single exception, given asylum to persons situated as described and exposed to the rigors of the Haytian government. However, he was entirely able to maintain his position on this subject, and during his entire term, although he found the custom of receiving refugees not only in the various legations but in the consulates as well, universal and uniform, he declined to take any refugee in his, and did not favor at all such action on the part of any subordinate American officer. This course of his resulted finally, not only in great advantage to the Haytian government in the preservation of its good order and peace, discouraging and preventing often revolutionary movements, but proved advantageous to his own government and others in that in such peaceful conditions of society and the undisturbed administration of the government, opportunity was afforded to all concerned for the quiet and appropriate consideration and orderly settlement of grave matters of international character and moment.

And yet, as dean of the diplomatic corps, he was so situated that communications frequently coming from the leaders of revolutionary enterprises, compelled his recognition while adding sensibly and materially to his duties. When perplexed and puzzled by revolutionary conditions, formidable and threatening, it was not infrequently the case that the government itself addressed him its communications when it felt its need of the counsel and sympathy of the corps. In either case Mr. Langston never failed to demean himself and influence the corps in such way as to secure the largest advantage of all interested, immediately or remotely. Such statements find full illustration and confirmation in the facts which are here recorded. Shortly after his arrival in Port-au-Prince, while Boirond-Canal was president of the republic, a revolutionary struggle headed by Boyer Bazlais and Edmond Paul broke out in that city, to the surprise and terror not only of the people generally, but of the government itself. In the absence of her Britannic majesty's representative, the American minister acted as the dean of the diplomatic corps. The government, ill prepared for this warlike and violent demonstration, hurried its messenger to the United States Legation with its appeal to the minister and his associates of the corps for counsel as to the course which it might be wise to pursue in the suppression of the movement, and for their assistance in good offices calculated to aid it in the accomplishment. It would use, if possible, the influence of the foreign representatives with those leaders to check and prevent the threatened slaughter of prominent officials and the inevitable destruction of property. Convoking his associates promptly, and explaining to them the conditions of the community, so exposed and defenceless for the moment, and the attitude of the government with its fearful responsibility, the acting dean accompanied the corps in a body to the national palace, where after a full, free conference, according to advice and counsel given it the government put itself at once and with vigor in such condition of attack and defence as that it found itself quite able to cope with and defeat the rebels, though led by two of the most influential men at that time in the republic. In this particular instance the charge of the government finally made upon the strongholds of the insurgents was furious and destructive alike of life and property. Quick, sharp and terrible was the work done. And, with the rout of Bazlais and Paul, with their co-conspiritors, the awful destruction of property and life had was witnessed in the utter ruin of ten solid acres of the very best part of the city of Port-au-Prince, and in the dead and wounded whose care, treatment and burial commanded the attention and efforts of the government, with the aid of relatives and friends, for several days. The flame rolling across the vast expanse of the city, devouring the richest, most costly and beautiful structures, public and private, were ignited and augmented by the heavy and deathly charges of the soldiery, with the Winchester rifles and cannon employed under order and by direction of the government. The house of Bazlais, where many of the insurgents, armed, concealed themselves and fired upon even defenceless citizens from ambush, was utterly demolished by attack and conflagration, while nothing of the home of Paul remained but the heaps of ashes which marked its site. It was in this struggle that General Manigat discovered not only his matchless loyalty to the government, but a Spartan, unflinching courage, which won for him the name of a brave and faithful soldier. In this struggle, too, because of his supposed loyalty to the government, attempt was made to kill General Lubin in the public street, as he walked by the side of his friend, the American minister, as they left the national palace. And it was in this outbreak of fury against the government, that for the first time, and perhaps the last in the history of revolutions in Haïti, the insurgents, through mistake doubtless, drew their guns upon the diplomatic corps as its members were passing in a body along the public street in front of the house of Boyer Bazlais. However, the guns were immediately taken down, as Mr. Langston warned those who drew them not to fire.

Routed and defeated, both Bazlais and Paul sought refuge in the English Legation, at that time in control of the vice-consul-general, Mr. Byron. Others of the insurgents sought protection in the French Consulate, and still others in those consulates and legations as were inclined to offer them asylum. None, however, found place in the United States Legation. Shortly after this occurrence, on permission of the government, Messrs. Bazlais and Paul, with certain other prominent and conspicuous members of their party, were conducted at midday through the streets of Port-au-Prince, under the protection of the foreign representatives who had given them succor, assisted by other members of the corps, with the acting dean, to the harbor, where taking ship, they were sent out of the country into exile. Located at Kingston, Jamaica, surrounded by many of their more trusted, reliable lieutenants and supporters, they undertook at once movements calculated to result ultimately in a broader, more comprehensive, and probably more successful revolution, which would overthrow, according to their purposes, President Canal and his administration. His term of office was now within ten months of its close. He would avoid, if possible, further destruction of property and life in his country. Accordingly, upon due consideration of the gravity of the situation, he quietly placed the government in the hands of his cabinet, and taking ship himself sailed away to a foreign country. Thus self-exiled, President Canal felt that in the abdication of power he might bring to pass a condition of things which without bloodshed and ruin might work, first the establishment of a wise and efficient provisional government; and secondly, the election of a person to the presidency without the intervention of the army or other force, upon popular choice and approval.

It will not be difficult upon reflection for any well-advised person, understanding the condition of the country, to believe that the representatives of all the foreign governments residing at this time in the Republic of Haïti, must have been put upon constant, anxious vigilance; and the diplomatic corps itself as a body, under the leadership of its wisest and most efficient member, whoever he may have been, upon such responsibility and duty as to tax its most vigorous, constant efforts. With a score of persons ambitious to be made president, each willing on the least encouragement from the army to attempt such movement as might promise him success, it is easy to understand and appreciate the delicacy of the situation, and how it required on the part of those who wielded influence and guidance, moderation, sagacity and wisdom. However, at this juncture of affairs, when the national welfare seemed to be quite upon the very verge of its ruin, the greatest man known in the modern history of the republic, formerly the secretary of state of foreign affairs and finance in the administration of Soulouque; subsequently the diplomatic representative of his government for many years at Paris, London and Berlin; a statesman of rare name and character; a lawyer of broad, profound and various accomplishment; a scholar of exalted attainment and rich culture; twenty odd years in exile, was called by popular voice, as by official designation under the provisional government, to his old position of secretary of state of foreign affairs and finance; and afterwards upon the united demand and choice of the p··· and the army, to the presidency of the republic. It is without satisfaction, certainly, to every foreign represe... ive then in Haïti, a member of the diplomatic corp... at he was permitted to bear in indirect but appropriate manner, in some cases a very humble, in others a larger, but in all a united part, as each was actuated by a common patriotic purpose, in the election of Gen. Louis Etienne Felicité Salomon.

He entered upon the administration of the government with the prospect and promise of continued peace and good order among all classes of the people. The unanimity of his choice, the enthusiasm attending his election and his general popularity augured that result. But he had not more than succeeded in the selection of his cabinet and the reorganization of the demoralized forces of the civil service, the army and the navy, before it became evident that an organized conspiracy of no small dimensions, with vigorous purpose, was being formed to attempt the overthrow of the new administration. Efforts to reconcile the leaders of past movements by decrees of amnesty and toleration seemed to work no change in their purposes, and reaching by correspondence those who would confederate with them in the country, the movement in its leadership and following became formidable and threatening. In spite of all words of warning and acts of the government with reference to its suppression, a revolutionary movement combining a large force, gathered principally from the southern sections of the republic, finding its chief, more conspicuous points of rendezvous at Jacmel and Jérémie, manifested itself in open, violent revolt. It even went to such lengths as to purchase, arm, man and dispatch a ship of war, which in its attempt to land at Jacmel was seized and confiscated by the government. After a few months spent in ineffectual attacks, here and there, upon the government forces, at every point defeated and vanquished, the rebels proposed through the diplomatic corps to make surrender in good faith to the authorities, upon condition that disbanding and surrendering their arms, its rank and file should be permitted, with the renewal of their allegiance in solemn earnest manner, to return to their homes and to their former condition of loyal citizens. After careful and thorough consideration, on the approval of the government and by arrangement formally and duly made, the diplomatic corps, the American minister being at that time as for some time past its dean, appointed as special commissioners to accomplish in the name of the government the service indicated, the dean, the German and the Spanish representatives, who having at the time war-vessels in the port of Port-au-Prince, employed severally his own ship of war for passage on that errand to and from Jérémie. It was in the neighborhood of this place that the rebellious forces, with their leaders, their arms and accoutrements, were collected, and where the ceremony of surrender, as conducted by the dean of the diplomatic corps, supported by his associates, was to take place.

Perhaps no more beautiful or noted enterprise was ever undertaken, and no sight ever had of any great national and international movement in Haïti, that so impressed the great body of the Haytian people, as this one made in behalf of good order and peace, as well as the maintenance and support of the government of the republic. It had become known far and near that the diplomatic corps had so managed the government authorities on the one part, and the rebels on the other, through their kind offices, that that body hoped through its commissioners to accomplish such reconciliation and amnesty as to promote and probably guarantee the general welfare. Some expressed confidence in the undertaking. Others seemed apprehensive lest even the government would show itself wanting in good faith, or the insurgents, and thus render all attempts in that regard abortive. The whole country watched the movement now with profound concernment.

All had been made ready and the commissioners, on a night as beautiful in the tropics as possible, had concluded to leave the harbor of Port-au-Prince for Jérémie and accordingly had gone aboard their respective ships of war, then anchored in the outer harbor of the capital. The moon was indeed in its light and glory the queen of the night. The stars were radiant in their magnificence, with every object in the harbor, great and small, easily discerned; while the waters of the sea, clear and translucent, were mirrors reflecting in all their added splendor every image which moved above and upon their faithful bosom.

At nine o'clock on this beautiful evening, amid the charms of a water scene unsurpassed in its magnificence and splendor the American man-of-war on which the minister of the United States had already taken his place, in its clear, full thrilling whistle, with certain naval manœuvres and displays decipherable only by those read in the secrets of the service, indicated its readiness to move on its errand of peace. Quickly responses came from the ships of war belonging to the German and Spanish governments, on which the other members of the commission had taken respectively their places, that they were ready, weighing anchors to follow. A ride of real pleasure in sight of a coast whose beauty under the circumstances could find few parallels, brought the ships to anchor at seven o'clock the next morning, in the harbor of Jérémie, facing a town of no mean name and character in the history of the republic. Shortly after going to anchor representatives both of the government and the rebellious forces came aboard of the American man-of-war to present their salutations and respects to the minister, who must as dean of the diplomatic corps take such conspicuous part in the ceremonies of peace and reconciliation about to be celebrated. Thence visits were made by the same persons to the other ships, on board of which they were welcomed by the foreign representatives who had been respectively commissioned as stated. At ten o'clock a matchless gathering was had in the public grounds of Jérémie. Here were the representatives of the foreign governments, those of the Haytian republic, a large part of the national army and the Home Guards, with the officers and men of the rebel forces, whose surrender would be made upon conditions already stated. Amid demonstrations of remarkable popular approval and applause the task which had been undertaken was formally and duly performed, and thus was ended one of the most extensive, threatening and destructive revolutionary movements known under Salomon's administration.

A little after mid-day, weighing anchors, the great ships of war which had now been employed as messengers of peace, quitted the harbor of Jérémie, after proper salutations of the port, and in honor of the great work accomplished, sailed for the capital, where the messages which they would bring were awaited with profound anxiety and interest. As the sun was setting they anchored once more in the harbor of Port-au-Prince, receiving those thundering salutes from the national forts, located about the capital, and the national ship of war then in port, which

392a

392b

PORTRAIT OF SALOMON, PRESIDENT OF HAITI.

made vocal the surrounding country, which felt and appreciated its emancipation, for the time certainly, from all those terrors which have always accompanied revolutions in Haïti.

The following letter from President Salomon, dated December 30th, 1883, as translated from his French, will show not only how he appreciated Mr. Langston's fidelity and ability as dean of the diplomatic corps, displayed in connection with this surrender of the insurgents, but his estimate of his services generally in the interest of the United States and Haïti;

LIBERTY.   EQUALITY.   FRATERNITY.

REPUBLIC OF HAÏTI.

Port-au-Prince, December 30th, 1883,
Eightieth Year of the Independence.

SALOMON,

PRESIDENT OF HAÏTI.

To Mr. John Mercer Langston,
   Minister Resident of the United States of America,
     and Dean of the Diplomatic Corps,
        MR. MINISTER:

It becomes my duty to thank you for the service with which you charged yourself for my Government in a mission entirely humane with respect to the insurgents at Jérémie, a mission which in conjunction with the consuls of Germany and Spain, you fulfilled as we fully recognize, with tact and ability.

Your predecessor, the Hon. Ebenezer Bassett, exerted himself to render more firm the bonds of friendship which so happily existed between Haïti, and the Republic of the United States of America. Such bonds have become daily more and more firm, thanks to your efforts, made constantly for the protection of your own citizens, and in accordance with which you have observed with respect to Haïti, the provisions of international law.

In my own name, and in the name of the country I thank you. Our desire so far as you are concerned, is that you remain so long as possible the representative in Haïti of the grand republic of the United States of America.

You will accept, Mr. Minister, the renewed assurance of my very exalted consideration.

                                                               SALOMON.

It proved, however, to be true that the movement which had thus been overcome and settled through the mediation of the diplomatic corps in the interest of all concerned, was not to prove the precursor of anything like protracted, continued peace in the country, and as early as the twenty-seventh day of March, 1884, Boyer Bazlais himself, with a large force, landing in Miragoâne and fortifying himself as strongly as possible, inaugurated a revolutionary attempt which covered several months in duration and cost the government large outlay of treasure, with great destruction of life and property. At last, completely surrounded on the land and sea by the forces of the government, without ability to secure provisions from any quarter, Bazlais and his men were forced from absolute exhaustion and starvation to surrender. During these months of struggle on the part of the government against the determined, unyielding, defiant rebel forces, the deepest anxiety, with the greatest care and discretion, marked the action of the diplomatic corps, adding very materially as well to its labors.

Unfortunately for the government and not a few foreigners, resident of Port-au-Prince, on return finally of the government forces from Miragoâne, flushed with the feelings of victory, certain of their numbers engaged themselves in riotous proceedings which resulted in the abuse of a large number of persons, some native and others foreign, and the death of a few, with large destruction of property. Among other persons outraged in this melée and who experienced losses of property, were several American citizens. The principal person among the Americans thus situated, was Rev. C. M. Mossell, the missionary of the African Methodist Episcopal Church, who with his wife and little daughter suffered such indignities and violence, with destruction of property, that the American minister upon his representations of the case to his government, was directed to and did make demand of the Haytian government, not only in full payment for his property destroyed but in settlement by payment of a large sum of money as

DIPLOMATIC AND CONSULAR SERVICES. 395

damages for the insults and abuses of himself and his family. The Haytian government was also held to pay for all property belonging to American citizens thus destroyed. At first effort was made by the government to treat such claims as not well founded and not falling within the limits of its responsibility. It soon discovered, however, that the demands in that behalf were made with intelligence, earnestness and purpose, and brought itself to good understanding thereupon and settled and paid the reclamations and claims, accordingly. Never were ten thousand dollars more justly demanded of a government, or more properly paid by it, than the sum thus asked and paid on behalf of the missionary named.

As illustrating still further the duties and labors constantly enjoined upon the representative of the United States, about this time an American captain aboard of his sailing vessel, on one of his regular trips from New York city to Port-au-Prince, was arrested on a charge of smuggling. His arrest was contrary to law, and he was besides harshly treated by the authorities of the port. Arrested Saturday afternoon, he was carried before the captain of the port, who while he refused to investigate the charge against him at once, declined to accept security for his appearance on the following Monday morning, although such security was offered in the sum of five thousand dollars by the consignee of the ship. Finally, however, the captain was hurried off to jail, where he was held in confinement, without the least justification. The Sabbath intervened and on the next morning, the American minister having had knowledge of the facts of the case given him, demanded the release of his citizen. As explained by the minister it was very apparent that the arrest and imprisonment were without warrant of the law. The officers of the Haytian government were not long in reaching a conclusion which accorded fully with the judgment of Mr. Langston, and the captain was set at liberty. No delay was made in bringing the facts of this case to the notice of the government of the United States, and upon its instructions, demand was made of the Haytian government in such form as to bring without anything like formidable objection full satisfaction to the American captain thus treated.

During his entire service exercising the double functions of diplomatic and consular character, and finally acting as *chargé d'affaires* near the government of Santo Domingo, Mr. Langston so demeaned himself and so conducted the business of his legation as to win not only the approval and commendation of his own government, but the respect and confidence of those near which it was his good fortune in the one case to reside for quite eight years, and in the other to manage American affairs for something less than two.

Upon the election of Hon. Grover Cleveland president of the United States in 1884, Mr. Langston tendered his resignation as minister-resident and consul-general near the government of Haïti and as *chargé d'affaires* near the government of Santo Domingo, to President Chester A. Arthur, to take effect January 31st, 1885. Although his resignation was duly accepted, no successor was appointed to him by the outgoing Republican administration. On the inauguration of Mr. Cleveland as president of the United States, the honorable secretary of state, Mr. Thomas F. Bayard, requested Mr. Langston to continue his services until such time, not distant, when the new administration could appoint, instruct and commission his successor. Accordingly on the first day of July, 1885, his successor having arrived, after full preparation for his reception and induction into office, Mr. Langston taking his own leave, introduced him to President Salomon, who gave him cordial, appropriate recognition.

The correspondence of Mr. Langston, diplomatic and consular, embracing thousands of dispatches bearing upon every subject of political and international significance, and covering every topic of commercial importance and relation respecting trade and navigation between the United States, Haïti and Santo Domingo, attests the care, propriety and wisdom with which he conceived, comprehended and ac-

DIPLOMATIC AND CONSULAR SERVICES.

complished any duty, special or general, committed to his charge. Hundreds of his dispatches have been published by the government in its formal diplomatic and consular reports; and many of them in less formal manner for the general advantage; while all of them were received and treated as possessing large importance and great value.

Of Mr. Langston's services and achievements in the first two years of his residence in Haïti, as minister-resident and consul-general of the United States, there appeared the following account, as published in "Our Representatives Abroad," in 1879. This estimate, so generous, impartial and intelligent, was written by one of the most accomplished scholars and eminent church officials on the continent. Its author is described, in the work referred to, in the following apt and truthful words:

"The following record of Mr. Langston's diplomatic and consular career has been kindly furnished for this work by Bishop James Theodore Holly, Episcopal bishop of Hayti, and one of the most distinguished colored men of the century. Bishop Holly has been a resident of Hayti for nearly eighteen consecutive years, fourteen of them as local missionary at the capital and the four latter years as bishop, having the general oversight of all the mission stations of the Protestant Episcopal church in Hayti. During ten of those years he was a member of the consular corps as consul of the Republic of Liberia at Port-au-Prince. For three more years he had a quasi connection with the diplomatic corps as secretary of Minister Bassett at the United States Legation in Port-au-Prince. Bishop Holly's personal acquaintance with Mr. Langston goes back to 1854, when he met him in a public convention at Cleveland, Ohio. These circumstances are here mentioned as indicative of the fact that Bishop Holly possesses peculiar opportunities for appreciating the influence of Mr. Langston in Hayti. We therefore accept with pleasure the following article from his pen:

"'Mr. Langston, on receiving the necessary instructions from the Department of State after his appointment (such as are usually given in all cases on such occasions), started without delay for his post of duty, and arrived at Port-au-Prince, November 21, 1877. He found Mr. Bassett, his immediate predecessor, making his preparations to vacate the post and return home. Mr. Bassett made arrangements with the Haytian government for the early presentation of Mr. Langston as his successor. This took place with the ceremonies usual on such occasions at the National Palace on the 27th day of November following.

"'The address delivered by Mr. Langston on that occasion produced a profound impression upon the president of Hayti and his ministers, and was published with the president's response in the official part of the *Moniteur*, the government newspaper published at the capital.

"'From this date Mr. Langston entered upon his official functions, which are both diplomatic and consular. Mr. Bassett had the unthankful task of beginning the work of bringing order out of the chaos that had long existed in the diplomatic and consular service of the United States in Hayti. Previous to Mr. Bassett most of the consular officers of the United States in Hayti were commercial agents, and there was not even at the capital any regular office kept for consular business or for the deposit of the archives of the legation. In remitting his charge to Mr. Langston, Mr. Bassett was able to install his successor into a tolerably well-organized office, containing the archives of the legation, and fairly equipped for the consular service. Much still, however, had to be done to regulate the relations between the consulate-general at Port-au-Prince and the subordinate consular offices at other ports of the island.

"'Mr. Langston undertook this work at once with the view of carrying it forward to completion, knowing that the promotion of the commercial interests of numerous citizens of the United States depended much upon the efficiency of this service in Hayti. The care of large numbers of American distressed seamen has also received his best attentions. Recently quite a number of shipwrecked sailors were on his hands, and a large amount of money had to be spent to clothe and board them, requiring much judicious management and delicate tact and discrimination in a place where outfitting stores for seamen and seamen's boarding-houses are unknown, the whole to be conducted in a manner so as not to needlessly waste the public funds set apart for this purpose, and to the satisfaction of the Department of State, charged with the control of this service.

"'The knowledge that Mr. Langston had acquired of men and things in the severe and laborious experience by which he has worked himself up to the eminent position he now occupies, aided by the legal acumen for solving the technicalities of the consular regulations, obtained by a long and successful practice of many years as a lawyer at the bar in Ohio, and as Dean of the Law Faculty of Howard University in Washington city, all this varied experience, we repeat, placed him in a position to bring to bear rare and singular powers to carry on to a successful completion the truly Herculean task before him.

"'After one year's effort the consular service of the United States, dispersed as it is over the whole island and employing ten consular officers, has been far advanced towards its harmonious unification and nearly reduced to practical working order, according to the requirements of the consular regulations. Mr. Langston feels it to be incumbent on him in his consular functions to make a diligent and serious study of Haytian finances and commerce in general, as well as of the internal resources and local industry of the island. One of the practical results, therefore, that he expects to realize from this more efficient organization of the consular service here will be his ability to furnish accurate and reliable information on all these subjects in his official reports to his government. Mr. Langston also avails himself of every opportunity, in his personal intercourse with the business men of the capital, to enhance American commercial enterprise in Hayti, by calling their attention to American manufactured staples. As the result of his efforts in this direction one commercial house at least has been induced to commence the importation of American print calicoes. Hitherto England and France have enjoyed the complete monopoly of this trade with Hayti.

"'On the other hand, he has also expressed the necessity upon coffee exporters here to take steps to prepare this article in a better manner for the foreign market than has been usual hitherto, and to send this Haytian staple thus nicely prepared in larger quantities for sale in the American market. The largest house here dealing in coffee is taking steps to follow this suggestion. It may also here be stated that France and England have hitherto enjoyed the monopoly of the coffee exported from Hayti. Such is the manner in which Mr. Langston, from a lofty sense of national patriotism, labors to promote the interests of his countrymen in Hayti by the faithful discharge of duties as Consul-General.

"'It now remains to add a few observations on his diplomatic relations with the government to which he is accredited. Into this sphere of his duties he carries the same high sense of devoted patriotism and does not fail to make it clear that he is here to represent the honor and dignity of a great government, and to sustain the world-wide reputation of a high-minded people.

"'It may be said as to the result of his open and frank deportment in this sense that the government of Hayti now feels fully assured from his representations, whatever may have been its fears heretofore, and however groundless these fears may have been, that the Great Republic of the North looks upon Hayti as a second sister in the great family of republics in the Western World, desires by all means to promote her welfare and would do nothing to aggrandize the Federal Union to the detriment of the national sovereignty of this Queen of the Antilles, eight hundred of whose sable sons took part in her own war of independence, under the banners of France, at the battle of Savannah in 1779. On this head we repeat Hayti is now fully assured and perfectly composed.

"'This sketch of Mr. Langston since his arrival in Hayti would not however be complete without speaking of his influence as a member of the corps of diplomatic consular agents accredited here by other powers, and of which he is subdean, and on one occasion acted as dean, in making the address in behalf of the corps at a reception of the president of Hayti, given in the National Palace. It is not too much to say that those agents have hitherto exercised prerogatives unheard of in any country save in the Ottoman possessions of the far distant East; and at times they have sadly embarrassed the government of Hayti in the exercise of its rightful attributions by bringing to bear a pressure upon it that almost totally ignored its sovereignty on its own soil over its own citizens. There is indeed a humanitarian side to this question that somewhat extenuates this broad statement. But the immunities claimed and exercised by foreign agents here have been pushed to the very verge of crying abuse. A foreign agent newly arriving in Hayti finds an *esprit de corps* already existing here among his colleagues that it is difficult to resist. Let it, however, be said to Mr. Langston's credit on this head, that such has been his lofty sense of justice and fair dealing towards a weak and struggling people, and such his high conception of duty in carrying out faithfully the generous sentiments of the great government and nation that he represents, that he will not allow himself to be a participator in anything that could wound the national susceptibilities of this feeble sister republic. Nevertheless he has not failed to endear himself to all his colleagues of the diplomatic and consular corps, who cannot but admire his high-souled principles.

"'One word more and this notice must be closed. We have now seen Mr. Langston at work in his official and semi-official consular and diplomatic duties. It may now be permitted to view him for a moment in his strictly private capacity as an American gentleman.

"'Mr. Langston is a philanthropist combining the broad and liberal views of true and progressive American republicanism. The starting-point of his life as given in his biography necessarily gave his character this bent in the most pronounced manner. Hence he arrived in Hayti with open and undisguised sympathies for them as a people whose national starting-point was so similar to his own as an individual. As he has made his way to honor and fame in the social and political circles of his native country, he desires to see the people of Hayti make their way in like manner to honor and distinction among the great civilized nations of the earth.

"'Profoundly convinced that the American standpoint of reviewing things politically is the best adapted to a rising people, he does not fail to make his views known in social circles here so as thereby to exert all the weight of his great influence towards helping onward and upward the progress of this people in the way of constitutional self-government and Christian civilization.

"'Encouraged by this influence the present government of Hayti feels to go forward with the curtailment of its hitherto large and oppressive military system, the promotion of civil administration, and the organization of a police force for correctional purposes. Under this impulse an election is now being held for representatives of the legislative body with two parties in the field, "Conservatives" and "Liberals," similar to the great political contests in the United States, and there are twice as many voters inscribed as ever before, thus showing the growing political education of this people on the model of American republicanism. In this way also he strengthens the hands of a large and increasing class here, who believe that there ought not to be any state-paid church in Hayti, but that each religious denomination should be entirely free from the State, as they are in the United States, being thus left for support to the individual contributions of their respective friends and members. As this class increases every day in Hayti, we may hope before long to see the concordat now existing between the government of Hayti and the court of Rome repealed, and the Roman Catholic church no longer supported by the State, but put on precisely the same footing as the different Protestant bodies that exist here, and just as they all exist in the United States.

"'Thus, aside from his official and semi-official duties, Mr. Langston, as the chief representative of the United States in Hayti, is so imbued with the spirit of American institutions and the genius of the American people, that a personal influence goes out from him, even in his private relations as an American gentleman, that is producing a salutary effect on the Haytian people and government, to the great and endless credit of the American nation and people, who have found in him such a worthy, high-toned and faithful exponent of their liberty-loving principles, accredited to a struggling people that sadly need the aid of such wholesome examples in the perilous task that they have undertaken to carve out for themselves a high and noble destiny.'"

CHAPTER XXV.

HIS SUIT AGAINST THE UNITED STATES GOVERNMENT FOR BALANCE OF UNPAID SALARY.

As between the American minister, Mr. John M. Langston, and the government of the United States, upon the close of his services, July 24th 1885, there arose a dispute as to the amount of his salary from and after the first day of July, 1882. When he was appointed minister-resident and consul-general of the United States to Haïti, the salary fixed by law was $7,500 per annum, payable in gold, and it is not to be denied that the amount thereof had some weight in determining Mr. Langston's decision to accept the position. Less than such amount, under the circumstances, would have induced, in all probability, the very opposite course— the non-acceptance of the situation. For it is true that not a single dollar additional to the salary, was appropriated by the government to meet any extraordinary social or personal outlay of the minister, and that too at a time and place when and where his necessary outlays for entertainments alone, of official and becoming character, were considerable. His case was by no means that of the British representative, who not only had large salary given him, but fit appropriation for meeting such expenses as those indicated. Whatever else is true, in respect to the diplomatic and consular representatives of the United States, it is a fact that they are never well paid, nor appropriately and fitly provided for. Hence, when one is appointed and accepts his situation at a salary, in view of which he makes his calculations for meeting the outlays connected with his office, he should not be disappointed, nor disturbed and annoyed by any change thereof, certainly by no unreasonable and unfair reduction. No personal or political consideration could justify such a course.

The attempt to reduce the salary from $7,500 to $5,000 per annum, was made by a Democratic House of Representatives, at the suggestion of one of its leading members, then chairman of the Committee on Appropriations, and in rebuke of the minister for certain party services which he had rendered while still representing the government abroad, in the national campaign which resulted in the election of Messrs. Garfield and Arthur as president and vice-president of the United States. To accomplish this end, without repealing the law which fixed the salary at the original figures named, the chairman of the Committee on Appropriations contented himself with appropriating, in lieu of that sum, the smaller one of $5,000, believing that this procedure would work the repeal of the law, and reducing, fix the salary in the sum appropriated. In other words, still, he believed by the act of simply appropriating a given amount, without any words of repeal of the old law, he could accomplish the two things of annulling the former law and establishing the salary at $5,000 by mere matter of appropriation. Subsequent action, however, discovered very plainly the absurdity of this position.

However, the Department of State notified Mr. Langston, on the passage of the appropriation bill, that his salary thereafter would be $5,000 per annum, and he must draw therefor, accordingly. Obedient in this as in all other respects, he made his drafts upon the government as if his salary was simply $5,000. But when he reached home in July, 1885, upon settlement with the government, he demanded, as he claimed, a balance due him of $7,666.66. From the very first he had held that while under the Appropriation Act he could only draw his salary covering the amount named, the government was responsible to him for the $2,500 per annum, as determined and fixed by the law under which he accepted his position. Therefore, he had credited duly the sum of $5,000 paid him, as indicated, and charged in his account the sum for which he made demand. When he presented this view of the case to the authorities of the State Department, of course they were taken by surprise and at once questioned the legality of his demand. They admitted however, that his view had so much reasonableness in it as to justify the reference of his claim to the auditor of the Treasury Department having such matters in charge. That officer soon reached the conclusion that the claim was not well grounded and refused to be influenced in any way by any opinion which might be secured thereupon from the attorney-general of the government. Indeed, every officer having any sort of concern with his accounts, contended that this claim could not be allowed, and that the minister must be satisfied with the salary which had been paid him. Really, every lawyer with whom he had conversation on the subject, questioned his ability to sustain his claim, with the exception of a single one.

But in no wise daunted; indeed, stout in his belief that his claim was well-founded and would be sustained to the last cent upon judicial investigation and decision, Mr. Langston employed the only attorney whom he found agreeing with him in his opinion, and brought suit against the government for the sum already mentioned. Commencing in the Court of Claims, a hearing was had in due season and the united judgment given in favor of the plaintiff. Of course, appeal was promptly taken to the Supreme Court of the United States, and without unnecessary delay, in fact with unusual promptness, the suit was brought to hearing and final judgment. In this court the judgment sustained the demand, and accordingly Congress appropriated and Mr. Langston was paid the full amount of his demand, with such interest thereupon as had accrued from the time of the judgment rendered in his favor in the under court.

It will be remembered that the Hon. A. H. Garland was the attorney-general of the United States government at this time. He, though of the opinion that Mr. Langston's claim could not be sustained, treated him and it with such kindness and consideration as to bring the ex-minister under special obligation, and he remembers this kindness and consideration in grateful manner.

Though Mr. Langston was himself a lawyer and a member of the Supreme Court of the United States, he employed as already stated, a lawyer of Washington city, of whose learning he had full knowledge. His attorney having prepared his petition instituting proceedings in such behalf in the Court of Claims, at its December term, 1884, pressing the matter with the most laudable vigor and earnestness, exhibiting at every turn signal ability and skill, brought it to the successful, favorable conclusion shown in the proceedings and judgment of the Supreme Court.

Mr. Langston has had professional relations with many lawyers of great learning and distinction, but among them all he has found no one of more amiable and courteous qualities of character, fidelity and cordial devotion to his client and his interests, cultivating larger assiduous care and skill, with abundant technical learning and knowledge, than his attorney in this case, George A. King, Esq. He therefore deems it his duty as well as his pleasure, as fit expression of his sentiments of obligation, to make full and distinct mention of him in this connection.

Mr. King was born in Minnesota, at St. Anthony's Falls, February 10, 1855, of English and Scotch ancestry. When nine years of age he came with his parents to Washington city, where he has constantly resided. He attended the public schools of the city till transferred to Gonzaga College, directed by the Jesuit Fathers, a school of prominence and influence, the number of whose students, quite large, showed its popularity. He attributes his success in business to the excellent course of instruction pursued at that college, and to the great kindness and wisdom of its instructors. He graduated, however, from the Columbian

College as early as 1870, taking the degree of A. B. in his sixteenth year, and that of A. M. in 1871; and in 1872 he graduated from the Columbian College Law School. By reason of his minority, he could not be admitted to the Bar till 1876. Meantime, he pursued the duties of a clerk in one of the first law firms of the capital.

In 1872, after a brief term of copartnership with his father in the law business, he established practice upon his own responsibility and account: and since that time having made special study of the various topics of international law and the claims of any officers of the government affected thereby, in respect of their salaries; government contracts and the law affecting them; military and naval claims against the government, and all questions of law and practice considered and enforced especially in the Court of Claims and the Supreme Court of the United States, he had established and sustained a large, important and lucrative professional practice. His success has been that of an earnest, honest, efficient, faithful and able lawyer.

In his religious inclinations he is liberal minded, as is shown in the fact that he is a conspicuous and influential member of All Souls, the leading Unitarian church of Washington city. As a husband, a member of society and a reliable faithful friend, Mr. King possesses a deservedly exalted and enviable reputation; and Mr. Langston, mindful always of his excellent services in his behalf, records with grateful appreciation these pleasant and agreeable facts. As a representative of a profession requiring the largest and most various talent and learning for its highest possible achievements, he expresses with special satisfaction the belief and hope that Mr. King, but a young man at present, will, ere he has reached his prime in life, have won for himself large and commanding place among the foremost and most noted members of his profession.

Mr. Langston deemed himself fortunate in the results of his suit, not only because he recovered a judgment in his favor, and thus secured the full payment of the amount which he demanded, but the rather because his opinion of the law with regard to the validity of his claim was entirely vindicated and sustained. This feeling was especially dominant in his mind by reason of the fact that the officers of both departments of the government having charge of his accounts—the State and Treasury—took positive and unqualified position against its payment, not hesitating to advise him against any suit, as they were confident he would be disappointed in his expectations and left to pay all costs. Even the learned attorney-general did not hesitate to offer him his gratuitous counsel that a suit would do him no good, that his claim was without legal support, and the court would so determine. It is not to be denied that Mr. Langston's feelings were something other than those of mere respect and gratitude, when he called at the conclusion of the case upon Attorney-General Garland, to thank him for the considerate manner in which he and his assistant attorney had demeaned themselves towards him in the suit. Congress had voted him, in its appropriation, the amount with interest as calculated by law which he demanded, and the government had transmitted to him its draft therefor. Feeling particularly happy in view of these circumstances, Mr. Langston called upon the excellent attorney-general to tender his acknowledgments for the professional courtesies which he had shown him, when moved by feelings of triumph in large measure, in a jocose way, but with special politeness, he exhibited his draft upon the government for quite $8,000 with the statement that it was a very handsome and desirable paper, not only beautifully executed in the engravings which it bore, but valuable in the dollars and cents which it represented. All this the learned attorney took in good part, and even appeared to be pleased at the result, as a great and good lawyer would naturally be, though defeated, when the law in its justice and power had vindicated and sustained the honest demand of a faithful public servant.

There was about this case a novelty connected with the interpretation of the law and its enforcement as sought by the claimant, which made it interesting from the very beginning. Many claims against the government of substantially the same character existed, but no officer of the government had ventured to assert for judicial investigation and judgment, any right of action which he held in such behalf. The case was wholly without precedent and must be planted upon original, untested principles and rules of the law, so far as the interpretations of the two acts of Congress having to do with the subject-matter were concerned. As decided, the case became at once as matter of precedent one of great importance and value. In fact, it has become by reason of the frequent references had to it, famous and celebrated.

This fact is abundantly sustained in a very recent reference to the case, as made by the Hon. Justice Brewer, in the opinion which he delivered on behalf of the Supreme Court of the United States in the case of Covington G. Belknap, appellant, vs. the United States, as follows:

"In the *Langston case* it appeared that the salary of the minister to Hayti was fixed by the Revised Statutes at $7,500, and that that sum was annually appropriated until the year 1883. In the statutes of two of those years, to wit, 1879 and 1880, it was expressly provided that the appropriation should be in full for the annual salary and that all laws and parts of laws in conflict with the provisions of the act should be repealed. In the years 1883, 1884 and 1885 there was simply an appropriation of $5,000 for the minister to Hayti. The plaintiff held the office from September 28, 1877 until July 24, 1885. Until 1883 he was paid at the rate of $7,500 per annum, but for the remaining years he received only the amount of the appropriation, to wit, $5,000 per annum. And this court held that there was nothing in the language of these last appropriation acts which could be satisfactorily construed as repealing the express language of the section fixing the salary at $7,500 per annum—a salary which had been recognized by Congress for ten years in its appropriations and by language in some of the acts clearly declaring that to be the salary attached to that office. Repeals by implication are not favored and it was held that the mere failure to appropriate the full salary was not in and of itself alone sufficient to repeal the prior act. And yet the court conceded at the close of the opinion that 'the case is not free from difficulty.'

"While not questioning at all the *Langston case* we think that it expresses the limit in that direction."

Mr. Justice Harlan delivered the opinion of the court in the *Langston case*, and concluded his opinion in the following words:

"The suggestion of most weight in support of the view that Congress intended to reduce the salary of the diplomatic representative at Hayti, is the improbability that that body would neglect, in any year, to appropriate the full sum to which that officer was entitled under the law as it then existed. On the other hand, it is not probable that Congress, knowing, as we must presume it did, that that officer had, in virtue of a statute—whose object was to fix his salary—received annually a salary of $7,500 from the date of the creation of his office, and after expressly declaring in the act of 1878 that he should receive that salary from and after July 1, 1878, and again in 1879, that he should receive the same amount from and after July 1, 1876, should at a subsequent date make a permanent reduction of his salary without indicating its purpose to do so, either by express words of repeal, or by such provisions as would compel the courts to say that harmony between the old and the new statute was impossible. While the case is not free from difficulty the court is of opinion that, according to the settled rules of interpretation, a statute fixing the annual salary of a public officer at a named sum, without limitation as to time, should not be deemed abrogated or suspended by subsequent enactments which merely appropriated a less amount for the services of that officer for particular fiscal years, and which contained no words that expressly or by clear implication modified or repealed the previous law."

Such is the opinion of the Supreme Court!

The record made in connection with this case, whether as found in the courts or in the proceedings of Congress, especially in the House of Representatives where elaborate earnest discussion was had upon the appropriation necessary to pay the judgment rendered by the court, is most interesting and instructive. On the whole, it would be found upon examination quite difficult to find a case decided latterly by the Supreme Court, which involves more concise and accurate features of interpretation and construction, with a larger but precise scope of application to all those subjects which by any legal possibility may be brought within its purview, than this one. And Mr. Langston feels that in prosecuting and maintaning it, he has accomplished a profitable public service.

CHAPTER XXVI.

HE ACCEPTS THE PRESIDENCY OF THE VIRGINIA NORMAL AND COLLEGIATE INSTITUTE.

WITH prior engagements arranged in acceptable manner to all concerned, after a brief visit to Petersburg and the institute, where the Board of Visitors of the school gave him welcome with full explanations of the work which might be done towards the education of the people by efficient, discreet management of its executive officer, and after his visit to and conference with the members of the Board of Education at Richmond, Mr. Langston accepted the presidency of the school tendered him and agreed to enter upon its duties at an early day.

He did not fail to appreciate and value the important business engagements which he was compelled to relinquish by taking this course. Nor did he fail to appreciate at its just estimate the loss which must be consequent upon the reduction of his actual annual income and prospective receipts in salary and commissions incident to and dependent upon the contract to which reference has been made, and which must be surrendered. It was an easy matter for him to discover the difference between receipts aggregating several thousand dollars yearly, in pleasant occupation, and fifteen hundred dollars, the salary attached to the position which he must occupy as president of the institute, while the labors to be performed would be confining and arduous enough. However, he felt and believed that in the new work to which he was called he would find opportunity and means for aiding the emancipated classes of his native State in a way and manner which he desired and would secure above all other things. Sacrifices of whatsoever character and however made were not to be considered in comparison with and against the privilege of doing something towards the Christian education and elevation of the classes alluded to. Hence the readiness and pleasure with which Mr. Langston accepted, under the circumstances, the presidency of the college to which he seemed to have been providentially called.

Indeed, for a long time Mr. Langston had hoped and desired that some opening in Virginia might be presented to him, educational if practicable, whereby he might be given the opportunity of employing any ability and knowledge which he might possess in substantial, advantageous manner for the good of the formerly oppressed and enslaved classes of the State. Often he had been urged to return thereto and make common cause with these people. More than once he had seriously considered the matter of buying from its present owner the old plantation of his father, and upon it erect a school of high standard for the education of the colored youth of Louisa County. At one time he went so far as to inquire the price at which the plantation could be bought, and made offer for it at such rate per acre as he deemed, under the circumstances, reasonable. His offer, however, was declined and the scheme abandoned.

Subsequently he had concluded that it was altogether probable, almost certain that he would not be permitted to return to the State in whose soil the dust of his father and mother reposes, to play any part in connection with any portion of its people, affecting in any way their lives and destiny. When this call came to him, unsought and without any previous hint even, in what he regarded as a most remarkable manner, with every inclination and ambition of his soul moving him to its favorable consideration, his acceptance in face even of pecuniary sacrifice and most agreeable professional employment, was with his temper of mind wholly natural.

The friends of the institution, those concerned in its success and prosperity, officially and otherwise, seemed doubly anxious to have Mr. Langston placed at its head. They seemed hardly willing to give him time to either fully and maturely reach his decision in the premises, or to arrange his business so that he might wisely and properly accept their offer. In a letter dated December 17, 1885, the superintendent of education of the Commonwealth of Virginia, employed in addressing him the following words:

"In my judgment, if your duty ever called you to assume responsibilities the call is now made, and that if you want an opportunity to serve your race and country you now have it, and I trust that you will consume no more time in considering but that you will come on at once and take charge of the institution."

Though the institute had been opened and students in limited numbers had been received and a number of teachers employed, it had not been duly and thoroughly organized. Besides, at the time of Mr. Langston's election considerable confusion, growing out of misunderstanding between the Board of Visitors and certain of the teachers existed. So much so that a friend of the school, indeed one connected with it of prominence and influence, wrote him in the following style and words: "We need your strong hand at the institute just now. All parties and classes desire you and the students have memoralized the Legislature to make you accept the position. The only hope of the institution from political rule and possibly from white management is in your acceptance." These persuasive and affecting words were conveyed to Mr. Langston in a letter bearing date December 10, 1885.

Shortly after this letter was received Mr. Langston was handed his commission.

His acceptance of the presidency of the institute seemed to give satisfaction to the Boards of Education and Visitors as well as the people of the State generally, and he received many kindly and flattering expressions in letters and otherwise to that effect. The superintendent of education for the State, Mr. R. R. Farr, addressed him on the subject at once the following letter:

> COMMONWEALTH OF VIRGINIA,
> DEPARTMENT OF PUBLIC INSTRUCTION,
> RICHMOND, Dec. 21, 1885.
>
> *Hon. J. M. Langston,*
>   *Washington, D. C.,*
>
> *Dear Sir:*
>
> I was very much gratified at the receipt of your letter to-day. You have done a great thing for your people, and have undertaken a work that I know you will make a success.
>
> I consider you a patriot in the true sense of the word.
>
> I was in Petersburg attending a meeting of the Board of Visitors when I received a telegram from the office informing me that you had accepted the presidency of the college and everybody was *delighted.*
>
> Your popularity is great and it is no mean thing to start the work on.
>
> I send you by this mail your *commission* and other usual oaths. You will come to Alexandria, qualify before a justice of the peace or notary, and forward the oaths to the secretary of the Board of Education with a request for leave of absence until the 15th of January, and it will be granted.
>
> We aim to have things so straight that the incoming Board can find nothing to complain of. As soon as you can qualify telegraph the office at *our* expense and I will make formal application for leave of absence, though you had better mention it in the telegram. Time is short and we must be prompt.
>
> You have relieved me of a great burden. I know time will demonstrate the wisdom of the Board in selecting you, and I trust that you will have a pleasant and successful administration.
>
> Very truly yours,
>   (Signed)   R. R. FARR.

Mr. Langston immediately qualified and made no delay in entering upon the duties of his office. His reception by the students, the instructors, the Board of Visitors and the entire Petersburg community, was cordial and flattering. His work was from the start, though important and laborious, unusually hopeful and promising. The officers, teachers and scholars all seemed ready to accept any changes which might be made necessary to promote discipline, improve the methods of instruction, and meet more fully any requirements needed for the wise and efficient application of any public funds used to advance the interests of the institution. The people of Petersburg feeling naturally enough special local interest in the success of the school, gave Mr. Langston every evidence practicable of their purpose to sustain him and their desire to have him introduce and maintain such authority and control of the school as would realize, probably, their anticipations and hopes, however exalted and lively, for the education of their youth.

The welcome given him by the citizens thus interested in the school located in its immediate neighborhood, was signalized by a banquet had in his honor, at which the leading people of society were present, and in sentiments, poetic and oratorical, manifested their cordial appreciation of the first commissioned president of the institute, which as they believed would now lead in the work of a high scientific and moral training of their sons and daughters.

The "Index-Appeal," the first daily paper published in Petersburg, in speaking of the banquet employed the following statements:

"The banquet given in honor of Mr. John M. Langston took place last night in the dining-room adjoining the Albermarle Hotel, and from first to last was a very gratifying success. Invitations to the number of one hundred had been issued, and those who participated comprised the most worthy and intelligent of the colored population of the city and State. Among those who were present were the following colored members of the Legislature: S. F. Bolling, Cumberland; William Faulcon, Prince George and Surry; J. R. Jones, Mecklenburg; Senator D. M, Norton, and Messrs Jordan and Harris. Other guests were Rev. Thomas Cain, rector of the board of visitors; Rev. Henry Williams, Jr., and J. J. Carter, King William County. The banquet hall was beautifully decorated with flags, among which was the one presented to the Petersburg Guards in 1873.

"The principal toast of the occasion was, "Our Guest," which was responded to by Hon. A. W. Harris, who gave a succinct and interesting sketch of the life and career of Mr. Langston. To this address he made response, saying among other things that he had come to Virginia to make, if possible, the institute the pride of the negroes of the country. He loved Virginia, and he would see her foremost again in the Union. He wanted to see the young white man and the young black one vying with each other in the work of making the old commonwealth what it ought to be. For his own part he would say: Let us leave nothing undone to make the young colored man complete in his scholarship and character."

With his election received by such general popular approval and applause, Mr. Langston entered upon his work of organizing the institute in all its branches, according to the most approved methods of instruction, pressing in every way a vigorous, wise discipline, so as to secure the best and broadest, various and most permanent results of good to his students. The whole school at once seemed seized with new vigor and determination. The instructors felt the inspiring presence of the president, and increasing from the beginning all students, old and new, pressed forward, exhibiting in every way diligence, even enthusiasm, in the prosecution of their duties.

The reputation of the school improved rapidly and its influence soon reached the most distant limits of the State. In the organic law of its creation provision was made for the attendance and instruction, upon special reduced rates of tuition, of state students, the number from each county being determined and approved by its educational authorities. This class of students was greatly increased and their influence was productive of large general growth in attendance. For it did seem to be true that the fact that a state student was admitted from a given county increased and intensified the desire, on the part of others, to come to the institute.

The standard of instruction was at once elevated, and efforts were made to improve the *morale* of the whole school. The first general lesson bearing directly on this subject given the students was formal and emphatic, founded upon the teachings of the Proverbs of Solomon as expounded by the president himself. To make the deeper impression, while certain that the students caught and understood the meaning of the lessons which he gave in such behalf, he selected several of the more advanced ones among them, girls and boys, and giving to each a subject suggested by the lesson, he required them to write and present to him essays and orations illustrating the maxims and teachings of the Moral Philosopher of Israel. Under his own direction and instruction he had the essays and orations thus produced prepared for public exercises held in the chapel of the institute. To these exercises the Board of Education of the State and the Board of Visitors of the school were invited. Their attendance gave special *éclat* to the occasion and the members of both boards seemed greatly pleased with what they heard and witnessed. At the close of the exercises, which lasted for quite two hours, Governor Lee, the chairman of the Board of Education, expressed himself from the platform in a brief address which he made, as being greatly surprised at the proficiency displayed by the students and their appropriate becoming demeanor.

In addition to the duties which concerned regular instruction in the various departments of the institute during the academic year of nine months, it was made the duty of the president with a sufficient number of his instructors and teachers, to conduct annually a summer teacher's institute at which all teachers of the colored public schools of the State were required to be present, and where they were to be instructed in the various appropriate methods best calculated to be employed for the easy, graceful and effective communication of knowledge upon the branches taught in their schools. It was expected too that all imperfections in their understanding of those branches would be corrected and improved in connection with lessons given the teachers.

Mr. Langston held his first teacher's institute during the first vacation following his appointment, and thereafter annually during his term of office. The attendance upon the institute in its summer sessions was throughout very large, the teachers manifesting their constant interest in its exercises by their orderly, appropriate behavior, and their earnest, diligent attention to the duties enjoined upon them. It was through the influence of these summer institutes also that the institution proper made large accessions to its numbers and increased and improved its opportunity for doing good to those in whose interest the government of the State had established it.

It is apparent from what has been stated that the Virginia Normal and Collegiate Institute is a state institution, founded and supported by state appropriations, and placed under the control and management of the state Board of Education. This board, in order to its wise and judicious conduct, provided as directed by the law for a board of visitors, consisting of six members, whose action was in no case final, but simply recommendatory, with its effect dependent upon approval of the Board of Education itself. When Mr. Langston arrived at the institution and took charge of it the Board of Visitors was composed of six colored men; and while they were all persons of limited educational attainment, they seemed confident of his ability to put the school on sound working basis and to conduct it upon such plans as to accomplish the objects of its creation. They assured him in very positive and unmistakable terms that he might rely upon their vigorous moral support.

The instructors were all young persons; some with small experience as teachers, and others now enjoying their first opportunity to engage in the work. All of them however appeared to be docile and ready to second all efforts which might be made to reconstruct and improve any methods of instruction or discipline necessary for the good of the students and the college. There had been misunderstanding, as already intimated, of such character between certain persons having in important sense control and authority in the management of the school and the Board of Visitors, affecting the good order of the students even, that it was necessary for the president to take his position with respect thereto at once and with decision. This he did; and with the discharge of a single person, a gentleman for whom he had entertained for many years very considerable respect, wise and efficient discipline was reassured in the peaceful, orderly, friendly relations of the faculty and students and the Board of Visitors. From that time all concerned accepted Mr. Langston as the master of the situation, and maintained towards him those relations of friendly feeling and respect which made his work, in the main, for the entire time that he remained president of the institute, pleasant and agreeeble.

The faculty was composed of five gentlemen and four

ladies; and the officers of the institute besides the president were a secretary, who took care of all records and proceedings of the institute; and a treasurer, whose labors were financial, covering the collection and disbursement of all funds. The number of students at first was not large, and some of them had to realize that their new president was a person possessing the sterner elements of authority and decision which he would maintain in his administration before they became profitably and intelligently reconciled to the new order of things. The number of such students however was small, and any opposition of feeling coming from that quarter soon disappeared.

Under the law creating the institution its work was divided into two parts; the first normal and the other collegiate. This implied really, first the normal department itself, with a training school; and then a college department, with a preparatory course calculated for training and fitting students for admission to the regular literary and scientific course of study. Of course courses of study fitted to the capacity of the students assigned to either of these departments and found in either the normal training school or the preparatory department, or in positions of greater advancement, calculated when wisely and thoroughly pursued to work the largest and best results to them, were carefully and cautiously considered and adopted. This work, difficult enough always, was attended with considerable anxiety in this case. However, it was soon and satisfactorily accomplished; and throughout the institution, teachers and students adjusting themselves to the new and improved condition, entered with earnestness and zeal upon the discharge of their respective duties.

Besides the ordinary studies of all the departments, lessons in music, vocal and instrumental, were given. The public exercises of the morning, the regular lectures on each recurring Thursday afternoon, besides occasional lectures during the week and the regular Sabbath afternoon lecture, were utilized to improve the students in all those matters of general understanding and knowledge which embrace such biographical, historical, literary, scientific, ethical and religious subjects as came within their comprehension and appreciation, and which were necessary for their permanent good. The public exercises were generally conducted by the president himself and the lectures delivered by him. The attendance upon both not only consisted of instructors and students, but ordinarily he had large and interesting promiscuous audiences, among whom it was no unfrequent thing to find many white persons.

The *esprit du corps* of the whole institution was soon changed and ameliorated, and the students, boys and girls, young ladies and gentlemen, not only discovered the new spirit and purpose which had taken possession of them in their dormitories, recitation-rooms and about the buildings and grounds of the institute, but in their manly and womanly, courteous, civil bearing and conduct about the city of Petersburg, where they were constantly seen and observed. Perhaps the highest compliment that the president and the students of the institute could have received was that paid them by an aged, venerable white gentleman of Petersburg, who stopping Mr. Langston in the street in the last month of the first year of his administration, said to him, "I take it, sir, that you are Professor Langston, the president of the institute; for your students pass my place in scores daily, and each one bears himself so much like you and is like yourself so polite and courteous that I have come to feel that I know you quite well and admire you. I have never seen you before, sir, but I have heard of you and your success in teaching, and have so constantly for the past year observed your students and their behavior that I do not need an introduction to you. However, I desire to present to you my respects and my hearty good wishes for your continued success."

Another testimonial borne to Mr. Langston's efficiency in his management of the institute, showing also the kindly treatment which he received at the hands of leading white men of Petersburg, is found in the following words employed among others by one of its influential citizens after listening to one of his lectures, and uttered in the presence of the faculty and students as well as a large general audience : " In your presence I want to thank your president for the good he is doing in breaking down race prejudice in this great democratic republic of ours. In his book, which I sincerely hope you have all read, he gave me more information about the negro race than all other publications it had ever fallen to my lot to see. President Langston is one of the broadest men in his views I have ever met. He is a thinker, a statesman as well as a scholar. * * * Thanking you kindly for your attention and wishing you well, I shall continue as in the past to take great interest in your school."

Elected and commissioned as Mr. Langston had been to the presidency of the college by a Republican administration of the state government, just passing out of power, and brought at once under Democratic control, it being wellknown that it was through the action of a Republican Legislature that the school had been established for the colored people, every friend of his and every supporter of the more advanced education of the colored youth was curious and anxious to know how he, an avowed and earnest Republican, and the institute itself, would be treated by the incoming Democratic power. Governor Cameron had promised Mr. Langston that nothing should be spared so far as he was concerned and had the authority, to make his situation in the school happy and prosperous. But now arose the question how a Southern man of the education, character, feeling and position of Governor Fitzhugh Lee, would treat the work of negro education in his State, especially so far as this school was concerned under its present management.

Accordingly the president, so soon as Governor Lee had been inaugurated and become actually *ex-officio* president of the Board of Education, visited him as well as the new superintendent of public instruction, and had with those officers a free conference with respect to the institute and their purposes and desires with regard to its management. He was entirely pleased with the treatment accorded him by the governor, and the promises which he made to do what he might to foster and sustain the school. The superintendent also expressed becoming solicitude for its success. However, with all this feeling of interest as expressed in the work, these gentlemen did not hesitate to let Mr. Langston understand that nothing like politics would be tolerated in the institution.

Governor Lee had not been in office long before Mr. Langston gave him special and pressing invitation to visit the institute and attend certain public exercises to be performed by the students. The invitation was promptly accepted, and for the first time in his life the governor attended exercises in the public chapel of a state negro college, and for the first time in the history of the negro race, in the State of Virginia, where its members had for centuries been slaves, the college was honored by the presence of this high official. The governor was accompanied on this occasion by the attorney-general of the Commonwealth and the superintendent of public instruction. The topics handled by the students in original essays and orations on subjects selected, as already stated, from the book of Proverbs, partook of high ethical, scholarly character. The visitors many of whom, especially the white persons present, attending such exercises now for the first time, seemed greatly delighted, and the gentlemen who had come the long distance from the capital to the institute to be present, were free in their expressions in public and private, of surprise and pleasure in view of what they had heard and witnessed. Governor Lee, as heretofore stated, was even more outspoken and positive than any other person, winning thus at once the sympathy and admiration of the whole school.

This occasion with such presence proclaimed in the notices given in the newspapers of the State with respect to it, proved to be of the greatest service to the institute in all its interests. It seemed to take therefrom a new and more desirable name and to extend its influence more generally and thoroughly among the better classes of those whose education and elevation it was designed to accomplish.

Thus favorably launched under the Democratic administration, with the chief officers of the government maintaining and discovering their interest in its prosperity, the institute grew in favor with the people, multiplying its students in regular attendance and the teachers who came from all quarters of the commonwealth to gain the advantages proffered them at the summer teacher's institutes. The first commencement exercises, had in June, 1886, discovered a condition of scholarly progress and accomplishment which were entirely satisfactory to the authorities and patrons of the college. The graduating class, though not large in numbers, displayed an excellence of training in all directions which gave increased and growing respect for the school.

Another year of successful experience was had, so far as the institution itself was concerned, under the management of Mr. Langston, although it was made manifest through certain expressions and behavior of parties in the Board of Visitors and in the Board of Education as well, that the liberality, freedom and impartial treatment which he accorded all classes visiting the school, white and colored, and the progress and fame which the institution was winning in the State, were creating a little uneasiness in the minds of the persons alluded to. However, by careful discreet management, the president brought the school in admirable condition in the best possible order to the commencement of 1887.

The graduating classes through the president of the institute gave Governor Lee a special invitation to be present at this commencement, and not only to present to them their diplomas but deliver to them the address usual on such occasions. It was not at first believed, even by the faculty of the institute, that the governor would accept the invitation and consent to perform the duty indicated. He did however promptly accept, and promised to be present, arriving at such an early hour as to witness the performance of every exercise. This he did, taking his place, of course one of honor, on the platform at ten o'clock in the morning, and remaining throughout the day up to four o'clock in the afternoon. On being appropriately introduced by the president, he formally presented the diplomas awarded to the graduating classes, and delivered to them an impressive, befitting and eloquent address. Even then he remained to the close of the exercises, receiving in appropriate and becoming spirit and manner the honor which the classes did him in their presentation, through the president, of a large beautiful bouquet of rare, rich flowers. It is to be regretted that his excellent address, in every way worthy of its author, the cause of education which he represented and the great State whose chief executive he was, cannot be given here in its entirety. By such demonstrations of personal and official, kindly, considerate feelings for the colored people of Virginia, Governor Lee has won many friends among them, who to-day entertain for him sentiments of the highest respect.

More than once after this visit Governor Lee referred in signal terms to what he had seen and heard at the institute, and how pleased he was at the interesting spectacle of educational purpose and endeavor which was presented there. In addressing the lawmakers of the State in his message of 1888, he employed the following paragraphs, in his allusions to its condition and prospects:

"At the Virginia Normal and Collegiate Institute, December 1, 1886, there were 162 academic students. On December 1, 1887, the number of academic students was 187.

* * * * * * * * *

"The Virginia Normal and Collegiate Institute is also in good condition. The attendance of teachers at the summer session of 1887 was 131, and of that number 129 were granted certificates. In 1886 there were eight graduates from the Normal Department; at the commencement of this year there were eighteen, all of whom are now engaged in teaching colored schools for the State. The work of this institute has been somewhat obstructed by the want of accommodations. The additional building however is nearing completion, and when finished the institute will, it is reported, have accommodations for at least 700 students. From a personal inspection of this institute I believe it is fulfilling its mission and carrying out the objects for which it was established."

At the time these statements were made by the governor, so far as the number of students was concerned, the condition and order of it, the institute was in its most flourishing and promising circumstances. The only serious difficulty which interrupted really its largest and best growth for the future was misunderstandings developing themselves now among the Board of Visitors with respect to the manner in which its affairs should be controlled and directed. In fact the double board feature in its management was unfortunate. It needed with the Board of Education no board of visitors.

It is not to be understood that Mr. Langston did not find drawbacks in number and character connected with the school quite sufficient to give him great anxiety from the first, and finally as they were not overcome as he had expected, to deter him. Among such drawbacks interrupting and hindering the work of the school, was the unfinished condition of its buildings; and hence the lack of suitable accommodations for over one hundred and twenty or thirty students. The incoming administration so far as the Legislature was concerned, seemed at first disposed to abandon the school, throwing the responsibility of its failure upon the Republican party, which having founded it had lost its power. At last, through the influence of Governor Lee and the Board of Education an appropriation, by no means liberal, was made for the completion of the chief and most needed building of the school. The work however in this respect was superintended and done with so little energy, efficiency and promptness as to leave the building largely incomplete even on the first day of January, 1888.

Another drawback which operated at once upon the change of administrations, tending to limit Mr. Langston's influence and to disturb his work, was found in the peculiar political condition of affairs in the State. The public sentiment of the people seemed to be on all hands favorable to the education even of the colored youth; but in so far forth as the support of this educational enterprise seemed to imply the endorsement of the Republican party, or any of its more conspicuous measures, there existed on the part of the opposing party constant, sometimes bitter opposition. The Virginia Normal and Collegiate Institute, as organized and conducted, with Mr. Langston at its head and the controlling agent in its management, was made the object of this feeling of opposition to such a degree and in such manner as to be environed by any other than an encouraging and sustaining power. Ultimately the opposition became so strong, outspoken and demonstrative that the powers and influences which Mr. Langston as president of the school was at first permitted to wield were curtailed, and he was left without authority and control necessary to accomplish the results proposed by its founders.

Other troubles arose during the last quarter of the school year of 1887, growing mainly out of certain unfortunate, imprudent conduct of two or three of the instructors—conduct which the president was compelled to notice and censure, even publicly, in order to the preservation of the good order and name of the school. Differences and disturbance connected with such conduct and the discipline enforced against it resulted in such feeling on the part of certain of the authorities and the parties immediately concerned as to make his situation no longer as pleasant and agreeable for him as could have been wished. However, it is to be understood that so far as the patrons of the school and the students were concerned, with the instructors generally and the principal officers in charge, Mr. Langston was loyally and faithfully sustained. His pupils exhibited towards him such devotion and adherence under these circumstances as under all others as to cause him, even as he dwells now in thought and remembrance of their conduct, to exercise towards them sentiments of the profoundest gratitude and the loftiest respect. They seemed to be in all respects related to him as his own children; and with regard to every girl and boy included in its membership during his control and management of the institute, he indulges the hope that he or she has either already reached or may hereafter the highest standard of womanhood and manhood in education and culture, with such position in life as to be abundantly useful, prosperous and happy.

CHAPTER XXVII.

HE RESIGNS THE PRESIDENCY AND LEAVES THE INSTITUTE.

AFTER the advent of the Democratic party to power in the State the old Board of Visitors was replaced by a new one composed of another set and sort of colored men. These latter ones, if not Democrats in sentiment and party affiliations, were persons who were quite disposed to follow the leadership of the superintendent of public instruction, who was, *ex-officio*, the chairman of their board. Narrow-minded and illiberal, full of prejudice against the colored classes, with strong feelings against their extended and various education, this officer was not disposed to sustain Mr. Langston in his opinions and purposes with regard to such exalted standards of training, mental and moral, as tended to develop the best conditions of manhood and womanhood in the case of those who were formerly enslaved. Exerting large influence in the control and direction of his associate members of the Board of Visitors, and holding the opportunity and privilege of explaining and advocating their judgment and views in the Board of Education, of which he was also *ex-officio* a member, he was so situated as to exert large obstructing and disagreeable power against Mr. Langston.

From the moment the superintendent fully comprehended the plans of the president and the exertions which he was making to give the school the best possible name in the achievement of the best practicable educational results, he did not hesitate to wield his influence and power in opposition to that end, controlling as fully as might be the members of the Board of Visitors. His real spirit was discovered in a statement made by him in petulant and bitter terms, when in addressing the president himself, he declared, "You have conducted this school in such manner that we cannot now take up a newspaper of the State without finding some allusion to it with complimentary mention of its work and accomplishments. It is even placed beside the state university itself!" While these words discovered the temper and feelings of their author, they contained a very high compliment to the president of the institute, and a very substantial and remarkable commendation of his work. And all this the superintendent would have known and felt had his mind not been beclouded by his unreasonable and unreasoning prejudices.

In this connection it is worthy of mention that the president, in what he supposed would be most agreeable and acceptable to the superintendent, made a great mistake. However, he did not discover it until it was too late. And now he relates it with no little feeling of merriment. As the Board of Visitors came to the institute from time to time to hold their stated and special meetings, often occupied for the whole day, it was customary for the president to have a private dinner prepared and served them. He did not make any distinctions on account of color or nationality; but invited the superintendent, a white Virginia gentleman of education and culture, exalted church relationships and Christian refinement, knowing that the colored members of the board and the colored officers, who were also invited to dine, could have no objection to that arrangement. Of course, the superintendent was given the seat of honor at the table. He could not however tolerate this arrangement; and was wholly dissatisfied with the conduct of the president, who put him in such disagreeable proximity socially with the colored gentlemen with whom he seemed very willing to serve and control in the meetings of the board. Nor was he indisposed to make himself comrade indeed of those persons in any effort finally which might embarrass the president. At last he declined utterly to dine with the persons referred to when invited to do so; either declaring that he had, or had already eaten, his lunch. Why having eaten with his colored associates once or twice he should thereafter decline to do so no one can explain, except upon the theory that his prejudices asserted their mastery even against a well-provided and appointed dinner. The influence exerted by a person, situated as the superintendent was, with his great powers and opportunities, in connection with an institution like the Virginia Normal and Collegiate Institute, could be so wielded as to accomplish many things aggravating and intolerable, calculated to disturb and hinder the work of an officer in Mr. Langston's place. No proof is needed on this point, and the effect of his conduct will be at once understood and appreciated.

It must be understood, however, that the influences which operated to disturb Mr. Langston's relations to the institution, making his stay there anything other than agreeable to him, were for the most part political. All others might have been overcome and he continued in service, but he would neither yield his political convictions nor hesitate as he deemed it proper to express and defend his party alliances. He was a Republican; and so he stated and declared without fear, according to his own judgment and his right and privilege as an American citizen. When he found that this was the real opposition to him, although pressed by a voice which seemed to be well-nigh unanimous so far as its patrons and friends were concerned, to remain at the institute and continue his services as its executive officer, he determined not to do so. After he had theretofore tendered his resignation on the twenty-third day of December, 1887, the examinations of the school preparatory to the holidays having been closed, he advised his faculty and students of his purpose to leave them.

Thereupon the greatest possible feeling manifested itself

in words and conduct of tenderest regard and affection, with the deepest sorrow and grief among the students, especially those of the more advanced classes. These feelings were largely shared by the professors and instructors; and so soon as his determination was made public, positive expression was had by the people generally, against any action taken by the Board of Visitors or the Board of Education tending to induce Mr. Langston's retirement.

The members of the faculty of the institute, all the students, and a large number of friends and patrons had assembled in the great audience room of the institution to listen to the last words of the president before they took leave, at the close of the fall term, for the vacation covering the Christmas and New Year's holidays just at hand. The president, in his address, concluding it, used the following words:

"I may not meet you again as a company of students in this capacity. Very soon my relations to the institute, as its president, must be brought to a close. Others will take you in charge. But though I go away from you, my interest in you and your welfare shall abide; and my prayers for your constant success shall be ardent and continuous. My stay with you, though brief, has been in many respects so pleasant that I shall not soon forget it. Had it been more useful it would please me better. I have, however, labored according to the measure of my ability and opportunities; and I leave you, thanking God if in anywise I have been serviceable in the least thing or manner to you. Committing you then to the keeping of the Infinite One who holds the destinies of us all according to His own benevolent purposes in His Almighty hands, I bid you, one and all, an affectionate farewell, with the most sincere wishes for your success, prosperity, and happiness. Ladies and gentlemen, students, farewell!"

When Mr. Langston had made known formally, as stated, his purpose of leaving the institute, even before the opening of the following term, the students made expression of their feelings of appreciation and affection for him in memorials, in form of preamble and resolutions, with appropriate addresses, which were received and adopted in the most unanimous, emphatic manner. Besides, a souvenir was provided by them in the form of a golden shield, significant in form, unique in its beauty, and rare in its richness,

RESIGNS THE PRESIDENCY.

bearing on either side in engraved characters and figures words and designs of tenderness and honor. In such manner the hold which he had upon the students and the attachment which they bore him were signally and strikingly expressed. These proceedings were gratifying in the most import sense to the retiring president, for they demonstrated the loyalty of those conducting them.

It is due the students and the patrons of the institute, indeed all persons concerned in its welfare, that such detailed account be given here of the occurrences alluded to as may do, at least, simple justice to their promoters. Hence no apology is offered for their exact presentation, even in their own words, of the expressions made in the memorials mentioned, consigned long since to the archives of the institute where they are preserved. The preamble and resolutions were encouched in the following words:

"Whereas, our most highly esteemed, respected and honored president. Hon. John Mercer Langston, LL. D., is about to retire from the presidency of the institution, which he has held for two years, accomplishing the greatest possible physical, intellectual, and moral results in the education of the colored youth, bringing the institution to the highest point of popularity, dignity and honor as designed by its founders.

"Whereas, endowed with the highest possible scholarly attainments, he has faithfully, zealously and effectually labored for the promotion of our interests, touching every phase of the true American ideal of education, instilling into our souls the great fundamental, eternal principles of virtue, integrity and honor, which are the secrets of success in the achievement of the grand and glorious results of manly and womanly endeavor;

"Whereas, appreciating his services to the youth of the State, feeling the most profound regret in the severance of his connection with the school;

"Therefore, be it resolved,

"1st. That we extend to Hon. John Mercer Langston our most heartfelt thanks for his matchless administration of the affairs of the institute, and his invaluable services in behalf of its students.

"2d. That we most cordially thank him not only as our president, but as the educator of the race for his unequalled utterances upon all questions pertaining to their welfare, making himself the champion of their cause.

"3d. That we bid him a hearty godspeed, in his future work—a work destined to place the negro upon the highest plane of citizenship—as enduring and lasting as the government itself.

"4th. That a copy of these resolutions be presented to Hon. John Mercer Langston, a copy to the institute, and a copy to the negro race of the country through the press."

Addresses were presented to President Langston, in the name of the students of the respective departments of the institution, by Messrs. W. H. Lewis, W. T. Sherman Jackson, and G. Herman Kyd. All of these gentlemen, students of the institute themselves, were representatives of the entire school, and each voiced the sentiments of the whole body of students.

Mr. Lewis, in his address, expressed among other things the following beautiful and eloquent sentiments: "The English tongue, so replete in the variety and beauty of its etymology, possesses no word, which at once pronounced, touches more deeply the diapason of human love, admiration, and esteem than the word *farewell*."

"Then it is that the chord of human sympathy and affection is strengthened by the sweet and tender recollections of long continued association, and our noblest feelings and aspirations assert themselves."

After dwelling upon those things which he claimed Mr. Langston had accomplished for the school, he closed that portion of his speech with these earnest and impressive words: "He came to the institute rich in character, wealthy in honor, and in brains a millionaire, bringing the fruits of a ripe scholarship and all the glories and embellishments of a great name," and continuing:

"At once the school sprang into prominence, as it were at one bound, from obscurity to fame. Since that time, she has been written about and spoken about as much as any other school upon the continent.

"With the rarest gifts and attainments, he has faithfully, thoroughly and entirely performed the duties confided to his care by the high and sacred trust of the State.

"He has given permanent shape and character to the only true and great ideal of negro education, which comprehends the whole field of learning, touching the very dome of thought.

"In his lectures, dealing exhaustively with the various subjects presented, he has impressed upon the negro youth gathered around him, the sanctity of the obligations incumbent upon them as American citizens, and all their rights, privileges and immunities connected therewith.

"He has imbued his students with that spirit, which is truly the secret of success in working out the grand and glorious results of manly and womanly endeavor.

" And I thank God that I have received a goodly portion of that spirit. I swear it now upon the altar of truth, that it shall follow me to the end of my career; for upon it depends all that I am, and all that I may hope to be in this life."

Concluding, Mr. Lewis employed the following touching sentences;

" But now comes the sad thought! He is about to retire from the presidency. What will be the effect upon us and our people ? True it will be, as I said to the governor of the Commonwealth, a calamity to us and our entire people; for he is the wisest and best educator that we have ever produced, and therefore we have no man so well qualified to succeed him as himself. * *

" Mr. President, how shall we fittingly thank you for the noble and self-sacrificing spirit with which you have so unceasingly labored for the upbuilding of all our interests ? * * * There is one thing at least we can do, Mr. President—vow now and here to be true to the negro—a people whose mission and destiny are the grandest on earth, and who claim no greater leader than John Mercer Langston." * * *

" Now, Mr. President, in the name of the students, allow me to thank you, yes, thrice thank you for your kind and fatherly care ; congratulate you upon the entire success of your administration, bid you farewell and wish you a long, happy and prosperous life in the service of your country, your race and your God."

The addresses of Messrs. Jackson and Kyd, like that of Mr. Lewis, were full of kindly expressions toward the president, of deep appreciation of his services, with utterances of profound regret in view of his retirement from the school. Extracts are not made from these addresses here because of the striking similarity in sentiment and feeling which they bear, necessarily, to that of Mr. Lewis. It is due their authors however to state that they were able and eloquent, eliciting, as did that of Mr. Lewis, the most cordial, hearty endorsement and applause of all who heard them.

In presenting the shield of honor, Mr. Winston Bell, a student of the institute, made the following address:

" Mr. President : I am commissioned by my school-fellows to ask your acceptance of this little token of their respect, appreciation and affection.

" We wish in some way to show our sense of your ability as a preceptor, and of your patience and kindness in dealing with the faults to which those varieties of the human species, called boys and girls, are proverbially prone.

" After some debate as to the best method of doing so, we concluded that the most befitting exponent of our feelings would be a memento to which we all could contribute, which, however insignificant its value might be, when measured by the magnitude of our obligations would agreeably remind you that we were indeed not ungrateful

"With our little gift, accept, dear sir, our warmest wishes for your health and prosperity.

"We hope to do credit to your tutelage. If we do not it is our own fault; for you have done your part faithfully and zealously.

"You have taught us to look up to you not only as a wise instructor but as a guardian and friend; and when we go into the world to turn to profitable account the lessons you have taught us, we cannot forget to whom we owe our acquirements, but shall ever remember you with filial regard as champion and prince of our cause.

"Sir, I feel as sensibly the loss that the institute sustains in your retirement from its presidency as any negro in our Commonwealth; but when I know that you will be called to a higher sphere and wider field of usefulness, I resign myself to fate.

"And, sir, imbued with Herculean strength and Socratic genius as you are, Virginia shall yet send forth an illustrious son of whom she shall be proud, and in whom the negro shall live and move and have his political being.

"I predict—even assert, that the day in which this State sends John Mercer Langston to the Congress of the United States she will have sent forth a star of the first magnitude and a man and scholar who shall do her perpetual and eternal honor."

The shield presented was designed by Mr. Charles H. Seales, one of the students, and made by the foremost jeweler of Petersburg, Virginia. Upon its face it bears the inscription: "*To our President, Hon. John Mercer Langston, L L. D., ex-Minister to Hayti.*" Upon the reverse side: "*From the students of the Virginia Normal and Collegiate Institute, Petersburg, Va., December* 23, 1887."

The exercises described as connected with Mr. Langston's retirement from the institute, from beginning to end were conducted in the most dignified, impressive manner, and the effect produced upon the minds of all present cannot be easily effaced. The general applause with which every utterance was received attested the deep, universal appreciation and respect entertained for him by all participating. The golden shield of honor was presented with such circumstances of solemnity and ceremony as to prove impressive in the highest degree, even increasing its value and the appreciation with which the one who was honored in its gift must ever regard and cherish it.

RESIGNS THE PRESIDENCY. 433

When the question of Mr. Langston's retirement was in debate simply, before he had determined to leave the institution, his students were so moved by the prospect of that occurrence, that they organized a committee composed of their own numbers, and addressed Governor Lee upon the subject with the greatest possible earnestness, urging his re-election and retention. The address presented was as follows:

"May it please Your Excellency:

"We come, first as citizens of the Commonwealth; secondly as students of the Virginia Normal and Collegiate Institute, to invite your attention to a subject which not only concerns our immediate and particular interests, but the interests of that class of citizens with whom we are identified; and not only the interests of a special class of citizens, but the interests of the entire State.

"For the perpetuity of a government of the people, for the people, and by the people, depends upon the education of its citizens.

"To this end the State has from time to time founded great institutions of learning at whose shrines her sons and daughters might worship and thus prepare themselves for the duties incumbent upon them as citizens. Among such institutions proudly stands the Virginia Normal and Collegiate Institute, an institute founded by an act of the Assembly of '82 for the higher education of the colored youth. Your administration has, so far, brought to her a successful era of progress. A gentleman and scholar of repute, a Virginian by birth, coming to her presidency, who when she was tossed about upon the waves of neglect and destruction and was about to go down in the maelstrom of death, assisted by your kindly hand rescued her from so imminently dangerous destiny, and placed her where she stands to-day. It is of him that we desire to speak, learning as we have through the press and otherwise, with profound regret, that it is the wish of those in authority that he should retire from the presidency. Though this seems to be manifestly true, from the non-action of the Board of Visitors with regard to the presidency at a late meeting, when every teacher endorsed him for re-election, we hope that it is not true and that ere his time expires he may be reappointed.

"President Langston is so earnestly and entirely devoted to the conservation of the best interests of the institution and our education that he has endeared himself in the strongest ties of devotion to every student.

"His ability, zeal and devotion make him in every way worthy and capable of the high and sacred trust of the State. And to force him to retire at a period when she is just beginning a career of usefulness to the State would be a calamity to us and our entire people. For we have no man so well qualified to succeed Mr. Langston as Mr. Langston himself.

"We are sure that his administration, marked by a judicious demeanor and fraught with most fruitful results, is beyond reproach and well deserving of the State.

"Therefore, in the name of the students associated with us in the institution, whose sentiments we represent *in toto;* in the name of hundreds of thousands of colored people whose children must look to this institution for an education; and in the name of the State itself, whose free institutions and Christian civilization we would conserve, we ask that our president be retained,

"We humbly implore you, Sir, as president of the Board of Education, as Governor of the State, whose administration has been one of the wisest and most peaceful in the annals of the Commonwealth, that it meet your approval.

"If you are the friend of the colored people, and who can doubt it, no act of friendship would be or could be, more appreciated than maintaining at the head of that institution the wisest and best educator that they have produced."

This testimony embraced and covered the judgment and feeling of those who were most deeply interested in the institute, and was expressed after the Board of Visitors had acted in the premises.

Brief as were Mr. Langston's administration and management of the Virginia Normal and Collegiate Institute, it will not be denied that he gained the confidence and affection not only of his students in regular attendance, all teachers coming to the several summer teacher's institutes conducted by him, the patrons of the school generally, but the entire people of the State wherever they had knowledge of his methods of instruction and his efficiency.

His discipline, though rigid and exacting when necessary, was on the whole so natural, mild, easy and affectionate, always showing that the object at which he aimed was the highest practical good of the student, wrought constantly not only a favorable standing for him with those immediately concerned, but becoming known to any interested in the matter of popular education, tended to enlarge and solidify his influence. Even the aristocratic and influential among the whites of the State were, as a rule not only not averse to him and his work, but manifested in many ways, as they became acquainted with him and it, their interest and favor.

So strong and unyielding was the attachment of many of the students, among these the most advanced and promising, for Mr. Langston, that when he left they quitted the institute. Many of them sought his counsel and direction as to the course which they should pursue for the future in the prosecution of their education according to the standards which he had impressed upon their minds. Among such students, Mr. Langston records the names of Messrs. William H. Lewis, W. T. Sherman Jackson, Winston Bell, Milton D. Brown, Charles H. Scales, J. E. Harris, C. H. Deanes, R. W. Brown, and others, at least a score. All these students have gone forward in the vigorous prosecution of their studies, no one of them neglecting the advice of their former president, as they have all asked and received it, as they have found it necessary. Several of them have already won graduations from collegiate and professional institutions and are now making their way, gallantly and successfully, in their different callings. Dr. R. W. Brown of Washington city, a practicing physician of unusual standing and influence for his age, is an admirable illustration of the class of professional men referred to. While Messrs. Lewis and Jackson, who as classmates graduated from Amherst College, June, 1892, and Bell and Milton D. Brown, now students, the former in the law department, and the latter in the medical department, of Harvard College, represent the larger class of the young men still engaged in prosecuting their studies upon a broad and various plan.

Such has been the record made by Lewis and Jackson in their course of study at Amherst College that it deserves special and particular note here by their old president and friend. It was through the influence of that friend that they were enabled to take such a course, and the fidelity and purpose with which they did their work make this notice entirely appropriate and profitable. Should it come to the attention of the noble white men who aided these colored students in the gift of their means and their kindly attention and encouraging care, they will read with satisfaction the estimate put upon their generous behavior by one who has always been profoundly interested in the education of colored youth, while grateful to the host of benevolent white persons in the United States who have done and given so much to contribute to this end.

Both these young men, classmates, achieved high standing in their classes and were honored by their fellow-students as well upon the field in games as in the recitation-room and the society halls. Lewis, while in college was regarded as its best orator, and was elected by his class to represent it on its memorable graduating commencement occasion in 1892. It is a remarkable fact that two young white men from the South, Messrs. J. H. Grant and S. H. Ransom, the latter a nephew of Senator Ransom of North Carolina, were his competitors for that exalted college honor. He was a member of the foot-ball eleven of the college three years. Such was the record which he made and the admiration which he won that he was made during his senior year its captain. In fact he is reckoned one of the best football players in the country, and is always given in the game responsible and trying position. Immediately after his graduation from Amherst he entered Harvard Law School, where he is now prosecuting his studies in the hope of graduating therefrom in 1895. Ex-President Seelye has been and is his special friend and adviser.

Mr. Jackson was graduated *cum laude*, and was a " rank man " throughout his course. He, scholarly and well behaved in every way won, fully the esteem and respect of his professors, fellow-students and classmates, and in connection with all class and college exercises as well as games, he received his full share of honors. He was director, secretary, vice-president and president of the Football Association, of which he was a member while in college. The offices named were all elective. He was also a member of the football eleven and athletic team for three years, and even now holds the championship of the college for the half-mile run. He held the championship for the half-mile run in the New England Athletic Association for two years of his college course. Upon his graduation his name as a student of rare accomplishment gave him place as a teacher, where he is now engaged, in the colored high school of Washington city. He can never forget Senator Hoar and his wife, who have been his good friends from the time Mr. Langston introduced him to them in 1885 up to the present moment. Of these benefactors in a late letter of his, he says: "While in college Senator and Mrs. Hoar took almost as much interest in me as a father and mother would have done. During my junior year (1890-1891), the senator invited me to spend a few days with him and his family at his home in Worcester. The more than cordial reception given at his home made me for the moment forget that there was any prejudice in this country. I was made to feel entirely at home. Nothing can ever make me forget Senator and Mrs. Hoar."

Interested as Mr. Langston has always been in a high intellectual, moral and Christian training for colored youth as the only means by which they might be brought to a wise, comprehensive understanding of their situation and duty as American citizens, and thus enabled to free themselves from prejudices which exist against them as brought, educated, cultured and refined, to take their places in general society, he would have been glad to remain in a situation where he could have spent his time and efforts to accomplish, so far as practicable, that result. However, as it seemed otherwise ordered as he feels by unwise and injudicious management on the part of those who really had neither knowledge nor solicitude to that end, he rests contented with the plaudit of those who were most deeply interested that as president of the Virginia Normal and Collegiate Institute, he did the work assigned him with diligence and fidelity, leaving the school at the end of his term with honor and success distinguishing his course.

CHAPTER XXVIII.

HIS NOMINATION TO THE FIFTY-FIRST CONGRESS AND HIS MEMORABLE UNPARALLELED CONGRESSIONAL CAMPAIGN.

IN passing through Farmville, the county-seat of Prince Edward County, one of the most populous and important counties politically, in the Fourth Congressional District, on his way to Salem, on the thirty-first day of December, 1887, a committee waited upon Mr. Langston as he remained on the cars, the train stopping for a few moments, and invited him to meet a company of gentlemen at that place on his return to Petersburg on the second day of January. On the first of the month he was to speak at Salem at a great emancipation celebration to be held there. This he did, and on the second day of the new year met his engagement at Farmville according to the invitation given him.

He met at Farmville at the house of a distinguished leading colored man of the community, a large number of substantial, foremost Republicans, white and colored, of Prince Edward County. In fact, there were present several persons, Republicans from the adjoining counties of Lunenburg, Powhatan, and Nottoway. He soon learned that the object had in view in this meeting was to advise him of the popular feeling prevailing, as was claimed, throughout the district in favor of his candidacy for the United States Congress. It had been reported that he intended, since he had left the Virginia Normal and Collegiate Institute, to abandon his residence in Virginia. The persons composing the gathering united in a solemn and earnest protest as his friends and the promoters of his political welfare, against that course, urging him in view of all the facts and the public feeling prevailing that he owed it to the people of his district, the colored people of the State and the nation, to remain where he was, ready to accept any duty or responsibility, with its honors, which might come to him.

Mr. Langston was advised that there was general and profound feeling existing in all parts of the district in favor of his nomination to Congress. He was assured that not only the nomination could be secured for him with comparative ease, should he remain and it be made known that he would accept it, but that his election would be just as certain as the nomination. He knew that the Republican party held an overwhelming majority of the voters of the district, and his friends here assembled declared in positive terms that he could be elected by even a larger majority than was usual. But over and above every consideration of this character, the whole meeting expressed in energetic, vigorous terms, the opinion that it was the duty of Mr. Langston to serve his race now in serving the people of the Fourth Congressional District, in which he had gained his residence and where his nomination and election could be assured beyond peradventure.

After full and free interchange of views on the subject indicated, with the positive assurance expressed, without the least contrariety of judgment as to the final result should Mr. Langston remain in the district and consent to be a candidate, moved by such considerations as those already mentioned, he agreed to give the subject immediate serious thought, and advise his friends at once as to the conclusion which he might reach. He asked however the privilege of consulting other friends, residing in other portions of the district, who were by reason of their situation and feelings qualified to give him a judgment, sound and well advised, upon which he could rely. This permission was granted him. Indeed the suggestion was received with the warmest approval, and the meeting ended with the feeling, quite apparent on all sides, that Mr. Langston would finally consent to serve his friends and his State, probably in Congress.

Upon his return to Petersburg, his home, he took such consideration of the whole matter and such observation of the whole field, with such information and counsel as he could secure, and having determined to remain in the district, advised his political friends that he would not only accept the nomination and election as they had suggested, but that he would take every necessary step to render both the nomination and election practicable by doing every honorable thing and meeting every just outlay proper to that end.

His friends, like himself, believed that in order to his success it would be necessary for him to enter at once upon a general canvass of the district, and thus announce, formally and in the most positive manner, his desire and purpose to engage heartily, practically and immediately in its politics. It was agreed, too, that it would be necessary in the canvass to have it distinctly understood that his success would be materially promoted by his election as a delegate from the district to the National Republican Convention to assemble in Chicago in the following June, to nominate candidates for the presidency and vice-presidency of the United States. With respect to both these matters there were full accord and purpose among all interested in their promotion.

His canvass was commenced without delay. Having completed other engagements so that he was wholly free to give his undivided, earnest attention to it, he planned and conducted a series of the most vigorous, aggressive Republican meetings ever known in the Fourth Congressional District. His speeches covered the whole field of Republican principles and measures, whose representative he claimed to be, and to whose support, with influence and vote, he invited every citizen who gave him hearing. His audiences, composed of all classes of the people, of every political complexion, were large, attentive and enthusiastic. He spoke at the court houses in every county and in the more prominent populous towns. Often he was heard by audiences whose numbers could not be accommodated in any public building, and were therefore addressed in the open air. But whether he addressed the people in doors or out, good order was constantly maintained, and undivided respectful attention given him.

He was first, then, brought forward as a candidate for election by the District Congressional Convention as a delegate to the national convention named. However, there existed, and was discovered eventually intense but limited opposition to him, in connection even with that delegateship. This feeling was shown by influential white Republicans, chief among whom was Gen. William Mahone, the chairman of the State Republican Committee, a resident of Petersburg and a man well known throughout the district, pugnacious and unyielding, who to defeat Mr. Langston was ready to adopt, and did adopt the most audacious, base methods. But when the convention met, as it did in Petersburg, it was altogether apparent that the great body of the delegates composing it was in favor of Mr. Langston as a delegate to the National Convention; and if permitted to cast their votes fairly and freely, would so declare. So true was this that when the convention assembled at one o'clock in the afternoon of the day named for its meeting, General Mahone himself appearing in the midst of the assembly immediately after its organization, on learning the trend and vigor of its general feeling advised and secured a recess until nine o'clock the following morning. This action was accomplished really through the cunning and chicanery of its presiding officer; and it was taken, as claimed, for the purpose of "purging and purifying the various delegations." These last words are the very ones employed by the promoters of the scheme which they sought to compass; and it is a fact that they did proceed with their work according to their purpose. They purged and purified the delegations by striking from each, so far as practicable, any delegate who they learned, or who they supposed would vote for Mr. Langston. But even after this "purging and purifying" process, had in the most open and shameless manner, it did not result in more than the lessening of the vote which Mr. Langston would otherwise have received. The vote cast for him finally was ample to work his election, and to utterly rout the schemers and plotters who devised and operated their designs against him. His election thus as a delegate, in spite of the opposition, gave him such standing and opportunity as to make him, in fact, the master of the situation.

In the first place, every delegate who had been maltreated by having his name stricken from the rolls of the convention and he replaced fraudulently by another, became at once the intense, vigorous friend and supporter of Mr. Langston. And every other delegate who had voted for him in the convention, learning of the manner in which his fellow delegate had been outraged and Mr. Langston abused, became intense and emphatic in his support of the latter for anything which he might ask or seek.

Immediately upon the adjournment of the convention, after Mr. Langston's election, he held by the assistance of the leading colored ladies of Petersburg, a great and magnificent reception at "Langston Hall," to which he invited every delegate of the convention and to whom he gave the most generous, hospitable entertainment, with abundant commendation and applause for the handsome conduct of its members which resulted in his triumphant election to the National Convention. At this reception no distinctions were made on account of color, and white and colored delegates for the first time in the history of Petersburg commingled freely and equally, apparently with the greatest satisfaction and pleasure. It is due the ladies officiating on this occasion to state that their management was so adroit, sagacious and suave, that at the close of the affair the campaign of Mr. Langston had been really and apparently successfully launched. No delegate, white or colored, coming from any county in the district, who attended the reception, went away without promising that Mr. Langston should have his earnest and energetic support.

NOMINATED TO THE FIFTY-FIRST CONGRESS. 443

In the National Convention which followed soon after the adjournment of the congressional one mentioned, the delegates of Virginia were divided in their support and vote for candidates for the presidency and vice-presidency of the United States. Mr. Langston, with several others, supported the Hon. John Sherman from first to last for the nomination to the presidency. In this regard he stood with the leaders of his party from Virginia, and his support of the candidate named was earnest, vigorous and persistent. Mr. Langston supported Senator Sherman for other than partizan considerations. He regarded him as being a great lawyer, a foremost statesman, and the first Republican in the country. He esteemed him, as above all other men of the republic, fitted by reading, experience and observation, to master and manage all those great questions affecting the general welfare, especially the free and just use of the ballot, which had very properly provoked popular concernment in both sections of the country. In his judgment, while no American citizen compared with him as the staunch and reliable friend of all classes of the South, no one possessed the availability as a candidate for the high honors proposed which distinguished him. He advocated, therefore, the nomination and election of the senator as a great American representative, peculiarly fitted above his fellows for the presidency of the United States.

At a certain point in the proceedings of the convention, when the name of the Hon. John Sherman had been presented by General Hastings of Pennsylvania for the nomination in a speech of great power and eloquence, and this proposition had been seconded in a speech of great brilliancy and effect by the Hon. J. B. Foraker of Ohio; and it became necessary, as many of his friends felt and believed, that Senator Sherman only needed earnest, positive and effective support from the South, when others from that section failed to respond, Mr. Langston, as the applause following the wonderful address of Governor Foraker had subsided somewhat, rising in his place claimed the attention of the convention, while he added any influence which he might possess to the support of the distinguished United States Senator of Ohio. He spoke as a delegate from Virginia, of course, and as a representative of the sentiment prevailing among the Republicans of the southern part of the country with respect to the nomination which the convention should make. His speech was characterized by the newspapers at the time as one of masterly power and marvelous effect. As an utterance pronounced in this deliberative assembly it was given at once high rank among the ablest and most impressive efforts of the convention, and it was received by the entire gathering in the most flattering and enthusiastic manner.

Although Senator Sherman was not nominated, Mr. Langston's course at the convention not only won for him large and commanding notice and consideration throughout the country, but gained for him the warmest possible popular favor in his own congressional district. On his return to Petersburg he was received by his friends with every manifestation of the most cordial and exalted pleasure and pride. He prosecuted without the least interruption, in increasing earnestness and vigor, his canvass for nomination at the Congressional District Convention to be held in the coming fall. During his brief absence from the district the ardor of his friends had not abated in the least. Hence it was that not long after the return of the delegates generally from the Chicago convention, certainly as early as the latter part of July, 1888, the proclamation was made, as against Mr. Langston, by General Mahone, followed by such white and colored Republicans, few in number, as he could control, that *no colored man would be allowed* to represent the Fourth Congressional District of Virginia in the Congress of the United States. In fact, on the thirty-first day of July, 1888, a conference was held at the house of General Mahone in Petersburg, at which all the devices and plans necessary, as was supposed, were concocted and adopted to defeat as well Mr. Langston's nomination as his election should he be nominated, against all odds. To accomplish this end there was to be adopted any violation of party rule or

NOMINATED TO THE FIFTY-FIRST CONGRESS. 445

usage, with the perpetration of any fraud upon delegates to the convention, or in its organization and conduct, deemed necessary. While to make their purpose doubly sure, they made outspoken and positive appeal to the Democratic party, then in masterhood of the polls, to initiate and sustain any trick or method, however base, calculated to gain that result. At this meeting the mode of counting the votes cast on election day, the interruption, hindrance and obstruction of all voters appearing at the polls with ballots which they would cast for the colored candidate, and such manipulation generally of ballots found in the several ballot boxes used in the various voting precincts as might be designed to accomplish Mr. Langston's defeat, were arranged and determined after elaborate and calculating discussion in that behalf. The manner of calling and conducting the local Republican conventions at which delegates were to be elected to the congressional, and the plans to be followed in either granting or refusing certificates of election in such cases, and the management and control of the congressional convention itself so as to defeat the nomination of the same candidate, were determined and announced at the same meeting, with the solemn injunction given the party leaders of each locality, especially the various county chairmen, that the "*nigger*" must be beaten at all events, in spite even of the popular wish and demand. Accordingly all sorts of methods, all however in keeping with the instructions given, were adopted as to the call and conduct of the local conventions; and the congressional convention itself, so-called, was finally organized and controlled in obedience to the understanding had at that time. With plans thus formulated and methods agreed upon, secret circulars containing positive orders to stop at no means however disgraceful or outrageous were issued to such persons, white and black, as agreed with General Mahone, the Republican party leader, especially to the chairmen of the various county committees of the district, that Langston must be defeated at all hazards, since no negro must be allowed to represent the district in Congress. Every conceivable influence therefore, whether of fraud or bribery, was exerted in every locality to compass the defeat of any person favorable to his nomination who was proposed as a delegate to the District Congressional Convention.

Where the people were overwhelmingly in Mr. Langston's favor, and no convention could be properly called and conducted without electing delegates representing this popular sentiment, the chairmen of the county Republican committees were ordered to prevent, first, the orderly assembling of the Republican voters according to usage ; and where it was not possible to do so, in the second place, to produce, in some way or other such confusion and disorder as to make it practicable to create contests which upon appeal must be settled by General Mahone, as chairman of the State Republican Executive Committee. It was well understood that in all these cases, right or wrong, he would decide against any single delegate or delegation favorable to Mr. Langston's nomination. Such a chapter of outrage and abuse, studied and planned, in violation of every principle, rule and usage of the Republican party, destructive of popular interest, party discipline and individual right, cannot be paralleled in the history of any despotic, tyranical, oppressive party management among any class of people, barbarian or civilized, in the world. And all aimed at Mr. Langston, solely and alone, because of his nationality and complexion. No account whatever was taken of his qualifications, his accomplishments, his record in public and private life ; his reputation and success as a scholar, a professor and president in at least two foremost colleges ; as founder and dean of the law department of Howard University ; as an office-holder of large, diversified experience ; a representative of his nation abroad in high and important diplomatic and consular capacity. No account was made of the learning, skill and success which marked his labors in these various capacities, and no respect paid to the popular enthusiastic demand which called him now from private life to public place. All such considerations must go for naught in the presence of that prejudice against him on account of his color, which neither had sense, reason nor justice upon which to defend itself.

But the methods adopted by General Mahone and his followers in this course of iniquitous and unexampled abuse reached their climax in a condition of fraud and outrage, as to the recognition of delegates to and the organization of the Farmville Convention, held September 19th, 1888, to nominate a Republican candidate for the Fifty-first Congress. For the enormity and shameless wickedness which distinguished their actions in this regard their conduct is absolutely without parallel in the history of party transactions however base, or political chicanery however mean or groveling. Any persons claiming to be delegates, coming from localities where the people had formally and regularly elected their representatives, were accepted and recognized as against the latter, upon the sole condition that they would vote against Mr. Langston. In other instances, where no delegates had been elected and no pretense was made to other effect, delegates who had been duly elected and who came with their certificates to such effect properly signed, were excluded and replaced by others at the will of the managers, because the former would support Mr. Langston. And thus General Mahone and his followers, claiming to be masters of the situation, undertook to constitute and control the convention according to their own designs and pleasure. But their highhanded, impertinent and mischievous conduct was not sustained, and their wicked designs, throughly exposed, wrought their complete utter defeat. They were caught in their own devices. For the duly elected delegates, in overwhelming numbers, refusing to follow their leadership while they condemned as they despised their counsels, acted in intelligent, patriotic manner, constituting, organizing and conducting at last the congressional convention in such manner as to realize the popular feeling of the district in favor of Mr. Langston.

General Mahone had come to Farmville, and had exerted himself to carry out through his immediate personal supervision and direction that part of the general plan which was determined, as already described, at the conference held at his house. He was surrounded too with a handful of irresponsible weaklings of the party, white and black, who were ready to do any base thing even which he might command. Of all the sorry gatherings, wanting in numbers, wanting in brains, wanting in influence, wanting in every characteristic and element found among high-minded and honorable men of any party whatever, this motley assembly, named a convention, headed by General Mahone himself, was the very flower and perfection. The upshot was defeat at Farmville; defeat at Petersburg; defeat throughout the district and at last defeat throughout the country upon the popular condemnation, censure and scorn of every intelligent and honest Republican in the land. In many instances and many localities of the district even the worst Democrats having rejected and spurned the copartnership of iniquity to which such Republicans had invited them, rejoiced at their defeat. Democrats of a higher sense of honor, in many cases, turned away from them even in the very beginning when their assistance was asked, with the withering question of the sharpest biting condemnation, "Are we dogs that we should do this thing?"

The regularly elected delegates, however, in full numbers, representing every county and voting precinct in the district, white and colored, assembled in due order at the opera house in Farmville on the day announced by the Congressional Committee of the district, and forthwith organized, appointing its usual temporary officers and committees, including the Committee on Credentials. Subsequently a permanent organization was effected, when the convention betook itself to the orderly consideration of the business which brought it together, and in due season proceeded to the nomination of a candidate for election to the Fifty-first Congress of the United States. Upon the count of the vote cast by the convention, it was discovered that in obedience to the general expectation John M. Langston had been made the candidate. The manner in which the result of the vote, as announced, was received, was flattering to the candidate in the highest possible sense. And yet the vote with which the nomination was made unanimous was even more desirable, as it discovered in its spirit and enthusiasm the certainty of his election.

At once a committee, large and impressive in its appearance and presence, was appointed by the convention to advise Mr. Langston of his unanimous nomination and to invite him to appear before it and express his purpose with respect to his acceptance of the honor and responsibility of his nomination. The committee waited upon him at his hotel, and after advising him of the action of the convention, invited him to accompany its members to the opera house, where the convention awaited his coming. His entrance was the signal for such outbursts of applause and demonstrations of welcome as would have gladdened the heart of any American patriot ready to serve his State and country in obedience to the desire and wish of his fellow-citizens. On his introduction to the convention such was the exhibition of popular feeling and applause that he could not proceed with his remarks for some moments. However, while the convention was enthusiastic and spirited, it was wholly orderly and attentive. Every word uttered by Mr. Langston was heard and profoundly appreciated.

In accepting the nomination he assured the convention that in the canvass he should pursue such course as became an honorable and devoted Republican; that he should seek to advance, while he defended, the principles of his party. If elected he should pursue such a course as a member of Congress as would tend to dignify and honor the name of his district and State. He declared that he should know no constituent of his by his former condition of freedom or slavery, nor by his complexion or nationality. An American by birth and responsibility, holding and advocating Republican principles and measures, he should do so as an American representative of broad liberal views and convictions. He deprecated, he said, any attempt which had been made to draw a line of demarcation against him on account of his color. He deprecated also, as he stated, any attempts which had been taken by designing Republican leaders even, to deceive and wrong the people of the district in their purpose and efforts to elect, in fair and honorable manner, delegates to the convention; and he expressed the hope that such leaders, though they should secure, as they had proposed and sought the assistance of leading Democrats, to prevent through fraudulent practices a fair vote and an honest count of it on election day, might change their purposes in that regard, and join finally the great body of honest, patriotic Republican voters in securing the election of the nominee of the convention. He closed his address amid deafening applause in the statement that whatever might be the opposition brought against him, however endangering to his success, or his life, he should meet it in earnest, courageous, manly manner, sparing neither time, effort nor money which might be employed in honorable, just way to compass his election while promoting the purposes of the convention, assured as he was that the people on the sixth day of November, 1888, would record their vote by an overwhelming majority in his favor.

Upon the adjournment of the convention Mr. Langston returned at once to Petersburg, where he was met by an immense concourse of his fellow-citizens of all classes and conditions, who awaited his arrival at the depot. Thence he was conducted by them with great parade and display as he rode in a carriage provided for that purpose, aptly decorated with United States flags and drawn by four white horses. The line of march covered the principal streets of the city and ended at "Langston Hall," from the steps of which, as arranged, he was met and honored by an audience of thousands of people whom he addressed and who ratified his nomination at the close of his speech by a unanimous vote of the most positive and emphatic character.

Perhaps never in the history of the country, in any section of it has any man been nominated to Congress in face of such stout, unscrupulous and defiant opposition; or whose nomination was finally made and ratified with such enthusiasm, unanimity and *éclat* as that of John Mercer Langston.

The Fourth Congressional District of Virginia is one of large size, consisting of eleven counties of great extent and well populated. The people consist of two classes, white and colored; the former, in the main, the old slave-holding class, and the latter, as a rule, excepting such changes as have taken place since their emancipation, the old slave class. The latter class with its descendants, largely predominates in numbers, so much so that the whole section of the district and adjoining counties are designated the " Black Belt of Virginia."

Petersburg, the chief city of the district, contains a population of twenty-five thousand; and while it does not equal in any sense a Northern or Western town of like size in business activity or thrift, it is a very pleasant place and one of more than average life and vigor for a city of the South. This place and its surrounding country, by reason of being the scenes of memorable military operations during the war, are now historical in an exalted and interesting sense. The people composing the population consist of the two great classes, white and colored, already mentioned. The latter class is numerically superior to the former. However, in all matters of business, trade and general industry, they are remarkably agreed and demean themselves towards each other in respectful, considerate manner. In politics there is a wide and marked difference between them. However, in this respect they seem to have agreed to differ. It is true that the town would, were a free and honest ballot enjoyed, like the congressional district, be constantly Republican in its character and administration—for the Republican vote being so largely in the majority would make it so. But what the whites lack in numbers in that behalf, in their purpose to rule, holding the ascendancy and control, they supplement in superior intelligence and power, using when it becomes necessary to that end, trick or fraud, intimidation, hindrance and obstruction at the polls on election-day. Such methods are adopted of course to gain Democratic control as against negro domination, so-called. And it is justified on the plea that otherwise ignorance and poverty would dominate intelligence and wealth to the damage of society. Upon this theory and the adoption of such methods the district and the city of Petersburg have been wrested from the Republicans, principally colored voters, and are held against them to-day.

Against this influence Mr. Langston was compelled to make his way from the city named to the uttermost extremities of the district, and from the very beginning. In his case however, known as he was and in fact feared, such influences were intensified and concentered in a combination and conspiracy which were formidable and apparently invincible. But in addition to even this concentrated, vigorous and fearful opposition he was compelled to confront and overcome other hostile opposing forces wielded by General Mahone and such white and colored Republicans as he could influence and direct. All of this last class demonstrated such inveterate and cruel purposes and sentiments against Mr. Langston as to make them assistant Democrats of the most active, persistent and dangerous character. Upon the loyal colored Republican vote of the district chiefly Mr. Langston had to depend, and his success or defeat must depend upon his ability to influence, secure and have counted justly and fairly, that vote. His organizations had for accomplishing such work, local and general, must be constituted with direct, positive reference to that end.

With such survey of the work which he must now perform, with diligent and wise study of the field, every inch of which he must cultivate, and with careful and critical understanding of the forces, intellectual, moral and political, which he must employ under the circumstances, he prepared himself for a contest worthy of and requiring the best manly and womanly elements of sagacity, moderation, courage, energy, perseverance, wisdom and power.

He discovered a threefold condition of affairs in the district which a person less sanguine, hopeful and determined than himself would have concluded was insurmountable.

NOMINATED TO THE FIFTY-FIRST CONGRESS. 453

The Democrats, who were utterly opposed to him and ready to inaugurate and wage a warfare that would accept, as it gave, no quarter, without forbearance and mercy, ready to recognize and adopt any unfair and illegal method of treatment to compass their purposes, had full possession and control of the election machinery of every voting precinct. They held every judgeship, as they did every clerkship of the election, and through their own appointee, controlled the registration of every voter. Thus supreme in its power and control it is easy to perceive how difficult it must have been to overcome such influences and authority wielded by such a determined party, devoid of any sense of right or justice, bent only on accomplishing its designs at any hazard.

Then the white Republicans generally, as Mr. Langston could well perceive, would employ every means in their power against him, going even to the extent of approving and sustaining any fraudulent proceeding undertaken in any way by any one to prevent his success. Of course, even after the small number of such white Republicans as might support him had been given full credit for that action, and any influence which they might exert in such behalf, it is easily understood that the task before him must have been rendered immensely more difficult and severe, even doubtful in its successful performance, by reason of the opposition noted. This consideration will be more fully appreciated when it is stated that this class of Republicans had always constituted the leadership of the party in the district, as to it were credited the brains and power which gave it name and influence. Lacking their support, as a rule, the burden which Mr. Langston was about to accept was weighty and hard to bear.

The colored voters had heretofore been under the control and direction of General Mahone. They had been wont to regard him as a leader whose mandates could only be disobeyed or questioned with defeat. Now for the first time his authority and leadership were to be confronted and defied by one of their own number even. They had seen first-class white men beaten and vanquished politically by his management and power. How now could they believe that any colored man could meet and overcome his cunning, skillful and powerful manipulations? And yet Mr. Langston saw and appreciated this condition and feeling and knew very well that they could not be treated lightly in connection with the duty which he must meet. Not one of these things, however, not all of them put together deterred him, although they did give him anxiety while they quickened and energized his wits and purposes.

Over against such conditions as these which have been indicated, Mr. Langston found many things true of his situation which gave him hope, even encouragement, to go forward with vigor and assurance in his canvass. In the efforts which he had made to secure election as delegate to the National Republican Convention and the results connected therewith, he had come to a good understanding of the genuine loyalty and purpose of those voters upon whom he must rely at last for support. He had learned that the colored voters of the district would sustain him with firmness and fortitude. He had learned that the women of the district, the wives and daughters of the voters, were as earnestly and heroically in his favor as the men; and that both these classes would demonstrate their possession of the best elements of heroes and heroines in their conduct to insure his success. Besides, he had found that the few white Republicans who would support him were men of character and principle, earnest and tenacious in their convictions of duty, with exalted and indomitable purpose to discharge it.

Other complications and circumstances which added materially to the difficulty of Mr. Langston's task were furnished in the fact that while each party had its regular nominee—the Democratic and the Republican—the Mahone faction of the latter presented its pretendedly nominated at their Farmville meeting, already alluded to, who they claimed as against Mr. Langston, whom they called "a bolter," was the regular nominee of the Republican party. Put in such a position and opposed, as a colored man who had no right to ask the vote of the people for election to Congress, and whose conduct in that regard was characterized and treated as an impertinence, he must have felt himself confronted by fearful odds. Certainly he was. But in no respect whatever was he daunted.

More than this, Mr. Langston knew that General Mahone expected and would probably secure the support of the National Republican Committee as against him, and from that source obtain large sums of money for campaign purposes in Virginia, the principal part of which he would use in the Fourth Congressional District, as he did, according to any necessities connected with his defeat. He understood too, entirely, what the moral effect would be as well as the material should the expectations of General Mahone be realized in that respect upon the whole State and district. He felt certain also that should the general receive such support, the National Committee would in all probability call upon Mr. Langston to allow them to settle the matter of his candidacy, and should he refuse to do so he would be counted and treated as in rebellion against the authority of his party. This refusal he knew very well would leave him to meet out of his own pocket every expense connected with his campaign, while it would cost him the sympathy and moral support as well of the committee as those of the Republican party generally. In view of all the facts stated, it is apparent to anyone exercising the most superficial reflection that Mr. Langston was confronted by a burden which required broad, firm and stalwart shoulders.

Mr. Langston was asked in due season to submit the legality and propriety of his nomination and candidacy to the National Republican Committee. This however he refused to do, claiming that since the Republicans of the district in regular convention assembled, by a unanimous vote had put him in nomination for the Fifty-first Congress, there was no power under the wise, accepted regulations of the party competent to call their action in question. He maintained that two courses only were left to him. One was to accept the nomination and make the canvass, employing all the necessary means honorable and proper to secure his election ; while the other was to decline the nomination and allow the Republicans of the district to take such other and further action in the premises as they might deem expedient and appropriate. In taking this position Mr. Langston weighed well every circumstance and fact connected with it calculated to embarrass, obstruct and render difficult and doubtful his election. But such was his confidence in the intelligence, integrity and purpose of the Republican masses, who had already honored him with a place in the National Republican Convention, and then with a nomination to Congress, that he had no fears of results against even all the influences described. He felt confident that by wise, judicious management he could not only control but secure for himself as the regular Republican nominee, and ultimately have duly counted, the Republican vote of the district.

So soon as Mr. Langston had concluded in the early part of January, 1888, to run for Congress, he had betaken himself to the work of addressing the people, organizing clubs, male and female, printing and distributing documents with reference to that end. He organized first of all a general committee composed of the most intelligent, energetic and reliable colored men, with two or three white ones, that could be found in the district. This committee had its headquarters in Petersburg, kept in a building large and commodious, purchased by Mr. Langston and dedicated to that purpose. Immediately after its organization and at its first meeting held in the building mentioned, this committee waited upon General Mahone, bearing him a communication from Mr. Langston in which he was advised that that gentleman had upon representations made to him by a large number of the foremost Republicans of the district, concluded to stand for nomination to the Fifty-first Congress. On returning to their headquarters the chairman of the committee reported in graphic manner the results of their visit, stating very distinctly that General Mahone had received them and their communication with no manifestation of favor. The whole committee however seemed the more determined to go forward with their work.

Thereupon Mr. Langston added to the property which he had already bought in Petersburg a beautiful place located in the heart of the city, with a large, convenient building containing a hall admirably adapted to all political purposes, sufficiently capacious to accommodate a large promiscuous assemblage, with ample grounds well suited for an immense out-door gathering. From the night that he held his first meeting in his hall it has been called and known as "Langston Hall." It has already been referred to and may be many times again, for it has become in connection with his political movements consecrated and noted.

Immediately following the organization of the general executive committee mentioned, whose duty and care concerned the whole work so far as Mr. Langston's campaign was concerned, other subordinate committees, county and local, were provided and given charge and direction of all movements and operations having to do with this object in the different voting precincts of the entire district. In the constitution of these subordinate committees special reference was had to the intelligence, efficiency and devotion of their various members. And it is subject of special grateful remembrance and gratification, that not one of these committees failed in the earnest and faithful discharge of every obligation enjoined upon it.

Besides these committees, popular organizations were formed throughout the district composed of persons who pledged themselves to give their labors, influence and vote to Mr. Langston. These organizations were Republican always in name and object. For while constant effort was made by certain designing persons opposed to his candidacy and election, to show and prove, as they claimed, that Mr. Langston was "a bolter" from his party, and only interested in his own selfish ends, he and his friends were determined by every act of theirs to demonstrate and sustain his loyalty to his party. These popular organizations were called, when composed of men only, " Harrison, Morton and Langston Invincibles," and where composed of women only,

"Harrison, Morton and Langston Female Invincibles." Thus it will be perceived from the titles of these political clubs that Mr. Langston did not stop at the organization of the men, but included in efforts in that regard the women. It was well, as he found very soon after the commencement of operations, that this course had been adopted, since it was true that the women could and did exert large influence in controlling and directing the men in their political purposes and conduct. Indeed, to this day Mr. Langston counts that his success in the district was more entirely due to the influence of its women than to any other single cause outside of the actual vote cast for him. These organizations proved to be remarkably popular and efficient and their numbers increased from the beginning to the close of the campaign.

On the tenth day of January, 1888, Mr. Langston made the first speech of his congressional campaign at his hall in Petersburg. From that time he continued his labors in speeches delivered in every prominent place in the district. Not a single day during the time occupied with the canvass was taken by him for rest and recuperation, and only two weeks of this time, which he spent in attendance upon the National Republican Convention held at Chicago, were employed in any other direction. Not during a single day did he find himself wanting in bodily and mental strength to meet every engagement; although he spoke, for the most part, in the open air, ordinarily to immense gatherings of the people. So far as the attendance upon his meetings was concerned there seemed to be no political feeling against him. Everybody appeared to hear him with entire satisfaction and his receptions were always enthusiastic and flattering. He did himself as a rule the heavy speaking of his canvass, occupying generally from two to two hours and a half in the delivery of each speech. He was careful as he was methodical in the presentation of all the fundamental, distinctive principles and measures of the Republican party sought to be given effect through state and national legislation. At every meeting he declared, with fulness and precision, the principles and measures which he should advocate in the interest of his district and State should he be elected. Nor did he fail to meet, with courage and fearless utterance, every charge made or objection offered against him personally by any Republican or Democrat. He vindicated the attitude which he had taken and maintained with arguments as cogent and irresistible as they were eloquent and acceptable. His whole manner wherever he spoke, under whatever circumstances, showed him confident and intrepid.

Mr. Langston was warned on different occasions that it might not be safe for him to attend meetings and attempt to address the people at several places in the district. At no time, however, did he pay any attention to such warnings. At each place from which he received intimations of this character he paid his visit and spoke without the least reserve or qualification of his remarks. It is due the people of the district to state that he was interrupted only once during his entire canvass; and then by certain white and black Republicans led by a foreign negro, who had been employed by the followers of General Mahone, in view of his ruffianly name and ruffianly capabilities. However, this interruption was soon quieted by the respectable white and colored persons present, Republicans and Democrats, who were not disposed to tolerate such base proceedings. In making hundreds of speeches in the various parts of the district, including every county seat, with repeated addresses at every such place, Mr. Langston was not only not disturbed or interrupted in any way, but heard with patience and respect. While the campaign so far as he and his friends were concerned was spirited, vigorous and persistent, and so far as the opposers were concerned, bitter and cruel in many senses and ways, no personal violence or brutal and savage disturbance was ever shown him except in the case already alluded to. It is to be as distinctly and positively understood that he did not abate at any time one jot or tittle of a fearless advocacy of Republican principles, measures and men ; or just, intelligent denunciation of any opposition made to his nomination and election by any pretended Republican or Democrat founded upon his complexion.

A notable instance illustrating these warnings with regard to personal danger to him just mentioned, occurred in connection with the second great meeting which he was to address at Dinwiddie Court House, on court day, in June, 1888. Here was a great Republican stronghold. In this county resided the leading colored man of the district, who had joined General Mahone and his white followers against Mr. Langston; and he and his friends sought to keep the colored candidate away from that meeting, well understanding that his attack upon their very citadel, their strongest fortress, would in all probability prove to be a demolishing force. Hence to keep him away from this meeting they concocted, in their cunning, the warning indicated, which they conveyed to him with no little circumstance of solemnity and solicitude. They were kind enough to state that there would prove to be great danger connected with his visit to their court house, and while they could wish that they were able to guarantee him full protection, they greatly feared they would not be able to do so. And they advised him accordingly not to attend and attempt to address the meeting. However, giving no heed to the suggestion, on the morning of the day on which the meeting was held Mr. Langston, taking carriage with three persons other than the driver with him—all staunch and brave friends, men who knew what danger was but who did not fear it—made his way directly to the court house, passing over the fourteen miles from Petersburg to that place just in time to be received and introduced to the five thousand people who composed his outdoor audience at twelve o'clock noon. He was received with demonstrations of enthusiastic deafening applause, such as demonstrated at once that he was in the midst of true, admiring and devoted friends. His introduction made in the happiest style by an educated, intelligent and eloquent young colored man, was the signal for another manifestation of feeling in his favor which was inspiring and assuring. As he took his place upon the platform further exhibitions of kindly sentiment and devotion to him were made, which occupied considerable time before he was permitted to proceed. He had only said, " Mr. President and fellow-citizens," when he was interrupted by the mercenary tool of those who had been so careful to warn him of the danger of his visit, by a question calculated to arouse feeling and disturbance against him. Before he could complete the first sentence of his address, this hireling, who was himself a negro, had interrupted Mr. Langston three times with questions of the same character and import. At this point the speaker pausing, advertised all present, in stern, earnest, but fiery manner, that he would not be interrupted by anyone during the delivery of his speech, and especially by any person whose action was manifestly intended to provoke disturbance which might result in violence. To the person who had interrupted him, he gave a warning which the audience appreciating, seconded and applauded in such manner and with such earnestness as to quiet utterly further molestation. Mr. Langston's speech, occupying quite three hours of solid time, covering all the general and special issues of the hour interesting to the people, was heard thereafter to the end, and was received by the vast assembly with manifestations of the profoundest and most intelligent approval. He was given after its delivery a warm and encouraging reception, with assurances that on election day the people of that county would give him a vote so large in its majority as to ensure him so far as they were concerned his election to Congress. The Dinwiddie meeting and its incidents are regarded and recorded as constituting a triumph of signal and memorable character, of which Mr. Langston and his friends are even to this day justly proud.

The campaign of 1888, in the Fourth Congressional District of Virginia, if one considers its *personnel*, the peculiar division of parties, the issues presented to the people, the mode of it's conduct, the manner in which Mr. Langston was treated both by the Democratic party and an intelligent, active and powerful faction of the Republican, and its final results, closing in his complete vindication upon popular verdict and vote, must stand among the most remarkable and memorable known in American political history.

Certain circumstances connected with this campaign, marking its unusual and memorable character, are worthy of emphatic notice. These circumstances concern the treatment which his opponents accorded Mr. Langston before the people; his own behavior and conduct; the alertness and vigilance, devotion and fortitude of his friends and supporters, and the ultimate complete triumph which rewarded his efforts, outlays and sacrifices.

Mr. Langston's nomination at all was dependent almost entirely upon the high qualifications which were ascribed to him, attesting his fitness for a place in Congress far beyond even the most talented white men of his district. He was, as claimed by his friends, specially ready, able and eloquent in debate upon all those questions which while they constituted the distinctive features of Republicanism, interested and controlled the masses of the people who sought his services. Just in proportion to the very degree that the Republican voters valued his services and would avail themselves of his ability and eloquence, the Democrats and the factional Republicans who opposed him feared and dreaded any influence which he might attempt to exert and wield through his speeches. The Democrats therefore, though they were obliged to recognize him as the regular nominee of the Republican party, refused according to a time-honored custom in the politics of the district, to divide time with him at any meeting which they held. They gave as the reason for such conduct that Mr. Langston was a colored person, and therefore it would be a condescension on their part to share time with him, which they could not afford. Learning that this was the feeling of the Democratic managers and orators, Mr. Langston accepted this condition of affairs without the least murmur of complaint, feeling and believing that he would be able at every county seat on court days or at any other time, and at any other prominent place in the district where a public meeting was held, to take and hold the audience against any Democratic speaker who might be produced. And so he did, whether the meetings were held in Mecklenburg County, Lunenburg, Nottoway, Prince Edward, Powhatan, Amelia, Dinwiddie, Brunswick, Greensville, Sussex or Prince George. While in the city of Petersburg his meetings held always at his own hall or upon its grounds, were large, enthusiastic, and attentive, wholly under the control of his friends and himself.

So far as the Republican faction was concerned Mr. Langston neither recognized it nor its would-be candidate as having such place legitimately in the canvass as to entitle either to such recognition as would be implied in a division of time with him. Besides, he understood very well that to accord such treatment would be in some sense advantageous to his opponents, while it would not be of the least possible service to him. The candidate of that faction could do nothing toward bringing him an audience, and nothing towards improving his opportunities for a full and fair hearing before the people. On the whole Mr. Langston lost nothing by the course pursued by the Democrats with respect to him, and could have gained nothing should he have shown his Republican opponents a different treatment. It was well enough that he was made entirely independent of both. The master of his own platform, he commenced and closed as he pleased, responsible only to the people who never failed to hear him to the end.

The success of Mr. Langston's meetings, like the success of his campaign in all other respects, depended not more upon the thoroughness and courage, the liberality and self-abnegation which he displayed upon every occasion and in connection with every movement, than the activity and watchfulness, the fidelity and spirit which distinguished the conduct of his supporters, especially those who constituted the working-force of his canvass. But it is to be understood of the colored people generally of the district that no class, whoever the individual who attempted to lead them or whatever the cause whose advocacy aroused their ardor and controlled their feelings, ever displayed, under any circumstances, larger devotion or more sterling, positive tenacity of purpose than they did in their support of Mr. Langston and the principles and policy which he represented. In fact, with the most limited exception of here and there a few members of that class, its whole strength was enthusiastically and unitedly given to him. Even colored men who had hitherto acted with the Democratic party, giving it with a consistency wholly inexplicable, from the day of their emancipation and enfranchisement, their support and vote, forgot their party allegiance and duty in their earnest and ardent determination to support the candidate of their own race and color. A prominent deacon of the Harrison Street Baptist church of Petersburg, a Democrat from conviction as well as the peculiar influences brought to bear upon him by his social and business relations, employed as he was by influential white men of that political faith and character, when inclined to vote for Mr. Langston and yet doubting as to his obligations in that regard, made the matter a subject of careful, serious, prayerful consideration. He did not cease his reflections and prayers in that behalf until, as he claimed, the Spirit of the Lord had revealed to him in the clearness of unmistakable sacred illumination that it was his duty to give both support and vote to the colored Republican candidate. This he did, so arranging for himself his ticket on election day as to vote for all the candidates of his own party except the Republican indicated running for the Fifty-first Congress. When this good deacon revealed his spiritual experiences and decision as regarded this matter to Mr. Langston, he did so with feelings apparently of special pleasure and comfort. It is due him to state that the Democratic candidate in the canvass was the son of his employer and one of his most reliable friends. While his course did not cost him his position, it discovered his manly, heroic devotion to what he conceived to be his duty. This case illustrates the conduct of more than one negro Democrat of the district who gave Mr. Langston his support and vote.

As the canvass waxed hot and hotter, the Republican faction under the leadership of General Mahone manifested increased life and vigor, making proclamation at every opportunity that they would buy negro votes enough to defeat the colored candidate. They claimed also that they were constantly supplied with all needed funds from the National Republican Committee, who were opposed to Mr. Langston's candidacy and election. All this occurred about the time when the agent of that committee had come into the district, as stated, to investigate matters and leave with General Mahone whatever amount of funds was deemed necessary to defeat Mr. Langston. Thereby, great, far-reaching, general anxiety was created among all classes, affecting as well the Democrats as Mr. Langston's supporters. The Democrats, while willing to support the Republican faction against Mr. Langston, or Mr. Langston and his supporters against that faction, in their conduct in either case were actuated and sustained by their desire and purpose to make themselves finally victors in the contest. At all events, they sought to maintain division in the Republican party itself in the hope of that result.

Hence it was that so soon as the condition described presented itself, with the anxiety connected therewith, the Democratic leaders fearing that Mr. Langston might become demoralized and abandon the contest, sought to reach him, and by promises and gifts of funds strengthen and sustain his purpose to wage to the last moment the fight in which he found himself engaged. To this end they employed an excellent, personal, Republican white friend of his, an inveterate opposer of General Mahone, Col. John W. Woltz, the editor and proprietor of the "Fredericksburg Free Lance," to see Mr. Langston and make known to him the willingness of those leaders to aid him in his canvass, proffering him means in large amount according to his necessities. These leaders of the Democratic party at this time had no idea that Mr. Langston was in such control of the Republican voters of the district that he was to be specially feared by them. They had no idea that he was controlling such voters so that General Mahone and his following constituted in fact a mere faction of the party, whose vote all told could not affect materially the final result, which justly considered would be favorable to Mr. Langston against and in spite of all other candidates. The Democrats were not a little astonished therefore when he not only looked with cold indifference upon their proposition, refusing utterly to give it a moment's consideration, and declining to put a dollar of Democratic funds in his canvass. On the other hand he assured his friend, Colonel Woltz, that he was able and would meet every expense connected therewith and would not give up the contest until the voters of his district had elected him to Congress.

Nothing disturbed, nothing moved his purpose to persist in the maintenance of his claims before the people as the regular nominee of the Republican party. He understood very well the spirit and aim of the Democratic party, and he was not ignorant of the weakness of the Republican faction, which was not behind in parade and show as to every item of strength it pretended to possess. About this time the Republican faction exposed its utter weakness in the district by its appeal to colored men living in other States than Virginia to lend their influence to Mr. Langston's defeat. Among the notable personages to whom this appeal was made stands most conspicuous Mr. Frederick Douglass, who was found quite ready to offer a cunning, false and base testimony against the colored candidate. More than once before his letter reached the district, Mr. Langston was advised of the purpose of his Republican opponents to bring down upon him the opinions and statements of one whose words would be utterly crushing to him. The name of that person was not at first given, although it was publicly stated that such one had been engaged to make a communication, that it would soon arrive, and after its publication in the district the colored voters would turn their backs in loathing upon the colored man who had presumed to assert his right to represent the district in Congress, contrary to General Mahone's permission. But all this did not specially disturb Mr. Langston. He defied the gentlemen who made these threats and dared them to produce their man with his statements. Finally the letter of Frederick Douglass with all its poor logic, irrelevant philosophy and false, malicious assertions, arrived and was distributed throughout the district. Its effect was simply to call forth from such persons as Bishop Hood, the presiding bishop of the African Methodist Zion church of the district, and Bishop James T. Holly of Port-au-Prince, Haïti, such replies thereto as to give Mr. Langston additional and formidable strength and influence among the people. Thus, indirectly, the communication did him an absolute service. But when it was answered by Mr. William H. Hamlin, one of the foremost young educated colored gentlemen of the district, in terse, sarcastic, vigorous refutation, its effect if it had produced any against Mr. Langston, was wholly overcome.

It is due Bishop Holly, formerly a resident of the United States, the greatest and the most learned of negro church officials now living, who bore such testimony to the ability, character and qualifications of Mr. Langston, whom he had known at home and abroad for quite forty years, that at least the closing paragraphs of his letter in that regard be reproduced :

"I, therefore, congratulate you, Sir, that you have had the moral courage to come forward and throw yourself into the breach, as a man of that race, yet with full national sympathies for the whole country, as a candidate for Congress in your native State.

"The number of men of African blood in Congress has been reduced from nine to two Representatives, if I mistake not. We must admit that the election of these men came rather prematurely, that is, before the race had sufficiently advanced from its previous servile condition to produce men of even average qualification for the posts to which they were elected. They, however, did their best ; did not disgrace the race, and therefore we owe them our gratitude. But such a limited meed of praise is not all that the occasion calls for. We must produce men for such posts in every way equal to the occasion, as compared with men of any other race that they may meet as colleagues in the halls of Congress.

"If this was the time and place I could criticize unfavorably some of your political acts in points where I take the liberty to differ from you in opinion, while conceding to you the same liberty to differ from myself. But after making this reservation, I think that it is beyond all question true, that you are the best qualified man, all things considered, that the race in the United States can now produce as Representative in Congress. Your long legal career at the bar, and as dean of a law faculty; your local experience in a municipal board, as an officer thereof, at the national capital; and your eight years' career in the foreign consular and diplomatic service of your country, have given you a rare and varied experience, such as none of your contemporaries of the same race can pretend to. Add to this your widely known oratorical powers as an effective public speaker and a ready debater, and you are thereby pointed out as the man, *par excellence*, of the race for the post for which you have had the patriotism to come forward and offer yourself. You have all the qualifications to raise the political dignity of your race, as well as to serve the whole country by your election to a place in the House of Representatives.

"Hence from the standpoint that I occupy on this question, and looking from this distance, it seems to me that it would be little less than the blackest treason to the cause of the colored race in America, for anyone of that race, under any pretext whatsoever, to oppose your election to the Congress of the United States; while every philanthropist of whatever nation, who desires to lift up a struggling race to the full dignity of manhood, should labor to carry you successfully through the approaching canvass.

"I am, my dear Mr. Langston,
"Yours very truly,
(Signed) "JAMES THEODORE HOLLY."

It is to be recollected now and always that it was early discovered in the campaign made in the Fourth Congressional District of Virginia in 1888, that the sole objection that could be or was made against Mr. Langston's nomination and election to Congress from that district was his color. The State of Virginia up to this time, while several colored persons had been elected from various parts of it to the House of Representatives and one or two to the Senate of the State, had not witnessed any attempt on the part of one of its citizens of negro extraction to secure his nomination and election to such high national position. It is not hard, therefore, to understand how a person of that class, as well known and as conspicuous as Mr. Langston had made himself in the State and nation, must arouse all the inveterate, intensified opposition of the whole State and district against his novel and unprecedented movement—and it mattered little whether the man who hated him because of his color was a white Republican or a white Democrat. The feeling of opposition and the purpose to defeat him at all hazards and by every means, honorable or otherwise,

NOMINATED TO THE FIFTY-FIRST CONGRESS.

were precisely the same. The wonder is that such opposition, intense and cruel in the beginning of the canvass, did not discover itself finally in such barbarous, hideous manifestations as to make it perilous for Mr. Langston to traverse freely the district and advocate his claims before the people; especially, subsequently to the publications had from Douglass and two or three negro leaders of the nation, who living outside of the State and district, affecting great regard for the Republican party and exceeding anxiety for its success, hired as they had been, according to report, which to this day stands unchallenged and uncontradicted, made their false and foul charges against him.

These falsehoods, however, as they were circulated through the parties who had secured them to answer their vile and selfish purposes, produced no serious effect of adverse character, since the great body of the electors of the district comprehended at once their design and trampled them as they deserved under their feet. While Mr. Langston despises and contemns their authors, as every honorable and true man must, he will exercise ever the profoundest gratitude of his whole heart toward those noble men who came to his defence in manly, masterly manner, and aided him in the maintenance of the cause of popular liberty and equal rights.

When one calls to mind how early and completely the negro was enslaved in Virginia; how long that institution was continued there; how he, held as mere property, reached in his personal and social status well-nigh brutehood itself; —and how the dominant class, proud of its origin, its noble blood in many cases, its chivalric character and name, conscious of a birth and destiny in masterhood, full of prejudices and predilections engendered and sustained by the keen sense of these facts, it will be hard to understand how in his remarkable undertaking Mr. Langston could hope to win, under such circumstances, the support of the former or the toleration of the latter class of the people in his canvass. This consideration will bear as it ought special significance when it is recalled that his district, so far as the wealthy white families, ex-slave-holding, are concerned, is populated chiefly with a class of people whose names and social connections show how far in character and influence they go back to the time when the chivalric, brave, honorable, hospitable Virginian was the representative of all that was noble, true and manly; to the time when certainly so far as his State, his country and his neighborhood were regarded, his word was the law, and all outside of his class, those below him in social existence, must accept it without question or debate. These families, glorying in the traditions which came down from the old, misty time of their greatness and power, now without brilliant or glorious environments in the change which has passed over all, composed those elements of the Democratic party which while they would not consent for a Republican, though white, could not tolerate, even in thought, the possibility of a Republican, dark-hued, tracing his orgin to the negro race, to represent their rich, intelligent, aristocratic *Virginia* district in the Congress of the United States!

The city of Petersburg numbers among its prominent, wealthy, cultured, controlling citizens many families of the class mentioned; and their great factories—tobacco, cotton, peanut, silk, wood, and other—testify how completely the the negro voter, yesterday a slave, to-day even a laborer and dependent, is under their influence and subject in important sense to their direction. Add to this the lesson taught the latter class from the day of its emancipation, that in order to succeed in party movement, it must be led and directed by some white man, who if not his friend in fact pretends to be, and one will have his conviction thoroughly settled in the opinions that the political elements with which Mr. Langston had to deal and which he must control, were difficult enough to reach by any means or exertions whatever; that they could not be reached and persuaded to support him without the most extraordinary and unparalleled efforts, vigorous, wise and persistent on his part and that of his friends. And yet whatever may be true so far as the white class was concerned, a reasonable number of whose votes were given him, it is true that the vote of the colored class was given him quite in its entirety.

His success with regard to the vote of the colored citizens is described aptly and forcibly in the words of a white Republican who opposed him throughout the canvass, doing all in his power to accomplish his defeat. His statements were made under oath, as he appeared to give evidence against Mr. Langston, and should have therefore special weight as showing the power which the latter wielded over the great body of the colored people who constituted the real Republican party of the district and gave it its overwhelming vote. The question was put to this gentleman by way of cross-examination.

"Then explain, if you please, how Arnold, the regular nominee of the party, supported by its entire organization in all its great influence, skill, management and outlay, ran so poorly in the district? *Ans.* For long months prior to the election, and for long months before the convention, Mr. Langston had, unopposed, been making a canvass in which he and his emissaries had insidiously and industriously played upon the passions and prejudices of the colored people, basing his claims to a seat in Congress, largely, on the fact that the negroes outnumbered the whites very considerably, and it was time for them to send one of their number to Congress. He aroused even the women, got up an immense religious fervor in his favor and aroused the prejudice of the large mass of the unthinking colored people to such an extent as I never witnessed before and hope never to witness again. It was at white heat in Sussex County the week prior to the election, so much so that I was impressed with the opinion and expressed it, that they would not then even listen to the Lord Jesus Christ, much less vote for him, if he were a white man and appeared against Langston. This feeling was intensified largely under the teachings and leadership of young colored men, who had no memories of the past which enabled them to properly appreciate what the Republican party had done for their race, hence no feeling of gratitude."

The words of another distinguished white Republican, made in official manner, were then quite natural enough: "With such feeling in the district the election of Langston was certainly to be expected." This opinion may not be doubted, in view of the record of population, total white and colored, of the district, according to the census of 1880, giving 56,194 for the former, and 102,071 for the latter, the difference being entirely in favor of the colored candidate.

In spite of every opposition, as a matter of fact, especially as the canvass neared its close, the supporters of Mr. Langston became as it were wild in their enthusiastic and vigorous determination to carry him triumphantly forward. His meetings became more numerous ; their attendance was increased, and such was the feeling exhibited on every hand in his favor that his opponents of all classes, though they greatly bestirred themselves, multiplying and intensifying their efforts to defeat him, could very clearly discern the success which must attend his labors. The tidal wave of popular feeling on whose crest he was borne was irresistible ! Even the Sabbath day gatherings, the very prayer-meetings of the most devout and pious, were converted into solemn occasions for the invocation of God's blessing upon the success of the cause which Mr. Langston represented. Thus he and his supporters came down to election day, the sixth of November, 1888, full of hope and confidence, with every arrangement made to poll on that day every vote possible in his favor, with such guards and protection thrown about them all as to make their honest and fair count a possibility and fact, in spite of every trick and fraudulent manipulation of his combined Republican and Democratic opposition. And that this proved to be the result, the historical record of the campaign fully attests.

As representatives of the class of persons upon whom with hundreds of others Mr. Langston relied in his campaign for advice, direction and active assistance, and toward whom he must ever exercise the most grateful feelings of obligation, he records here the names of Messrs. David A. Batts, R. H. Hampton, Ross Hamilton, R. J. Jones, Matt N. Lewis, Lee Reed, W. H. Hayes, Scott Wood, Charles Scott, Joseph Meade, Moses Burrows, N. T. Goldsberry, W. W. Worsham, H. C. Green, Green Harrison, Herbert Lambert, J. W. Smith, T. L. Jones, Clay Bagley, C. L. Bethel, W. D. Evans, George King, Tazewell Branch, George Bragg, Joseph McFunn, T. J. Venable, Jack Funn, J. W. Brown, E. W. Brown, Madison Lowry, E. D. Bland, John M. Brown, John N. Robinson, Junius T. Archer, William Booker, William Gray, W. W. Williams, Thomas H. Brown, J. C. Booker, William T. Crowder, Pleasant Goodwyn, A. J. Smith, Robert F. Hartwell, Frank N. Robinson, Samuel Bolling, Baxter Guy, David L. Brewer, William H. Jackson, W. E. Grigg, John W. Tucker, Richard R. Townes, John A. C. Stevens, G. H. Dabney, J. L. Sweatt, York Harris, A. J. Gray, C. W. Davis and Revs. Henry Williams, Henry Madison, C. B. W. Gordon and William Bassett. The following ladies, among others, showed themselves to be of great efficiency and service in the canvass, controlling, indeed, hundreds of votes, with their associates, for Mr. Langston; Mrs. Richard R. Townes, Mrs Richard Mayo, Mrs. Robert H. Epps, Mrs. Henry Williams, Mrs. Mary M. Jennings, Mrs. Clementine Bartlett, Mrs. C. L. Bethel, Mrs. George King, Mrs. C. E. Epps, Mrs. Matt N. Lewis and Mrs. Doctor Webb. Nor are such white Republicans, as Col. James D. Brady, Col. John W. Woltz, D. L. Selke, T. E. Wilkerson, W. H. Weiss, A. B. Batts, T. D. Redd with others, not numerous but earnest, true and brave, who served Mr. Langston and the cause which he advocated as they might, to be omitted from this roll of honor, upon which their names are now recorded in grateful remembrance of their manly, patriotic and noble conduct.

CHAPTER XXIX.

ELECTION DAY IN THE FOURTH CONGRESSIONAL DISTRICT, NOV. 6, 1888, AND HIS CONTEST FOR A SEAT IN THE FIFTY-FIRSTH CONGRESS.

THE State of Virginia has witnessed no political campaign more important to it and the nation than that of 1888. Messrs. Harrison and Morton, as the representatives of Republicanism, asking the support of the people of the United States for election to the presidency and vice-presidency, and Messrs. Cleveland and Thurman, the standard-bearers of Democracy, asking promotion to the same high positions on the vote of the nation, were competitors in a political contest with few equals and no superiors in its significance and importance. And at no time in the history of congressional elections did greater consequences depend upon success in the elections to the party which had saved the Union, and which must be held responsible for the perpetuity of its free institutions. Hence it was that from one end of the republic to the other, in every State in the Union, the most strenuous efforts were made by the friends and supporters of the one and the other set of candidates to secure beyond peradventure their election to the high offices named. As to the election of members of the House of Representatives, it was everywhere realized that success in that regard was quite as indispensable for the general good of the country, would the Republican party enter upon practical control of the nation. Under such circumstances, with such fearful responsibilities confronting the voters of the Commonwealth who were naturally moved by feelings of profound determination and enthusiasm, the campaign referred to was inaugurated and conducted.

The sixth day of November, 1888, the closing day of the campaign, dawned upon Virginia and the Fourth Congressional District of the State with popular feeling, politically, at fever heat. It is true that the work of the Republican party of the State had neither been wisely organized nor vigorously conducted. The voters of that party had been largely left to take care of themselves and their own interests, while their chief leader of the State wasted his time, as he spent too much of the funds appropriated for the general work, in local quarrels and struggles calculated to disrupt and defeat the party. The Democratic party, on the other hand, had left no effort untested nor any outlay neglected necessary to give it success in the State, and of possible triumph in every congressional district. Democratic orators had employed everywhere such utterances as tended to arouse beyond precedent popular purpose in favor of their party; and the press, metropolitan and country, had demonstrated in displays of large and various ability and tact its determination to do its utmost to achieve Democratic success.

The advantage resulting to the Democratic party from the misunderstandings, the quarrels and divisions of the Republicans, was quickly and earnestly seized and turned to the largest and most positive account and profit. Especially was this the case in the Fourth Congressional District, where the Democratic party could only hope for success upon division of the Republican party and the fraud made possible thereby, as tolerated and sustained by the white Republican leaders. The fact that there existed differences between leading Republicans in this congressional district, working a condition of things which seemingly rendered it possible for the Democratic party to gain it in the election, and thus make certain its success as well in the State by a large and emphatic majority, increased the intensity and activity of its purpose and efforts to accomplish that result. That feeling will be appreciated when it is stated that the Democratic party played in this district its most desperate game, even that of transcendent shameless fraud, to compass the victory at which it aimed. Pledged itself to the frauds necessary to compass Mr. Langston's defeat, it did not fail to hold its associates in that iniquity, though Republicans in their party affiliations and pretentions, to a full and complete discharge of their obligations. Thus Mr. Langston, on election day, found himself confronted by a conspiracy of such double character, forceful and formidable, as to stagger for the moment even his own strong and unyielding faith in his ultimate success. He never doubted the purpose of the people to give or offer to give him their votes. The only matter about which he had misgiving as he witnessed the condition of things about the polls on election day, was whether he would be able, at last, with all his precautions to overcome the tricks and frauds which were to be perpetrated against him. The double agencies and influences wielded against him were the keen sharp instruments of those skilled in their use, while crafty and cunning in the concealment of their misdeeds.

With the vote polled as Mr. Langston knew it would be if given freedom and fair play, he had no question as to results. But hindered, obstructed, intimidated, refused, and finally, where accepted, fraudulently and wrongfully counted and credited by election officers, all of whom were pledged to that iniquity and outrage, how could he hope to secure and maintain justice in the case! Anticipating this condition of things, he and his friends had armed themselves with such means of gaining and holding the facts connected with the organization and conduct of the polls; the hindrance, obstruction and intimidation of voters; and the reception, refusal to count and credit of ballots, as would give them power to present, legally and with effect, all the facts respecting such transactions.

Of course, it was necessary in order to do this, to make large and expensive provision for the work to be done; and at the same time make such selection and employment of agents as would ensure the wisdom, skill and efficiency of its accomplishment. The district contained over one hundred voting precincts. Six wards were organized and manned, in the city of Petersburg, where both the Democratic leaders and the chief promoters of the Republican faction hoped to perform with the greatest ease and success any fraudulent project which they might devise against Mr. Langston. For each of these voting precincts and for every ward, wise and efficient scrutiny and surveillance were indispensable, with the service implied, performed by persons of courage, fidelity, intelligence, tact and devotion—devotion in full measure to the person to be served and the cause to be promoted. But in addition to these indispensable qualities in the agents indicated it was found necessary to so instruct all voters who would cast their ballots for Mr. Langston that when they had either accomplished their purpose, or had been refused that privilege, or for any reason had been prevented from doing so, the fact could be made known at once and recorded. Hence the voters were instructed first of all, when they had presented the ballot and it had been received and deposited in the ballot-box, to so declare in such way in such audible voice as that the bystanders, including any persons employed especially for the purpose, might make record of such announcement. If a vote was refused like course must be pursued ; and if the voter was prevented from voting by any means whatever he must, before leaving the polls, report the fact to those employed to take care of that matter. Thus instructed, all the voters of the district who intended to cast their ballots for Mr. Langston approached the polls on the sixth day of November, 1888. There the voters found, duly armed with ballots, at least two persons who had been employed as distributors of tickets for Mr. Langston ; two persons seated, one on either side of the window through which the vote was passed to the judges of the election, duly provided with the means of taking the name, residence and vote of every elector who gave Mr.

Langston his support; and where any voter found refusal made him, or prevention in his vote, such facts were also noticed and a record thereof kept by the same persons. Thus at every polling place in the district Mr. Langston had employed four persons, who acted, two as clerks and two as the distributors of his tickets, whose duty it was, in addition to the services named, to maintain a strict observance and keep an exact record of all that was done and said to disturb the voter and prevent in any wise the honest and fair vote intended by the elector, cast, or otherwise, for him. It is a fact that in many cases good and true friends of Mr. Langston volunteered their assistance to these persons. In three or four instances at least, certain efficient and faithful women did good service in that behalf. Here it should be noted that in nearly every case where the voter himself by reason of his ignorance, or want of understanding as to his duty in the premises, needed help, he was promptly aided by his more intelligent wife or daughter. It will be perceived from this statement that Mr. Langston had in actual employment on election day quite five hundred persons, giving their attention and services to his interests especially, as connected with the election. With the fewest number of exceptions, the persons thus employed were colored men whose education, intelligence and general qualities of character rendered them competent and efficient for the maintenance and performance of the trust and duty confided to them.

When the fact is recorded in becoming emphasis, with full effect of its truthfulness, that Mr. Langston on election day was confronted by the most formidable odds in that two of the first white men of his district were his competitors and opponents—men of the first social position among the dominant classes of the State, wealthy and influential—sustained in their purposes and efforts to defeat him not only by the white community generally, but by the judges, clerks, supervisors and officers of every sort and kind of the election, with all determined to perpetrate even the blackest fraud to compass that end, the exercise on his part of all the care, caution and labor possible will be certainly justified and commended. Otherwise he must have met with utter and entire failure, as was expected and desired by all those Democrats and Republicans who opposed him.

With such men as Mr. E. C. Venable, the regular nominee of the Democratic party, and Judge R. W. Arnold, the nominee of the Mahone faction of the Republican party, running against him, with their friends in full control of the polls throughout the district and in every ward in Petersburg, competent and willing not only to accept and credit those candidates with every vote that could by any means, fraudulent or other, be given them, Mr. Langston undertook and maintained a work in opposition to them, fraught as one might have supposed, with the direst calamities. Nothing but Providence and the wisest, most skillful, energetic, determined purpose and labors could have saved him against such untoward odds.

It is not practicable to follow the line of conduct, base and fraudulent, pursued in every voting precinct against Mr. Langston throughout the district. The facts connected with that conduct and its results in the sixth ward of Petersburg alone, the ward in which he lives and where the great body of the voters, above all others, were his friends and supporters, must suffice.

In that ward, the polls fully manned under the law, with every officer of the election present, were duly opened and voting commenced at the usual time. Not later than nine o'clock in the morning Mr. Langston visited the polls to cast his vote for the regular Republican ticket. He was confronted at once by the remarkable fact that so far as the Republican colored voters were concerned, the approach to the ballot-box had already become blocked and access thereto rendered impossible. This condition was caused by the unheard of and unjustifiable arrangement whereby two approaches had been ordered and established for voters coming to the polls; one for white persons, Democrats and Republicans, and another for colored voters, Republicans, of course. Indeed, had it not been that place was given to

Mr. Langston out of special consideration at the head of the line of colored Republican voters, it would have taken him, starting from the foot of the column, where he would have been obliged to take his place, over three hours to make his way up to the window through which he must pass his ballot to the judge of election.

This arrangement was made for the express purpose of preventing the free, ready and prompt vote of Mr. Langston's supporters, and was operated with the least possible compunctions of conscience and with the greatest vigor and advantage against him. It was understood that all persons coming forward in the line set apart for white voters would cast their ballots against him, either for Mr. Venable or Judge Arnold. Hence in the case of these voters, such control could be exercised as to give them full advantage of time and opportunity, at the expense of the colored voters, who were thus so situated that they could easily be kept back, with seeming fairness, to accommodate their white fellow-citizens. With this unusual condition of things adopted and maintained throughout the day, when the polls closed at sundown in the evening, besides the colored voters who becoming discouraged had gone home without voting, one hundred and fifty of them stood in the line with Langston ballots in their hands, anxious but unable to cast them. All that could be done under the circumstances was to take the names of such voters, with their residences and their ballots, upon the back of each of which the voter wrote his name, as witnessed by the clerks employed by Mr. Langston. These ballots put together carefully in a package, sealed up, and cautiously guarded and preserved as sworn to and certified by the clerks mentioned, were conveyed to the Committee on Contested Election Cases for their examination and use. It is apparent that this procedure was cunningly devised and instituted for the very purpose indicated and wrought great and serious damage to Mr. Langston. He lost by it hundreds of votes.

But this was not all. Where votes were cast for him in large numbers, when the polls were closed and the count was had, manipulations were made so as to give Mr. Langston the smallest vote cast for either of the three candidates. This could be done with the greatest possible ease, since no person friendly to Mr. Langston was allowed to witness the opening of the ballot-box or the counting of the votes. Hence when the vote of this ward was announced—a ward in which the combined vote of Mr. Venable and Judge Arnold would not reach, as everybody knew full well, one hundred—the following figures were given: Venable 352—Langston 139—Arnold 160. The figures here were, without the least doubt, taken out of their proper places, as they ought to have been credited to the respective candidates, and made to answer the purposes named; that is, the figures given Mr. Venable belonged to Mr. Langston, those given Judge Arnold belonged to Mr. Venable, and those given Mr. Langston belonged to Judge Arnold. Not only did the general political conditions, with the popular feeling of the ward, show this, but the results in every other ward in the city of Petersburg and throughout the city demonstrate the correctness of the same opinion. For while it is true that Mr. Venable, the Democratic candidate, was credited with a larger number of votes in every ward than Mr. Langston so as to insure his election beyond peradventure, Judge Arnold was given a much smaller vote than Mr. Langston in every ward except the sixth. Upon the general vote of the city the Democratic judges upon their count gave Mr. Venable 2,259 votes—Mr. Langston 1,273—Judge Arnold 694. Of course, pursuing such a course, the judges of election in this ward affected the greatest possible care for the wise, just and honest management of the votes cast. So that after they had completed their count and credit of the votes to suit themselves, in accordance with their fraudulent purposes, they called in a large police force to guard and protect them as they bore the ballot-box with its sacred treasure from the voting-place on the corner of Gill and Halifax streets to its safe, impregnable deposit in the court house! How apprehensive these custodians of the popular will appear!

to be lest a score or so of Langston's friends should attempt to disturb them while conveying the ballot-box to its place of safety! Such fears could only find place in minds pricked in the consciousness of their own sense of wrong-doing, which they would attempt to conceal by hypocritical pretense of just behavior.

On election day, in all parts of the district wherever voting was had and Mr. Langston had his agents at work in care of his interests, they met and had to overcome the like conditions of fraud found in the sixth and other wards of the city of Petersburg. However, they were met and controlled so successfully that when the whole vote was counted and declared, Mr. E. C. Venable, the Democratic candidate, was awarded the certificate of election by a plurality of 641 votes over Mr. Langston. Judge Arnold was really not in the contest at all, so small was the vote given him, amounting in the whole district to only 3,207, as counted by his Democratic friends and accomplices. The vote, as credited by them to Mr. Venable, was 13,298, and that credited to Mr. Langston 12,657, showing a plurality in favor of the Democratic nominee upon an unchallenged count, as manipulated and declared by the Democratic judges and election officials, as stated. It is true, however, could the vote of the district have been polled freely, and counted and credited honestly, Mr. Langston's majority over the combined vote of both Mr. Venable and Judge Arnold would have exceeded five thousand.

It is true, that election day closed upon the efforts of Mr. Langston and his friends with the record of fraud made by the Democrats and the Mahone Republican faction, as already stated. But from the returns made to Mr. Langston at his headquarters in Petersburg, from his clerks especially, representing the conditions under which the election had been conducted, the votes received or rejected, the manner of their manipulation and credit, with accurate and complete records made in that regard as attested and confirmed by the same persons, he was thoroughly convinced that he had received, in fact, such a vote in the district as to assure his election, and that the fact was susceptible of the most convincing legal proof. With full explanations made in that belief to his large number of friends who gathered about him, manifesting by word and act their deep solicitude and concern for his success, he did not hesitate to state that his election was entirely certain and that he would in proper time, and by accepted legal methods, convince all concerned of that fact. Thereupon at one o'clock, early in the morning of the seventh of November, accompanied to his home by his friends, he after bidding them good-bye amid their congratulations and cheers, retired shortly thereafter, fatigued and worn, to seek the rest which was now due one who had carried the anxieties and fears, with the hopes and expectations, of a day which shall ever remain in his thoughts as in his affections, memorable, though trying beyond any other he ever knew.

On the day following the election it was very apparent to all interested in the subject, that of the persons disappointed in view of the returns made by the Democratic judges of the district, General Mahone and Judge Arnold were the chief and most annoyed. They had staked not only money but judgment and unstinted effort and influence upon the result. They had concluded and believed that in view of the general conditions of the district, with the Democratic party through its official agencies and leaders to assist them, they could so overwhelm Mr. Langston in disastrous defeat that they would retire from the contest with new and additional honors in the victory which Judge Arnold's election would bring them both. But it was not so ordered. Instead, through the neglect and indiscreet management of General Mahone, chairman of the Republican State Executive Committee, the State itself had been lost to Harrison and Morton, and won by Cleveland and Thurman by a plurality of only 1600 votes, showing that with proper diligence, effort and outlay, it might have been carried for the Republican candidates. Besides, in spite of their fraudulent and humiliating combinations with the Democrats to defeat Mr. Langston, whom they constantly characterized in their vulgar, ungenteel style, as a "bolter," Judge Arnold had received in the district and was credited with a vote which showed him the man of all others to whom the people refused their support, thereby marking him as the leader in fact of a rebellious faction of his party. But the keenest and most intolerable wound of all came to these men from the fact that on the face of the returns as made, the person of all others whose defeat General Mahone desired and sought had discovered such vote in his favor as to make it certain that the people had sustained him with remarkable unanimity against every adverse influence. And more, it was evident upon the vote given him that when he had exposed and established the frauds which had been perpetrated against him by the connivance and assistance of these disappointed and dissatisfied Republicans, he would win at last his election, with all the honors and emoluments connected with it.

The opposition and hostility of feeling manifested on the part of the Democrats generally, and the faction of the Republican party, with respect to the nomination and election of Mr. Langston, did not abate a whit, either in their intensity or vigor, at the close of the campaign. As it became known that he would make contest for a seat in Congress, these feelings seemed to deepen and spread themselves among the classes indicated; and when his notice had been served upon the Democratic candidate who had already received the certificate of election, these feelings of opposition and hostility did really reach their highest point of intenseness and vehemence. They were pictured in the "spleen and sour disdain" of those who opposed him—their very countenances, the bearing and conduct which distinguished them indicating their determined purpose to defeat him, regardless of consequences, right or wrong.

The consciousness of the truth and the justice which distinguished Mr. Langston's claim, and their appreciation of the vileness of their own deeds, appeared to create in their minds the bad resolution to spare no efforts, to hesitate at the adoption of no cunning which their ingenuity could devise to save them against the exposures of the frauds which they knew they had perpetrated. They feared an investigation and would adopt any means to prevent the results which must inevitably follow in its wake. They could but feel that duly conducted under the law, with openness and fairness, it would undoubtedly eventuate in favor of the person who was the subject of their hatred and enmity. The last thing which his opponents could endure—that which they could not even contemplate without indescribable dread and fear—seemed to be the seating of a colored man in Congress as the representative of the district.

There were still many things which these opponents held within their reach, under their influence, and largely under their control, which they seemed able to so manage and manipulate as to give Mr. Langston the greatest possible trouble, even thereby so obstruct, hinder and prevent his efforts in a contest as to accomplish at last his defeat. One has only to recollect the agencies necessary to be employed —their number, character, ability and circumstances—in a contest originating in a great congressional district like the Fourth of Virginia, to understand and correctly estimate this assertion. It is only necessary to add that all such agencies are vulnerable, especially in a case like this of Mr. Langston's, to every sort of social influence and exaction.

Eleven counties, with more than a hundred voting precincts, compose this congressional jurisdiction, in different parts of which frauds, as claimed, lurked, were located, and must be detected and exposed according to law and by accredited judicial methods. It is apparent that the first thing needed would be able, skillful, and faithful lawyers; not one, but in this case many. Besides, in order to the wise and due taking of the testimony with its appropriate authentication for use, many officers appointed to that duty by the State would be as indispensable as the attorneys. It is easy to perceive that attorneys and officers located, as in this case, principally white men connected with the general community by social relationships of long standing and tenderness, would be vulnerable and sensitive to any ostracism which the opponents of Mr. Langston might seek to bring upon them should they in their professional or official capacity undertake to serve him. Such an attempt was made and in several cases wrought its natural consequences. It is hard for one to really understand such a condition of social influence and power, and yet it requires the least experience to awaken his sensibilities to the full knowledge of their effects.

In the city of Petersburg, Virginia, and in the district in which that city is located, constituting the chief business center, attorneys are not wont to have offered them large retainers, or to receive large pay for their services. Ordinarily business is of a less important character, and lawyers are in the habit of asking and obtaining such renumeration for their labors as would seem to be under the circumstances reasonable only. Understanding and appreciating these facts, Mr. Langston had felt that he might employ at usual accepted rates even the very best attorneys located in the district. He did not realize that so great would be social influence brought to bear upon any, even the leading members of the bar, that they, or any one of them, would refuse an unusually liberal retainer under any circumstances, from him. He asked, therefore, in confidence several of his friends to call upon perhaps the leading lawyer of the Petersburg bar, and secure for him his services. He was astonished to learn that this lawyer, a Republican of known character, learned, able and influential, and though active and laborious by no means wealthy, declined to give him his services. An honorable and worthy man as he was, Mr. Langston had not felt that any influence, social or personal, could be brought to bear upon this attorney which would lead him to refuse his professional services to any person of character and means who needed them. He certainly could not reach that conclusion in view of the name and position of the person who occupied that exalted place in the community and at the bar.

Mr. Langston, although his friends reported to him that the attorney declined to serve him, fearing that they might not have stated his desire and the conditions of the case with sufficient clearness and precision, covering at the same time the assurance that prompt pay for every service would be made, including a reasonable retainer, called upon him himself in the hope of being able to make such representations of his feelings, with the offer of retainer and promise of payment in the premises, as to secure his services. However, upon Mr. Langston's own presentation of the case, he still declined; and when asked whether he had been retained upon the opposing side, he answered promptly that he had not. And when offered a retainer in the shape of two five hundred dollar bills, should he consent to become the leading lawyer in the conduct and management of the case, he still refused, saying: "I cannot take your case. I am, socially, so related to those who are opposed to you that to do so would cost me and my family so much in the severe ostracism which would be meted out to us, that I cannot do it. Mahone would never forgive me!"

Putting his one thousand dollars back in his pocket, Mr. Langston left the office of the learned attorney, taught a lesson of which he had not entertained the least conception prior to the interview detailed. He was profoundly impressed now that other agencies, quite as potent, though impalpable, as fraud, intimidation, obstruction, hindrance of voters, and foul manipulations of ballots when cast, were to be met and overcome by him. The social influences, stronger than any other in many senses, were being operated against him. How could one bear, even the best among the learned lawyers, the denial and loss of past kindly recognition by families of character and standing, whose friendship, association, hospitality and influence were valued! Few men of any class, certainly few lawyers, even of the bravest character morally, can be found able to meet that social influence, and in defiance of it give their services to an unpopular client who represents an unpopular cause.

In his fear of social ostracism for himself and family, the learned attorney who thus declined to serve the colored aspirant for congressional honors had forgotten that his would-be client was a person of fair standing in the community, a gentleman of education and refinement, and a lawyer who had reached such position through his laborious successful efforts in practice in the courts of a neighboring State, where he had been educated and resided for many years, that he had become several years prior to this time, a member of the Supreme Court of the United States, and thus in fact a member in good and regular standing of the great American Bar. Besides, the would-be client of this learned attorney appeared neither in the attitude nor garb of a pauper, craving services as a matter of professional charity. Nor did he come as one, for the time being even, without the necessary funds to pay any retainer which might be demanded. He had even property, real and visible, abundant to make good all charges of the attorney for his services, located within the jurisdiction of the court, where he might bring with ease any suit to recover any balance due him at any time. But what signified such considerations in the estimation of this attorney with the apparition of social ostracism confronting him, shaking its terrifying finger in his face! The attorney thus frightened from duty has small, too imperfect and limited conception of his obligation to the members of civil society, who have given him his honorable professional character and made it possible for him to win name and recompense by its legitimate and appropriate cultivation! A would-be client of honor, competent to meet every professional obligation, is not to be denied the ablest, the best, the most faithful legal aid when it is required, whether a dominant class in the community be pleased with his politics or justify his honorable aspirations.

Now Mr. Langston realized that here was a difficult, aggravating and annoying matter which confronted him upon the very threshold of his contest. He could not import attorneys! Would he be able at last to employ the skillful and the efficient of the local profession so as to answer his necessities? His first experience in this respect had filled his mind with dark, portentous misgivings. And as he wended his way homeward the question came and went, each time making deeper furrows in his gushing sensibilities, Will the enemies of justice and right, through their selfish social influences, finally shipwreck the honest ballot of a loyal constituency?

Mr. Langston's visits to other lawyers were quite as edifying and interesting as that already described, and resulted, for precisely the same reason, in all save a single case, in the same manner. In fact it really seemed to be true that efforts were being made to render it utterly impossible for him to employ any one of the recognized first-class lawyers of the district. Where they were not retained they were brought under such social fear as to make it impossible to secure even for lavish outlay their services. He did succeed, however, in employing a person who while he had no name as a lawyer and no standing at the bar connected with labors in practice before it, felt that he could be admitted, and with very little effort make himself equal to the task of wise, efficient and successful management of this case of contest. This person felt that it was necessary however to employ two certain lawyers whom he named to give him besides any legal assistance which he might require, protection and support against social, ostracising influences, which might be wielded, otherwise, to the discomfort and annoyance of himself and his family. This was the only person with whom Mr. Langston could even at great outlay, and as indicated, in rather untoward conditions, employ for his service. The gentleman had had some experience with one or two election cases, and his knowledge gathered therefrom, with his natural vigor of intellect and strong common-sense, with his intimate acquaintance with the district itself in every voting precinct, and with quite every white and colored man residing therein, as he might be assisted by other learned and skillful lawyers, and especially sustained by the two whom he named, was able really to render useful service in the case. He was, therefore, employed, as Mr. Langston could do no better, and the other two lawyers were retained upon conditions of unusual character involving the payment of large retainers and great sums for services. An ordinary business man, acquainted with the charges of extravagant American lawyers, would have the astonishment of his nature stirred to its very depths, should Mr. Langston disclose to him the fabulous amounts which were demanded and which he agreed to and did pay the three lawyers referred to for their services. But the circumstances were such that he could do no better, and must comply with the demands imposed or fail. Notwithstanding their exorbitant terms, after the preparation of the notice of contest served upon Mr. Venable, every one of them confined his labors to the taking of testimony—a service not difficult of performance nor requiring special or commanding talent—in the district, principally in the city of Petersburg. Finally, compromise, arrangement and settlement were made with two of them whereby they were paid in full, upon their receipts and acquittances, and relieved from further responsibility in the case.

It is not to be understood from anything said here that Mr. Langston would find fault with his attorneys so far as their actual services in the district were concerned. He notes the circumstances connected with their employment and the unusual demands which they made upon him to mark and emphasize the difficulties which confronted him in the matter of securing competent lawyers, even in a case of the character and importance of the one which he represented.

Among other attorneys employed by Mr. Langston were three young colored gentlemen—Messrs. James H. Hayes, Matt N. Lewis, and Scott Wood—who discovered in addition to their learning and tact large activity, efficiency and fidelity, doing the work assigned them with skill, industry, promptness and satisfaction. The example and conduct of these young lawyers are especially commended. The first is a member of the Richmond, and the other two members of the Petersburg bar.

With notice duly served upon Mr. Venable; the different localities at which frauds, with other acts which affected the validity of the election returns, were perpetrated, determined; the witnesses to be examined selected; the next thing in order was to employ a suitable number of subordinate judicial officers, especially notaries public, before whom the examination of the witnesses might be conducted. Mr. Langston's success as to the engagement and service of these officers was, on the whole, of satisfactory character. Nevertheless social influences were exerted, in no unmistakable manner, to prevent certain persons of more prominent position in the community from serving him. They failed, however, for the reason that the service in this case as respected these officers was promising and inviting. Hundreds of witnesses must be examined; the testimony to be taken would be voluminous; and the amount to be paid to each notarial officer employed, in ready cash, would be large and desirable. These officers of Petersburg and the district, as a rule, were not inclined to allow even threats of social ostracism to deter them and thus disturb their labors while costing them the loss of their prospective gains. The officers employed by Mr. Langston not only discovered excellent ability, promptness and fidelity, but courtesy and kindly bearing which deserve emphatic note and commendation.

The array of attorneys appearing for Mr. Venable, from the very beginning, was in numbers and character imposing and formidable. They had all engaged, apparently, in the contest more for love than fees, and were determined that no stone should be turned the movement of which was calculated to shed the least light upon any frauds which had been committed. They discovered the purpose to throw every obstruction possible in the way of securing full and complete evidence in Mr. Langston's favor. The obstructions which they cultivated with the most constant assiduity, zeal and purpose, had to do with the intimidation of the witnesses and the extended, continued, unheard of protraction of the cross-examination of many of them. These lawyers, all of whom were by birth and education Southerners of the extreme Democratic school, understood full well how easy it was to intimidate an ignorant and dependent person who had all his life been a slave and who had been in the habit of regarding white persons as sustaining to him the relation only of masters and mistresses. Upon witnesses of this class they sought to impose their tricks of intimidation. Generally, however, while they did create in some cases a little delay, they did not as a matter of fact affect the character of the testimony given by the witnesses. It was in the case of such witnesses as Messrs. J. A. C. Stevens, Thomas H. Brown, Pleasant Goodwyn, David L. Brewer, A. J. Smith, Matt N. Lewis and Frank N. Robinson, persons who had acted as clerks and ticket distributers for Mr. Langston on election day, and whose testimony, clear, direct and convincing, could not be met by any legitimate means, that the opposing attorneys by adopting the methods of useless, irrelevant and frivolous cross-examination sought to consume time so as to prevent within the limit allowed by law, the introduction and submission of the evidence, which presented in anything like fullness, must have sustained the case of the contestant while it would expose in alarming manner and with frightful features the frauds which had been perpetrated.

Not to dwell upon the other cases mentioned in detail, it may be stated of that of Mr. Frank N. Robinson, that he was called and sworn as a witness at twelve o'clock, on the thirty-first day of January, 1889. His examination, so far as his testimony concerned his direct statement, consisted of eight questions. The cross-examination was then commenced, and was continued until late in the day of the fifth of February—six days—and was prolonged by the asking of three hundred and sixteen questions, nine-tenths of which were without the least significance and were employed only for the purpose of consuming time, the hope being, without doubt, that by that procedure Mr. Langston might be forced to forego the opportunity of submitting his evidence in such completeness as to sustain his case. After the three hundred and sixteenth question of his cross-examination had been put and answered, Mr. Robinson, while upon the witness-stand, was arrested and taken into custody by a deputy United States marshal by virtue of a warrant or capias falsely and maliciously sued out by two attorneys-at-law, representatives of Mr. Venable, who had appeared and participated professionally in his cross-examination. Their complaint, on oath, was that the witness refused to testify in the case. His behavior had been in every respect genteel, courteous and obedient. The outrage perpetrated against the witness was without parallel, while the injustice attempted against Mr. Langston was glaring, atrocious and despicable.

The chairman of the sub-committee appointed to consider and report upon this case, very truthfully and pertinently stated in commenting upon this outrage:

"An examination of the record shows the absolute falsity of this charge. The witness maintained under the most provoking and insulting cross-examination remarkable self-possession and dignified courtesy, and the only explanation of this outrageous conduct on the part of the contestee's counsel must be that they hoped by their perjury to intimidate other witnesses from taking the stand to expose the frauds by which their client obtained the certificate of election."

Mr. Matt N. Lewis was another of Mr. Langston's witnesses, who though not abused by charge and arrest, as Mr. Robinson was, was kept upon the stand in a cross-examination which covered thirteen full days; and in the eight hundred and nineteen questions put to him the entire political history of Virginia was canvassed. This abuse of the witness did not weaken his testimony in the least. It rather served to strengthen and render more effective its strong and unimpeachable features.

The charge made against Mr. Robinson was fabricated and feigned. The abuse done Mr. Lewis and other witnesses whose cross-examinations were unduly protracted and vexatious could not be justified by any consideration of necessity or judicial usage. Delay only was sought in this unheard of procedure. Without it a hundred witnesses might have told how loyally and bravely they had voted for Mr. Langston. The delay thus created and the denial of opportunity thus wrought, took from them that privilege—and this was the base object had in view.

Witnesses who appeared to testify against Mr. Langston, as summoned by Mr. Venable, were both Democrats and Republicans; but all of them of and from the classes who had opposed the colored candidate in the canvass, perpetrated frauds and voted against him on election day. In the evidence which they were called to give they were swearing in self-defence, testifying to save themselves against their own illegal and fraudulent conduct. They knew full well that the vindication of their own conduct could be found only in their successful support of the Democratic candidate. Testifying thus in self-defence, as they were moved by sentiments of hate and hostility, they proved themselves to be not only voluntary and ready, but quick witnesses, dexterous in any turn or shade needed in their testimony designed to disappoint and defeat the colored man whom they had so basely and treacherously opposed.

Among the witnesses introduced and sworn by Mr. Venable were two colored men, lieutenants of General Mahone, active and vigorous supporters of him in whatever plans or methods he might adopt in opposition to Mr. Langston. It was amazing to witness the bitter, dogged spirit in which these two men testified, as well in their direct as their cross-examinations, against him. Though both claimed to be intelligent and worthy Republicans, opposed of course to any discriminations made adversely to one on account of his color or nationality, they asserted themselves against Mr. Langston with surprising vigor in the very spirit of hostility and bitterness employed by their white Virginia chief. They much preferred that Mr. Venable should be seated to seeing Mr. Langston given place in the Fifty-first Congress of the United States; and, accordingly, each of them volunteered his testimony to that end and gave it with a sort of pride and satisfaction that must have been to an intelligent, patriotic colored person, or his friend, entirely astonishing. The names of these gentlemen are not recorded here. It is enough that they figure so conspicuously on the wrong side, in the record of the case as made and established forever!

As soon as Mr. Langston had received notices of witnesses, Republican in their party affiliations, whose testimony was to be given in favor of his opponent, he wondered why General Mahone himself was not placed upon the stand and examined in behalf of the contestee, Mr. Venable. The general occupied such a conspicuous, leading position in the ranks of the hostile Republican faction; played such general and important directing part in all that faction undertook and did against Mr. Langston; was so intimately related to all the enterprises of the Democratic party in that behalf as well and had such knowledge of every voting precinct and everything that was done in each, that he seemed to be of all others the most competent, and therefore the most desirable and serviceable witness to be found among the Republicans who were bent upon Mr. Langston's defeat. It has been, constantly, a subject of surprise that he was not, for the reasons indicated, called to testify.

But notwithstanding all the difficulties and obstructions which confronted Mr. Langston, growing out of the inimical feeling and opposition which prevailed against him, he succeeded remarkably under the circumstances in securing, formulating and presenting in reasonable quality and quantity such testimony, the effect and tendency of which were to settle the case of contest in his favor. However, after the testimony had all been taken and transmitted, as required, for consideration by the Committee on Contested Elections appointed by the House of Representatives for that purpose; and the case had, with sixteen others, been taken up in this committee, the hostile feeling which had shown itself in the district throughout the campaign, at the polls on election day and in connection with the examination of witnesses, manifested itself even at the national capital. The members of the House itself, and those who composed its committee, were made to feel its presence. Of nine cases of the seventeen brought to the attention of the committee, that of Mr. Langston was the eighth; and at every stage of its progress the feeling indicated discovered its detestable and annoying effects. Finally, so potent was its influence, operating so insidiously and with such fell purpose that it reached even, as believed, the very attorneys employed by him, so that the majority of the committee heard and considered his case with very little interest, because the lawyers who presented it discovered the least earnestness and exhibited the smallest amount of real ability in its management. Indeed, the person who had been employed and who was by special appointment to make the chief and leading argument in the case for him assigned this duty to another attorney and refused to argue the case, even after the attorney whom he had employed to represent him had utterly and signally failed in his opening address to the committee. The same person, though contrary to Mr. Langston's earnest wish and desire, emphatically expressed, was permitted to make the closing argument in the case ; a poorer and weaker effort, if possible, than the opening one. Mr. Langston has always feared that untoward influences caused all this unexpected action. However, the facts upon which the case rested were so patent and so clearly and distinctly brought out in the testimony submitted that those members of the committee who gave it the least thought and consideration saw that the merits of Mr. Langston's claim were of such character and importance that they deserved more than passing notice; that they were worthy of sincere, deliberate examination and decision. And Mr. Langston must ever feel that he is under lasting obligation to the able, learned and thoughtful members of the committee, who in spite of the inadequate, really unprofessional, disloyal and weak efforts of his attorneys, apprehended, understood and appreciated the strong and effective points of the law and facts presented in connection with his contest. He must ever feel that otherwise the influences and agencies which had been directed at his defeat in the district, failing there, would have so effectually displayed their power against him at the capital as to compass at last the design at which his opponents aimed.

But even after the committee had reported in clear, distinct, favorable manner in the case, as early as June 16, 1890, it really seemed that the influences which were operative against the consideration and adoption of the report would prove to be all-powerful and invincible. At one time Mr. Langston and his friends had well-nigh reached the conclusion that the case might not be settled for a long time; probably not at all. Influences of unusual power, far-reaching and persistent, were brought to bear upon every Republican member; while the hatred and opposition of every Democrat in the House were rendered thereby more intense and unyielding. Hence the report which had been submitted was delayed and its consideration postponed for quite three months. All this time the opposition was gathering strength and marshaling its forces for a deadly struggle. The Democrats had taken great pains to notify the Republican members of the House that they never would consent to the seating of Mr. Langston: that they would not by their presence in anywise aid in maintaining a quorum of the House for that purpose; and disaffected Republicans had announced in plain and emphatic terms that they would not even give their countenance and support to that proceeding.

Thus warned the speaker of the House, the Hon. Thomas B. Reed, and its leaders, chiefly responsible for its character and action, could see and appreciate the duty which confronted them. At one time all these persons were apprehensive that it might be impracticable, even impossible, to secure and hold a sufficient number of Republican members to constitute the quorum indispensable for independent party action in the case. But there came a change in public sentiment with respect to it, which reaching the Republican members of the House, especially the leaders, so aroused and fortified their purposes on the subject as to bring them to the determination to secure and hold the quorum necessary for action. The resolution thus formed and acted upon brought the required number of Republican members to their seats in the House.

The case, as reported from the committee, was taken up for final consideration on the sixth day of September, and after seventeen days of unexampled struggle it was brought on the twenty-third to a decisive vote, which resulted in the adoption of the two following resolutions as recommended by the committee:

"Resolved, that E. C. Venable was not elected a representative of the Fifty-first Congress from the Fourth Congressional District of Virginia, and is not entitled to a seat therein.

"Resolved, that John M. Langston was elected a representative of Congress from the Fourth Congressional District of Virginia, and is entitled to a seat therein."

The first resolution was adopted by a vote of one hundred and fifty-one to one, the speaker counting a quorum as present; and the second without division; when Mr. Langston was sworn and took his seat in the House of Representatives amid demonstrations of enthusiastic Republican approval and applause.

When the final vote was being taken in the case, and prior to and during the administration of the oath to Mr. Langston, every Democratic member of the body had left his seat and gone from the hall of the House, refusing utterly to be present to witness the ceremony of his admission. The sight of one whole section of the body absent, while the body itself was engaged in usual legitimate business, the vacant seats of the Democrats gone testifying of their second feat of secession, was quite unique and novel enough to merit in all its black details a lasting record of infamy.

Not a single Democratic member of the Fifty-first Congress of the United States was in his place in the House of Representatives on the twenty-third day of September, 1890, when Mr. Langston took his place in that body!

Upon the consideration and adoption of the resolutions of the committee resulting in the decisive concluding procedure of the House in the case, the foul and malicious spirit which had shown itself all along in malignant manner against Mr. Langston reached its most desperate display.

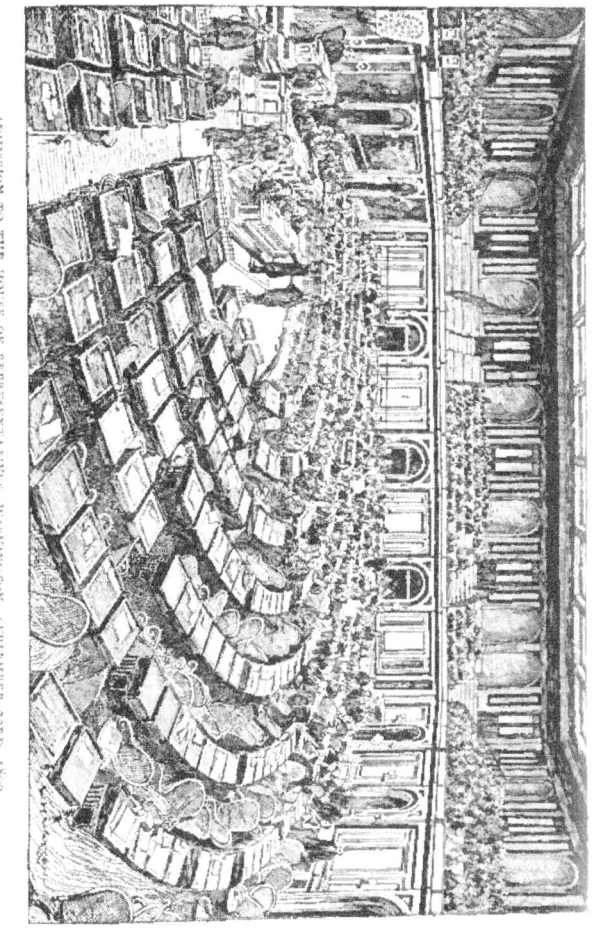

ADMISSION TO THE HOUSE OF REPRESENTATIVES, WASHINGTON, SEPTEMBER 23RD, 1850.

498b

It was noted in the united, determined purpose and action of the Democratic party, whose conduct against him, unfaltering, resolute and unseemly, was utterly illegal, rebellious and indefensible. It was witnessed in the outspoken opposition of a single Republican, who was so becrazed by it that in opposition to the judgment and interests of his own party and to his own probable defeat spoke and voted with the Democrats. Two other Republicans were so controlled by the same influences operating against Mr. Langston that while they gave their presence to maintain the quorum of the House, through fear and cowardice, refused to support by their votes the sentiments of their party associates and the judgment and desires of their constituents. The three Republicans referred to have no standing to-day in American politics! Their mistake was fatal!

If special mention and personal commendation be due to any single person above and beyond all other Republican members of the Committee on Contested Elections for intelligent, vigorous, persistent and successful efforts in behalf of Mr. Langston, both in the committee and in the House, that honor belongs, without question, to the earnest, able and efficient representative of the State of Wisconsin, the Hon. N. P. Haugen. As a member of the committee his labors as chairman of the sub-committee appointed to specially consider and report upon the case were indefatigable, searching and discriminating; and as he made discovery of the facts and figures which sustained Mr. Langston's claim, he was brave and manly in his advocacy and defence of them. Indeed, he was not long in his investigations of the case before he discovered and appreciated its full truth, and comprehended with clearness and just understanding the spirit and significance of every movement made against the contestant, whether inaugurated by Democrats or selfish, designing, negro-hating Republicans. His conduct in the case challenges the highest admiration, and deserves the most unstinted praise of every one interested in its wise and just decision.

The great majority of the Republican members of the House supported Mr. Langston in his claims with intelligence, firmness and patriotic purpose. And from the speaker down, these persons deserve positive, hearty approval and eulogy for their behavior. The leaders of the House, Messrs. Thomas B. Reed, the speaker, William McKinley, Jr., Julius C. Burrows, Joseph G. Cannon, Robert R. Hitt, Henry Cabot Lodge, Elijah A. Morse and Charles H. Grosvenor, not to mention others equally deserving, who displayed their sense of justice as well as their appreciation of individual worth and long years of consistent Republican devotion, by the wise and manly performance of their full duty in this case, are worthy of such distinct and signal mention as accords with their great and commanding reputation and influence.

Perhaps the inconsistency demonstrated by the Democratic members of the House in leaving their seats as already described, was not more marked and signal than that of their return, one by one, except now and then they came in groups, to their places, after Mr. Langston had been given admission. They could not bear to witness his approach; they would not be present at his entry; and yet when they might have gone home and ought to have done so to maintain their consistency, they returned with all the grace accordant with Democratic usage; and several of them even went so far as to give the colored representative cordial greeting with congratulations upon his success. Every one of them, however, treated him finally most respectfully, and recognized him as a member in full and proper fellowship with themselves.

The welcome which Mr. Langston received on entering the Fifty-first Congress from the Republicans who had supported him, was considerate and cordial to a degree certainly unusual and exceptional. When it was found that the seats on the Republican side of the House were all occupied, he was at first informed that it would be necessary for him to accept a desk on the Democratic side, among the gentlemen who had declined to witness his admission. To this he was disposed at first to object, feeling that his presence in such juxtaposition might, if not to himself, create feelings of uneasiness perhaps to some of the gentlemen members who had fought him with such desperation of purpose and hostility. He was, however, at once relieved of any embarrassment in that regard by the kind, cordial treatment of the Hon. Theodore E. Burton, representative of the Cuyahoga district, Ohio, who offered him his own seat on the Republican side. He accepted this very gracious offer and found himself pleasantly and eligibly located by the side of his excellent personal friend, Hon. Henry P. Cheatham of North Carolina, and in the neighborhood of a company of most worthy and agreeable gentlemen, all Republicans, who accorded him marked consideration and respect.

The announcement of the action of the House through the public press provoked widespread, remarkable comment upon this case. This was natural; for from the very beginning, by reason of its peculiar character and surroundings it had commanded general popular attention. The progress of its consideration before the Committee on Elections, and its protracted and tedious consideration by the House, marked as it was in all its stages by the most active, vigorous party opposition and rancor on the one side, and earnest, positive partizan support on the other, tended to create in connection with it such popular interest as to render it noteworthy and famous. The whole country watched, as it awaited, with deepest concern its termination.

Of course the same division of sentiment that was found elsewhere marked the expressions made about the case by the various journals of the country. Many advocated Mr. Langston's claims in earnest, able terms. Others as emphatically and positively opposed them. It is a remarkable fact, however, that while most of the leading Republican papers gave him their support there were not a few Democratic partizan ones which expressed themselves, in cautious, careful manner, in his favor as well.

The day following his admission to the House Mr. Langston received congratulations in letters and telegrams coming from all sections of the country, so numerous that were he permitted to publish them according to his desire, they would constitute a volume of great size, and prove to his friends, certainly, to be of peculiar and striking interest. It would tax a person of the largest ability, one possessing the most unusual powers of expression, a very genius in that respect, to record and proclaim the feelings and sentiments of Mr. Langston in view of the great kindness and consideration shown him by those who rejoiced with him in his success, and honored him in their congratulations. He can only express to them through this means his profoundest lasting gratitude.

On the morning of the twenty-fourth of September, the day following his admission to the House of Representatives, the seat of Mr. Langston was beautifully and strikingly decorated with a profusion of flowers, costly bouquets, presented by his friends and admirers. One of these was of special significance, representing in its floral composition the sword with which he had met and overcome his opposers, and the broom of destruction with which a good Providence had swept them out of his pathway to victory. To the friends and admirers who thus honored him he would tender sincere, hearty acknowledgments. Nor would he fail or neglect to record his generous appreciation of the honor done him by the thousands of people who proffered the evidences of their great joy at his success in their unexampled popular serenade, given him at Hillside Cottage, Washington city, D. C., and their matchless reception, so distinguished for its dignity, its good order and its marvelous attendance, held in the great African Methodist Episcopal Metropolitan church of the national capital.

Thus was ended a case of contest, every feature of which marked it as peculiar and unique. The persons concerned, the one representing the Democratic and the other the Republican party, one white and the other colored, both the very best representatives of the respective classes from which they came, and both Virginians of well-known names and character, would alone give it under the circumstances, unusual, important significance and interest. But above all mere personal considerations stands the exalted, overshadowing fact that in this contest the legality, the purity and the perpetuity of the honest popular American suffrage were involved. The decision, therefore, made by the Republican House of Representatives in view of the facts which constituted its history, places this case, unlike any other recorded in the annals of the nation, in a position from which it shall ever reflect the dignity and glory of the justice and the philosophy of equal rights, the sure and impregnable foundation upon which it was based and rests.

CHAPTER XXX.

HIS CONGRESSIONAL EXPERIENCE AND RECORD.

ALTHOUGH his contest was protracted and tedious, characterized by unheard of filibustering operations which tended greatly to delay its settlement, Mr. Langston was ultimately given his place in the Fifty-first Congress under such remarkable circumstances and with such *éclat* as to put him at once in conspicuous and influential position in the body. The demonstrations in his favor on the Republican side of the house were so general, quite unanimous and enthusiastic, as to make him feel that the obstructions thrown in his way and the unexpected delays had in his case so far from being merely vain and frivolous had been providentially turned to the largest significance and the amplest recompense. His reception and treatment were something ecstatic; and the generous sentiment and purpose generated by the triumphant settlement of his case made it easy enough to take other and immediate action in the Miller-Elliot contest, resulting in the seating of the former; and thus presenting, after so long time, the refreshing sight of three colored members, Cheatham, Langston and Miller, in the House of Representatives.

Betaking himself to the close and critical observation of the general conduct of affairs in the House; witnessing and studying the manner in which business was introduced, considered and determined; applying himself to diligent and careful reading of the parliamentary regulations by which the body was governed in its proceedings; listening with becoming attention to the addresses, marking even the attitudes of distinguished members as they offered their views, pro and con, upon measures had under debate, it did not take a great while for Mr. Langston, with large and varied experience at the bar, in deliberative assemblies of which he had been a member, with his general knowledge of affairs, to realize that though he was a member now of a most august assembly, he might count himself quite at home among his distinguished associates. He understood fully, however, that no man could figure in that body, gaining name and influence, without possessing and displaying much more than ordinary talents. It was apparent to him that here was a field in which one might employ in connection with his labors all the learning, practical wisdom and eloquence which he might command; while to be useful as a member of the body he must possess unusual general understanding of national and international affairs.

The Fifty-first Congress had among its members several of the foremost leaders of the Republican party and not a few of the more prominent members of the Democratic. Its leading members were strong men, possessing not only large native endowment but broad and various learning and commanding address and eloquence. Thoroughly versed in parliamentary affairs, with experience and knowledge of all the abstruse difficult things connected with service in the House, they were admirably fitted for assuming and maintaining controlling place and influence in its deliberations. In fact, with such leaders as indicated, the body as a whole was one which discovered in its sayings and doings as a rule remarkable character, efficiency and power. No history of the Fifty-first Congress, however, shall ever be written which does not give the most conspicuous places connected with it, so far as leadership, the introduction and adoption of great measures, and the efficient and effective management of its deliberations are concerned, to Thomas B. Reed, its famous speaker, and William McKinley, Jr., its noted Republican leader upon the floor of the House.

The large, learned and able company of Republicans, members of the body, such as Cannon, Grosvenor, Lodge, Rowell, McComas, Morse, Caldwell, Haugen, Hitt, Dolliver, Burton, Henderson and Houk, not to name others of like rank and influence, are worthy of special mention by reason of their eminent and effective services.

On the whole the Fifty-first Congress, for many reasons connected with its history; the various important measures adopted by it and which must ever illustrate its record, shall occupy memorable and exalted place in the annals of the nation. When it is recollected that this Congress was composed of many of the great foremost leaders of the Republican, and quite a number of the more prominent members of the Democratic party, and that its record is distinguished for several important enactments of far-reaching character, as the famous McKinley Tariff Law, no well-advised, impartial person will think of doubting this statement.

It has been felt by many persons who understood well how bravely and consistently Mr. Langston had always served his party; and who understood too very well that he had been elected by a large majority to Congress, upon it securing to the party even the electoral vote of his State for Harrison and Morton, that his case ought to have had prompt consideration and early decision. By delay therein, as such persons claimed, through his absence from the House his district was unduly denied proper representation, and Democratic interests were advanced both in a party and individual sense. This delay not only put in jeopardy the future prospects of the party in the district and the State, as was claimed, but gave to the Democratic representative the perquisites of the position and his salary for the time he was allowed to remain a member of the body, with opportunity to say and do by tongue and vote all he could against Republicanism. While the truth and force of these feelings and opinions cannot be met by argument in such fulness and positive character as to relieve entirely those who entertained them, it is wise to credit those earnest and sagacious Republicans having this case—

with at least sixteen others, all involving more or less difficult questions of law and fact—with such understanding and conduct as seemed under the circumstances considerate and proper; especially, since they must have fully appreciated the character and measure of the opposition which was being felt and exerted against Mr. Langston. All things considered, the Republican members of the Committee on Elections deserve the largest credit for their management of the case ; and the House signalized its devotion to Republican principles at last, in the large, comprehensive American sense, in its action which resulted in the favorable consideration and adoption of its report.

On his return to the district at the close of the first session of Congress, Mr. Langston's friends and supporters gave him a warmth of reception and cordiality of treatment in view of his success which were truly marvelous. Weeks of his time were occupied in receptions given at his home in Petersburg to those who came from all parts of the district, anxious to pay him their respects and listen to explanations from him designed to show how he had made effective the vote which they had so bravely and defiantly cast for him as their representative. Often when overjoyed in view of his statements, they expressed themselves in such terms of friendly feeling and applause as to affect him even to tears.

During the whole recess subsequently to the last weeks of September and the early days of October, 1890, Mr. Langston was occupied in visits to different parts of the district, at each place holding and enjoying conferences with such friends as were by reason of their fidelity to him and their superior judgment as to persons and the wants of their special localities, competent to advise him with respect to the distribution of any patronage which he might secure from the administration. This was a subject which under the circumstances, was found to be quite delicate enough, requiring careful judgment and just, impartial discrimination. His colored supporters must have their claims duly considered. His white friends must not be neglected. And the whole matter must be so discreetly managed as not to incur anything like well-founded and damaging criticism from his Republican opponents. With regard to this whole subject however, his success was apparent and admirable. The colored electors were really proud of the office-holders of the district representing their class; and the white ones were wholly satisfied with what was done in that regard for them. Whatever may have been the case with respect to the latter class as to holding office during all the past, it was a new thing, novel and curious, exciting great interest generally and special satisfaction and pleasure on the part of the former, from whose numbers postmasters and other officers were now for the first time appointed and commissioned to duties, responsibilities and emolument in those capacities. And it is not saying too much to affirm that Mr. Langston's labors resulting in such conditions unheard of heretofore, added materially to his general popularity and the fervor of its expressions made by those and their friends who were specially served. Having accomplished such results in the district there was certainly general profound satisfaction felt in view of the action of the House of Representatives in seating the first and up to this time the only colored congressman from Virginia; while no one was found to express harsh and vulgar opposition thereto, except those Republicans of the district, white and colored, who had manifested in every possible way their desperate opposition to Mr. Langston. The Democrats of the district took the defeat which had come to them as a matter of course, against which they could not and ought not to have expected any other result. With such general contentment gained so quickly and prevalent in the district, the assurance of a common and irresistible support of Mr. Langston was apparent and positive. His first victory, with its results, seemed to give promise of other signal and certain successes in the future.

Returning to the capital on the opening of the second session of the Fifty-first Congress, Mr. Langston gave prompt and regular daily attendance thereupon, from the beginning to the close. He was honored by the speaker of the House in an appointment as member of the Committee on Education. This committee was composed of able and agreeable gentlemen, representatives of both political parties. He attended every meeting of the committee and was greatly benefited by association with its members. He was treated by them all with marked consideration, and his views, presented upon any subject commanding the attention of the committee, were received with most respectful, appreciative attention.

Treated considerately and cordially by his associates, members of the House; finding himself in pleasant surroundings in view of his reasonable, general understanding of the rules and regulations governing the body in its proceedings; with usual and growing interest in every matter and measure of ordinary character requiring attention; and with profound special concernment in certain pending measures, Mr. Langston was found ready for intelligent, earnest work as a member of Congress, both as he was called to duty in his committee-room and in the House itself. So far as all subjects of importance were presented, considered and adopted or rejected, he showed himself at ease as to his knowledge. Loyal to his party he sustained it, as a rule, upon every proposition involving any distinct party issue with influence and vote, and yet he did so always upon judicious, well-grounded personal judgment.

The second session of the Fifty-first Congress, commencing on the first day of December, 1890, lasted only three months. And yet by reason of his attention and diligence the record made by Mr. Langston therein in that time was sufficient to show the bent of his mind and understanding as to public affairs, and to indicate the rank which he might take as a representative finally, if permitted to remain in Congress for any length of time.

The petitions, resolutions and bills formulated and presented by him represented a variety of subjects, and embrace several important matters of general interest.

The first petition presented by him was that of John H.

Brooks and forty-two others, citizens of the District of Columbia and the States of Maryland and Virginia, praying for the reimbursement by the government of the depositors of the Freedmen's Savings and Trust Company.

The second petition was that of the United Presbyterian Church of Cannonsburgh, Pennsylvania, against opening the World's Fair on Sunday.

The third was the petition of Catherine Pringle and others, praying for indemnity against certain Indian depredations.

And the fourth the petition of certain citizens of Richmond, Virginia, for the passage of House Bill 639, to rehabilitate the merchant marine of the United States of America.

The resolutions introduced by him were: First, one asking a report of the honorable attorney-general of the United States upon any action had in his department, to enforce the Acts of Congress, passed May 31, 1870, and February 23, 1871. The resolution reads as follows: Resolved, That the honorable attorney-general of the United States be requested to transmit to the House of Representatives all communications, orders, directions and instructions which have been made, issued or given by him to any United States district attorney, marshal, or deputy marshal, commissioner, or other officers, with regard to the institution and prosecution of any suits, of whatsoever character, under the act to enforce the right to citizens of the United States to vote in the several States in the Union, and for other purposes, passed by Congress, May, 31, 1870, and the act amenadatory thereto, passed by Congress, February 23, 1871, and to communicate to the House the results of any suits instituted and prosecuted as stated.

This resolution was duly referred to the Committee on the Judiciary and by that committee, having been favorably considered, was reported to the House and adopted.

The second resolution introduced by Mr. Langston was a joint one providing for amendment of the Constitution of the United States in the matter of suffrage and the mode of electing presidential electors, representatives and senators to Congress, and reads as follows:

Article XVI, Section First. That all elections for members of Congress, senators of the United States and presidential electors shall be by the people of the several States, under such laws as Congress shall enact ; *provided*, that no elector shall be allowed to vote at any such election who cannot read and write the English language, and the basis of representation in each State shall be reduced in the proportion which the number of those allowed to vote shall bear to the whole number of male citizens twenty-one years of age in such State.

Section Second. That Congress shall have power to enforce this article by appropriate legislation.

This resolution was referred to the Committee on the Election of President, Vice-president and Representatives in Congress. There was no sufficient time for its consideration, the session of Congress being entirely too limited, and adjournment was had without action upon it.

The resolution embodying as it does new propositions, subjects not heretofore adduced for congressional consideration, received notices of the press, with such comments, sometimes for and at other times against it, as to show its importance and the propriety and necessity of its presentation.

Among other bills introduced by Mr. Langston—several for the relief of various citizens of his own and other districts—the most important was one to provide for the establishment of a national industrial university for the education of colored persons residents of the United States. No apology is offered here for the presentation of the bill in its entirety as drawn and submitted. Its object is of such transcendent importance as to justify its careful and thorough reading and to warrant its insertion as follows :

A BILL.

To provide for the establishment of a national industrial university for the education of colored persons, residents of the United States.

Be it enacted by the Senate, House of Representatives of the United States of America in Congress assembled, That there shall be established within any State of the Union where unappropriated public lands may be found convenient for such purpose by the Government of the United States a national industrial university for the education and training of colored persons, residents of any State of the Union, male or female, desiring to attend such university seeking an education, academical, collegiate, and professional, with instruction and training in any special industrial occupation or trade, mechanical or other.

SEC. 2. That ten thousand acres of any public lands wherever located, as selected by the board of commissioners hereinafter created, shall be appropriated and set apart as the site and for the purposes of said university.

SEC. 3. That there shall be appropriated, out of any moneys in the Treasury of the United States not otherwise appropriated, one million of dollars to erect buildings, to fence and otherwise improve the lands of the university, and to supply furniture, apparatus, and tools, mechanical and industrial, with general outfit therefor.

SEC. 4. That there shall be appointed by the President of the United States, by and with the consent of the Senate, a board of commissioners consisting of fifteen competent citizens of the United States whose duty it shall be to select the land hereinabove described to be set apart as the site of the university, to improve such lands, erect the necessary buildings thereupon, provide the necessary furniture, apparatus, tools, and outfit, and make all arrangements of every kind and sort, including the appointment of necessary officers, president, professors, instructors, and teachers, with all employees for said university.

SEC. 5. That the members of said board of commissioners shall hold their positions during good behavior, and as vacancies shall occur in said board by death, resignation, or otherwise, the same shall be filled by appointment made by the remaining members thereof; and such commissioners shall receive no compensation for their services, but all necessary and legitimate expenses incurred by them, or any one of them, in connection with the university, shall be paid.

SEC. 6. That the board of commissioners shall make and enforce all rules and regulations for the government of the university in all of its departments : *Provided*, That no person shall be accepted as a student therein who shall not enter into a contract himself or by his or her parent or guardian to pursue, upon such terms as may be prescribed, the courses of the academic, collegiate, professional, or industrial departments, respectively: *And provided further*, That no person, male or female, shall be received as a student in such university who shall not agree in advance to pursue the industrial as well as scholastic courses prescribed, and of which he or she shall make choice, for the entire term, and in the manner and upon the conditions provided therefor.

SEC. 7. That it shall be the purpose and aim in this university to educate and to train young men and women in all the branches of the highest scholarship and in all the callings of general industry, art, and trade, fitting all students graduating therefrom for the best possible industrial effort and scholarly professional labor in life. And any student graduating from such university, qualified as indicated, upon approval of the board of commissioners, shall receive a diploma signed by the chairman of said board and the secretary, under a seal which shall be provided and used by the university.

SEC. 8. That the board of commissioners hereinabove provided for and their successors shall constitute a body corporate, empowered to sue and be sued, to contract and to be contracted with, to receive, to hold, and dispose of in its own interest for the benefit of the university, all property bought, given, or bestowed by bequest or devise: *Provided*, That all powers herein vested in said board of commissioners shall be exercised solely and alone for the purposes hereinbefore mentioned to advance the objects and maintain the work of the university.

SEC. 9. That the board of commissioners shall proceed without delay, upon their appointment and commission, to organize with a chairman and secretary of their own members, with such committees for service as may seem to be necessary and practicable to discharge the duties enjoined upon them herein, and so soon as the university shall be made ready for use, which period shall not exceed one year and six months from the date of their appointment and commission aforesaid, said board of commissioners shall notify all persons concerned by public advertisement that said university is ready to receive students. And thereafter said board of commissioners shall make annual report to the Commissioner of Education, through the Secretary of the Interior, as to the condition, progress, and success of said university, in all of its departments.

The importance and necessity of such legislative national action cannot be exaggerated when the educational and industrial wants of the colored youth of the country, and the general benefits of their improvement in such directions are duly estimated and considered. The bill was duly referred to the Committee on Education, and had time permitted it would have been given thorough, critical examination with favorable report, and in all probability passed by the House.

Another bill introduced by Mr. Langston was one to provide for the observance of the twelfth day of February and the twenty-seventh day of April, respectively, as national holidays, in memory and honor of the great national benefactors, Lincoln and Grant; and to give the people of all classes and conditions both the leisure and the opportunity to do so in such reasonable and proper manner as seems to accord with the great services and the eminent worth of the statesmen and heroes named.

In addition to the petitions, resolutions and bills introduced by Mr. Langston, which, as might be necessary, would have had his explanation and support in connection with their consideration and passage, he must be credited with making two quite full and elaborate speeches, upon the national elections law and the rehabilitation of the merchant marine of the United States.

It was through the kindness of the Hon. Louis E. McComas, a representative from the State of Maryland, who had charge of the appropriation bill for the District of Columbia, that Mr. Langston was given the opportunity of making his first speech in the House, under such circumstances and upon such a subject as to give him a very attentive hearing and a most cordial reception. He spoke, as stated, in favor of the national elections law; and was heard in the most flattering manner by every member of the House, Republican and Democrat, as he vindicated the American ballot in its purity and power, claiming that any action of the national government necessary to its preservation and protection was constitutional and imperative. Hence the action of the Republican party in that regard was to be approved and applauded. His speech was received with demonstrations of warmest approbation, and upon its conclusion, at the expiration of one hour allowed him for its delivery, he was made the recipient of many cordial and commendatory expressions.

Of his effort at this time many comments of the press were made and might be adduced. One however alone shall be reproduced here. It sufficiently explains his position, illustrates the character of his address, and describes the manner in which he was treated as well as the impression which he seems to have made upon his auditors. "The Cleveland Leader" of January 17, 1891, employs in its issue of that date, in referring to the doings of the House of Representatives, the following remarkable expressions in commenting upon Mr. Langston's speech:

LANGSTON ELOQUENT.

THE COLORED VIRGINIA CONGRESSMAN MAKES A MEMORABLE SPEECH IN THE HOUSE. HE BRINGS MOISTURE TO THE EYES OF HARDENED OLD BOURBON MEMBERS.

[Special dispatch to the Leader.]

Washington, January 16.—The sensation which relieved the tedium of an otherwise dull day in the House was a speech by Mr. Langston, the colored member from Virginia, whose admission was so long and fiercely contested by the Democrats at the last session. Evidently Mr. Langston had some things

MAKING HIS FIRST SPEECH IN THE HOUSE OF REPRESENTATIVES, JANUARY 16, 1891.

514b

in his mind that he wanted to say on the race question. The only way by which he could do it was to have time yielded him on the District appropriation bill and then use it in his own way. This is what the Democrats have been doing for a week past. In the early part of the session to-day Rogers, of Arkansas, made a speech on silver, and Shively, of Indiana, one against shipping subsidies. Perhaps it was no more than fair that Langston should take a little license and wander far from the subject under consideration. Mr. Langston made a speech that was eloquent and effective. It would not be an exaggeration to say it was brilliant. No sooner had he warmed to his theme than members on both sides laid aside newspapers and pens and turned their chairs around to look and listen. No higher compliment can be paid him than to state the fact that he commanded the close attention of all in the chamber, Democrats and Republicans alike.

There are not five men in the House who can talk as well as Langston. He speaks extemporaneously, without even notes, and his command of language is masterly. No doubt there are scores of Democrats in that body who would give a year's salary for half as good a gift of oratory. When he began the Democrats showed a disposition to ignore him, but he compelled them to hear him, and before he had finished a dozen such Bourbons as Stockdale and Hooker of Mississippi, Breckinridge of Kentucky, and Stewart and Lanham of Texas, were over on the Republican side listening intently to his every word. It is scarcely credible, but it is true that he caused the eyes of some of these case-hardened Democrats to moisten by his impassioned appeals for justice to the black men and to the white men of the South who are proscribed because they are Republicans.

Mr. Langston had the floor for more than three quarters of an hour. The Republicans applauded again and again, and when he closed some of the Democrats joined in the ovation that was given him. Among those who shook his hand and offered congratulations was Hon. Amos J. Cummings, a New York Democrat. Mr. Langston had not expected so warm a greeting from such a source, but his native wit prompted the response: "You are very near the Kingdom, Mr. Cummings."

The second address was made from a deep sense of patriotic duty. An appeal from leading citizens of wealth and influence of his own State, especially from the several Chambers of Commerce, urging his support in speech and vote in favor of the bill pending in the House providing for the rehabilitation of the merchant marine of the United States, was made to him by letter and otherwise. He therefore prepared himself and made the speech accordingly. Of this effort it is only necessary to say that it was received in appreciative manner, offering a fit opportunity to display as well his logical as his rhetorical powers in its preparation and delivery. As made and published in the "Congressional

Record" and subsequently in pamphlet form, it gave Mr. Langston increased influence and favor both with his associates in the House and the large majority of the people of his State. In this address he displayed entire mastery of the subject, illustrating and impressing his views with large information, facts, figures and conditions of the American merchant marine, gained in his extended and protracted observations and experiences as consular-general of the United States; displaying in the advocacy of the measure the profoundest earnestness and interest.

As a member of Congress Mr. Langston was treated by the president of the United States, the several members of the Cabinet and the chief officers of the various departments of the government with whom he had official intercourse and associations, with marked kindness and respectful consideration. His success in locating applicants for office, residents of his district and State, at home, in Washington city, and even abroad, was certainly as great as that of any other member of Congress; and by pursuing a wise and judicious course in that respect he made many friends among both white and colored constituents. He gave more than a score opportunity to locate themselves at service in the national capital, where they might pursue advanced courses of study of ordinary collegiate and professional character. He situated others in the same city where they were able to prosecute such lines of artistic and mechanical occupations as accorded with their desires and interests. One case of the last class mentioned deserves here special note. It is that of a young colored man of Sussex County, Virginia, who located by Mr. Langston in the Navy Department as an apprentice, pursued with unusual proficiency and success his trade as an engraver. He has been permitted to remain in his place for over three years, and has reached such a stage of advancement as to make his position a very desirable one and his services useful to the government. The walls of Mr. Langston's home are ornamented by two productions, engravings of this young black man, which testify of his genius, power and application. This young man, Mr. Theophilus A. Parham, the forerunner of his race in this country in the calling to which he has dedicated himself, shall, if studious and diligent, gaining the success which seems to be in store for him, serve his people in such a way and measure as to make him indeed their benefactor as well as their representative, in a most dignified and honorable occupation.

The second was the short session of the Fifty-first Congress and its adjournment came only too soon. However, its closing scenes witnessed by whomsoever can never be forgotten. Its end was announced in a most eloquent, telling and effective address by the speaker, Hon. Thomas B. Reed, delivered in his happiest and most pleasing manner. No such occasional address was ever received with greater satisfaction and more enthusiastic applause. His utterance was to the ears of all Republicans, abounding as it did in truthful, ringing sentiments, the sound of exulting triumph. And the popular, soul-stirring airs, "John Brown's Soul" and "America" bursting forth upon its close spontaneously, as it were, from the hearts and lips of the members and the vast audience whose voices swelled the choruses, seemed veritable pæans of immortal hilarity and joy!

Had Mr. Langston been permitted to continue as his own successor in the Fifty-second Congress, his district through his agency and influence would have been represented in the national military and naval schools of the United States, at West Point and Annapolis, by at least two young scholarly colored persons. He made special effort to accomplish that purpose before the close of the Fifty-first Congress, but was unsuccessful, the honorable secretary of the navy holding that the matter must be passed to his successor. This seemed hard indeed, since the same officer had allowed the person who held Mr. Langston's seat illegally for so long a time during his contest, to send a young white man from a Democratic family of the district to one of these schools without even giving any colored youth of the district the opportunity of competing, in fair and scholarly contest, for that place.

Such was the record made by Mr. Langston in the brief term of his actual service during the second session of the Fifty-first Congress, that he was, in fact, unanimously renominated by a popular Republican conference held in Petersburg when the Republican Congressional Committee of the district had refused to convoke the regular nominating convention of the fall of 1891, and thereupon in the election which followed he was returned to the Fifty-second Congress by a large majority of the honest, reliable votes of the district. Although the majority by which he was thus elected was beyond question certain and decisive, he would not make contest for the seat because the Democratic party, holding a majority in that Congress, as moved by deep-seated hatred and opposition against Mr. Langston and sustained by every influence and effort which Mahone and his deluded followers could exert, would not give the case fair hearing, or decide it upon the accepted principles of law and the facts. Mr. Langston verily believed, and his friends and supporters endorsed his opinion, that whatever might be his showing upon the law and facts in the matter of contest against the Democratic member who had already received the certificate of election, his efforts would prove to be ineffectual and his labors wholly abortive. He knew very well that he could secure nothing like justice in the premises, with the Democratic party holding entire control and mastery of the House.

Mr. Langston, so far as his friends and supporters are concerned, has not lost in any sense the least particle of his great influence in his district; nor has the feeling in favor of making him its representative in Congress abated the least. Accordingly, in 1892, he was elected without a dissenting voice by the Republican District Convention a delegate to the State Republican Convention, at Roanoke, and a delegate to the National Republican Convention, at Minneapolis, Minnesota, to nominate candidates to the Presidency and Vice-presidency of the United States. He acted as the representative of his district in both the State and National Conventions, to the acceptance and approval of his constituents. Subsequently, at the last Congressional District Republican Convention held at Burkeville, Nottoway County, Virginia, in the fall of 1892, with delegates present representing every county of the district and the city of Petersburg elected by order of the Republican District Committee, he was unanimously and enthusiastically nominated by the party as its candidate for election to the Fifty-third Congress. Influenced by considerations of party interest Mr. Langston declined to accept this nomination, and advised that under the circumstances the party of the district would be more likely to elect and secure a seat for its candidate in Congress should a white person of name and influence, distinguished for his party loyalty and the acceptance and defence of its principles and measures, be put in nomination. In this judgment he was finally cordially sustained, and permitted to name the person who should be the candidate. He did name a good and reliable white Republican as he believed, and that person was upon his withdrawal and recommendation nominated by the convention. It is believed generally in the district that Mr. Langston's judgment in that matter was wise; and had it been acted upon to the end the person nominated by his assistance would have been elected to the Fifty-third Congress by the usual Republican majority of the district. It is doubtful, however, whether he could, under the circumstances, have secured from the state authorities the certificate of election, or finally upon contest, his seat in the House of Representatives.

The feeling of bitterness and opposition existing on the part of the Democratic party of Virginia and the district, sustained as it has been by Mahone and such white Republicans, falsely so-called, against Mr. Langston, has been so unyielding and persistent that though popular with the electors of the district he has not deemed it prudent, latterly, to make the least endeavor to gain political preferment so far as the nomination and election to Congress are concerned. It is apparent that though nominated in the most unanimous and emphatic manner, he must incur all the doubts and hazards connected with an election fraudulently conducted, with account of the ballots dishonestly and mischievously made.

It is to be hoped, however, and greatly to be desired that ultimately, and at a day not distant, the political elements and forces of the district as well as those of the entire State, will be so improved, reconstructed and reorganized under new and better legislation and honest management, as to insure justice and honorable dealing in all elections, local, state, and federal.

520a

520b

HILLSIDE COTTAGE, WASHINGTON, D. C.

CHAPTER XXXI.

HILLSIDE COTTAGE AND HIS FAMILY.

PRIOR to the removal of his family from Oberlin, in 1871, and its location in Washington city, Mr. Langston had purchased convenient grounds in the neighborhood of Howard University and erected thereupon a beautiful, unique Swiss cottage, with other appropriate improvements, adequate and proper for its accommodation. This property in all its appointments, improved after the best modern methods and styles, with buildings designed and erected upon plans of approved and attractive architecture, besides being eligible in situation, is impressive and inviting in appearance. Located upon the south side of a beautiful elevation looking towards the Capitol, and fronting a government reservation of ten acres ornamented with original forest trees of oak, maple and hickory, besides other artificial attractions, Hillside Cottage offers to its occupants and visitors all that is pleasant and agreeable in rustic and urban life combined.

The house, cottage as it is, Swiss in its plan and structure, is a three-story frame building with fourteen rooms, with which, as necessary, are connected large, spacious and airy closets, including a spacious well-ventilated and lighted basement, thoroughly dry and healthful, as well as perfectly convenient and suited to every ordinary domestic purpose. The premises are situated at the corner of Fourth and College streets, and the house is entered from the former street, upon which it fronts, by a broad, long vine-covered porch, which not only adds materially to its beauty but to the convenience and pleasure of the family. The internal arrangements of the house so far as its general sanitary conditions are concerned embrace every approved modern convenience. And though it has been occupied for twenty-two years, built in good first-class substantial manner of excellent materials, it is in all respects well-preserved and in thorough repair. Besides, Mr. Langston and his family take great pride in their home, and do whatever they may to preserve it while adding to its value and beauty in every possible manner.

The grounds, which embrace within the fences surrounding them a full acre of valuable land, besides being furnished with all necessary out-buildings, as barn, stables, hennery, and well-house, built on plans and styles in keeping with the residence, are so ample as to offer opportunities for gaming-places, as the croquet-ground and tennis court, and yard ornamented with flowers, shrubs, evergreen and fruit trees of various varieties.

As one approaches the premises his sight rests first upon a long row of shade trees, hard and silver maples, planted twenty-two years ago, now grown large with spreading beautiful boughs, standing upon the outer edge of the pavement fronting and extending along the whole length of the grounds on Fourth street, opposite the public park. Besides furnishing ample shade to the residence and premises, these trees add immensely to their value and their beauty. Inside of the yard, among the ornamental trees, is found a French magnolia, sent from France by a friend to Mr. Langston twenty years ago, now well grown and perfectly acclimated. Beautiful always as bearing the richest green satin-appearing leaf, while in its annual abundant, magnificent, fragrant blossoms, rare, choice and matchless, it is attractive and impressive in the highest degree. Among others stand four towering beautiful trees—a spruce pine upon the rear of the premises, marking them from that point; a classic sycamore in the northwest corner of the grounds, lifting its sightly lofty branches above every tree upon the place and marking it above all others from that point; a white birch and a sweetgum, set in conspicuous places in the front yard, all presented to Mr. Langston by the Hon. Charles Sumner, in 1882; and which were located upon the premises through the directions of the senator, to answer the purpose especially of marking the place in front and rear, according to his own conception and taste. Of these four trees, gifts of Senator Sumner specially valued by Mr. Langston, he never tires of talking to his friends and visitors. He always speaks of the classic sycamore, inviting attention to its rare beauty, telling how the donor presented it to mark his place, assuring him that it was the sort of sycamore-tree up which Zacchaeus climbed to see Jesus as he passed. Indeed, it would be difficult to find Mr. Langston more eloquent upon any subject than these trees and his exalted opinion of the great senator, who gave them to him.

Of fruit-bearing trees, standard and dwarf, bushes and vines, the apple, pear, cherry, peach, quince, gooseberry, raspberry, blackberry, with various varieties of grapes, figure most conspicuously. These fruits appearing annually in large abundance are handled by Mrs. Langston, whether for canning, preserving, or distribution among her visitors and friends, with special profit and pleasure. In fact she discovers large interest and activity, with reasonable advantageous results, in the care and cultivation of every flower, plant and tree upon the premises.

Among the things specially valued at Hillside Cottage, in addition to those already named, are first the abundance of excellent spring and cistern water so connected by pumps with the house as to furnish easy and ample supply for all purposes ; and next a large hennery always supplied with a goodly number of fowls of best breeds whose products prove always to be advantageous and desirable. In the warm seasons of the year, Mr. Langston never fails to invite his guests to seats in his well-house, where as he claims he can present them, in either glasses, tin-cups or gourds, draughts of the best, coolest, clearest, most refreshing and health-giving spring-water that can be found in the country. Thence he is wont to invite his visitors and friends to the inspection of his hennery and thrifty pretty broods of fowls, hens and chickens. Often he points out some special cock or hen, sometimes both, and interests all present in noting and explaining the excellent qualities of the rare and superior breeds of which he speaks. Just now his hennery is distinguished for a cock and hen of rare beauty and choice qualities known as the Silver Duck-wing breed, noted for its unusual laying, breeding and fighting qualities, presented to him by a Virginia white Democratic friend.

In view of its situation upon the southern slope of what is known as University Hill, and the architecture of the residence, Mr. Langston's Washington home, where he and his wife spend most of their time, has been named by him Hillside Cottage.

Mr. Langston's family proper consists, as already stated, of Mrs. Langston, one daughter and three sons. The eldest daughter born at Oberlin, sickened, died and was buried there before the family left that place. No other death so far as the offspring have been concerned has occurred; while it is true that the children have all been distinguished by strong, firm, robust conditions of body, and enjoyed generally excellent health. They have grown to womanhood and manhood, and marrying according to their desires and judgments, have settled with their several families in different sections of the country.

Arthur the first-born, having completed his education at Oberlin College, graduating therefrom with high honors and subsequently locating himself as a teacher in the colored public schools of St Louis, Missouri, has continued in that occupation, rising gradually in position, responsibility and control, until to-day he is principal of the Dessalines school of that city. In his present position he has a large number of teachers subject to his direction, with hundreds of pupils who constantly feel his controlling influence as their instructor. As a teacher and principal, besides showing himself competent and efficient he discovers the largest earnestness and enthusiasm in his work. He devotes his entire time to his school engagements, mastering all new methods and enlarging and diversifying his knowledge of all subjects commanding his attention; and thus while he wins exalted growing influence with the officers, he improves constantly his relations to the parents of his scholars.

But while his position as an educator in the community is deservedly high and influential, he occupies a most desirable place in popular esteem and respect as a man and member of society. He is a member of the leading social club found among the colored people of St. Louis. This club is composed of many of the foremost colored gentlemen of that city, persons of wealth and culture, well known in the community and noted for their integrity and good character. This club is known as the "Home Club," and at this time Mr. Arthur D. Langston is its president.

He married shortly after he had settled in St. Louis, taking as his wife Miss Ida M. Napier, of Nashville, Tennessee, the daughter of Mr. and Mrs. William C. Napier, whose prominence and influence as conspicuous foremost members of colored society in the capital of that State are well known and appreciated. Miss Napier was not only a young lady of prepossessing, attractive characteristics of body and mind, naturally, but by more than ordinary thorough, various training had in part at Fisk University, in her native city, and subsequently at Oberlin College, is a person of most refined and agreeable culture. She has cultivated largely, and succeeded with unusual proficiency in mastering the art of music, and besides singing well she performs with grace, ease and effect upon the piano. Being an only daughter no outlay or pains were spared to perfect her education.

The fruit of this marriage has been two splendid young boys. The elder named in honor of his grandfather John Mercer Langston, and the younger in honor of his uncle, his mother's brother, James Carroll Langston. These boys are, respectively, aged fourteen and twelve years, and are remarkably advanced in study for their ages. They are promising in health and bodily strength, and while each discovers his peculiar talent and taste for special branches of study and art, both possess strong marked general intellectual character, with self-reliant qualities of constitution and admirable native temper.

Arthur's family is well constituted, with their residence permanently established in St. Louis, where having made many good and reliable friends, they are the recipients of their cordial respect and constant honors.

Ralph E. the second child of his parents, completed his education principally at Oberlin College, where besides a thorough academic course he pursued a regular business training, graduating from one of the most prominent commercial colleges of the country. Subsequently he worked as an apprentice at the Government printing office, Washington city, D. C., and after mastering his trade, continued his services there for several years. During this time he married Miss Anna Pearl Jackson, the daughter of Mr. and Mrs. James Jackson, residents of the national capital—a family well known and highly respected by the foremost people of that city. This family occupies especially prominent place among the members of the St. Augustine Roman Catholic church, of which they are all members.

Miss Jackson possessing a good education, as she had gained it in the public and parish schools of her native city, is distinguished for her musical accomplishments and her knowledge of domestic arts and industry, elegant and usual, indispensable to successful and wise management of her household. After his marriage, Ralph removed with his wife to Nashville, Tennessee, where he resided doing a furniture business for several years. Thereafter he returned to Washington city, where his family at present resides.

Among the most beautiful and attractive, intelligent and promising little girls found in the public schools of Washington is Nettie Matilde Langston, the only child of this marriage. Bright, yet docile and well-behaved, she is so far as her grandparents are concerned, on both sides, the

526a

526b

PORTRAIT OF MISS NETTIE LANGSTON.

object of their greatest delight and satisfaction. She is equally the object of the deepest affection and pride of her parents. She is eleven years old only, but manifests all those traits of character and mind which give promise of an excellent womanhood marked by extraordinary intelligence, charm and usefulness.

Of the father and mother it is to be said, that while they are themselves unusually fine looking, intelligent and affectionate persons, they with their little daughter constitute the *personnel* of a most interesting happy family.

The only living daughter of Mr. and Mrs. John M. Langston is Mrs. James C. Napier. Though younger than either of her brothers named, she was first to marry ; and as already stated heretofore, in connection with her wedding, is located in Nashville, Tennessee, where her husband is engaged in the practice of the law. Her brother Arthur married her husband's sister, and while the one family resides in St. Louis and the other in Nashville, a cordiality of intimacy and intercourse exists between them which constitutes a bond of brotherly and sisterly feeling, drawing and holding them constantly together. Since Mr. and Mrs. Napier have no children, and because they entertain constantly such deep affection and interest in the family of their brother and sister, they cultivate every opportunity possible to demonstrate their anxiety and purpose to promote the general education and welfare of Arthur's and Ida's children. Indeed, the young boys find themselves really as much at home with their uncle and aunt at Nashville, as in St. Louis with their parents.

Mr. and Mrs. Napier live in comparatively easy and comfortable circumstances, occupying deservedly exalted and desirable position in general society in the city, the state, and the country of their residence. Mr. Napier cultivates with diligence and vigor, constantly, his profession, never failing to give such attention to politics as a Republican, and general affairs as would become an American citizen of intelligence and patriotism. Mrs. Napier besides giving constant attention to such social pleasures and duties as command her attention, shows herself an efficient and consistent worker in enterprises connected with the Congregational church of her city, of which her husband and she are members. Besides, she interests herself in matters of education, never failing to aid by advice and substantial support often, persons seeking situations as students in Fisk University or other schools. Possessing as she does an accomplished musical education, with a deep, rich contralto voice of great power, she is frequently invited to take part in musical entertainments, often of public and general interest. Such is her public spirit that it would be found difficult to learn of her making refusal where she might in any way serve a humane, Christian end. In whatever enterprise she engages she is always sustained not only by the approval of her husband but by his earnest and cordial support. Indeed, their tastes, judgments and affections are thoroughly mutual and reciprocal.

The only daughter of her parents, the very life of their household when at home, the pet of her father who both admires and loves her, she has compensated in large measure for her absence from them during the fifteen years of her married life, by her constant, cordial weekly correspondence, as a rule, and regular annual visits between the families, she generally visiting Hillside Cottage at least once every two years, and occupying the apartments known as hers, which are constantly kept in readiness for her.

Mr. and Mrs. Napier, two in number only, constitute in and of themselves a very small though very happy family. However, their home, so pleasant and agreeable in every way, is never without visitors and friends who share their generous hospitality with pleasure and delight.

Frank Mercer, the youngest child of the family, was educated in part at Oberlin and West Newton, Massachusetts. A boy of excellent appearance, good native ability, with engaging and pleasant manners, he made many friends at home and school, who always discovered great fondness for and lasting attachment to him. Though a boy of remarkable spirit naturally when aroused, he was ordinarily in temper and manner lamb-like, so much so that he early won from his sister and brothers the nickname of Lamb, by which they address him even to this day. Though he did not take a regular academic or college course of study, he is so thoroughly educated in the common advanced branches of English education and is so well read in general history and current literature and has had such observation of men and things in travel at home and abroad, that he shows himself always in conversation or in the use of his pen, however exercised, a man of intelligence and well-formed judgment.

No one of the children had larger personal constant association with his parents, especially his father, at home and abroad, than Frank. Being the youngest child, for that reason and because his society was particularly agreeable during his sojourn in Haïti, Mr. Langston had this son with himself and wife more than once and for protracted periods at Port-au-Prince. It was in that city, in the midst of the most favorable surroundings for that occupation, that he studied and mastered the French language. He became a great favorite in this island country, both among Americans found there and Haytians. During one of his visits, when smallpox prevailed as an epidemic in Port-au-Prince, he was stricken down by the disease, and had it not been for the kindly constant professional attentions of Dr. Terres and his mother's unremitting careful personal nursing, like thousands of others in that city he must have died. He was prostrated by the disease in its most frightful confluent form; and his recovery under the circumstances, though he had every attention and care, was regarded as truly miraculous. Fortunately, by the use of burned sulphur employed as a disinfectant neither Mrs. Langston nor any other member of her family or any attaché of the legation took the disease.

At another time, and subsequently, he was with his father and mother abroad in the same city, when the yellow fever suddenly making its appearance among foreign residents, produced the greatest possible excitement and fear. There happened to arrive at this time in the harbor of Port-au-Prince, opportunely indeed, an English ship bound for New York city, on which Mr. Langston with some difficulty secured passage homeward for his wife and son; so as to gain for them escape from the epidemic, which soon became prevalent and of which he was himself very shortly after their departure, stricken down, narrowly escaping finally with his life. Within a few weeks after their arrival at home, learning through mistake that the husband and father had died of this disease, they were filled with deep regret that they had left him, feeling that had they remained to care for and nurse him he had not died. Upon the joy which came to these loved ones when they learned the truth as to his escape from death under the circumstances, Mr. Langston will not dwell.

It was after Frank's return home at this time that he secured, through the influence of his father, a situation in the Government printing office, where he pursued and mastered his trade as a bookbinder. He worked thereafter for some time in the government service, but finally established himself by assistance of his father in a book and stationery business in Petersburg, Virginia. Here he did a thrifty but small trade, winning in connection therewith many friends and patrons.

Subsequently, at the earnest and pressing invitation of his brother-in-law and sister he made his residence for a short time in Nashville, Tennessee. After about one year he married Mrs. India Watkins of Town Creek, Alabama, where he made his residence and established himself in a small grocery business. Mrs. Watkins, the lady whom he married, is one of the most intelligent, refined and worthy women found among the colored people of her neighborhood and State. She possesses superior native endowments with unusual general acquirement. She is well known and beloved by Frank's family, and is welcomed among them as their daughter and sister.

As the result of their marriage a pretty little baby girl, not yet two months old, has been born; and bears, as suggested

530a

PORTRAIT OF MRS. J. M. LANGSTON.

by its grandfather, Langston, the name of Carrie Cornelia, the given names of its grandmothers, Mrs. Langston and Mrs. Smith, united. Located in their own home, in the far South, where they are respected and honored by a large circle of faithful and devoted friends, Frank, his wife, baby girl and mother-in-law, constitute a loving, happy and prosperous family.

With all the children married and settled in different parts of the country, each pursuing such line of life as seems to be agreeable and useful, Mr. Langston's family is, as it has been for the past ten years with a single exception, composed of himself, his wife, his wife's sister Mrs. Sara K Fidler, and Miss Janie M. Percival. From the beginning this family has been one distinguished in all respects for the fortunate conditions of its constitution and the happy results of its judicious and sagacious management. In view of these facts Mr. Langston has always felt himself peculiarly blessed, and has constantly credited his wife in that behalf with the exercise of her great native and improved sagacity and wisdom in such a way as to accomplish these result. In dealing with her children from birth, through the stages of their early and advanced education to manhood and womanhood, she cultivated in the case of each, at home and abroad, such discipline and control with such moderation and observance of any peculiar temper or tendency of feeling or thought as to maintain over each her authority and motherly influence. Her mode of government was discovered not so much in the exercise of authority in any case as in her affectionate regard and interest manifested in the case of each child. It is not recollected in the household that she ever severely scolded or punished, bodily, one of her children. To-day there is not one among them who does not affectionately honor, praise and bless her, and not one who does not deem himself happy in her association and companionship.

Mrs. Langston has always shown herself a befitting sympathizing companion of her husband, giving her influence and support to him in every concern of private life, and every enterprise of public moment which have commanded his attention and efforts. Without a difference of feeling and purpose, harmonious and united in their general views as well as their political and religious convictions, entertaining high hopes with respect to their race, impressed with the obligation and duty which rest upon them with respect to its amelioration and elevation, they have striven under all circumstances to so order their conduct, wherever living, as to exert a good influence, no more upon their own family than upon the general community and any members of colored society constituting the great body of their friends and associates. She has not failed to so impress all who have known her, and who have been brought within the limits of her acquaintance and influence as to add materially to the good name and popularity of her husband.

As to inmates of the family, Mr. and Mrs. Langston count that they have been very fortunate. For the last ten years of her life, Mrs. Sara K. Fidler, the only sister of Mrs. Langston, resided with them at Hillside Cottage. She was greatly beloved by every member of the family, and being a woman of large and varied scholarly accomplishment, discreet and judicious in her treatment of the children, with ample means so that as prompted by her love and generosity she could in many ways indulge and gratify their desires, she exercised over them an effective, improving and desirable influence. She always sustained in intelligent and noted manner the discipline of the household, insisting to each child that the wishes and judgment of its parents must be strictly and cordially observed. Thus she aided very greatly in the wise management and education of the children, while her superior knowledge and experience made her, though younger than Mrs. Langston, quite a counsellor, almost equal to a mother, in the direction and control of all those weighty matters which pertain to responsible domestic concerns.

When Mrs. Fidler died, in 1886, the whole family mourned their loss of one who was esteemed, respected, honored and loved as an affectionate and devoted sister, a loving and indulgent aunt, and a considerate and valued friend. Her memory and her example of personal purity, noble Christian life and self-sacrificing interest in those around her, are treasured as precious and worthy legacies endearing her to them all forever.

Miss Janie M. Percival has been an inmate of the family for over twenty-five years. She is an English person who by her discreet and circumspect, useful and Christian conduct, and many good offices as a companion in important sense, and constant assistance of Mrs. Langston, has made her membership of the household advantageous and desirable. While she has won the confidence and affection of every child and grandchild she has gained and retains the good opinion and lasting friendship of the parents. No guest or visitor at Hillside Cottage has come and gone without carrying away the highest and most constant feeling of respect and favor for her. Thoroughly versed in all the ways of intelligent sound domestic management, appreciating and cultivating, as opportunity permitted, every wise economic dealing in household affairs, industrious, energetic and good natured, she has been and is in every material way of incalculable service and benefit to the family. Every member of it respects, honors and values her as a reliable, worthy friend, accepted indeed in full membership of the household.

Situated as indicated, while Mr. Langston spends much time at Petersburg, Virginia, where he makes his residence, he and his wife maintain their home in Washington city where one or the other, frequently both, are found spending their time in such employments, with entertainment of their large circle of friends and acquaintances, as accord with their duties and desires. Given to the cultivation of literary and artistic habits, fond of the weightier matters of thought and science, they find themselves at home with the large and valuable collection of works, English, American, French and other, which compose the select, rare, general and professional library which Mr. Langston has accumulated during the past half century.

Without special bodily infirmity or weakness, indeed

possessing and enjoying reasonable health and strength for persons of their ages, Mr. and Mrs. Langston are not wanting either in activity or vigor, physically or mentally. They possess strength and power, in full measure, for all needed useful daily exertion. Mrs. Langston is under sixty years of age, and Mr. Langston has not yet reached his sixty-fifth year. As time adds to their years they become even more grateful to their friends and fellow-citizens who have contributed in influence and effort to give them name, standing and honor in the country. They pray constantly, that as in the past they have been fortunate in all the ways of life they may so continue in all the future, cultivating integrity, sound discretion, Christian fortitude and moderation, with just appreciation of all friendly favor and kindly consideration. And thus through a good Providence be permitted to close their days, maintaining the respect and affection of all who may know and honor them.

Of all the persons who in 1834 left the old Virginia plantation for Ohio, the child of the company, now an old man, is the only survivor. And he is delighted that he may make just mention in these reminiscences of his relatives and friends composing that company, all of whom have gone to their long, deep sleep!

Made in the USA
Coppell, TX
01 April 2022

75762325R00312